Chicago
Business
and
Industry

# CHICAGO BUSINESS AND INDUSTRY

## FROM FUR TRADE TO E-COMMERCE

### Edited by Janice L. Reiff

THE UNIVERSITY OF CHICAGO PRESS    *Chicago and London*

**Janice L. Reiff** is associate professor of history at the University of California, Los Angeles. She is coeditor, with James R. Grossman and Ann Durkin Keating, of *The Encyclopedia of Chicago*, also published by the University of Chicago Press.

The University of Chicago Press, Chicago 60637
The University of Chicago Press, Ltd., London
© 2013 by The Newberry Library
All rights reserved. Published 2013.
Printed in the United States of America

22 21 20 19 18 17 16 15 14 13    1 2 3 4 5

ISBN-13: 978-0-226-70936-9

Library of Congress Cataloging-in-Publication Data

Chicago business and industry: from fur trade to e-commerce / edited by Janice L. Reiff.
    pages cm
    "Collection of essays drawn from the Encyclopedia of Chicago"—introduction.
    Includes bibliographical references and index.
    ISBN 978-0-226-70936-9 (paperback: alkaline paper)   1. Chicago (Ill.)—Economic conditions—Encyclopedias.   2. Industries—Illinois—Chicago—History—Encyclopedias.   3. Business enterprises—Illinois—Chicago—History—Encyclopedias.   I. Reiff, Janice L., editor.
    HC108.C4C537 2013
    338.09773′11—dc23                    2013000269

♾ This paper meets the requirements of ANSI/NISO Z39.48-1992 (Permanence of Paper).

# Contents

## III. Chicago's Businesses

## IV. Working in Chicago

# Acknowledgments

A book like *Chicago Business and Industry* rests heavily on the efforts of many people, all of whom deserve recognition and my thanks. First and foremost among these are my coeditors of the *Encyclopedia of Chicago*: Ann Durkin Keating and James R. Grossman. They imagined Chicago in new ways and translated that wonderful city and its people into both a print volume and an online reference work housed at the Chicago History Museum from which this volume is derived. Michael Conzen's remarkable contributions as the cartographic editor for the *Encyclopedia* are readily apparent in the maps, drawn by Dennis McClendon, and reproduced in this volume. The many contributions of managing editor Douglas Knox are less immediately visible, but neither the original *Encyclopedia* nor *Chicago Business and Industry* could have come to fruition without his deep knowledge of the city and the original project, as well as his organization of its materials so they could be reused here. Mark R. Wilson also deserves special mention. As a research assistant for the *Encyclopedia*, he researched and wrote many of the understudied industry entries and much of the original business dictionary, which served as the basis for section III of this volume.

I cannot overstate the Newberry Library's contribution to the *Encyclopedia* and this volume. The institution generously shared its copyrighted materials from the *Encyclopedia*, and its staff helped bring *Chicago Business and Industry* to completion. Daniel Greene, Vice President for Research and Academic Programs—who also worked as a research assistant on the *Encyclopedia*—provided me with a place to work and financial support for the illustrations. Also at the Newberry, Carmen Jaramillo, Jennifer Thom, and John Powell each offered important assistance. Russell Lewis of the Chicago History Museum once again demonstrated the cooperative spirit that gave birth to the original *Encyclopedia*. A word of thanks also goes to the University of California, Los Angeles, and especially to the University Library for its superb digital collections, which made updating much easier to do. The University of Chicago Press and especially Jenny Gavacs and Paul Schellinger guided this project from idea to book.

The individual authors whose original contributions to the *Encyclopedia* reappear here also deserve my gratitude and admiration. Almost a decade has passed since I did the final editing of their entries for the *Encyclopedia*, and in rereading all and updating many of them, I was once again impressed by the quality of their scholarship. I hope the updates, when appropriate, kept the quality of the original work intact. I am only sorry that the space limitations of this volume did not allow the inclusion of even more of the entries from the original *Encyclopedia of Chicago*.

Finally, I want to thank my brother and sister-in-law, Terry and Kate Reiff, who regularly provided me with a place to stay while in Chicago to work on this project. Even more, I want to thank my Chicago nieces and nephew—Sarah, Olivia, and Bradley—who made those visits far more enjoyable.

# Introduction

Cities, it is often claimed, drive the economy. They gather raw materials and goods from their surrounding regions, frequently process and rebundle them, and forward them on to other cities for consumption, redistribution, and further processing. The transportation and communication hubs that they host connect people domestically and internationally. Their large populations create the consumer demand on which retail business thrives. Construction to sustain their metropolitan growth and the infrastructural requirements to keep them working properly provide jobs for millions. Money flows through cities and the financial institutions that make their homes there. The mix of people and opportunity located within urban areas make them centers for cultural, educational, and technological innovation.

At the same time, the economy shapes the cities that help to drive it. Engraved in every urban area are the relics of the economies that encouraged them into being, spurred their growth, and, too often, fostered the decline of neighborhoods and even whole cities. Evidence of changing economies and their effects are visible in the locations and landscapes of cities, in the people who lived in them, and in the homes and buildings where those residents lived and worked. Train tracks and roads serve as physical reminders of the movement of natural resources, finished products, and people that sustained urban development. Brownfields—landscapes difficult to redevelop because of earlier environmental degradation—offer glimpses into what particular eras valued and what might be risked, knowingly or otherwise.

This volume, a collection of essays drawn from the *Encyclopedia of Chicago*, offers its readers an opportunity to explore that reciprocal relationship between metropolitan Chicago and the economy during the city's history. Several features distinguish this collection from the *Encyclopedia* itself. First, it is organized topically to provide particular perspectives on the relationship between the economy and the city. The first section, "The

Economic Geography," explores the relationship between the physical spaces of Chicago and its economic development locally, nationally, and globally. The global view presented in several of the essays offers insights into the ways that Chicago's location in terms of international economic systems, natural resources, and the development of the North American continent fueled the growth that made Chicago one of today's "global cities"—cities that are most important for the flow of world finance and trade. The other essays in this section explore the many ways in which the distribution of economic activities within the metropolitan area shaped the social contours of the region and the ways in which changes in the local and global economies affected particular areas within the region.

The second section, "The Business of Chicago," focuses on Chicago's business and economic history by first offering overviews of the historical development of Chicago as a center for business and innovations in business and then through the experiences of key segments of the economy. Its essays intersect with the larger themes of the first section, but do so within the context of some of the region's most important economic sectors. They provide insights into important business trends like globalization by documenting the Chicago meatpacking industry, which sold its locally processed products to consumers living around the world, and the evolution of the region's once-booming local steel industry, which is presently best represented locally by the North American headquarters of the world's largest steel company. The essays in this section also provide insights into what it meant and continues to mean for the city when old industries disappear and new ones arise.

"Chicago's Businesses," the third section, surveys the histories of some of the city's most representative and iconic firms. More limited in scope than the business dictionary in the *Encyclopedia of Chicago*, this section complements the previous one. If a particular firm's story is well-represented in the broader essay of "The Business of Chicago," it may not appear here. Some firms may appear in both, especially if they made Chicago famous (or infamous), were unique in their reputation or impact on the city or the larger national economic landscape, or illustrate broader economic trends that have affected Chicagoland. Conversely, if a firm that captures the history of its industry in Chicago appears in this section, a more general industry essay may not appear in the previous section. Taken together, however, the sector and firm entries offer a panoramic sweep of Chicago's business landscape.

The last section, "Working in Chicago," considers Chicago's economy from the perspective of the jobs that sustained those businesses and the men and women who worked those jobs. It draws from the *Encyclopedia*'s more comprehensive essays that speak to work and closely related issues like training, unemployment, unionization, and leisure. These essays help to put a human face on the economic developments that shaped Chicago.

Each essay, small and large, relates a particular story about Chicago's economy. Taken together, these stories create a picture that is greater than its parts. Readers are encouraged to explore that larger picture by following their own paths through the essays to pursue their individual interests. By beginning with the essay "Global Chicago" and moving to "Agricultural Machinery Industry," "Agriculture," "Food Processing," "Lumber," "Meatpacking," and "Railroads," one can see Chicago's evolution from a colonial, mercantile economy to an economy based on its agricultural hinterland, which transformed the city into what historian William Cronon has called "Nature's Metropolis." A different combination of essays drawn from all four sections will document the city's phenomenal physical and population growth as it became a center of North American industry, home to the large factories that became symbols of America's industrial age and that led poet Carl Sandburg to describe Chicago as the "city of broad shoulders." In reading the essays dealing with the manufacturing and service industries along with entries on firms within those sectors, one can see the changes that took place between 1950, when manufacturing provided 37.5 percent of jobs in the Illinois counties that are part of the Chicago metropolitan area, to today, when only two firms among the city's largest employers (Abbott Laboratories and Motorola) do substantial manufacturing, with much of their manufacturing done at facilities outside the Chicago area. Reading the essays most closely tied to the parts of the economy regularly in today's news will provide a detailed look at how the impact of the new global economy is affecting Chicago and Chicagoans.

To capture the economic turbulence and change of the new century, many of the essays have been updated from the original *Encyclopedia of Chicago*. It was clear to many of the authors when they submitted their essays for the 2004 *Encyclopedia* that their most contemporary observations were capturing Chicago in a period of enormous economic change. Peter A. Coclanis, in his "Business of Chicago" essay, states it succinctly: "Chicago in many ways and for many people remains even today the 'I will' city 'that works.' Whether it will remain so in the future as capitalist market integration intensifies in our increasingly 'borderless' economic world is the challenge facing Chicagoans in the generations to come." David Moberg, in his essay "Work," echoes a similar sentiment: "As far as the future of work in Chicago is concerned, the 'City of the Big Shoulders' has become the 'metropolis of the big question mark.'"

The updates made to these earlier essays document that change, still very much in progress. Most of the updates appear in "The Business of Chicago" and "Chicago's Businesses" sections, in part because change takes place faster in individual firms than in the landscape or in the nature of the workforce. Because this volume rests on the enormous research of individual authors in the *Encyclopedia*, the names of whom appear with the essays, every effort was made to leave their original contributions intact.

Updates were added most frequently at the end of essays and can be recognized by their dates. Generally, anything that refers to something after 2002 was updated for this volume.

This strategy makes this volume up-to-date, at least until the waning months of 2011. It also illustrates the constantly shifting economic environment that confronts the region's residents, businesses, planners, and governments. However, it also means that some of the city's "hottest" companies do not have their own entries in the section "Chicago's Businesses" because new companies were not added for this volume. In no sector is this more noticeable than that of high tech. Parts of that story appear in the histories of corporations and sectors that have moved into high tech. The "Electronics" essay, for example, highlights Chicago's involvement and leadership in the development of electronics equipment from the telephone to the television to computers to chip making and back to cell phones. Motorola's corporate history ends with its 2011 split and Google's purchase of one of the new companies.

Groupon (group coupon), the Chicago-based electronic commerce firm that figured prominently in the business press in 2011, does not have its own corporate entry. Using the guidelines for the *Encyclopedia of Chicago* that stipulated number of employees, revenues, and long-term significance as requirements for inclusion, it would not have appeared. Yet this firm, which was founded in 2008 and was once described as America's fastest-growing company, is part of Chicago's new economy, providing discount coupons electronically to consumers throughout the United States and around the world. In its choice of office location and investments, Groupon also reflects the changes to Chicago's previous economy. Its offices are in the former Montgomery Ward catalog building, and its cofounders were among those who purchased the Wrigley Building on Michigan Avenue in 2011. Future development of that property will show whether, as local reporters speculated, one of Chicago's most famous buildings will become an incubator for new high-tech firms.

Groupon is only one of many such businesses that are reshaping the economic landscape of the Chicago region and that have fueled the city's aspirations to become the Midwest's Silicon Valley. Some, like AllScripts, began offering one service and flourished by taking a leading role in the incorporation of digital technologies. Launched in 1986 to market prepackaged medications to physicians to dispense directly to patients, AllScripts grew into one of the world's leading providers of electronic medical records and information systems. Others, like Orbitz—an online travel service launched in 2001 with the support of major airlines—have flourished and supported the development of other tech innovators in Chicago. Some of the successful start-ups like EveryBlock—a web service for neighborhood discussion and block-level information developed and headquartered in Chicago—have been bought by firms elsewhere that saw the value of the ideas imagined and implemented here. Still others, like GrubHub—which since 2004 has made it possible for consumers to order food from restaurants online and have it delivered to them—have been able to use their profits and infusions of venture capital to expand by purchasing other firms and tapping new technologies like those associated with smart phones and other mobile devices.

The success of these firms has depended not only on their founders' visions and their market appeal; it has also depended heavily on capital investments. Investments from outside of Chicago have always been important for the city's economic development. The railroads, for example, could not have been built without financial assistance in the form of land grants from the federal government and huge infusions of money from both foreign and U.S. investors. There is no essay in this collection, nor in the *Encyclopedia*, that attempted to encapsulate the story of where these diverse investments came from over time and across industries. The task of doing so was simply too daunting for a short essay. However, the importance of hedge funds, private equity companies, and other such capital investment firms is visible in many of the updates for this volume, as their influence and importance grows in the current economic environment. A few of these local firms, with longer histories in Chicago, have their own entries in the "Chicago's Businesses" section. References to other firms such as Sam Zell's Equity Group Investments or Warren Buffett's Berkshire Hathaway appear in the histories of local firms that have been purchased, reorganized, privatized, or closed in the last four decades. Those references, dispersed as they are, document the important role that these investments firms have played in shaping Chicago's contemporary economy, especially in the borderless economic world to which Coclanis referred.

Although evidence of that world is visible in many of the essays, none encapsulates it quite as well as the updated essay on commodity markets. The electronic trading that made the famous trading "pits" largely unnecessary along with the merger of the Chicago Mercantile Exchange and the Chicago Board of Trade (as well as their New York counterparts) into the CME Group Inc. and CBOE Holdings Inc. have shown what a borderless economic world means for two of Chicago's most iconic firms, the origins of both having depended on Chicago's regional and global role over a century before. Even more revealing of this new environment was the 2011 threat by the CME Group to relocate to another state. Long and complex negotiations between the CME Group, the city of Chicago, and, most importantly, the state of Illinois followed. The result was a change in the state tax code that reflected the CME Group's worldwide business and prompted the company's decision to stay in Chicago.

Those negotiations had much to do with civic pride; the idea of the Chicago Board of Trade being located in Florida would be a blow to the city's ego and its aspirations as a global city. But, equally important, it has to do with jobs and politics. This is not a volume about Chicago politics, but the updates suggest that they are as important today as in earlier periods that are well documented in the *Encyclopedia of Chicago*. Politics were instrumental in bringing new corporate headquarters like Boeing and MillerCoors into Chicago. They have been critical in negotiations with unions about labor costs at McCormick Place in an attempt to keep the large conventions coming to Chicago that provide jobs and contribute to the revenues of the city and its businesses. They have been front and center in the battle over Chicago's Walmart Stores, a firm that has a record of putting smaller establishments out of business and offering jobs with low wages and limited benefits, even as it promises to provide retail outlets to areas of the city with few retail outlets and with jobless rates much higher than most of the metropolitan area. By 2010, according to *Crain's Chicago Business*, Walmart, with its more than 21,000 jobs in the area, was Chicagoland's sixth largest employer.

The other large employers in the Chicago area also reveal the importance of the political world for work in contemporary Chicago. The top employers are all governmental: the U.S. government, the Chicago Public Schools, the city of Chicago, the state of Illinois, and Cook County; the CTA and the University of Illinois at Chicago make the list as well. Other large employers and the economic sectors that they represent have been very visible in the political debates raging over the U.S. economy and the government's role in it. Representing the banking industry, JPMorgan Chase and Bank of America, relatively new players in Chicago, are among its largest employers. The health care industry, another topic of intense political debate, is represented in the list of top employers by Advocate Health Care, Resurrection Health Care, Rush University Medical Center, and the city's large universities with substantial medical schools and hospital operations: the University of Illinois at Chicago, the University of Chicago, and Northwestern University. In these and other sectors, what happens politically will certainly have an effect on Chicago's economic role as both a regional city and as a global city.

The final update and reorganization of this work lies in its bibliography. It features the most readily available and important books for understanding Chicago's economy over its history. It also includes the most recent efforts to document and explain the new economy. Readers of this volume are encouraged to consult them to learn more. They should also revisit the *Encyclopedia of Chicago* or its online version at http://www.encyclopedia.chicagohistory.org to trace the economic impact of the topics presented here back into individual communities, political debates, and a wider range of activities that also contributed to the economic environment Chicago helped to drive and that, in turn, shaped the city and region over the last three centuries.

# I. The Economic Geography of Chicago

# Chicago's World—Within a Day's Travel

Chicago's relations with the wider world changed as its transportation links extended its geographical reach. The white areas on these four maps show how far a person could travel from Chicago by scheduled service in a 24-hour period, calculated for four dates at 50-year intervals since early in the city's history. In 1850 travel was restricted to lake and canal boat, stagecoach, and a single railroad line west of the city. Consequently, the zone of access with a day's travel reached little farther than Peoria, Milwaukee, and some other local centers within the region. By 1900 railroads had supplanted all other means of fast long-distance travel, and Chicagoans could reach most of the remainder of the United States and some parts of nearby Canada and Mexico within a day. In 1950 air service had joined railroads to extend 24-hour travel from Chicago (often in combination) to much of North and Central America, as well as some localities in Western Europe. By 2000 this combined reach, together with road service, had effectively expanded Chicago's reach to much of the rest of the well-populated world.

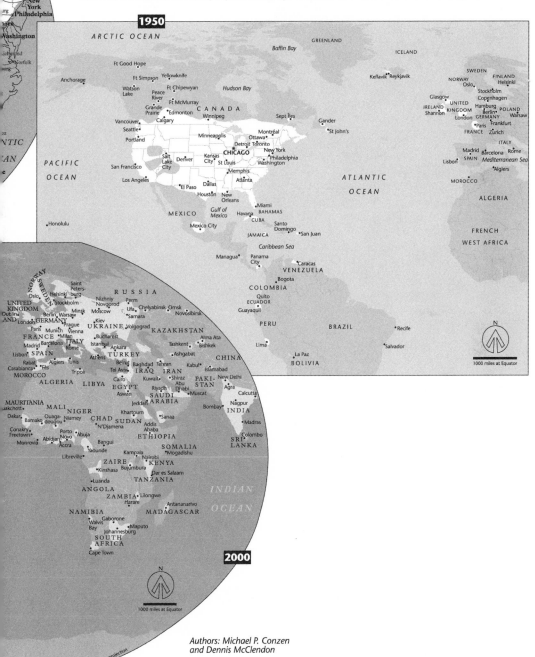

Authors: Michael P. Conzen
and Dennis McClendon

© 2004 The Newberry Library

# Global Chicago

For most of human existence, no city existed on the southwestern shore of Lake Michigan. Chicago arose there within the thinnest sliver of human time. But having been willed forth, Chicago became a prototypical American product, built from scratch and in a hurry, a time ball of urban dreams a mere 175 years old. And well before its own centennial, in its precocious size, itchy dynamism, and rough edges, Chicago had become what Frank Lloyd Wright called the "national capital of the essentially American spirit." As Chicago's material presence and power have grown, a parallel world has arisen to shape the outlook of its citizens, the reach of its physical prowess, and the outer bounds of its influence.

This essay maps that world by considering Chicago's role within the territorial economies of its region, the nation, and the globe, as well as its cultural institutions, intellectual creativity, and projected identity. Chicago redefined its spheres of influence, both internal and external, in five distinct but related stages.

## NEW WORLD COMING: 1780–1832

"Chicagou" came to life as one of several meeting points linking the diverse habitats of the Great Lakes with Indian portage routes to the vast Mississippi Valley. A nexus of periodic trade for centuries among Indian peoples, it acquired new meaning as European explorers, fur traders, and adventurers pounced on its regional advantages. As the fur trade swelled in the late eighteenth century, Chicago formed as a loose community of Indian, French, and American traders distinguished by their long-distance ties, biracial households, and pragmatic cohabitation. It was a society dependent on consumer demand a continent and an ocean away, yet its isolation bestowed congenial self-governance upon its members.

This multi-ethnic world came under pressure from advancing colonial interests, reflected in the strategic establishment of Fort Dearborn in 1803. As the fur trade declined and American settler interest grew, the small but relatively successful integrated community quickly succumbed to the relentless influx of white frontier opportunists intent on quickening the trade in European commodities and transforming the Middle West into a farmer's paradise. This world had no place for indigenes set in their ways.

## MERCHANT COMING: 1833–1848

The city of Chicago was born on the promise of a canal capable of providing cheap transcontinental water access from Lake Michigan to the Illinois River and whatever additional transport links might then follow. The Illinois & Michigan Canal had a difficult birth, spanning a quarter century of planning, funding, and construction. Unlike the Erie Canal, Chicago's 97-mile-long waterway was built through a virtually unpopulated region, ahead of demand. Yet the canal's very imminence spurred settlement along its margins and brought hoards of speculators and capable businessmen to its Chicago terminus, many from New England and New York, with much-needed eastern capital in their pockets. Not surprisingly, then, Chicago's commercial links during the wait for the canal were primarily with the northeastern states of the Union. Most traffic came by lake, though intrepid travelers also journeyed overland through southern Michigan and northern Indiana.

A strange geometry of external relations paired this economic and cultural link to the East with political power emanating from the southern sections of Illinois, home to the governor and legislative influence over internal improvements. Little did these politicians realize how geographically lopsided the long-term benefits of canal construction would be, although Abraham Lincoln rightly stressed that any benefit for northern Illinois would indirectly aid the rest of the state. Had state representatives farther south known how astounding Chicago's growth would be during the quarter century to follow, and how fatefully it would etch the social and political divide between the city and "Downstate," they would surely have hindered the canal's completion. As it was, Chicago at first developed as a terminal lake port awaiting the opening of transport avenues to the west and south, already savoring the prospect of huge increases in interregional trade. The immense confidence in the future shown by Chicago's fast-accumulating entrepreneurial class spurred speculative real estate bubbles of unprecedented scale, and this confidence spilled over into other business activity.

The built environment of Chicago combined an odd mixture of boomtown flimsiness and incipient solidity. The former could be seen in the countless utilitarian homes and stores constructed of wood—going up daily by the score—while the latter characterized the proud new government structures, such as the courthouse, customs house, post office, and several elegant churches. Chicago built itself in the image of eastern cities of the day, full of Greek revival architecture and tall spires, as well as Federal-style commercial blocks that would have looked at home in Boston or Philadelphia. It was a merchant's town, focused on the business core strung along both sides of the main stem of the Chicago River and benefiting from the federal government's financial help in straightening the river's mouth. Considering that the state canal commissioners (who controlled all canal land sales in the city environs) drew up and implemented the city plan—together with the canal works themselves, the river improvements, and the infrastructure provided by the establishment of federal services—one could be excused for regarding early Chicago as quite the government town. Such priming of the pump, together with the rush of private capital from outside, ensured the city's future.

Chicago possessed no clear urban margin. Land sales and lot subdivisions were so lusty and widespread that houses and businesses tapered off indiscriminately into the countryside. Yet the place was too small and pedestrian-based to have suburbs. Chicago grew to more than 20,000 residents by 1848, a burgeoning community of new arrivals and transients preoccupied with getting and spending. Institutional development proceeded slowly, with a tilt toward commerce, especially among the newspapers. Self-made men built mansions filled with imported exotica. More complete cultural refinement would come later.

For all the tenuous new wealth, when the canal opened and the first short railways were constructed, the physical world of Chicagoans was still decidedly local. The range of travel within a 24-hour period confined travelers to a sphere that barely penetrated the Illinois Valley and the southern districts around the base of Lake Michigan. The year 1848, however, was pivotal. The canal and first railroad west brought sudden agricultural bounty to the city from this new hinterland, and Chicago prospered as a transshipment center. This led to the formation of the Chicago Board of Trade and subsequently to its system of futures trading on wheat and corn deliveries. Balloon-frame construction, strikingly associated with Chicago, forever changed Americans' access to inexpensive homes, and other auguries of an innovative urban environment began to make their appearance. Chicago had begun to define itself as a midwestern metropolis, not just an eastern reproduction.

## INDUSTRIAL COMING: 1848–1894

While the canal triggered Chicago's takeoff to sustained growth, the concentration of long-distance railroads during the 1850s, '60s, and '70s gave the city its regional power within the national economy. The railroads permitted Chicago to surpass the longer-established and proud city of St. Louis for control of trade in the great continental interior and the Far West and underwrote a dramatic industrialization of the metropolis that placed it at the forefront of American modernity by century's end. St. Louis was not the only rival; Chicago also eclipsed the older Queen City of Cincinnati and hobbled the chances of contemporary rivals such as Indianapolis and Milwaukee. St. Louis had seemed perfectly situated to serve as the central transfer point for the continental nation, but it was Chicago instead that fully grasped its own potential as the hub of western land routes and the industry-friendly water routes of the Great Lakes to the east. The radiating of trunk railroads from Chicago in all directions by the 1890s brought all manner of business to the city and gave its residents unparalleled choice in connecting with other places, making it a national center both economically and culturally. Chicagoans could now reach the bulk of the continental United States within 24 hours, a boast no other city's boosters could make.

The 1890 U.S. census listed Chicago as the country's second largest city (after New York), a fact surely attributable to Chicago's commercial ascendancy, but also to its strategic annexations of surrounding townships during the year prior to the census. This happy conjunction of affairs was not unimportant in securing the epochal World's Columbian Exposition for Chicago a mere two years later.

What the annexations only underscored, however, was the rapacious industrial development that Chicago and its outlying satellite communities had attracted by the 1890s. From the agricultural machinery industry (embodied by McCormick's reaper firm) of the late 1840s, to the giant meatpacking sector (the Armour and Swift companies) that emerged from the Civil War, and the manufacturing of complex machinery and railroad equipment (at George Pullman's Palace Car Company, for example) in the 1880s, Chicago industrialized on a gigantic scale. The economics of steelmaking came to favor a two-way system of iron and coal exchange through the Great Lakes shipping network that diffused the industry from Pennsylvania to the Middle West and to Chicago in particular. Railroads and steel undergirded a broad industrialization that transformed Chicago from a merchants' town into a metropolis of heavy industry with all its job-creating implications. Chicago became a factory city simultaneously for producer and consumer goods, which it could distribute in all directions. In 1848, Chicago had been dependent for most of its sophisticated manufactured goods on eastern imports; by the 1890s, Chicago competed with eastern cities in most categories of mass production. It was also becoming a banking center of national importance.

Physically, Chicago in this period developed a star pattern set within a giant wheel of satellite settlements. First, industrialization created a commuter city, a web of residential enclaves bordered by a latticework of industrial corridors, all woven together by mass-transit sinews that thrust the city outward in vectors along commuter railroad lines and selected streetcar routes. The railroads gave birth to bedroom suburbs strung like beads along lines out from the central city. These commuter spokes of the metropolitan wheel connected with outlying towns (Waukegan, Elgin, Aurora, Joliet, and Gary) that had industrialized in their own right. Suburbs born on a grand scale were functionally dependent on Chicago in all but local governance, and outlying cities came within Chicago's daily orbit. A centripetal metropolitan world pulsating on a daily basis had begun to emerge.

The Great Fire of 1871 propelled Chicago's urban core into a modernizing mode. The center would be built with immense solidity (balloon-frame wood construction had all too easily become kindling) and, increasingly, to great heights as tall buildings became technically feasible and businesses came to favor their operational efficiencies and symbolic potential. The core also gained culturally, as civic and business leaders began to create an institutional structure for the arts, science, and letters through the founding of permanent performing companies (e.g., the Chicago Symphony Orchestra, 1891), libraries (e.g., the Newberry Library, 1887; Chicago Public Library and Crerar Library, 1897), museums (e.g., the Field Museum, 1893), and universities (e.g., University of Chicago, 1892) to humanize somewhat the raw face of this upstart behemoth. What kept the metropolis raw were the gross inequities of large-scale capital in an age of robber barons getting rich from abundant cheap labor where people were sometimes made to work in scandalously unsafe conditions. The worker unrest of 1886 and the Pullman Strike of 1894 were explosive high points in a long struggle between labor and capital in Chicago that paralleled and punctuated its rise to industrial might.

## SECOND COMING: 1894–1968

Chicago's meteoric rise to replace Philadelphia as the nation's second largest city conditioned Chicagoans to expect their city to catch up with and surpass New York in short order. And it was not simply a matter of uncontrolled boosterism. Using a heartland-rimland model of urban supremacy in the deployment of natural resources, a University of Chicago geographer confidently predicted just such an outcome in a 1926 address before the Commercial Club of Chicago. While his predictions were not accurate, they reveal a recognition of the power of massive industrialization to propel the metropolis forward in size and complexity on the basis of coal, steel, and (later) petroleum. For the first two-thirds of the twentieth century, Chicagoans believed in the unfailing virtues of mass production in centralized facilities in central locations, and shaped their city to proffer these conditions. Chicago became the great western anchor of a vast heavy-manufacturing belt stretching from Massachusetts to Illinois. To the west, north, and south lay the immense resource regions to supply it with raw materials—corn, wheat, cattle, lumber, iron ore, coal, and petroleum—with Chicago as consumer and funnel to eastern markets, as well as dispenser of manufactures to these staple-producing regions.

From 1900 to 1970, Chicago functioned as a complete national-scale metropolis, with particular sway over a continental interior extending to the Rocky Mountains and beyond. By 1950, Chicagoans could travel to four continents in a single day's journey, thanks to planes and trains. New York had more international ties and better links with the national hinterland when only one extra-local connection was needed, but Chicago was its only serious competitor and trying hard to cut the margin.

Chicago's world was enlarged socially, too, by the diversifying regions around the world from which it drew its new population elements. A ceaseless procession of new migrants piled into Chicago's growing factories. Eastern and southern European immigrants streamed through East Coast ports of entry and headed straight for the capital of the midcontinent. Subsequently, African Americans headed north in unprecedented numbers from the penury of southern cotton fields. All added to an already multicultural city long dominated by Yankees, the Irish, and Germans. For some from overseas—such as the Swedes, Lithuanians, and Danes—Chicago became the second city for their ethnic community in the world, a veritable exclave of emigrants with new lives and new allegiances.

The world that Chicagoans created in the region during this long period of industrial hegemony was characterized by rising densities in developed districts, infilling between the spokes, and aggressive expansion into the urban fringe, pushing it back until the metropolitan wheel became more like a giant crescent extending inland from the lakeshore. As the suburbs proliferated, an anti-urban bias pitted them increasingly against the central city, socially and politically. The spread of the automobile offered individual freedom, until the next encounter with gridlock. Superhighways were inserted into the metropolitan frame, disrupting community life in the tight neighborhoods where expressways were pushed through, while creating wholly new axes for urban development beyond the built-up zone.

Chicago flowered in this period as a center of literature, art, design, and performance. From the novelists of the early twentieth-century Chicago literary renaissance to the rise of Chicago blues music, from the advent of the Art Institute to the rise of opera, ballet, and the popularity of theater, Chicago invented, presented, and reconfigured its feisty urban culture to the world. Through boom and depression, peace and war, expansion and segregation, this cultural awakening created a canon of works that reflect the energetic, convoluted, contested social worlds of the time and something of the identity of the place. Above all, Chicago projected a hunger for and celebration of modernity, best captured in the technological wonders of the 1933 Century of Progress Exposition and the continuous record of architectural innovation from the earliest steel-skeleton skyscrapers to the Miesian-lessness of slab-style architecture that culminated in the totemic Prudential Building.

But it was a fractured modernity, tolerating racial injustice, housing segregation, job discrimination, and political demagoguery. Urban planning came of age, became bureaucratized, and, despite successive clarion calls for collaborative regional visions (beginning most notably with Daniel Burnham), stopped, stupefied, at the municipal boundary. As suburbs prospered on Federal Housing Authority mortgage subsidies and became increasingly diverse in vision, social character, and environmental appeal, the central city inherited all the problems of an aging infrastructure, threatened tax base, and divided people. Moreover, the connected city was also the visible city: the 1968 Democratic National Convention gave the world an eyeful of America's social cleavages and provided a glimpse of Chicago's unsettled world.

## GLOBAL COMING: 1969–2004

The world has been globalizing for centuries, but only since the 1970s has electronic connectivity gone meaningfully global for businesses and individuals. In this human environment, with its boundless competition for resources and markets, cities must strive to be global in their connections, if not always in assets and urban reputation. Chicago ranks with New York and Los Angeles as one of the world's ten "alpha" cities in most inventories of global economic hipness. This status has been earned through a combination of old-fashioned, cumulative development of economic and social infrastructure critical to international operations, as well as through painful readjustments in the last three decades of the twentieth century to metropolitan deindustrialization, particularly severe in the central city. While industrial loss afflicted the Rustbelt as a whole, Chicago emerged tolerably well to compete in a new environment of diversified, globally positioned, high-tech industries, as well as to develop its financial and corporate services institutions. While losing much of its banking independence, Chicago sought to buttress its role as a home to international corporate headquarters. New York far outdistances Chicago in this field, but the move of the Boeing Company to Chicago in 2001 suggested the city's continuing viability at the highest levels of global business support.

In a world in which individuals can communicate via satellite signals with others almost anywhere in the world, the reach that a traveler can personally extend around the world in 24 hours remains a measure of social and societal significance. In 2000, such a traveler from Chicago could penetrate all six settled continents (although by no means reach all other important cities). Air travel has become an American norm for global and interregional movement, and Chicago's possession of strategic and busy (sometimes too busy) O'Hare International Airport has been key to its global connectedness.

Whether or not Chicago has reached a stage of "postmodernity," the metropolitan crescent has become an ever-farther-flung web of regional settlement. Exurbs—residential subdivisions sitting amid cornfields with no visible support from nearby urban services—scatter across the countryside 100 miles from downtown Chicago and send commuters to the outer fringes of the metropolitan employment web. Frequent direct daily express bus service connects residents of Madison, Wisconsin, and central northern Indiana with flights leaving from O'Hare Airport. Nearly 7 million suburbanites inhabit the margins of Chicago, which struggles to retain and add to its own 2.7 million residents. This world is one of ever greater anonymity, congestion amid sprawl, efforts to maintain costly infrastructure, and strangely skewed or nonexistent conversations among communities, political and cultural, in the metropolitan web, as parochial worlds seek distance from one another's problems.

As Chicago's suburbs have aged, the central city has learned at least some lessons in recapitalizing the built environment. Something of a renaissance has taken hold in Chicago's public governance, approach to services, and official outlook on city viability and livability. That renaissance has been driven at least in part by demographic changes that occasionally transform minorities into majorities. But it has also been driven by a certain discipline imposed by global competitiveness to put on an attractive face for visiting conventioneers, tourists, and other contributors to the urban economy. The city has become festooned with wrought-iron fences, median planters, and other elaborate street furniture, as well as spectacular nighttime lighting effects on tall buildings and other landmarks. Gentrification and new-town/in-town developments have penetrated large swaths of the once-tired urban core, crossed racial lines, and received municipal support through tax abatements and the effective privatization of neighborhood street parking.

## RETROSPECT

Chicago's world has expanded exponentially over time, in physical, psychological, symbolic, and practical ways. The metropolitan "neighborhood" of greater Chicago has more people crammed in and strewn about than ever before; they move about with greater speed and frequency; there are vastly more things to acquire and aspire to; there is more choice of what to do and what to be interested in—and greater difficulty in comprehending the complexity of it all. Psychological time and distance and the pace of life have been redefined many times. Contemporary Chicagoans are worlds away from their predecessors, even those just a few generations back. Could Jean Baptiste Point DuSable, the I&M Canal Commissioners, Marshall Field, Jane Addams, Theodore Dreiser, and Anton Cermak possibly have imagined the character of Chicago as it existed at the opening of the twenty-first century? How much more difficult is it to realistically imagine the Chicago world they inhabited?          *Michael P. Conzen*

# Economic Geography

American cities grow or decline because of their roles in the national economy. The village of Chicago became the country's second largest city in 1889 because it captured many of the fastest-growing sectors of that economy. Businessmen and politicians enhanced Chicago's geographical position at the eastern edge of the nation's agricultural heartland, making it the center of multiple transportation networks. These supported wholesale trade and manufacturing, which spurred the city's growth. Industry determined the physical development of the city itself, preempting space for zones of commerce and manufacturing and channeling the expansion of residential neighborhoods. During the twentieth century, new economic trends undermined Chicago's position; decentralization favored suburbs over cities, and the rise of the South and West created new centers of competition for the most dynamic sectors of the economy.

Chicago developed because its site was convenient for commerce. For hundreds of years, American Indians gathered each summer to trade where the Chicago River enters Lake Michigan. In 1673 the French explorer Louis Jolliet recognized Chicago's potential for wider trade: it sits on a low divide between the drainage areas of the Great Lakes and the Mississippi River, and only one large portage breaks an all-water route between Lake Michigan and the Gulf of Mexico via the Chicago, Des Plaines, Illinois, and Mississippi Rivers. During the rainy season, the "Chicago Portage" between the Chicago and Des Plaines Rivers could be traversed by canoe. Jolliet suggested cutting a canal across this portage to link the Gulf and French Canada, but French officials ignored him.

Chicago's first permanent resident, Jean Baptiste Point DuSable, settled near the mouth of the Chicago River in the late 1780s to take advantage of this geography to trade with the Indians. In 1795 the new United States government also recognized the site's potential and acquired a piece of land, six miles square around the mouth of the river, by treaty with the Indians. Fort Dearborn, erected in 1803, secured the site for Americans. Trading eastern manufactured goods for furs established a base for Chicago's economy, consistent with DuSable's more limited enterprise. After 1819 the American Fur Company, headed by John Jacob Astor in New York, monopolized the fur trade of Chicago and the Great Lakes region. From this point, Chicago's economy was tied to national and international markets and financing. By the late 1820s, overhunting depopulated the game of Illinois, and the American Fur Company left Chicago for points farther west. Rather than wither, however, the village of fewer than 100 residents began its rapid expansion as others saw new opportunities in the site.

National business and political leaders created the conditions for the rise of Chicago in order to develop the country's western territories. When New York's Erie Canal connected the Great Lakes to the Atlantic Ocean

# Economic Origins of Metropolitan Chicago's Communities

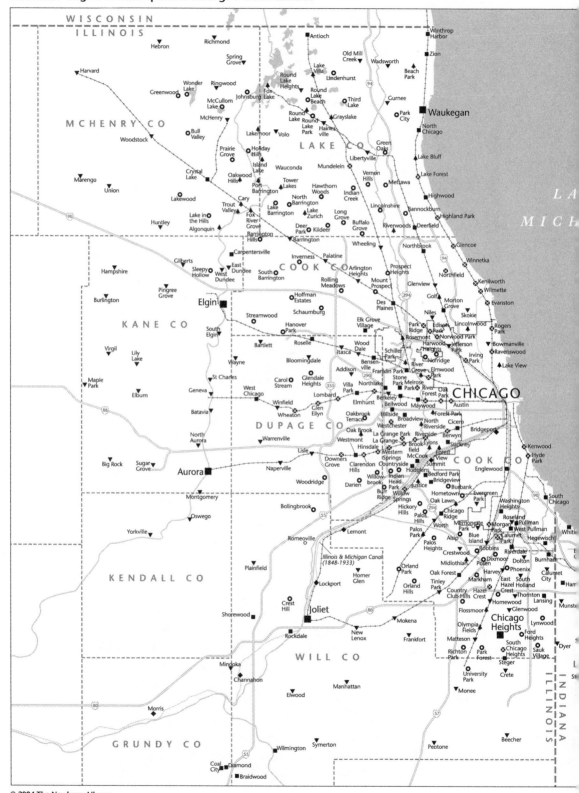

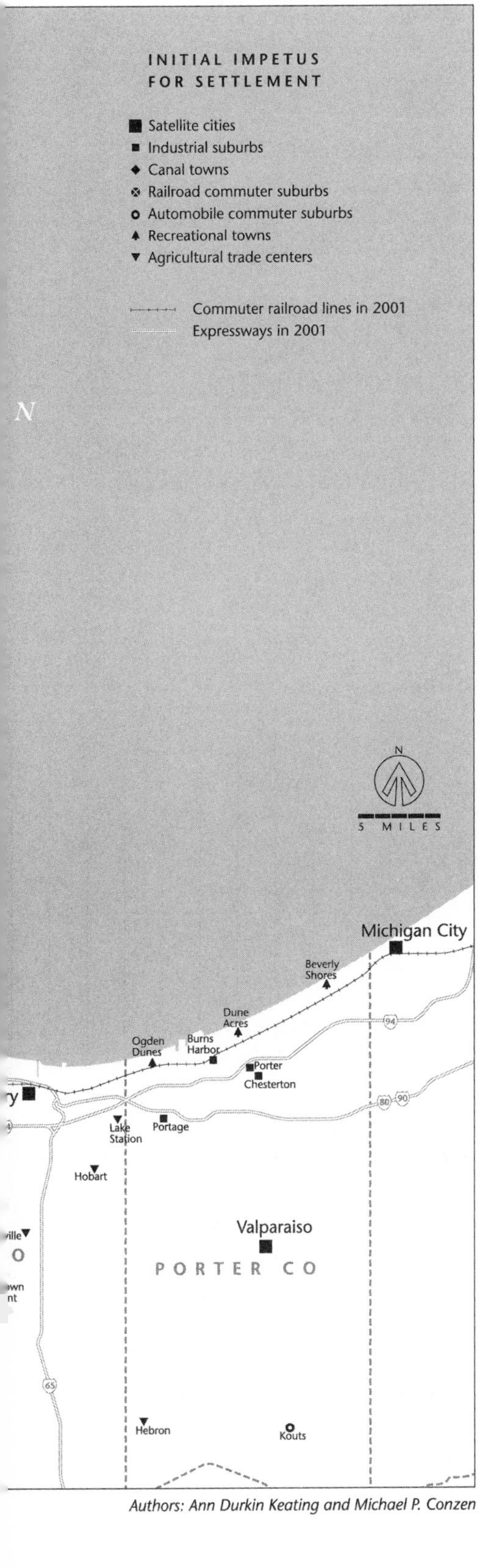

*N*

N

5 MILES

Michigan City

Beverly
Shores ▲

Dune
Acres ▲

Ogden   Burns
Dunes ▲ Harbor
        ■      ■ Porter
               Chesterton

⊗ 94

80  90

y ■

Lake    ▼ Portage
Station

▼ Hobart

ville ▼          Valparaiso
○                     ■
wn
nt          P O R T E R   C O

65

▼ Hebron          ○ Kouts

*Authors: Ann Durkin Keating and Michael P. Conzen*

The classification of community types displayed on this map is based primarily upon entries in the *Encyclopedia of Chicago*. Identifications reflect the initial impetus for clustered settlement beyond agricultural use, effectively the initial step in the urbanization process. Note the relationship between history and geography. Eight old industrial satellite cities ring the metropolis at a distance of about 25 to 40 miles, while old agricultural trade centers stud the region as a whole. Canal towns line the Illinois & Michigan Canal heading out of Chicago to the southwest, while communities that started as railroad suburbs line the major commuter railroad corridors. Later automobile-era suburbs fill in many of the interstitial spaces. Industrial suburbs of varying age appear with greater frequency on the Near West and South Sides of the metropolitan area, while recreational towns are more abundant to the north and northwest.

in 1825, they searched for a port at the western end of the lakes to serve the potential trade with new settlers. Eastern businessmen and Illinois politicians revived Jolliet's vision to connect the lakes to the Mississippi through Chicago, and in 1829 state legislators began planning the Illinois & Michigan Canal.

For easterners to settle northern Illinois, however, the Indians had to be dispossessed. In 1833 the federal government pressured the united Potawatomi, Chippewa, and Ottawa nations to cede all their lands east of the Mississippi River, opening the path for easterners to seek their fortunes in northern Illinois.

Chicago had no natural harbor, but the sandbar at the mouth of the Chicago River created a sheltered spot for boats. The river became a federal harbor in 1834, when government aid for cutting a channel across the bar, constructing piers, and dredging made the river into the port of Chicago. The state authorized construction of a canal in 1836, and bonds sold well to eastern capitalists. From the mid-1830s, Chicago developed as a transfer point—shipping midwestern agricultural products to New York and eastern manufactured goods to farmers on the plains.

While many people came to Chicago to engage in this trade, others came because they believed a city would develop around the port. Real estate speculation fueled town development in nineteenth-century America and was an important avenue to wealth. Speculation in Chicago real estate boomed in 1835 in anticipation of the construction of the canal. Several thousand people, including many New Yorkers, migrated to the city. William B. Ogden, Chicago's first mayor, came to oversee a relative's real estate investments and bolstered their value by developing transportation facilities. He promoted the first swing bridge to span the Chicago River and link the North and South Sides of the city. In 1836 he helped found Chicago's first railroad, the Galena & Chicago Union, to connect the port to the lead mining center on the Mississippi.

Although most Chicagoans were involved in trade or real estate speculation, some established factories to process the farm produce and natural resources that were shipped to the city. In 1829 Archibald Clybourne began meatpacking, and a lumber mill settled near his factory on the North Branch of the Chicago River. The city's first manufacturing district developed there, with the river providing transportation and waste disposal.

The national economic depression of 1837 halted work on the canal and the railroad. Trade atrophied, and Chicago land values plummeted. In 1840 Chicago was a small city of more than 4,000 people, with the outline of the transportation network that would make it the center of wholesale trade in the West. Once the national economy revived in the mid-1840s, Chicago's potential came to fruition.

Eighteen forty-eight was a key year for the city—the canal was completed, the first railroad opened, the telegraph reached town, and the Chicago Board of Trade was founded. The canal facilitated trade in bulky goods, not only farm produce but also coal from southern Illinois to fuel the city's homes and industries. Initial plans called for a deep-cut canal to allow boats to pass directly from the lake to the river system, but lack of funds led supporters to settle for a narrow, shallow one. This reinforced Chicago's position as a transfer point where goods were switched from lake boats to barges. Traffic on the canal peaked in 1882. In the long run, Chicago's development as a rail hub was more important for its dominance in wholesaling.

Private companies built railroads radiating out from Chicago in all directions to tap the farms of the Midwest. By 1856, ten trunk railroads ended in Chicago, making the city a breakpoint for railroad traffic as well as waterborne trade. Tracks paralleled the river and canal to facilitate transfers of goods between railroad cars, canal barges, and lake ships. The wholesale traders set up along the river on South Water Street to direct this commerce. By 1854 Chicago claimed title as the greatest primary grain port in the world, and the grain elevators lining the river dominated the skyline. The grain trade grew rapidly as a national speculative futures market developed. The telegraph made such a market technologically feasible, but the Chicago Board of Trade made it a reality. It created standards and measures such as grades of wheat along with an elevator inspection system, giving eastern capitalists enough confidence to invest in grain sight unseen. The lumber trade also boomed, as lumber from the midwestern woods was shipped by boat across the lake to be milled in the city. A huge lumber district, with sawmills and extensive storage yards, developed on the Chicago River's South Branch. After milling, the lumber was shipped by rail mostly to the West to build farmhouses, barns, and fences.

Chicago merchants combined wholesale and retail operations; they sent dry goods to small stores throughout the Midwest and kept stores in the city center for travelers and residents alike. The large retailers congregated on Lake Street, and Chicago's department stores developed as these establishments enlarged and diversified. The downtown rose around the wholesalers and retailers with hotels, restaurants, saloons, and less reputable businesses to service traveling men and conventioneers.

Although the wholesale trade was the most important element in Chicago's economy until the 1870s, industries for processing agricultural and raw materials also developed. Pork—salted, pickled, and otherwise preserved—was the primary product manufactured for easterners. At the same time, Chicago businessmen saw the potential of producing goods for farmers in Chicago rather than acting as middlemen for eastern manufacturers. In 1847 Cyrus H. McCormick opened his reaper works and initiated one of the city's most important industries—agricultural machinery.

The Civil War extended the advantages conferred by geography and human initiative. St. Louis, an older and larger city, was Chicago's rival for the western trade. Chicago's railroad network was making the city more attractive to shippers, but Union forces delivered the decisive blow to St. Louis when they closed the Mississippi River during the war. Trade that shifted to Chicago did not return to St. Louis after the war.

Contracts for supplies for the Union forces also stimulated Chicago enterprise, especially among the meatpackers. The packing plants, scattered around the city, had always been a nuisance because they created pollution. Now huge numbers of animals driven through the streets caused total congestion. Chicagoans wanted the plants moved, and the packers needed more space for pens and better access to railroads to minimize production delays. Chicago's first planned manufacturing district—the Union Stock Yard—opened in 1865 to solve these problems. The packers and the railroads chose a site just outside the city limits at 39th and Halsted Streets. With access to the canal and major railroads, it was the prototype of future industrial developments that would move to the edge of the city in search of space and better transportation.

By the end of the Civil War, Chicago was poised to build on its dominance of midwestern trade and its manufacturing base. Growth came quickly, as the completion of the transcontinental railroad enabled the vast expansion of Chicago's potential market. Federal subsidies underwrote this rapid development, in the form of land grants to railroads laying new track. Once again the joint efforts of politicians and businessmen secured Chicago's future. As the eastern terminus of important western railroads and the western terminus of eastern railroads, Chicago remained the central transfer point for people and freight. In the next decades, railroad building devoured more of Chicago's physical space, and rights-of-way guided the siting of industry and residences.

The Great Fire of 1871 decimated the center of the city, but it did not slow development. It spared most of the outlying areas, including the manufacturing district, the lumber district, the Union Stock Yard, the grain elevators, and the railroad freight terminals. This infrastructure supported the rapid rebuilding of the central business district and residential neighborhoods because it gave eastern investors who financed reconstruction confidence that the city would recover and investors would profit.

From 1870 to 1920, Chicago was "the metropolis of the West," the hub of transcontinental trade and the most dynamic center of manufacturing for the new national market. In the 1870s, Gustavus Swift financed the development of the railroad refrigerator car, enabling meat butchered in Chicago to be shipped fresh to the East. He established sales offices and refrigerated warehouses in eastern cities and launched a national advertising campaign to overcome consumer fears about meat that was not butchered locally. Other newcomers to the city, like Philip D. Armour, followed his lead, until Chicago's "Big Five" packing companies controlled the nation's meatpacking industry. By 1900 these companies were expanding internationally, both exporting Chicago products and opening subsidiary plants abroad.

As production at the stockyards increased, the residential neighbor-hoods around the factories grew polluted and congested. The slums of Packingtown were peopled by poor workers, primarily immigrants from central and eastern Europe who struggled to support their families and sustain their cultural traditions. Large working-class neighborhoods characterized by industrial pollution, congestion, poverty, and cultural diversity developed wherever industry located.

By 1890 Chicago had a population of more than 1 million people and had surpassed Philadelphia to become the second largest city in the nation and the second largest manufacturing center. The diversity as well as the size of its industries spurred this development. Manufacturing based on the trade in agricultural commodities, like brewing and baking, flourished. The furniture industry developed from the lumber trade; it prospered even after the woods of the northern Midwest had been decimated and the lumber trade declined in 1880s. Established industries like agricultural machinery also expanded as other manufacturers followed McCormick to Chicago. The creation of International Harvester from these companies in 1902 capped Chicago's leading position in this industry.

New industries such as iron and steel production also pushed Chicago ahead of other cities. The North Chicago Rolling Mill produced the city's first steel rails in 1865 but soon relocated to South Chicago. This move signaled not only its need for more space but also a new factor in the city's economic geography. The transcontinental railroads skirted the bottom of Lake Michigan, and production costs were minimized for manufacturers who obtained access to both lake boats and railroads by locating there. The new steel plant, which later became the United States Steel South Works, anchored the north end of the vast iron- and steel-producing district that developed along the lake from South Chicago to Gary, Indiana. Like the stockyards, it attracted workers, especially immigrants from eastern and southern Europe, and created new neighborhoods on the fringes of the city.

Industries that used iron and steel—including those that manufactured machinery, machine tools, and railroad cars and equipment—also developed, most frequently near the steelmaking district. George Pullman, who manufactured railcars, saw the potential of the area around Lake Calumet; major railroads ran nearby and the lake provided an inland harbor accessible to Lake Michigan by the Calumet River. He built the town of Pullman on the western edge of the lake in 1881 to house his workers and a new factory. Unlike most of Chicago's manufacturing districts, Pullman's model town was neither polluted nor congested. It became a tourist attraction—a vision of what people wished the city would be. No other manufacturers followed Pullman's lead in building decent neighborhoods, although others followed him to the Calumet region. In 1889 and 1893, Chicago annexed all these suburban districts as well as extensive territory to the north, more than tripling its area.

Although the combination of space and transportation drew some industries to the edges of the city, many still found the resources of the old central city more useful. Garment manufacturing was one of Chicago's most important industries, and Chicago led the nation in the production of men's clothing, thanks to firms such as Hart Schaffner & Marx. Garment makers settled in lofts west of the downtown near Chicago's poorest neighborhoods, because the cheap labor of women and children was their most important requirement.

Perhaps the most important resource of the central city was the concentration of modes of communication. Chicago's printing and publishing industry, second only to New York's, developed with companies such as R.R. Donnelley & Sons, which located near the downtown because of the demand for business information and the proliferation of commercial journals. Chicago businessmen who pioneered and came to dominate a new form of trade—mail-order houses—also utilized this concentration. Montgomery Ward was first in the field, but Sears, Roebuck & Co. became even larger. This revolution in retailing used printed catalogs to reach out to individual customers in rural areas and created white-collar "factories" in the center city—office buildings full of clerical workers who processed orders that arrived by mail and filled them from huge warehouses situated on the river and the railroads.

The continuing vitality of the old core was most apparent in the central business district, known as the Loop after 1882 when it was encircled by a cable car line. Chicago banks had expanded quickly after the Civil War; the city ranked second nationally in banking, manufacturing, wholesaling, and population by the end of the century. Large banks now joined the Board of Trade and the Stock Exchange to make LaSalle Street Chicago's financial center. The concentration of public transportation in the Loop enhanced its retail potential, too, as middle- and upper-class shoppers enjoyed easy access from outlying residential neighborhoods. The department stores moved from Lake Street to State Street when Potter Palmer developed the latter as a fashionable street in the late 1860s. Stores such as Marshall Field's and Carson Pirie Scott reached a new level of elegance, appealing to the prosperous clientele created by the city's expanding economy as well as to the growing tourist trade. To serve the tourist trade, the Loop provided hospitality and entertainment for every taste—from the elegant Palmer House to the cheapest transient hotels, and from the best theaters to the infamous Levee, Chicago's vice district. Tourism hit a peak in 1893, when Chicagoans hosted the World's Columbian Exposition.

The growing demand for office space in the Loop led upward because of the constricted area. The skyscrapers of Chicago became the symbol of business success and set the architectural fashion for central business districts throughout the country. The Loop's clerical and managerial workers used public transportation to commute to a variety of residential neighborhoods. Districts of boardinghouses and apartments for those without children and middle-class housing for families sprang up in a ring around the inner areas. Construction was the city's largest employer, and real estate speculation was still a major avenue to wealth. Some contractors, such as S. E. Gross, built large developments of single-family houses, comparable in scale to more recent subdivisions.

To maintain their economic prominence, Chicagoans sponsored more transportation improvements, like the Chicago Sanitary and Ship Canal, built in the 1890s to replace the obsolete Illinois & Michigan Canal. Like comparable projects, it boosted industrial development outside the city limits. The Chicago Outer Belt Line Railroad, completed in 1887, facilitated freight traffic and spurred manufacturing in Chicago Heights, Aurora, Joliet, and Elgin. Although outlying areas had always attracted industry, the implications for Chicago changed in the twentieth century. When the city limits reached already established communities such as Oak Park and Evanston, Chicagoans found the path to expansion blocked. After 1900 outlying communities resisted annexation to Chicago, and the metropolitan area developed as an integral economic unit without political control or social unity. The limits on Chicago's development were set.

After 1920 the suburbs grew faster than the city. New transportation, the car and the truck, encouraged the suburbanization of people and industries and reversed the century-old pattern of increasing concentration in the city. Railroads spurred suburban development, but always along their rights-of-way. Cars and trucks allowed industries and people to disperse throughout the area. This provided the large tracts necessary for the single-floor factories that utilized continuous-flow automated technologies.

As deconcentration increased, however, the metropolitan economy also experienced new competition. Detroit monopolized the most important new industry of the early twentieth century: automobiles. Even more significant were long-term shifts in regional development; the Midwest stagnated as the West and the South boomed. After 1920 cities in the Sunbelt enjoyed the advantages in location and transportation that previously had stimulated midwestern economic growth. Chicago businesses reeled during the Great Depression of the 1930s and then boomed because of World War II defense contracts, but the regional shift determined the long-term trend in economic growth and hence in population, and in 1990 Los Angeles surpassed Chicago as the second city in population and wholesaling.

Chicago's economy did not fall behind for lack of leadership or innovation. Businessmen and politicians fostered transportation improvements such as the Mississippi-Illinois Waterway to accommodate modern barge traffic. Chicago port facilities modernized, although, like many economic functions, they did so by moving out of the center of the city. After the Cal-Sag Channel between Calumet Harbor and the Illinois River opened in 1922, Calumet Harbor replaced the Chicago River as the city's port. Chicagoans also embraced new technologies and developed Midway Airport in the 1920s, making Chicago the breakpoint for cross-country air traffic as it was for water and rail. The country's largest airline, United, headquartered in Chicago. To maintain the country's busiest airport after World War II, Chicagoans developed the larger, more modern O'Hare.

The building of the interstate highway system in the 1950s and 1960s helped the area's economy initially, because the first expressways paralleled existing forms of transportation and reinforced older metropolitan areas. Transcontinental bus lines routed through Chicago, and the largest company, Greyhound, established its headquarters in the city. The Chicago area also became the country's leading trucking center. The interstate system intensified the attraction of suburban locations for industries, however, especially south of the city, where the major east–west and north–south routes met.

Between 1920 and 1970, the Chicago area retained most of its traditional industries. In 1954 it even surpassed Pittsburgh, the old leader, in iron and steel manufacturing, producing one-quarter of the nation's output. Production remained high in machinery, primary metals, printing and publishing, chemicals, food processing, and fabricated metals. The consumer electronics industry expanded greatly, as firms such as Motorola, Zenith, and Admiral captured a significant share of the market for radios and televisions. The first big loss, however, was meatpacking. The industry had been decentralizing since the turn of the century, as Chicago companies shifted to multiple plant locations in western cities, closer to the feed lots. The Chicago stockyards closed in the 1960s.

Although the area's industrial economy remained strong, the city's did not. Companies closed aging factories in the city and shifted work to new suburban plants. The McCormick Reaper Works was demolished in 1961; production was taken over by a new plant south of Hinsdale. Many new

Chicago has experienced three fundamental phases of economic development, reflected in the geography of its changing land use. Before the Civil War, Chicago sprang up as a highly successful merchants' town at the base of Lake Michigan, its future assured by the opening of the Illinois & Michigan Canal and the first railroad tracks laid westward. The commercial heart of the town developed along the Chicago River, which offered easy transshipment between lake vessels, canal boats, and train cars. Wholesale and shipping businesses crowded South Water Street; financial services located on Lake, Dearborn, and Randolph Streets; and lumber dealers lined the North and South Branches of the river. Between the Civil War and the Second World War, Chicago developed into a manufacturing city of staggering proportions, and industry of all types spread across the urban area. Most plants clung to the waterways and the proliferating railroads, which crisscrossed the city without hindrance. By the turn of the twentieth century, the cheap, marshy lakeshore lands of the South Side attracted a disproportionate amount of heavy industry. For all its diversity, Chicago's manufacturing pattern was dense, urban-oriented, and tied firmly to the central city. In the last half of the twentieth century, as the region experienced significant amounts of industrial decentralization and outright loss, Chicago's metropolitan economy turned markedly to service provision and restructuring for the information age. This was aptly reflected by 1990 in the highly bifurcated pattern of office space: a vast concentration of commercial offices in the Loop business district offset by a widespread scatter of office parks and commercial space in the suburbs, tied closely to the expressway network as it had evolved by then. The geography of office development is the obverse of the old industrial pattern.

# Chicago's Evolving Economic Geography

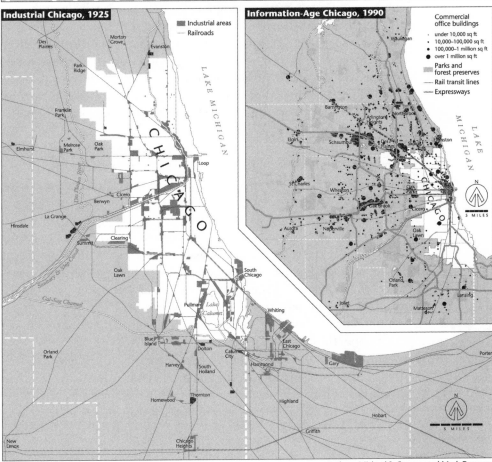

## Mercantile Chicago, 1854

Railroad shops
Galena & Chicago Union RR
Passenger station
Kinzle
Freight depot
*Chicago River*
Hospital
South Water
Passenger station
Lake
Market
Market
Dearborn
Market
Despaines
Jefferson
Clinton
Canal
West Water
Market
Franklin
Wells
LaSalle
Clark
Randolph
State
Wabash
Michigan
Court House
Washington
Madison
Illinois Central RR

- ■ Banks
- □ Exchange offices and brokers
- ● Forwarding and commission merchants
- ■ Lumber dealers
- □ Coal merchants
- ▽ Provision dealers
- ▲ Grocery dealers
- ⊕ Ship chandlers
- ⊛ Expresses
- ▨ Area beyond original townsite

N
500 FEET

*LAKE MICHIGAN*

## Industrial Chicago, 1925

- ■ Industrial areas
- — Railroads

Des Plaines
Morton Grove
Evanston
Park Ridge
Franklin Park
Elmhurst
Melrose Park
Oak Park
CHICAGO
Loop
Cicero
Berwyn
La Grange
Hinsdale
Summit
Clearing
Oak Lawn
South Chicago
Pullman
Lake Calumet
Whiting
Blue Island
Dolton
Calumet City
East Chicago
Orland Park
Harvey
South Holland
Hammond
Gary
Homewood
Thornton
Highland
Hobart
New Lenox
Chicago Heights
Griffith
Porter
*LAKE MICHIGAN*
*Des Plaines River*
*Sanitary & Ship Canal*
*Cal-Sag Channel*

## Information-Age Chicago, 1990

Commercial office buildings
- · under 10,000 sq ft
- • 10,000–100,000 sq ft
- ● 100,000–1 million sq ft
- ⬤ over 1 million sq ft
- ▨ Parks and forest preserves
- — Rail transit lines
- — Expressways

Waukegan
Barrington
Arlington Heights
Northbrook
Elgin
Schaumburg
Des Plaines
Skokie
Evanston
St Charles
Wheaton
Oak Park
CHICAGO
Oak Brook
Cicero
Aurora
Naperville
Oak Lawn
Orland Park
Lansing
Joliet
Matteson
*LAKE MICHIGAN*

N
5 MILES

N
5 MILES

*Authors: Michael P. Conzen and Mark Donovan*

industries, such as Sara Lee's frozen foods, began in the suburbs. As jobs became more plentiful outside the city, people migrating to the Chicago area often settled in the suburbs, bypassing the city entirely. This was only true, however, if the migrants were white; because of discrimination, African Americans were restricted to the city. Out-migration accelerated after 1950, when the city's population peaked at 3.6 million people. White people followed the jobs, as Chicago's share of the area's manufacturing dropped from 71 to 54 percent between 1947 and 1961.

The history of the Loop reflects both the struggle to remain competitive and the process of deconcentration. Financial institutions stayed on LaSalle Street, though not all retained their dynamism. The Chicago Board of Trade stayed on top of the national futures market by creating innovative contract markets in new fields such as financial instruments. Chicago banks, however, serviced the Midwest, and they grew slowly, in step with the sluggish regional economy. Beginning in the 1950s, many corporations moved their headquarters out of the downtown skyscrapers to suburban "campuses." Headquarters thrive on quick access to air transport, and O'Hare drew them out of the Loop to the northwest suburbs. Most notable was Sears, which left after trumpeting its success by building the world's tallest skyscraper. The Loop's tenuous economic situation is reflected in the building booms and busts since World War II, which left some of the world's most innovative skyscrapers often half empty.

The Loop's retail functions also ebbed. Marshall Field's and other Loop department stores opened their first branches in the suburbs in the 1920s. City officials replaced the cluttered and decaying South Water Street with Wacker Drive in the 1920s, but new construction in the Loop virtually ceased for decades while North Michigan Avenue became the Magnificent Mile. Suburban competition became intense in the 1950s with the opening of shopping malls. Loop retail trade declined, but the Loop continued to attract conventioneers after the construction of McCormick Place Convention Center. Loop hotels, theaters, and museums drew tourists to the lakefront of the central city.

Since 1970 the character of Chicago's metropolitan economy has been transformed; both manufacturing and wholesaling play a lesser role than in the past. Chicagoans hoped to gain international commerce with the opening of the St. Lawrence Seaway, but the oceangoing trade was not as successful as projected. Furthermore, foreign competition undercut many manufacturing companies. Older plants in Chicago closed first; newer ones in the suburbs followed. Some corporations, even giants such as International Harvester, failed. Both central city and suburbs suffered, as the area lost almost all railcar and agricultural machinery production and most of its consumer electronics industry. The steel industry declined precipitously but has since rebounded; at the end of the century it employed, however, only one-third as many workers as it did in the 1970s. A high-tech corridor has developed in the western suburbs, but most of the new industries are centered elsewhere.

The service sector is the source of most new growth for the metropolitan economy. The old central city is almost totally dependent on business services and tourism for its vitality. Where the river empties into the lake, a Ferris wheel replaces the grain elevator as a symbol of what makes the city great. The diversity of the area's economy remains a strength, but its future, like its past, will depend on national and international economic trends. Chicago was geographically well situated to become the capital of the Midwest. It retains this position, but the old dream of dominating the continent has died.　　　　　*Susan E. Hirsch*

## Retail Geography

Retail geography has been a component of the evolving urban landscape of Chicago since the formal incorporation of the city in 1837. Historical records do not identify the first retailer in the city, but clearly the first major concentration of retail stores was located along Lake Street. Accounts of the Lake Street retail environment from the 1840s emphasized the rather slapdash construction of the stores and the coarse interactions between the dry-goods dealers and their customers. Despite the fact that Lake Street was one of the first streets in the city to be covered with wooden planks, travel up and down the street was at times quite difficult because of the heavy amount of animal and vehicular traffic in the area. The problem was exacerbated by bulky merchandise (such as building materials) that would extend beyond the wooden sidewalk into the main thoroughfare. By the mid-1850s, the intersection of Lake and Clark Streets was the nucleus of Chicago's retail environment. Here residents and travelers could find a bevy of goods ranging from ice skates to nails. Mirroring broader trends, several stores began to specialize in certain goods, such as haberdasheries and stores that only sold women's hats.

The South Water Street Market, located on the banks of the Chicago River, emerged as an important center of activity for food distribution throughout Chicago. This wholesale center was supplied by ships arriving from all around Lake Michigan. Photographs from the 1860s depict a scene much like the one found on Lake Street. Numerous carts and horses transported materials and goods from the ships to the wholesale retailers located on South Water Street, many of whom sold directly to mobile greengrocers, who would later sell the produce from the back of their own horse-drawn carts. As the population of Chicago began to disperse, this type of mobile retail business became increasingly difficult, though it would persist in modified form into the twentieth century. By the early 1870s, the South Water Street Market was becoming an almost impossibly difficult place from which to transport goods around the city. Members of the local business community, particularly those in the real estate industry, sought solutions from city leaders, but the question of South Water Street Market's future would not receive an official response until the early 1920s.

## Chicago's Retail Centers in 1948

Authors: Michael P. Conzen and Dennis McClendon
© 2004 The Newberry Library

In the middle of the twentieth century, shopping in the Chicago region was still resolutely urban. It had developed around the historic business core of the city, which still accounted for an overwhelming proportion of total retail sales. It spread along major streetcar routes within the city, a seemingly endless string of family businesses, chain stores, and department store branches at key intersections. Beyond that, small retail concentrations were to be found in the downtowns of the region's satellite cities and the trackside business clusters of the railroad suburbs. The spread of the automobile at first simply reinforced this historic mass-transit-based pattern, because the plethora of city streets and slowly rising urban congestion limited the impact of the private car.

## Chicago's Retail Centers in 2000

Authors: Michael P. Conzen and Ann T. Natunewicz

© 2004 The Newberry Library

By century's end, shopping in metropolitan Chicago had been revolutionized. First, shopping plazas with off-street parking began the concentration of retail land use into favored nodes. Commercial strips incorporating such plazas also proliferated, especially along major arterial streets. But it was the building of the metropolitan expressways in the 1950s to 1980s that fundamentally realigned shopping locations for Chicagoans by providing widespread access to the new shopping malls and regional supermalls. By 2000 there were at least 23 regional malls within the contiguous built-up area. Most of the old commercial ribbons along major city streets atrophied, except where foot traffic remained strong, and downtown Chicago retail businesses faced severe competition from suburban competitors, leading a number of department stores to close in the urban core, having repositioned their sales space in the outlying malls.

The next crucial development in the shifting retail geography in Chicago was the movement of the Field, Leiter & Co. store from Lake Street to the increasingly fashionable and business-friendly area developing along State Street. The development of State Street as a retailing mecca was aided by Potter Palmer, the Chicago mercantile king, who built an extravagant hotel at the corner of State and Monroe Streets and persuaded the city council to widen State Street. One contemporary observer, acknowledging planning efforts in Paris, referred to Palmer's work as the "Haussmannizing of State Street." But most important to the retail community in Chicago was Palmer's role in persuading Field, Leiter & Co. to move into a rather ostentatious building on State Street.

It is difficult to overestimate the importance of Marshall Field on retail merchandising. Along with stocking dry goods in the Field, Leiter & Co. store at the corner of State and Washington Streets, Field constantly maintained a stock of high-quality and cosmopolitan products, such as women's handbags and the latest fashions brought over from Paris. Field also helped maintain a loyal customer base through such innovative policies as a money-back guarantee and a competent and reliable delivery service. These customer-friendly policies were complemented by an almost astonishing array of ancillary services, such as children's playrooms, writing rooms, tearooms, and stenographic services. Marshall Field also kept a shrewd eye on the wholesale trade by contracting with the architect Henry Hobson Richardson to design a wholly modern wholesale goods distribution center at Adams and Wells Streets in 1885.

By the turn of the nineteenth century, most of the large-scale retail merchandisers had secured a place on the State Street corridor in the Loop. Along with Marshall Field's, Carson Pirie Scott and other large department stores had large and expansive emporiums that utilized large metal-framed display windows to showcase the wide variety of goods that they offered. Other prominent department stores included Mandel Brothers, the Boston Store, Rothschild's, Siegel, Cooper & Co., and the Stevens stores.

Arising at the same time as these magnificent edifices along State Street were the substantial retail centers in neighborhoods around Chicago. These retail businesses tended to reach their densest concentrations near transportation junctions, particularly near where the rapid transit lines intersected with major street railway transfer stations. Two of the most important examples of this trend toward retail aggregation and clustering were 63rd and Halsted Streets in Englewood, and Lawrence Avenue and Broadway Street in Uptown. As affordable and efficient transportation encouraged residential expansion around these increasingly popular areas, there was concomitant development within the retail environment. While many of these community and regional retail centers of activity would see their greatest flowering from the 1920s to the early 1950s, their presence within the urban environment was apparent by the first decade of the twentieth century.

In the years before World War II, a new mode of retail geography began to develop in suburban Chicago. Older inner-ring suburbs that were intimately linked to the city by a network of interurbans also developed clusters of retail establishments at junctions of major transfer points. Oak Park followed this pattern quite neatly, with a high concentration of major retailers at the intersection of Lake Street and Harlem Avenue, including a branch of Marshall Field's. At the same time, many other suburbs were building intricate and elaborately executed retail complexes that catered primarily to people with automobiles. One of the earliest such retail developments in the nation was Lake Forest Market Square in Lake Forest. Designed by the architect Howard Van Doren Shaw and constructed in 1916, this blend of retail and office space with residential apartments offered extensive parking facilities. The other early well-known retail development that catered to automobiles was the Spanish Court in Wilmette. Constructed in 1926, this innovative development was also built with the understanding that many of its patrons would arrive by automobile.

Despite the increased competition from retail developments outside the city of Chicago, the downtown area maintained its dominant role as a major regional retail center of the first order. Even as late as 1958, it sold eight times as many shopping goods as the largest regional center within the city (located at 63rd and Halsted) and had ten times the total retail sales of this particular regional shopping district. While the downtown area maintained its position atop the city's hierarchy of retail centers, the central business district accounted for only 15 percent of all retail sales within the city of Chicago. Many of Chicago's neighborhoods were well served by a nexus of available retail options around major arterials, often including a small department store (such as a Wieboldt's or Goldblatt's) and a variety of other retail businesses.

Planned retail developments became increasingly popular after World War II in the Chicago metropolitan area, though few were built within the city for several decades. One of the most well-known planned retail centers was Evergreen Plaza, located right outside the city limits at 95th Street and Western Avenue. Evergreen Plaza was developed by real estate mogul Arthur Rubloff, who had initially conceived of such a plan in 1936. When it was finished in 1952, Evergreen Plaza had approximately 500,000 square feet of retail space and 1,200 parking spaces. Cars could easily pull in off the street into the parking lot, and the plaza also featured a conveyor belt that transported groceries from the supermarkets to a parking-area kiosk.

While many of these retail developments were built to accommodate a growing suburban population that was moving out to well-established suburbs in the metropolitan area, still other planned retail developments were built in conjunction with towns that were built totally from the ground up. Park Forest Plaza was a well-received example of this emerging retail-complex style that sought to mimic a previous era in the history of town planning. At Park Forest Plaza, the architects Loebl, Schlossman and Bennett placed a landscaped court amidst a circle of shops and surrounded the entire area with parking.

In the city of Chicago, many retailers in neighborhoods faced with widespread demographic shifts fell on increasingly hard times throughout the 1960s and 1970s. Former areas of robust retail spending, including many of those on the South and West Sides, found themselves plagued by arsonists, robbery, and a general decline in the socioeconomic makeup of their clientele. The city of Chicago attempted to alleviate the dwindling returns of these neighborhood retail centers by diverting automobile traffic from the main area of pedestrian traffic. While this policy might have been successful in Oak Park (which created a small downtown pedestrian mall in 1974), it was met with resistance and apathy by shoppers and retailers alike along State Street, which was turned into a "pedestrian-friendly" street in 1979 and then restored back to accommodate traffic in 1996.

Many of the city's formerly vibrant neighborhood retail areas continued on a downward spiral through the 1980s and 1990s. Planned retail developments such as Ford City on the city's Southwest Side seemed to siphon business away from surrounding neighborhoods rather than drawing nearby suburbanites into the area. Large-scale retail developments in the suburbs continued emerging throughout the late 1970s and early 1980s, with several notable examples, including the Old Orchard Mall in Skokie and Woodfield Mall in Schaumburg, drawing city and suburban residents. Many of these malls began to offer a diverse set of amenities such as children's playgrounds, valet parking, and senior citizen days.

Another retail development, the "big-box" retail store, began to situate itself within both the urban and suburban fabric in the 1980s and early 1990s. Like many of their historical predecessors, these massive single-story structures were frequently located at significant transportation junctions, such as the confluence of major highways or freeway exits. While big-box retail developments remained popular through the 1990s in the city and surrounding suburbs, the Loop has a seen a new influx of contemporary retailers, many of them occupying prime retail space along State Street. Along North Michigan Avenue, the much-heralded "vertical malls," such as Water Tower Place, remain popular and highly visible destinations for tourists, suburbanites, and Chicagoans.        *Max Grinnell*

# II. The Business of Chicago

## Business of Chicago

Business and Chicago have been inextricably bound since the city's beginnings in the early nineteenth century. Although there is no truth to the story that *Chicago* is Potawatomi for "let's make a deal," economic and business concerns have not merely shaped but have also determined Chicago's destiny for almost 200 years. After an initial period of settlement and environmental/economic accommodation, the city entered into a remarkable phase of economic expansion between about 1850 and 1930. Chicago's economic performance since that time has been less impressive, but the city, having adjusted to a series of economic shocks and dislocations in the 1970s and 1980s, remains the most important economic and business center in the interior of the United States. Indeed, with its increasingly diversified economy, metropolitan Chicago appears well poised to continue as the economic powerhouse, if not the growth engine, for the greater Midwest.

European penetration of the Great Lakes region began relatively early during the so-called Age of Discovery. By the late seventeenth century, numerous Frenchmen—most notably Louis Jolliet and Jacques Marquette—had explored the area along the southwestern shore of Lake Michigan. Throughout the eighteenth century, the area's marshy grounds were traversed by various trappers, traders, "projectors," and "adventurers" from Europe and elsewhere in the Americas. The intensity of European and African commercial penetration increased markedly in the early nineteenth century, illustrated in stylized form by the establishment, destruction, and reestablishment of the Fort Dearborn site on what is now Michigan Avenue in the period between 1803 and 1816.

Until recently, few scholars viewed Chicago's early development in a fully commercial framework, arguing instead that slow, desultory, rather aimless economic encounters among traders, frontier farmers, Indians, and government contractors of one type or another characterized the area's economy until the 1830s. The same scholars then contend that during the 1830s Chicago experienced a wild period of boom and bust, based on furious but ultimately unsustainable land speculation, before establishing a firm foundation as a trading center in the 1840s.

Today most students of the economic development of the southern Great Lakes region, including Chicago and environs, consider the area from the start in the context of an expanding capitalist market in the Western world. The fur trade, military installations, public investment in infrastructure, private real estate speculation, and the marketing of farm products, however prosaic and seemingly petty, are all viewed as expressions of the region's gradual, piecemeal and incremental, but ultimately inexorable incorporation into capitalist financial and product markets of extra-regional, national, and even international scope. When considered in this way, Chicago's development after 1830 seems not as sudden and abrupt and less implausible. This is not to suggest that Chicago qua Chicago was foreordained or inevitable, merely that, given American capitalism's nineteenth-century trajectory, the development of an urban center such as Chicago somewhere in the southern Great Lakes region of the Midwest is readily understandable.

By the early nineteenth century, an expanding capitalism was transforming the area economically from a site of irregular or intermittent cross-cultural trade in resources and "preciosities" to a site of regular, routinized production and exchange of agricultural commodities and manufactured goods conducted and organized under Euro-American auspices. Such expansion manifested itself in a variety of ways: in state formation and in the build-up in the administrative capacity of the U.S. government in the region; in the capitalist state's increased police powers and its move to monopolize organized violence; and in rising public and private investment in transportation infrastructure. The completion of the Erie Canal in 1825 was particularly important in this last regard, for by linking the Great Lakes with Buffalo, Albany, and by extension with New York City and the Atlantic world, the canal at once signaled and helped to bring about a shift in the locus of economic power in the Old Northwest Territory from the Ohio Valley to the southern shoreline of the Great Lakes, from Cincinnati and Louisville to Cleveland and, increasingly, to Chicago. The Erie Canal did not do this all at once, of course, but with its completion and early success, visionary entrepreneurs began to sense and, more importantly, to invest in the future of cities on the Great Lakes' southern shores. These investors were as prescient as they were vigorous, but in retrospect it is clear that the Great Lakes region generally and the Chicago site specifically were good bets in the first half of the nineteenth century.

One might begin with resources, not merely because they were bounteous in the Midwest—although they certainly were—but because the particular constellation of resources available in the Great Lakes region was remarkably appropriate for rapid economic development in the nineteenth century. There was the soil, for example, of great natural fertility, and water in almost unimaginable and seemingly inexhaustible quantities. And there were prairies, pancake flat and most fortuitous in the coming age of the railroad, as well as vast deposits of iron ore and coal, which proved propitious as America turned to steam and steel.

A formidable stock of social and cultural resources complemented these natural resources. Settlement was dominated by farmers and artisans who, whether of Yankee or German origins, were accustomed to disciplined labor, rational calculation, and patient accumulation. Equally determined migrants from other lands followed and, despite vast differences in cultures and traditions, either bought into, or at least behaved in a manner consistent with, the economic and social expectations and ethos of their Euro-American neighbors. Such resources, conjoined with the relatively liberal and egalitarian developmental policies associated with the midwestern states, help to explain both the rural and urban opportunities available in the southern Great Lakes region and, ipso facto, the region's inflows of labor and capital. Indeed, the area was nothing if not ready for what the novelist Richard Powers has aptly referred to as the "tireless nineteenth century."

If the best opportunities early in the century were still in the procurement of raw materials, cross-cultural trade, government contracting, and land speculation and development, commercial agriculture soon entered fully into the mix. Along with commercial agriculture—small grains and cattle plus corn and hogs, most notably—came increased trade and the beginnings of what might be called Chicago's agro-industrial complex. Because production, exchange, and consumption were closely, even organically linked in the Midwest (unlike the case in the American South among other places), town and country—or, more accurately, field, forest, and factory—fostered and supported one another in a mutually ramifying, virtuous economic cycle. Well before 1850, even before the much-ballyhooed completion in 1848 of the Illinois & Michigan Canal connecting Chicago to the Mississippi River system via the Illinois and Chicago Rivers, the city on the southwestern shore of Lake Michigan was emerging as one of the more important urban nodes in the Midwest's regional economy. Chicago's population grew accordingly, from about 200 inhabitants in 1833 to almost 5,000 in 1840 and nearly 30,000 in 1850.

Yet resources, impersonal market forces, and capitalism's "systemics" cannot fully explain Chicago's development. Despite the city's many locational advantages, an equal number of disadvantages—poor drainage, endemic disease, a late start—had to be overcome if the city was to outcompete other commercial centers to become the jewel in the midwestern urban crown. Here, many scholars point to yet another advantage that Chicago enjoyed over its rivals: an advantage in human capital, specifically in entrepreneurship.

Whatever attribute or complement of attributes one chooses to emphasize in defining entrepreneurship—risk receptivity, vision, creative innovation, deal making, enlightened management, and the like—Chicago-ans have never seemed lacking. Although some economists assume that economic behavior is entirely positional, and that sociocultural qualities such as entrepreneurship are randomly distributed among human beings, Chicago's early history suggests otherwise. In this regard, it is most instructive to plot Chicago's historical trajectory against the trajectories of some of its early urban rivals, places with more or less similar structures of opportunity, places such as Kenosha, Racine, and even Milwaukee and St. Louis. The historical differences among these places cannot be attributed solely to structural factors, locational differences, first-mover advantages, timing, or luck. A residual remains, some part of which arguably is explicable by invoking entrepreneurship.

In any case, in the 1830s and 1840s, risk-receptive, visionary, creative, deal-making businessmen and -women were busy making Chicago work. Not only was the city establishing a hinterland; it was beginning to develop entrepôt and manufacturing functions—trading, milling, butchering, tanning, brewing, distilling, sawing, planing, and, most portentously, fabricating products for local, regional, and, in some cases, extra-regional markets. In so doing, Chicago and Chicagoans—aided by governmental policies supporting development and a legal system promoting the "release of entrepreneurial energy"—were setting the stage for the amazing period of economic expansion about to unfold.

Chicago's economic dynamism between the 1850s and the 1920s is the stuff of legend. Seldom before in world history had an urban center grown so rapidly, been transformed so dramatically, or captured and conveyed the regnant spirit of the age so thoroughly. Chicago had developed big shoulders indeed by the 1920s, and this development was due more than anything else to sweaty work and heavy lifting. In the age of industrial capital, Chicago had become America's industrial capital and would remain so for most of the twentieth century.

The city's will to power—one of Chicago's official mottoes, revealingly, is "I will"—can be said to have begun, metaphorically at least, in 1847. In that year, a Virginia native named Cyrus Hall McCormick migrated from Cincinnati to Chicago and brought with him a business enterprise, the McCormick Harvesting Machine Company, which captured and embodied the epoch of Chicago's industrialization. Not only was the factory that McCormick established in 1848—the McCormick Reaper Works, located between North Water Street and the Chicago River, just east of what is now Michigan Avenue—large and centralized, but its metal-fabricating technologies and the agro-industrial tenor and cast of the products produced were avatars of the city's subsequent manufacturing orientation. McCormick later marketed its products not just in the Midwest or even the United States, but all over the world.

Between 1850 and the 1920s, Chicago was transformed—or more accurately and actively, it *transformed itself*—from an earnest little regional trading node in the interior of the United States into the nation's second largest city. Served only by the Galena and Chicago Union in 1850, the city was the greatest railroad center in the world by 1856. In possession of only rudimentary manufacturing facilities at midcentury, Chicago formed the core of one of the most heavily industrialized regions on earth before 1900. A nice little trade, distribution, and supply center for Great Lakes' farmers in 1850, Chicago had extended its hinterland into the Rockies within a few decades and developed into a world emporium before the turn of the century. How and why?

As the American economy grew, the northeastern quadrant of the United States—the area east of the Mississippi River and north of the Ohio River—came to constitute the nation's manufacturing core. As transportation and communications improvements linked the West more closely with other regions, Chicago, well positioned to take advantage of such developments, began to assume more and more economic functions, of greater and greater sophistication and complexity. The city's growth and dynamism began to seem irresistible, inexorable, inevitable: the juggernaut of the southern Great Lakes, indeed, of the United States. Wherever one looks—transport, trade, finance, manufacturing, services—one finds Chicago on the move. The city's primacy in the U.S. transportation system grew, for example, with the simultaneous, mutually reinforcing development of the West and the American railroad network. As a "gateway" to the West, moreover, Chicago benefited both coming and going, serving as a staging point (commercially and financially in particular) for migrants heading west as well as a collection and processing point, later on, for the fruit—or, more accurately, the grain and meat—of their labor. At the same time, Chicago's economic relationships with its immediate hinterland in the Great Lakes region intensified as well, with the city's mercantile community not merely facilitating but, in many cases, making possible increased production and consumption in the region.

As the city's population grew, internal multiplier effects came into play: more people meant more construction, provisions, services, entertainment, and so on, which, in turn, led to more jobs and more people, and perforce to iteration after iteration of the same process. Chicago's population grew from just under 30,000 in 1850 to about 300,000 by 1870 then to almost 1.1 million by 1890. By 1910 the city's population had doubled again to almost 2.2 million, and Chicago's population grew by another 55 percent or so over the next two decades, approaching 3.4 million by 1930. Some of this growth came from annexation, but most was "real," the result of natural increase (an excess of births over deaths among the resident population), rural migration (from the Midwest and, increasingly, from the South), and from foreign immigration (particularly from southern and eastern Europe).

For all its railroads, western connections, trade and commerce, and internal multipliers, Chicago between 1850 and 1930 evokes images of manufacturing, the heavier the better. However important the Illinois Central, Sears, Roebuck & Co., or the Board of Trade—and they were important—in the mind's eye, Chicago during this period butchered hogs, made tools, and stacked wheat. With apologies to Carl Sandburg, Chicago meant iron and steel, too; and furniture, clothes, and tobacco; as well as 1,001 other manufactures. In 1890 Chicago was the leading center of slaughtering and meatpacking, lumber production, and furniture manufacturing in the United States. By that time, the city was also the nation's leading manufacturer of foundry and machine-shop products, the second leading manufacturer of clothing and apparel, the third largest manufacturer of tobacco products, and a leading producer of iron and steel, industries that would grow dramatically in the years to come.

By 1930 Chicago had become even more of a manufacturing town. Moreover, many of the early processing activities—sawing and planing lumber, milling, and meatpacking—lost ground in relative terms to higher-order industries based on metal fabrication, particularly the fabrication of iron and steel. In 1930 the "Chicago Industrial Area"—comprising a five-county region in northeastern Illinois and adjacent Lake County in northwestern Indiana—was the second largest manufacturing region in the United States, behind only the "New York City Industrial Area," which had over twice as many people. In per capita terms, Chicago's value of manufacturing product and value-added by manufacturing exceeded New York's in 1930, as did the manufacturing proportion of the labor force. In qualitative terms, too, vast differences distinguished the two regions: Chicago was America's center of heavy industry; New York, the center of light industry. Chicago, in the eyes of Chicagoans and non-Chicagoans alike, typified large-scale, centralized, capital-intensive, heavy industry.

This view of Chicago is not so much wrong as incomplete, both in terms of the city's manufacturing sector specifically and of its economy as a whole. Although the electrical machinery industry, iron and steel production, and machine-shop and foundry production constituted the three largest components of Chicago's manufacturing economy in 1930, employment in other less "brawny" manufacturing sectors was extremely significant as well. There were, for example, over 30,000 Chicagoans employed in the clothing industry in 1929, over 25,000 employed in printing and publishing, and another 18,000 employed in the furniture industry. If many Chicago workers labored in huge integrated mills—the average number of wage earners in Chicago's 36 iron- and steelmaking facilities in 1929 was 1,261—many other Chicagoans toiled in much smaller manufacturing establishments. One of the great canards about American industrialization is that by the late nineteenth century all of the manufacturing action was occurring in big vertically or horizontally integrated units controlled by large corporations. In reality, much of America's manufacturing output continued to come out of small- and medium-size family-owned firms, producing small "batches' of specialized goods. In Chicago, such firms could be found everywhere but seemed to be located most commonly on the West and North Sides, with big mills dominating production on the South and Southeast Sides of the city.

As Chicago's manufacturing sector evolved, as its output became at once more varied and more sophisticated, the markets for manufactured goods produced in the city changed as well. With the relative shift away from processing activities and toward fabricating industries, the city was increasingly able to pursue import substitution policies and to export fabricated goods (rather than just raw materials, agricultural commodities, and processed manufactures) out of the region. By the 1920s, electrical machinery, iron and steel products, machine tools, and fabricated metals from Chicago were being sold not only throughout the United States, but all over the world.

Chicago's formidable industrial prowess provides a ready explanation of the city's economic dynamism between the 1850s and 1930. But the city's expansion and growth during this period, before this period, and after this period owed much to trade and finance, to transportation-related

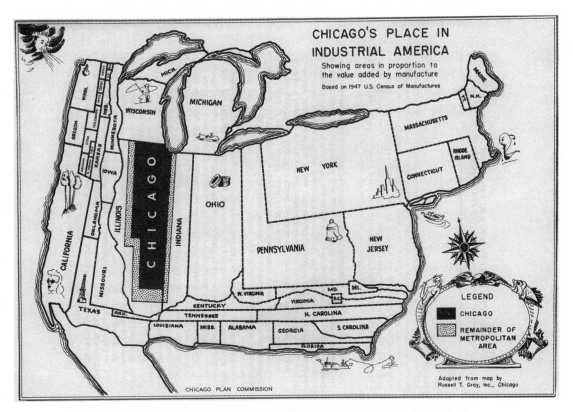

Chicago's place in industrial America, 1952. This cartogram captures Chicago's industrial dominance in the United States even as factories started moving to the suburbs and the Sunbelt and as the city's traditionally important industries like railroads and farm equipment began to decline. © Chicago Plan Commission. Courtesy of the Chicago History Museum (ICHi-37022).

activities, and to a variety of service activities. Chicago became the Midwest's great wholesale and retail emporium during this period and retained many of its marketing functions for areas farther to the west. Its bankers and financiers provided credit and financial services for much of the region, and the city's commodities exchanges, however controversial, helped bring greater order and stability to American agriculture. Chicago remained the leading railroad center in the country, and, as the U.S. automotive-industrial complex became increasingly centralized in the Great Lakes region, Chicago came to play a leading role in the automobile and trucking industries too. Finally, as the city's population grew wealthier and more sophisticated, Chicago began to invest more in human capital—in education and in health care, most notably—and to spend more on sports, entertainment, and the arts, that is to say, on cultural capital. As a result, service-related activities—the food, beverage, and lodging industries, for example—grew as well. All in all, Chicago, circa 1930, was at its apogee. Would this mighty city's amazing growth ever end?

This question is more difficult to answer than appears at first glance. On the one hand, the city has clearly experienced some periods of tough economic sledding over the past 70 years. Like most other cities in the industrial Midwest, Chicago suffered terribly during the Great Depression, as the demand for Chicago-made capital goods and consumer durables plummeted. Similarly, both the city and the entire metropolitan region have been hurt by the decline of jobs in heavy industry over the past 30 years—the region lost a staggering 188,000 jobs in this sector during the 1980s alone. On the other hand, Chicago's economy grew robustly during the Second World War, for most of the period between 1945 and the early to mid-1960s, and during the 1990s. Chicago's economic performance, once amazing, has been solid since its apogee. To appropriate and adapt a conceptualization initially developed by historian John Higham, the period can be seen as one in which the city moved in economic terms from "boundlessness" to "consolidation."

Demographic as well as economic data support the theme of consolidation. Although the growth rate of the *city* of Chicago has been negligible (and, at times, negative) over the past 70 years, the Chicago metropolitan area has grown at a robust rate over much of the period. According to the 2000 census, greater Chicago constituted the third largest metropolitan area in the United States, behind only Los Angeles–Riverside–Orange County and the New York City–northern New Jersey–Long Island metropolitan conurbation. As such, metropolitan Chicago, with more than 9 million inhabitants, is still by far the largest urban center in the "flyover district" of inland America.

Metropolitan Chicago's economy has experienced relatively robust growth for much of the period too, despite severe problems related to industrial readjustment and restructuring during the 1970s and 1980s. Indeed, the Chicago area's economy as a whole continues to perform well, and, in some ways, Chicago's more diversified and balanced economy at the turn of the twenty-first century is healthier and more stable than ever before. Even the situation in manufacturing is more complicated than often assumed. Manufacturing has declined in relative terms in the Chicago area, particularly the manufacturing proportion of the area's labor force, but total manufacturing output has continued to grow, and the Chicago Standard Metropolitan Statistical Area ranks third behind New York and Los Angeles in most measures of industrial might. Chicago remains, according to almost every index, one of the most important industrial areas in the United States and in the world. Given Chicago's continuing importance as a center of trade, finance, and transport—air as well as rail and highway—how does one evaluate and interpret the modern economic experience of (metropolitan) Chicago?

One important consideration in attempting to answer this question is the relationship of Chicago to the Midwest. Unlike the situation during the period of Chicago's great ascent, the Midwest since the 1930s has been in a period of relative decline. The income elasticity of food, generally speaking, is low, which, not surprisingly, hurt the agricultural Midwest; and with the expansion of capitalist markets in the United States and national economic integration, relatively underdeveloped or undeveloped American regions—in the South and West in particular—began to develop rapidly. To some extent, their development came at the expense of older regions, including the Midwest. In an efficient capitalist economy such as that in the modern United States, standard economic theory predicts that costs of production will converge with growth rates over time. Areas with very high growth rates, such as the Midwest in the late nineteenth and early twentieth century, would not be expected to sustain those rates as other areas developed, but to slow down and decline in relative terms over time. This is more or less what has occurred in the southern Great Lakes region, including metropolitan Chicago, since the 1930s.

Indeed, when one compares Chicago's structure of economic opportunity in the post-1930 period with the opportunities afforded the city in the period between the 1850 and 1930, one is struck by how much more constrained and limited Chicago's possibilities and options have been over the past 70 years than during the period of the city's ascent. Chicago's rise was in large part an expression, if not the embodiment, of the Midwest and its manifold resources: flat, fertile prairies during the great age of agricultural and railroad expansion; coal and iron ore during the age of steel; food, fibers, and raw materials during a period of rapid population increase, urbanization, industrialization, and economic growth in the United States. To be sure, since the 1930s the U.S. economy has continued to develop, but hardly in the same way. The Midwest's comparative advantages have proved less compelling, and Chicago and Chicagoans have had to live with this painful, unvarnished truth. One can argue that metropolitan Chicago has fared pretty well under the circumstances, and that both the city and its inhabitants deserve high marks for devising and implementing sound development strategies and displaying considerable entrepreneurship.

Chicago has maintained a strong, increasingly high-tech industrial profile, for example, and has remained a center for wholesale and retail trade, distribution, and industrial and commercial exhibitions. The city has a huge presence in publishing, and it is one of the leading centers of finance, banking, and insurance in the United States. Chicago, moreover, is still the major transportation node for the nation's interior: O'Hare International remains one of the busiest airports in the world; the city handles more railroad freight than any other U.S. city; Chicago has excellent highway connections and massive trucking and intermodal transport capacity; and it is a major inland port. With the opening of the St. Lawrence Seaway in 1959, Chicago became a world rather than a lake port.

Chicago has survived depression and war, the postwar boom, the retrenchment and restructuring of the 1970s and 1980s, and the go-go 1990s with a good deal of its pride and prosperity intact. Although it will likely never again experience a period resembling 1850–1930, and although the city faces countless economic challenges—poverty, inequality, declining infrastructure, and insufficient investment in human capital, for starters—Chicago in many ways and for many people remains even today the "I will" city "that works." Whether it will remain so in the future as capitalist market integration intensifies in our increasingly "borderless" economic world is the challenge facing Chicagoans in the generations to come.                                         *Peter A. Coclanis*

## Innovation, Invention, and Chicago Business

Joseph Schumpeter drew a compelling distinction between invention and innovation. Invention is the creation of something new, a new good or service, but what really matters for economic growth is innovation, the act through which these new ideas are successfully introduced to the market. Cyrus McCormick of Virginia improved upon his father's invention in the 1830s. He brought reaper production to Chicago in 1847 and introduced the machines to prairie farmers. Ray Kroc was not the inventor of fast food; he was the innovator. The market in which McCormick sold reapers was one that was just beginning to grow from local to national. The market in which Kroc sold hamburgers was one that grew from national to global. What precipitated these changes were continuing improvements in transportation, production, and communication. Any examination of inventors and innovators in Chicago's business history necessarily involves these improvements.

At incorporation, Chicago was still tied to the fur trade, a business that avoids cities as readily as fur-bearing animals try to avoid people. Early businessmen John Kinzie, Gurdon Hubbard, and John Clark were involved in the fur trade, but they anticipated that something more substantial would arise at the mouth of the Chicago River than a government fort and traders' cabins. An early innovator named George Dole arrived from Detroit in 1831. The following summer the firm of Newberry and Dole erected what is thought to be Chicago's first frame building used for business—specifically, the slaughtering and packing of cattle and hogs. While slaughtering for local consumption had taken place in Chicago for some time, Newberry and Dole were the first to pack meat for export. In 1839 the firm began shipping wheat from Chicago's first grain elevator, which was located at the north end of the Rush Street Bridge. Consequently, Dole is generally credited with being the father of Chicago's meatpacking industry as well as of its shipping, warehouse, and elevator systems. He innovated the market mechanisms that would make Chicago a major transshipment point.

William B. Ogden, another early innovator, arrived in Chicago in 1835 to manage property that his brother-in-law and others had purchased. After selling roughly a third of the property at substantial profit, he moved into transportation. He played a major role in the completion of the Illinois & Michigan Canal. He was the president of the Galena & Chicago Union Railroad and several other railroads that eventually became the Chicago & North Western Railroad, and of the National Pacific Railroad Convention held in Philadelphia in 1850. He also was the first president of the Union Pacific Railroad Company, the first mayor of Chicago, and the president of the Chicago branch of the State Bank of Illinois.

Ogden also played a role in bringing the McCormick Reaper Works to Chicago. Robert McCormick of Virginia first developed the reaper. His son Cyrus continued to work on the concept and moved to Cincinnati in 1845. Two years later, with Ogden's financial encouragement, he moved to Chicago to locate the firm at the heart of the emerging wheat-growing region. McCormick entered into a contract with Ogden in 1848 to distribute reapers to most of Illinois, Indiana, Michigan, Kentucky, and Tennessee. The McCormick firm developed a number of innovative business practices. It established agency relationships with local businessmen, who promoted the use of reapers. It was one of the first enterprises to offer a written guarantee on every machine. It offered a free trial period during which dissatisfied customers could get a refund of the stated purchase price and offered credit as part of the terms of sale.

As more people and goods arrived to contribute to, and to benefit from, Chicago's growth, Ogden and others formed the Chicago Board of Trade in 1848 to promote Chicago's commerce. They promoted harbor improvements, tolls on the Illinois & Michigan Canal, and a land grant for the Illinois Central Railroad. From the beginning, the grain trade involved speculation. By the time farmers were able to harvest their crop and ship it as far as Chicago, water transportation on the upper Great Lakes was coming to an end for the winter. This meant that much of the grain would be shipped in the spring. The board facilitated the development of futures markets in which crops could be purchased well in advance of their delivery.

Members of the Board of Trade, along with other Chicagoans, sought a resolution to the city's most serious problem—mud. In 1855 Ogden and the other members of the newly formed Board of Sewerage Commissioners planned a coordinated sewage and drainage system; Chicago became the first North American city to construct a comprehensive sewer system. The innovative plan, designed by Ellis Sylvester Chesbrough, called for an intercepting, combined sewer system that emptied into the river. Drainage was to be accomplished by gravity, but Chicago's flatness created a problem. This was resolved by the simple but costly expedient of having the city raise its level. As construction progressed away from the river, sewers were laid at the level necessary to accomplish gravity flow. Earth was then packed around them, and new streets were constructed above the sewers. Much of the fill was obtained by dredging the Chicago River in order to lower and enlarge it. Building owners had to find a way to raise their property to the new level. George Pullman, who invented a technique for raising buildings during the enlargement of the Erie Canal in his native New York, moved to Chicago. Part of Chicago folklore is that guests in the Tremont Hotel were not disturbed when the building was raised about six feet.

Inevitably, the Chicago River became polluted as a result of the new sewer system. The pollution spread into the lake until it reached the water supply intake. By 1860 Chicago's sewerage commissioners, concerned with the offensive condition of the Chicago River, suggested diverting river water through the Illinois & Michigan Canal. It is customary to date the formal reversal of the Chicago River to 1871, when work was completed that deepened the canal and increased the pumping capacity at the Bridgeport end. In fact, beginning sometime in the 1850s, the river was reversed under normal conditions through the operation of the original Bridgeport pumps. From that time on, the city invested in additional works to keep sewage away from its Lake Michigan water supply. In 1889 voters approved the Sanitary District Enabling Act, which led to the construction of the Sanitary and Ship Canal, essentially a larger version of the Illinois & Michigan Canal. Innovation continued into the twentieth century. In the 1970s, the Tunnel and Reservoir Plan, better known as "Deep Tunnel," included construction of larger sewers and underground reservoirs to hold storm water rather than allow it into the lake.

The Chicago River divided the city into three parts, impelling Chicagoans to become leading innovators in bridge technology. The first bridge, constructed in 1832, was a fixed span that could not be opened and therefore was placed where it would not interfere with the part of the river used as a harbor. It ultimately was replaced by a series of drawbridges, swing bridges, and pontoon bridges that proved unsatisfactory. By the turn of the twentieth century, engineers determined that the trunnion bascule bridge, based on a seesaw principle, was the ideal solution to Chicago's bridge problems. That principle, built into the Tower Bridge in London, was modified to such an extent that bascule bridges came to be built in the "Chicago style."

While the railroad was not invented in Chicago, it was important to Chicago's economic development. By the late 1860s, rail connections were available from the Atlantic to the Pacific via Chicago, and the growth of the railroad network fostered commercial development. Because of its position on this network, Chicago became an important livestock market. Initially livestock were traded at Chicago and shipped live to eastern markets, since that was the only way to assure fresh meat in those markets. By 1864 the livestock trade had grown so large that the burgeoning individual stockyards were considered a nuisance to the public and a costly burden to the railroads. Chicago encouraged the development of a new site by banning stockyard activity from the city limits. The Union Stock Yard opened for business in 1865. Nine railroad companies subscribed the vast majority of the $1 million cost, but every railroad entering Chicago was connected to the Union Stock Yard.

Refrigeration was the critical innovation that transformed the livestock business. It changed meatpacking from a local business operating largely on a seasonal basis to a national business operating year-round and centered in Chicago. It contributed to a large increase in the operating scale of these firms by expanding the packers' operations beyond manufacturing into distribution and by-product utilization. Around 1868 George Hammond of Detroit shipped eight tons of beef in a refrigerated car that had been designed for fruit shipments. While there were problems, Hammond was so confident of the technology's potential that he moved his operation to Chicago.

Gustavus Swift resolved the major marketing problems associated with shipping dressed beef. During the winter of 1877, Swift shipped a few carloads of dressed beef in regular cars with the doors left open so the cold air would keep the meat refrigerated. As a result of this experiment, Swift learned the advantages of shipping dressed beef in refrigerator cars, and he recognized this would require a major expansion in plant and equipment. When the railroads refused to produce refrigerator cars, Swift undertook the task on his own. Other packers began shipping refrigerated dressed beef east, often in Swift-built cars. Meat was shipped to refrigerated warehouses in big cities and distributed in smaller places in refrigerated "peddler" cars.

Such vertical integration, which contributed to the growth in the size of Chicago firms, was also pioneered by another meatpacker. In 1884 Armour & Co. purchased the Wahl Brothers glue works in Chicago and began funneling a large quantity of bones and low-quality hides into this plant. The same year, Armour hired a chemist to investigate the various alternative uses of animal wastes. Eventually, all the large packers were involved in such activities as soap production and selling hides to the leather industry and tails to the paintbrush industry. They also filled the bottom of the refrigerator cars with such goods as butter, eggs, and cheese. The large packers began buying the wastes of small packers; Armour, notes historian William Cronon, "built his empire on waste."

Like the meatpackers, the Pullman Palace Car Company innovated a new type of railcar. In 1859 George Pullman entered into a contract with the Michigan Central Railroad to fit two old passenger cars as sleeping cars. Pullman's initial car was like those on other lines; it consisted of a series of bunks and was used only at night. Four years later, he produced the first "Palace" car, one that could be used by day as well as for sleeping. Beginning in 1880, Pullman planned and constructed the model town that bears his name.

Retailing was the bailiwick of one of Chicago's major innovators, Potter Palmer, who arrived from New York in 1852 and opened a dry-goods store with several unorthodox practices. Other merchants largely rejected what has been termed the "Palmer system." Palmer insisted that his goods be displayed in an attractive manner, both in the store and in print advertisements. He allowed customers to take merchandise on approval and offered generous exchange provisions including a full refund. Perhaps just as importantly, he emphasized the continual introduction of new goods and, wherever possible, attempted to become their exclusive agent. In 1865 Palmer entered into partnership with Marshall Field and Levi Leiter. Palmer left the partnership in 1867; Leiter, in 1881. By then the firm of Marshall Field & Co. had become a leading dry-goods firm and a pioneer department store, the most complete retail establishment west of New York City. The Palmer system remained, in Field's phrase, to "give the lady what she wants."

In 1865 Field, Palmer, and Leiter hired Aaron Montgomery Ward, who had quit his job in a Michigan general store and moved to Chicago. Two years later, he took a job as a traveling salesman for a similar firm in St. Louis. Living among the farmers, Ward got the innovative idea that through direct-mail marketing he could make the goods enjoyed by city dwellers accessible to people living in small towns and on farms. He hoped to keep prices competitive by buying directly from manufacturers for cash and saving the expense of retail outlets and salesmen through mail order. He also recognized his business location would have to minimize the cost of transporting the goods. He chose Chicago. The fire of 1871 delayed the start of business until 1872, but Montgomery Ward & Co. proved an immediate success. The initial circular advertising the company's existence and the products it offered was one page; by 1886 the illustrated *Buyers' Guide* had grown to 304 pages. Success breeds imitation: Sears, Roebuck & Co., founded in Minneapolis in 1893, moved to Chicago two years later when shipping from Minneapolis proved impractical. Its 532-page catalog included housewares, saddles and buggies, and sporting goods, along with the watches and jewelry that reflected the firm's origins.

Another series of business innovations facilitated the extension of electric power throughout the Midwest. Samuel Insull, an Englishman who once served as secretary to Thomas Edison, believed electricity was a natural monopoly. In 1907 Insull, who had purchased most of the competing firms in Chicago, reorganized Chicago Edison as Commonwealth Edison and took the logic of his argument one step further. Using the holding company device pioneered on nineteenth-century railroads, he assumed control of entire territories by forming holding company upon holding company. Cash from the sale of stock in one company financed the next. At its zenith, Insull's Middle West Utilities Company controlled as much as one-eighth of the nation's electrical power and delivered it to 5,000 towns in 32 states and Canada. Among those who took advantage of electrification were Charles Yerkes, who put together Chicago's urban transportation system and introduced electric trolley cars, and Essanay Studios, which made motion pictures in Chicago before the film industry moved to Hollywood.

Chicago firms were also innovators in the emergence of the electronics industry. In 1928 Paul Galvin started a small company that produced battery eliminators for battery-operated home radios, but, as that market dwindled, he became one of the earliest producers of car radios. The name "Motorola" comes from the conjoining of motion and radio. The company also produced walkie-talkies, a product line that Robert Galvin, the founder's son, followed while moving the company into the emerging field of electronics. As early as the 1950s, Motorola was innovating in the emerging field of cellular telephones. The company also produced two-way radios, pagers, and microchips. Motorola's 68000 series of microprocessors became the heart of the workstation market and the brains of the Macintosh computer.

In the twentieth century, automobiles, trucks, and air transportation pulled economic activity away from the confluence of lake and river. The suburbanization of business began as early as the 1920s, but the trend accelerated after World War II, as the population also increasingly suburbanized. By 1970 half the population in the Chicago metropolitan statistical area lived in the suburban ring. The first pieces of what became the Interstate Highway System were the expressways built as spokes out of the city, much as the railroads had been a century earlier. Falling transportation costs have allowed a corporation's headquarters to separate from its production facilities. A town like Oak Brook, because of its easy access to an airport, is home to an amazing number of headquarters operations—and Ray Kroc's (McDonald's) Hamburger University.

Chicago's "hometown airline," United Airlines, like many other Chicago firms, is not native to the city. In the 1920s, Carl Fritsche of Detroit, in conjunction with Clement Keys of New York, determined to raise $2 million to start an air-transport company in the hope that Detroit would become to air transport what Chicago was to rail. National Air Transport's first flight was in 1926. In the fall of 1928, during a period of several air-transport company mergers, Boeing and Pratt & Whitney created a holding company that adopted the name United Aircraft and Transport the following year. They wanted a connection between Chicago and New York and, in 1930, obtained National Air Transport, with whom United was doing cargo transfers at Chicago. The headquarters of United Airlines were located in Chicago because the airmail routes were established on the basis of the rail lines.

Many of Chicago's most vibrant, innovative enterprises in the twentieth century are oriented toward research. In the early 1920s, hospital administration and purchasing were developing specialties, and the American Hospital Supply Corporation (AHSC), incorporated in Chicago in 1922, grew with those specialties and the highway system. Foster McGaw assumed leadership in 1946, and AHSC grew into a corporate giant with a national warehouse system. With the changes in the health care market in the 1980s, AHSC merged with Baxter Laboratories.

Baxter got its start in 1929 when a Californian, Don Baxter, developed a baffle to prevent reflux in IV solutions under vacuum. Baxter became friendly with Harry Falk, who in 1931 got financial assistance from his brother, Ralph Falk. Harry moved to Glenview to begin sales. The small firm, through the leadership of William Graham, adopted a strategy of seeking specialty market niches and found several. In 1952 they were one of the first firms involved in the commercial marketing of human blood plasma. Four years later, Baxter agreed to help Willem Johan Kolff develop the market for the artificial kidney. Similarly, they worked with the University of Minnesota Medical School in developing the first heart-lung oxygenator, a key component of open-heart surgery.

A second successful health products firm is Abbott Laboratories. Many of the early medications were "nauseous mixtures," fluid-based concoctions. In 1888 Wallace C. Abbott began producing pills with measured doses in a room above his Ravenswood pharmacy. His business soon expanded. The Abbott Alkaloidal Company was incorporated in 1900 and changed its name to Abbott Laboratories in 1915. The company introduced Nembutal, a sedative-hypnotic, in 1930, and a few years later Abbott scientists discovered Pentothal, an intravenous anesthesia.

The Manhattan Project, a government research project that led to the development of the atomic bomb during World War II, has left its legacy on research in Chicago. Although the project involved many scientists across the nation, the metallurgical laboratory of the University of Chicago developed the only known method for the production of plutonium-239. It was at the university that Enrico Fermi was successful in producing and controlling a chain reaction in December 1942. Atomic research remains the focus of considerable research at Chicago universities and sites such as Argonne National Laboratories and Fermilab.

Ray Kroc's hamburgers are now sold where McCormick's reapers once harvested. Yet for all the change, Schumpeter's dictum still holds—what really matters for economic growth is innovation. The continued health of Chicago business depends on its ability to attract innovators.

*Louis P. Cain*

**Accounting.** Chicago's emergence as a major center of professional accountancy began during the 1890s. Initially, Chicago businesses relied on semiprofessional bookkeepers who were usually ill-prepared to develop innovative responses to the bewildering measurement problems associated with new technologies, legal contracts, transactions, management practices, or organizational forms.

A major focus of the early drive to professionalize accounting centered on the founding in 1897 of a state professional association that later became the Illinois Society of Certified Public Accountants. Public accountants provided three distinct services: (1) certification of financial statements; (2) consulting services concerning accounting systems; and (3) tax compliance and planning services after the passage of the federal corporate excise tax (1909) and the federal corporate income tax (1913). The Illinois licensing law (1903) was similar to New York's—both required an examination and practical experience—but the Illinois law provided for reciprocal licensing for practitioners certified in other jurisdictions. Besides encouraging more competitive markets, reciprocity facilitated the building of branch offices and interstate practices.

A unique aspect of Chicago's leading accounting practices was the importance of consulting. The central role of consulting was illustrated by the experience of two early public accounting firms that eventually grew to be giants, Arthur Andersen & Co. and McKinsey & Co. The initial impetus came from a plethora of small- and medium-size businesses in the Chicago area whose managements were often skilled in either manufacturing or marketing but were not knowledgeable about finance and accounting.

To help clients overcome these weaknesses, Arthur Andersen created a new service in the 1920s known as financial and industrial "investigations." These were specialized studies employing accounting analysis to evaluate markets, organizational structures, plants, or products. Besides assisting business operators, they were also used by bankers in planning mergers or new securities issues. In 1932 this proficiency led to Andersen's selection as the monitor for the financial restoration of Samuel Insull's bankrupt utilities empire. Beginning in the 1960s, Andersen Consulting registered strong, sustained growth because of the advent of new opportunities attributable to the use of electronic data processing. Under the leadership of Leonard Spacek, the firm assisted clients in converting from manual-mechanical to computer-based accounting systems. In 1989 Arthur Andersen & Co. elected to spin off Andersen Consulting, later renamed Accenture, which had grown to become the world's largest consulting practice. The remaining firm, known simply as Andersen, lost its accounting business suddenly in 2002 because of its association with a financial fraud scandal at Enron Corporation, one of its clients. At that time, many of Andersen's largest international offices joined the firm of Deloitte & Touche.

McKinsey & Co. was formed by James O. McKinsey, a CPA and University of Chicago professor. McKinsey's pioneering *Budgetary Control* (1922) established the intellectual underpinning for a service specialization that supported the formation of his firm three years later and eventually drew it into consultancy. Although budgeting was a practice then thought primarily relevant to the fund accounting procedures of governmental enterprises, McKinsey demonstrated that it also had great utility in business planning and control. The firm avoided the controversy over audit independence that developed in the 1970s, having completely abandoned its accounting practice in 1935. McKinsey & Co., headquartered in New York, gradually diversified into strategic planning services and became one of the world's largest management consultants.

Chicago also became an important center for accounting education and research. Foremost in this regard was the University of Chicago, which in 1922 was the first U.S. institution to grant a doctoral degree in accounting. Historically, its scholarly agenda was shaped by two initiatives taken in the allied discipline of economics. The first was the long-standing interest of professional economists during the Progressive era in the cost structures of monopolistic and oligopolistic business enterprises. The Interstate Commerce Commission, the Federal Trade Commission, and a host of state regulatory boards sought a better understanding of the economics of high-fixed-cost businesses in order to curb monopoly power or to assure the equity of rate bases. These concerns affected the program in accounting through the emphasis placed on budgeting and cost and managerial accounting. The second initiative began in the 1950s with the rise of positive economics under the leadership of Milton Friedman and others. This aspect had its greatest impact on accounting through the theoretical work of Franco Modigliani and Merton Miller on the functioning of efficient capital markets.

The accounting program at Northwestern University, on the other hand, developed more directly in response to the needs of practice. The Northwestern program was founded after the passage of the Illinois CPA law to meet the need of local firms for college-trained accountants. Its closeness to the profession was reflected by the fact that its two earliest chairs—Seymour Walton, of Joplin & Walton, and Arthur Andersen—were both leading practitioners.

Another dimension of accounting education in Chicago involved the activities of proprietary academies and extension institutes. Proprietary schools like the one founded by Seymour Walton after he left Northwestern concentrated on providing rudimentary training in bookkeeping on a part-time basis to the city's large force of clerical workers. It functioned as an adjunct to the local high schools that lacked a commercial arts curriculum. A variant of the proprietary school was the extension institute, which imitated the approach of the city's great retailer, Sears, Roebuck. The LaSalle Extension University supplied accounting education via mail order beginning in the 1910s. Eventually, both types of institution were found wanting in preparing candidates for careers in professional accounting, and state licensing authorities mandated the completion of a bachelor's degree as a prerequisite for sitting for the CPA examination.

A fourth development was CPA firm–sponsored professional education. Initially this took the form of staff training designed to standardize practice procedures among new hires. An early example of such tutelage was the in-house development programs established by Arthur Andersen for his junior accountants in the 1920s. In the 1970s, with the introduction of continuing education requirements by state licensing boards and by the quality-control standards mandated for practices by the American Institute of Certified Public Accountants, firm training also became focused on assuring the continued technical competency of those in the profession. The extent of this training became clear when Arthur Andersen & Co. acquired a former college campus in suburban St. Charles for these purposes.

By the end of the twentieth century, strong connections had been forged to the global economy through the competencies of Chicago's accounting and educational organizations. Branch offices of the world's largest accounting firms employed thousands of Chicagoans and provided services for its businesses. In these and other ways, professional accounting has been deeply intertwined with the developments that have shaped Chicago.                    *Paul J. Miranti Jr.*

**Advertising.** Even though New York City has always been the center of American publishing and broadcasting, Chicago became, by the beginning of the twentieth century, the heart and soul of American advertising. Chicago's advertising leadership was forged from the city's unparalleled success in personalized mail-order cataloging, nurtured by its pragmatic business attitude, and accelerated by the Midwest's democratic culture.

Chicago mail-order pioneers Montgomery Ward and Richard Warren Sears were the first great catalog copywriters. After the Great Fire of 1871, Ward began publishing well-illustrated catalogs with product testimonials and personalized copy. By 1883 his catalog advertised a stock of goods worth a half million dollars. Sears and his partner Alvah Curtis Roebuck claimed $53 million annual catalog sales in 1907 based on a circulation of about 5 million catalogs annually. Sears wrote nearly all of the copy himself.

The shift of advertising to the Midwest was stunning. In the 1860s and 1870s, only about 5 percent of the nation's advertising came from west of

THE **EXTENSIVE** ADVERTISING AGENCY OF COOK, COBURN & CO. IN THE KENDALL BUILDING, SKETCHED DURING BUSINESS HOURS. (*See page* 54.)

Advertising agency Cook, Coburn & Co. interior, in the Kendall Building, 1874. This early Chicago advertising agency was located at the corner of Dearborn and Washington. From *Land Owner*, April 1874. Courtesy of the Newberry Library.

Philadelphia and New York City. By 1906, 45 percent of all nonlocal advertising in the nation originated west of Buffalo.

One Chicago ad agency—Lord & Thomas—overshadowed all the rest, achieving greater national influence and notoriety than any other agency in the United States. Albert Lasker started at Lord & Thomas in 1898, became general manager in 1904 at a salary of $52,000 per year, and within a decade owned the agency. He traveled the city in a chauffeur-driven yellow Rolls Royce and maintained a suburban estate with a staff of 50. Lasker hired the best copywriters in the business and taught them that advertising was "salesmanship in print"—probably the best-known definition of the advertising business in twentieth-century America.

Lasker sold the public on the idea of orange juice (people previously only ate oranges), built brands such as Goodyear and Van de Kamp's, established a "records of results" department that monitored its clients' advertising impact with catalog-response precision, and even used advertising to help defeat Woodrow Wilson's League of Nations. Advertising legend David Ogilvy rightly ranked Lasker as one of the "six giants of modern advertising."

The most legendary American advertising copywriter was Lord & Thomas's Claude C. Hopkins. In his popular autobiography, *My Life in Advertising* (1927), Hopkins captured the populist style of Chicago advertising as literature for the common people. Hopkins is probably the father of consumer advertising for branded goods. He dubbed Schlitz the "beer that made Milwaukee famous," created unparalleled brand equity for Palmolive soap and Pepsodent toothpaste, wrote the "shot from guns" slogan for Quaker Oats, and invented free product sampling through print coupons. Hopkins also penned the most influential book ever written about advertising—*Scientific Advertising* (1923).

Lasker sold Lord & Thomas in 1942 to three employees (Messrs. Foote, Cone & Belding). Fairfax Cone led the new company into an unparalleled era of creative broadcast advertising. The agency built some of the most successful broadcast advertising brands of all time, including the "Hallmark Hall of Fame," Clairol's "Does she or doesn't she?" and Dial soap's "Aren't you glad you use Dial?" Cone's client-sponsored broadcast programs helped make superstars out of such performers as Frank Sinatra and Bob Hope. Cone also led the Chicago advertising industry into public philanthropy, supporting the University of Chicago, opera, and many other endeavors.

The other great modern Chicago ad agency was the Leo Burnett Company. Burnett started the agency in 1935, mortgaging his house in the midst of the Great Depression. In 1989 the agency claimed $3.2 billion annual billings and maintained offices in over 40 countries. Burnett's television campaigns included the Jolly Green Giant, the Pillsbury Dough Boy, Charlie Tuna, Tony the Tiger, and the Marlboro Man. *Advertising Age* ranked Burnett the third most influential person in the history of American advertising.

The *Chicago Tribune* was third nationally among newspapers in total advertising linage from the 1920s into the 1950s, creating and placing ads for thousands of its retail customers. *Advertising Age*, the best advertising trade magazine in the world, was started in the Windy City in 1930. The magazine's critical style set the standard for business journalism across the country.

By 1980 advertising was among the largest industries in Chicago, with 8,000 employees in over 500 agencies and $6 billion in revenues. Writer and sociologist Hugh Dalziel Duncan called Chicago the nation's home of "commercial magicians and priests of consumption." Chicagoans turned consumption into a "token of an infinitely expanding future of bigger and better things" that people must buy. Chicago businesspeople understood that "the power of style in America is derived from its power to *communicate* to others . . . our power to spend freely and frequently."

*Quentin J. Schultze*

**Agricultural Machinery Industry.** In 1847 Cyrus McCormick decided to consolidate manufacture of his reaper in Chicago. Since developing the first successful reaper in 1831, McCormick had tried selling it through regional licensees who also manufactured the machine. This approach had worked poorly, often producing inferior machines and always producing inferior financial results. McCormick also recognized that the future of American agriculture lay to the west and that Chicago—with the railroad to Galena nearly complete, the Illinois & Michigan Canal soon to open, and a telegraph link to the East Coast about to be in place—offered the best location from which to build his business.

On August 30, 1847, McCormick, in partnership with Charles M. Gray (later mayor of Chicago), bought three lots on the north bank of the Chicago River. The two immediately began construction of a factory to build the McCormick reaper. By 1850, with the McCormick factory in full operation, the U.S. census reported 646 people working in the agricultural implement industry in Chicago.

Chicago soon attracted other machinery producers, including George Esterly of Heart Prairie, Wisconsin, who built a Chicago factory to produce his grain header, and John S. Wright, who made a self-rake reaper developed by Jearum Atkins. But the sharp financial panic of October 1857 destroyed or crippled many of McCormick's competitors. In 1860 his factory occupied 110,000 square feet of floor space and, with more than 300 workers, employed nearly a fifth of all wage earners in Chicago's agricultural implement sector.

During the next decade, employment in the sector grew quickly—the 1870 census found nearly 4,000 working in agricultural machinery establishments—but the McCormick Company, though still the largest single employer in the Chicago implement industry, had stagnated. Its products were ill-suited to a shift among many farmers to combined machines that could efficiently harvest both grain and hay, the latter much in demand to feed the livestock in America's burgeoning cities. McCormick harvesters also technically lagged behind specialized self-rakes used for harvesting small grains. As a result, McCormick had shrunk to a regional firm, selling principally in upper Midwest states.

On January 25, 1871, Cyrus McCormick bought 130 acres on the South Branch of the Chicago River, where he hoped to build a new factory. But the Great Fire of 1871 put the whole future of the company into question when, on October 9, it destroyed the entire old factory. Within days Nettie Fowler McCormick, the young wife of 62-year-old Cyrus, was on the new site, where she ordered the resumption of full production. Within two years, the new McCormick Works replaced the old factory. At the same time, the company management, much influenced by Nettie McCormick, refocused on building the business, and the company began to regain ground. By 1880, with McCormick the largest agricultural machinery producer in Chicago, area employment reached nearly 7,000, a fifth of the national total.

A few years earlier, William Deering, a retired merchant from Maine, had come to Plano, Illinois, to superintend another reaper factory his old friend Elijah Gammon had purchased. Deering settled in Evanston the following year, and after buying control of the company in 1878, he moved it to Chicago in 1880. The William Deering Company soon rivaled the leading McCormick Company, and the Deering factory on the North Branch of the Chicago River employed nearly as many workers as the McCormick plant on the South Branch. A second reaper company was organized to take over the old factory in Plano, but it also relocated to the Chicago area. In 1893 the Plano Company built a new factory in West Pullman.

In the mid-1880s, as McCormick management tried both to gain closer control over the production processes and to wrestle with the impact of a severe national recession, labor unrest grew rapidly. As a result, the McCormick Works faced several major strikes. During one, police used brutal tactics to defend non-union workers from attacks by strikers as they left the plant on May 3, 1886, leading directly to the protest meeting the next night at Haymarket Square, where a bomb killed seven policemen. Only a few years later, however, McCormick proudly went through the tumult surrounding the Pullman Strike with no troubles at all; by then the company paid among the highest factory wages in Chicago and enjoyed high worker loyalty.

In 1902 these three companies—McCormick, Deering, and Plano—together with two others, came together to form the International Harvester Company (Navistar after 1986). The new company controlled more than 80 percent of world production in grain harvesting equipment. International Harvester quickly expanded its Chicago-area facilities. At its peak, in the 1920s and 1930s, the company had six major manufacturing facilities in the Chicago area (plus a steel mill in South Chicago), covering 440 acres, and accounting for a large share of the nearly 23,000 workers in Chicago's agricultural machinery sector in the 1930 census. This accounted for more than half the national total of 41,662.

This was the high point of the industry in the Chicago area. The Great Depression took a heavy toll, and after World War II both International Harvester and the broader industry undertook all of its expansion outside the Chicago area. As a result, the Chicago-area plants were increasingly outdated and uneconomical. In the 1950s, the McCormick Works was progressively closed down, and the agricultural machinery industry no longer held a significant place in the Chicago-area economy.    *Fred Carstensen*

**Agriculture.** Although agriculture was practiced by Native Americans living in the area, it was not until settlers from the eastern United States arrived that Chicago began to emerge as the agricultural leader of the world.

The years between the first schooner load of grain to leave Chicago in 1839 and the 1865 opening of the Union Stock Yard defined Chicago's agricultural heritage. The opening of the Illinois & Michigan Canal, the construction of railroads, Cyrus McCormick's and Obed Hussey's competitive manufacturing of grain reapers and other implements, the beginning of the Chicago Board of Trade, and the extremely favorable growing seasons of 1849, 1850, and 1851—all combined to strengthen Chicago's importance to the agricultural business community.

Likewise, developments after the American Civil War maintained Chicago's role as the leading agricultural city. Development of the refrigerated railroad boxcar, dredging and expansion of the city's harbor, and the establishment of the corn and livestock belt expanded the agricultural prosperity and reputation of the city.

Chicago's "big shoulders" were broadened with each swing of the farmer's scythe. Grain was and remains at the very center of Chicago's agriculture. Wheat—and later oats, barley, rye, and corn—filled the bellies of livestock and ships alike. Grain culture spread westward from Pennsylvania and Ohio and reached peak production on the prairie lands of Illinois in the 1850s and 1860s. Here, the development of technology for planting and harvesting, combined with the fertile soil and almost perfect climate, produced bumper crops on an annual basis. By 1860 Illinois was the number one producer of both corn and wheat.

Grain farmers benefited from the ever-expanding transportation system for getting their crop to market. Oxen-pulled carts on crude roads were replaced by horse-drawn wagons on the plank roads of the 1830s. These in turn became obsolete with the opening of the I&M Canal in 1848 and the subsequent railroad construction westward from Chicago in the 1850s. What had been a difficult journey of three or four days to transport a wagon full of grain from the Fox River 35 miles west of Chicago was now a several-hour trip by train to the city.

This mass movement of grain resulted in the commingling of grain at railroad stops and barge tie-ups called elevators. There, a farmer's grain was carefully weighed and graded, with like grades being elevated into large commingled overhead bins. From these bins, gravity provided the impetus and wooden chutes quickly filled the waiting railroad cars and barges. While the elevator created another middleman between the farmer and the purchaser, it facilitated a more reliable delivery system, provided a means to accommodate a larger harvest, minimized the loss of grain to a single seller, and provided for the speculator, who could easily buy or sell the stored grain.

Speculation on the price of grain and other agricultural commodities has been a critical component in Chicago's agriculture. The Chicago Board of Trade has been the platform allowing access to markets within the United States and throughout the world. Historically, it has provided price stability, setting the minimum price for agricultural commodities and stimulating interest and reinvestment in agricultural businesses. While farmers saw speculators as making money off their labor, the Board of Trade facilitated working capital being available for farmers to utilize.

The Chicago Board of Trade provided similar support for the growing beef cattle and hog industry of the mid-1800s. As the railroad link between the eastern markets and the increasing number of midwestern and trans-Mississippi producers of livestock, the Union Stock Yard became the largest facility of its kind when it opened in 1865. Just as wheat production had moved westward, so had the production of hogs, stripping Cincinnati in the early 1860s of its self-proclaimed status as Porkopolis. Following the arrival of Armour, Swift, and other meatpackers, the Union Stock Yard was easily handling 8 to 9 million animals each year by the mid-1870s.

This post–Civil War commercial growth brought expansion to the city and its population. Feeding this population and supplying transport materials within the city limits was a large agricultural endeavor unto itself. Following the Great Fire of 1871, vegetable and dairy operations moved

Mexican workers in Willow Springs, 1917. Chicago's demand for agricultural, railroad, and industrial workers in the 1910s combined with the social upheaval of the Mexican Revolution to spur migration from Mexico to the Chicago area. Pictured here are Mexican immigrants working in agricultural fields in Willow Springs, 1917. Photo: *Chicago Daily News*. Courtesy of the Chicago History Museum (DN-0068516).

outside city limits. Vegetable and chicken farms could be found arcing from South Holland to Maywood. Dairy farms developed in DuPage, Cook, and Lake Counties and in the closer-in areas of Will and McHenry Counties. Creameries and milk-processing facilities were constructed along existing railroad lines, and special milk trains transported this commodity for processing. Hay and oats were cash crops for farmers in the outlying counties, as they were vital for feeding and maintaining the tens of thousands of horses used in Chicago each day. The hay market in Chicago was a huge endeavor, with the Union Stock Yard feeding its livestock 100 tons of hay each day during its peak seasons, in addition to the corn that was fed to select holdings.

After the fire, horses remained the only farm animal permitted to stable within the city limits. They provided necessary cartage between warehouses and businesses, made livery services possible, pulled milk and street peddlers' wagons and fire and municipal vehicles, and performed hundreds of other tasks, including functioning as personal transportation. The waste from these horses was in excess of 40,000 pounds each day.

In 1872 New Yorker Franklin J. (F. J.) Berry established a small but successful horse market at the corner of Michigan Avenue and Monroe Street. By 1886 Berry was selling 4,000 horses annually. In October 1888 he moved his operation to the Union Stock Yard and by 1895 was selling 27,000 horses annually. His success was due to his innovative sales method: horses brought in by the rail carload were sold individually in a weekly public auction. This method, which allowed Illinois to dominate the national horse market from the late 1880s through the late 1920s, continued into the twenty-first century.

The interest in and specialization of the Chicago livestock market continued well into the twentieth century. Agricultural fairs and specific breed expositions, including the numerous agricultural pavilions of the 1893 World's Columbian Exposition, assisted in this promotion. Beginning in 1878, a "fat stock" show was held annually, always in the fall, in order to promote and identify the best examples of purebred species. This evolved into the International Livestock Exposition in 1900 and continued on an annual basis until 1975. J. H. Sanders, founder of the *Breeder's Gazette* in 1881, and son Alvin worked closely with the various large breeders and individual breeders' associations to create this uniquely large, very successful market and exposition.

In the twentieth century, changing technology and the expansion of the Chicago region's population continued to adversely affect the daily role of agriculture. The Union Stock Yard began declining in the 1950s as better methods of carcass transportation decentralized the meatpacking industry away from the midwestern transportation centers. Two decades later, the Union Stock Yard itself fell victim to recession and closed. Meanwhile, large grocery store conglomerates with their own independent supply and distribution systems facilitated the demise of most local fresh-produce growers.

Today the Union Stock Yard gate stands as almost a lone sentry against the urban and suburban sprawl that has claimed hundreds of thousands of acres of prime farmland in the collar counties. At the end of the twentieth century, agricultural production continued on a handful of grain and dairy farms that once numbered in the thousands. The recent interest in more wholesome food has sustained a hundred or so seasonal farmers' markets throughout the Chicago region. Specialized products such as free-range chickens, ostrich, llamas, buffalo, and organically grown herbs and vegetables are raised on suburban farmettes. Throughout it all, the South Water Street Market has continued to be the best source of fresh fruits, vegetables, and herbs for midwestern restaurateurs and independent, upscale food stores. And the CME/Chicago Board of Trade remains a powerful influence on the world's agricultural markets, despite the fact that most area residents are three to four generations removed from the family farm. Thus, it is these specialized products along with the vastness of the world's grain trade that will define Chicago's agricultural industry for the future.                                                  *Chas. P. Raleigh*

**Airlines.** Chicago's geographic location and established position as a major transportation center have made the city attractive to the airline industry from its beginning. The roots of the industry lie in the transport of mail for the U.S. Post Office. By the 1920s, the U.S. Post Office contracted with fledgling airline companies to fly mail throughout the country. Chicago was a pivotal location from the earliest establishment of the Contract Air Mail routes.

Development of the early commercial airline industry grew from a combination of a federal infrastructure of navigation systems and regulations, local boosterism, and private investment. In the 1920s and 1930s, communities built airports as a matter of civic pride and attracted private airline companies by promising modern facilities and room for expansion. Chicago's most important airports, O'Hare International and Midway Airport, have been operated by city government.

One of the first municipal airports was Chicago Municipal Airport, built in 1927 to replace Maywood Field, the airstrip used for airmail. That year Chicago Municipal Airport was a single cinder runway with one square mile of land available for expansion 10 miles southwest of downtown. By 1929 the airport maintained its own post office, stationed a division of the Illinois National Guard, and handled 32 arrivals and departures of passengers, mail, and cargo daily. Chicago Municipal Airport cost $10 million to develop. By 1932 it was the busiest airport in the nation and for years claimed the title of World's Busiest Airport. In the early 1930s, it was also the birthplace of the Air Line Pilots Association. In 1949 Municipal Airport was renamed Midway Airport to commemorate the famous battle in the Pacific. In 1940 the air transportation industry in Chicago employed 822 men and 303 women in both commercial and government jobs; by 1950 the industry employed 3,711 men and 1,431 women.

To compete as an international city, however, Chicago needed an airport with greater growth potential. In 1946 the city purchased over 1,000 acres of land northwest of the city. O'Hare opened its $24 million terminal for commercial passenger traffic in 1955. The airport covered 10 square miles. O'Hare soon dominated Chicago's aviation system, with its capacity for handling the new jet airplanes, international flights, and military aircraft through its unique paired tangential runways, which allowed for simultaneous takeoffs and landings on six runways. Despite its remote location in cornfields 22 miles outside of downtown, O'Hare soon usurped Midway's title of World's Busiest Airport. By the early 1960s, O'Hare handled 8 million passengers a year. In 1960, 7,845 men and 3,392 women worked in air transportation in Chicago.

Starting in the 1960s, most scheduled commercial airlines shifted their operations to O'Hare from Midway, causing an economic downturn for the Midway community and a boom for the suburbs surrounding O'Hare. The construction of several expressways accessing the newer airport linked it to both the city and suburbs. Suburbs surrounding the airport—such as Rosemont, Bensenville, Addison, and Elk Grove Village—experienced tremendous growth in population and in light manufacturing and service industries, air freight businesses, and the hospitality industry.

In the late 1990s, approximately 75 commercial, commuter, and cargo airlines served Chicago at Midway and O'Hare. At the beginning of the twenty-first century, United Airlines and American Airlines provided the majority of commercial scheduled service at O'Hare; Southwest Airlines anchored service at Midway, which was substantially renovated in 2001. In 2010, O'Hare served nearly 67 million passengers; Midway, over 17.5 million.

The pivotal role of the airline industry in Chicago's economy cannot be underestimated. The city's growth as a center of light industry as well as banking, consulting, and other white-collar businesses has been linked to air access at O'Hare, Midway, and, until it was closed in 2003, the city's lakefront airport, Meigs Field. In the early 1990s, Chicago's airports directly employed over 50,000 people, and the industry generated an estimated 340,000 jobs in the metropolitan area through service to visitors and companies that depend on the airports for their existence. Public transportation by elevated train to O'Hare was finished in 1984 and to Midway in 1993, providing easy access to both airports from downtown and other parts of the city for both travelers and workers. Jobs at the airports are split between Chicago residents and suburbanites, although suburbanites take home the majority of personal income earned at the airports. By 2010 the city estimated that the two airports created 540,000 jobs and $45 billion in economic activity. Additionally, since 2001 when Boeing moved its headquarters from Seattle to Chicago, the administrative center of the U.S. largest airplane manufacturing has contributed to the city's economy.

Despite the economic benefits to suburban Chicago, its relationship with O'Hare has grown tense over issues of noise, growth, and density. In the 1990s, politicians, airlines, and residents began to debate the creation of a third major airport in the far south suburbs, as well as expansion of O'Hare. By the early twenty-first century, expansion efforts again focused on O'Hare. By 2011 its neighbors and largest carriers had acquiesced to expansion plans and agreements; O'Hare expansion was under way.

*Liesl M. Orenic*

**Automobile Manufacturing.** Although two early automobiles were exhibited at the World's Columbian Exposition of 1893—the prototype Morrison electric and a gasoline-powered car from Germany—horseless carriages didn't receive much notoriety until the *Chicago Times-Herald* offered $5,000 in prizes to the winner of a round-trip race between Chicago and Evanston two years later. The race attracted considerable attention because two cars were able to finish despite the fact that a storm had deposited a foot of snow on the Chicago area two days earlier.

What was possibly the nation's first auto show was held in conjunction with the race. A modest 12 automobiles were exhibited in a donated Studebaker Company wagon and buggy showroom on South Wabash Avenue. Annual auto shows at which builders exhibited production and futuristic vehicles did not begin in Chicago until after 1900. Except during major wars, they continued through the end of the century. Road races and "reliability runs" intended to demonstrate the durability of motor cars were also popular in the early twentieth century.

The 1895 race in a way marks the beginning of Chicago's auto manufacturing industry; at least six local tinkerers tried to build vehicles for the race but were unable to complete them in time. In the final five years of the nineteenth century, at least 22 local companies were formed to build and sell horseless carriages, and at least 12 got their vehicles into production.

Although Chicago never quite rivaled Detroit as the nation's auto capital, during the first decade of the twentieth century, no less than 28 companies produced 68 models of cars in the Windy City and its environs. Chicago's industrial base, which included a profusion of machine shops able to turn out automotive components, established the city as a center of manufacture of automobile parts through the twentieth century. The fact that the city was a railroad center enabled customers to travel to Chicago from all over the Midwest to buy cars built locally as well as in Detroit. In the decades before rural roads were paved to permit intercity travel by auto, out-of-town customers would buy cars along Auto Row south of the Loop and ship them home by train.

Many early manufacturers also built light delivery trucks, which for a time provided more of an impetus for the conversion from horsepower to motor vehicles than did autos because they were less expensive to operate than horse-drawn drays. Trucks also enabled Chicago to reduce pollution from dung and urine deposited by horses on the streets and to avoid epizootic diseases that decimated urban horse populations in the late nineteenth century. Several auto manufacturers, such as International Harvester Company and Diamond T Motor Car Company, successfully converted to heavy truck production. International Harvester, which became Navistar Corporation in 1986, was one of the nation's largest builders of large trucks and school buses.

A motorized farm buggy known generically as the "highwheeler" because of its wagon-style wheels was developed in Chicago, which became the center of manufacture of that type of car between about 1903 and 1912, when the Model T Ford drove it from the market. Holsman Automobile Company, International Harvester, Staver Carriage Company, and Sears, Roebuck & Co. combined built nearly 18,000 highwheelers in Chicago. Sears sold them through its catalog.

Woods Motor Vehicle Company manufactured more than 13,500 electric and dual-powered cars between 1896 and 1918, when it went out of business. Other well-known Chicago auto manufacturers included Checker Motors Corporation, a taxicab builder that moved to Kalamazoo, Michigan; Yellow Cab Manufacturing Company, one of auto-leasing company founder John Hertz's ventures; and Thomas B. Jeffery & Co., a bicycle maker who developed the Rambler automobile and moved his manufacturing operations to north suburban Kenosha, Wisconsin. The Rambler was the most popular car developed in Chicago. More than 4.2 million were sold between 1902 and their discontinuance in 1969 by the successor American Motors Corporation. As the twentieth century ended, the Rambler factory in Kenosha was used to build engines for Chrysler Corporation autos.

The auto manufacturing industry in the Windy City began to decline by World War I as Detroit-made cars became dominant, although the Chicago area remained an important center for auto parts and steel used to make cars. At the beginning of the twenty-first century, Ford Motor Company maintained an assembly plant in Hegewisch, and Chrysler Corporation maintained one in Belvidere, but the last Chicago manufacturer of consequence was the Elgin Motor Car Company, which built 16,784 conventional cars in suburban Argo (Summit) between 1916 and its bankruptcy in 1924. In 1946 Preston Tucker organized his company and planned to build the "Torpedo" in a factory located in what is now the Ford City Shopping Complex in the West Lawn Community Area. Detroit was so dominant that he had no chance of success. The company was bankrupted in 1949 after producing only 51 vehicles.     *David M. Young*

**Automobile Parts.** The manufacture of automobile parts was never one of Chicago's largest industries. Nevertheless, the history of the auto parts industry cannot be written without Chicago-based companies. The production and distribution of car and truck parts employed thousands of area residents engaged in delivering many of the approximately 15,000 parts used in a modern automobile.

In 1900, when the nascent automobile industry was still closely related to the bicycle industry, Chicago companies such as the Western Wheel Works and Smith Steel Stamping were among the earliest makers of parts for gasoline-powered vehicles. As the auto industry grew at an explosive rate, new parts makers sprung up in and around the city. During the 1920s, as many as 600 companies in the Chicago area made auto parts and accessories. Most were quite small, and many went out of business or were bought out by larger firms. Still, metropolitan Chicago boasted dozens of small-scale manufacturers and distributors of auto parts through the end of the twentieth century.

Several Chicago companies—including Stewart-Warner, Maremont, and BorgWarner—became leaders in various sectors of the industry. Stewart-Warner, a maker of speedometers and other gauges, was descended from the Stewart Company, a Chicago company founded in 1905, and the Warner Instrument Company, which originated a year earlier in South Beloit, Wisconsin. By the 1970s, Stewart-Warner employed about 5,000 people in the Chicago area. Another local industry leader descended from Maremont, Wolfson & Cohen Inc., which was established in Chicago in 1903. In 1933 this maker of truck yokes and springs became Maremont Automobile Products Inc. and manufactured shock absorbers, mufflers, and other parts. The largest and best known of all the Chicago-based auto parts companies during the twentieth century was BorgWarner Corporation, created from several midwestern auto parts makers in 1928. BorgWarner saw its annual sales rise from about $54 million in 1929 to over $600 million by 1957. During the 1950s, it supplied many of the new automatic transmissions installed in the vehicles assembled by Detroit giants such as Ford. By 2005 when it moved its headquarters from Michigan Avenue to Auburn Hills, Michigan, the company was selling nearly $2.5 billion worth of auto parts annually and employing a global workforce of over 13,000 people.

By the late twentieth century, intense global competition in the auto parts industry made it difficult for local manufacturing firms to prosper. BorgWarner, despite its continued growth, no longer manufactured as many parts at local plants. Some companies were forced to retrench. Oak Brook's Champion Parts Inc., once the leading independent American rebuilder of parts such as carburetors and alternators, was having trouble remaining profitable in the 1990s. Navistar International—the descendant of International Harvester that sold truck engines and parts as well as finished vehicles—trimmed domestic operations and opened overseas factories to reverse large losses and return itself to profitability. Warshawsky & Co., an auto parts catalog company based on the South Side, laid off about 500 workers when it closed a large warehouse in 1996. Other local parts makers, including Maremont and Broadview's Robert Bosch

Corporation, became subsidiaries of foreign companies. At the end of the twentieth century, Chicago-area companies continued to participate in what had become a highly competitive global industry.     *Mark R. Wilson*

**Banking, Commercial.** Chicago's economic growth reached the point that it needed banking institutions just at the time that a fierce debate over banks and paper money engulfed the nation. Although the Bank of Illinois already was operating in 1817, chartered banking was not authorized until the following year, by the 1818 Illinois Constitution. The state bank closed ten years later, when its notes plummeted in value. The bank's notes failed to maintain their value for a number of reasons: the bank failed to maintain sufficient gold and silver; there was a fire that destroyed the bank, followed by a robbery of the temporary quarters; and changes in state law made it difficult to collect debts. Banks received their charters from the state legislature, and this process made the chartering of banks a highly political process. Under the charter provisions of virtually all states, banks were permitted to issue notes based on gold or silver coin called *specie*. When a bank could not redeem its notes in specie, it had to close, a problem many Illinois banks faced after the panic of 1837, at which time the Second State Bank, created in 1835 with a branch in Chicago, also failed. Most Chicago banks failed during, or shortly after, that panic.

These circumstances generated a hostility to banks throughout the Old Northwest Territory and might have doomed Chicago to slow growth, starved for credit, had it not been for the appearance of "private" (i.e., unchartered) banks. One of the first of those was created by Gurdon Hubbard, under the title Hubbard & Balestier, in the 1830s. More important was the bank of George Smith, a Scottish land speculator and investor, who played a crucial role in the city's early financial history. Smith created the Scottish Illinois Land Investment Company in 1837 by investing in Chicago properties, and in the process of handling the real estate business, the company started to discount bank notes from other cities and states. Although the company split in 1839, with Smith moving to Wisconsin, his banking activities shaped Chicago.

Smith reentered banking in Chicago later that year, first by creating the Wisconsin Marine and Fire Insurance Company and second by founding George Smith and Company in Chicago. The latter was not a chartered bank, and therefore could not issue notes, but it could circulate certificates from the Wisconsin business. Smith called his certificates "checks," and by 1842 "George Smith's money," redeemable in specie, was in sharp demand throughout the Chicago region. Within two years, all Illinois banks other than Smith's had disappeared. By 1854 George Smith's banks supplied nearly 75 percent of Chicago's currency.

The Illinois legislature passed a "free banking" law in 1851 in which a bank no longer had to obtain a charter from the legislature but could secure a general incorporation charter from the secretary of state. The first

Chicago bank under the new constitution, the Marine Bank, appeared that same year and developed close ties with William Ogden and other influential Chicago leaders in railroads, industry, and real estate. The appearance of the Marine Bank was followed shortly by the Merchants and Mechanics Bank, then, rapidly, eight more institutions. As a result of the new law, Illinois banking capital nearly quadrupled in the mid-1850s.

Although Chicago witnessed 204 business failures during the recession following the panic of 1857, less than 10 percent of Illinois's banks failed, and the politicians praised the banking system for its performance. However, in 1858 Chicago bankers started to refuse the notes of "country banks," many of which were backed by bonds from the South. The discounting of non-Chicago notes and the continued collapse of the country bank notes' value led to calls for the abolition of all banks in the state. Instead, the problems were addressed with reforms in the free banking laws.

With the passage of the National Bank Act (1863), Chicago added five new nationally chartered institutions, all developed out of existing private banking houses. Illinois encouraged large "unit" banks—epitomized by the Central Trust Company of Illinois, which opened in Chicago in 1902 as a "big bank for small people." Its president, former U.S. comptroller Charles Dawes, opposed branch bank legislation at the state and national levels. The national banks were created first and foremost to finance the Civil War, and thus gained important advantages over state banks in securities acquisition and sales. In 1891, for example, Chicago's First National Bank took $1.2 million in the city's bond issue—the entire amount. When the bank's bond department could not handle mortgage or real estate loans, the bank organized a "security affiliate," First Trust and Savings Bank, to deal specifically in securities. This represented a revolution in securities financing and was quickly copied by New York institutions, which referred to it as the "Chicago Plan." Later, during the Great Depression, critics of the banking system pointed to the interlocking of banks with securities affiliates as a cause of the weakness that led to the banking collapse in the 1930s. In fact, this system strengthened the banks by giving them more flexibility in their portfolios. Since only the state bank was allowed to have branches, its failure effectively ended branching in Illinois.

Chicago bankers also led the way in creating a system for preventing panics through the Chicago Clearing House. James B. Forgan of First National Bank initiated the new clearing system in 1905 and ran it effectively. Clearinghouses allowed the city's banks to settle all their outstanding obligations with each other at the end of each business day. This enhanced information transmission among the banks and reduced the risk of panics. After the panic of 1907, however, many concluded that only a national "lender of last resort" could prevent future panics, leading to a reform movement. Forgan served on the Currency Commission of the American Bankers Association and helped shape the reform legisla-

Milwaukee Avenue State Bank failure, August 1906. Crowd gathered outside the Milwaukee Avenue Bank at 739–47 (formerly 409–15) Milwaukee Avenue during its August 1906 failure. Photo: *Chicago Daily News*. Courtesy of the Chicago History Museum (DN-0003927).

tion that became the Federal Reserve Act of 1913. Forgan, meanwhile, had found a way around the branch bank restrictions by establishing new, but clearly related, unit banks in areas outlying Chicago, thus forming an early "chain" bank—the second most efficient form of banking next to branching. Chain banks, unlike branch banks, might have the same owners, but they could not commingle assets or liabilities: each, essentially, had to stand on its own. This was a weaker structure than branching, because branch banks could shift assets around to "trouble spots."

After the creation of the "Fed," Chicago was designated a headquarters city of a Federal Reserve District Bank, and the city's national banks soon opted to have Chicago designated a central reserve city in the new system, under which all national banks had to carry a 25 percent reserve. That attracted the balances of banks designated as country banks to Chicago, which, by 1914, had $205 million in interbank balances, or nearly six times more than in 1887. George Reynolds's Continental and Commercial National Bank of Chicago was the leader in handling correspondent business. Banks already had started to specialize in either commercial operations—which financed agriculture, trade, and businesses—or large-scale capital investment, often through a syndicate of many institutions, to build railroads or other capital-intensive enterprises.

After 1900 Chicago emerged as a major source of investment funds. By this time, a difference had emerged between "investment banks" (such as J. P. Morgan), which dealt extensively with providing start-up capital for large, new enterprises, and commercial banks, which provided loans for business operations on a more short-term basis. From 1900 to 1928, Chicago's banks, most of which were commercial banks, underwent a period of rapid expansion, with aggregate net worth growing nearly sixfold. During that same period, the nation's percentage of total banks made up of national banks shrank from 60 percent to 36 percent, indicating the strong advantages offered by state charters, including lower capitalization requirements. Like bankers in other major cities, Chicago's financial leaders had no reason to see a threat in the near future: in the 1920s alone, Chicago banks marketed $2.5 million in public utilities, and at the end of the decade, Chicago stood behind only New York and London as a great money center.

But the correspondent system that had generated much of that growth rebounded negatively with the city's banks when the agricultural downturn of the 1920s caused the collapse of many unit banks in farm states. Their balance withdrawals started to weaken Chicago's major institutions. After the Great Crash of 1929, a national banking panic materialized. Research suggests that the complaints about banks' "speculation" causing the crash were exactly wrong: banks with securities affiliates, such as First National, were less likely to fail than banks *not* involved in the market. There were exceptions, of course: the collapse of Samuel Insull's Midwest utilities empire helped weaken the Continental Illinois Bank. From 1929 to 1930, more than 30 Chicago banks went out of business. In addition, more than 100 banks sought to strengthen themselves through mergers. In 1931 the collapse of Insull-related securities spread through the banking community, with runs forcing 25 banks to close in a matter of days. Research has suggested that most of the failures between 1930 and 1933 resulted more from weakening portfolios related to government securities they held than to declining real estate prices that might indicate poor management of mortgage lending.

By 1933 President Franklin Roosevelt concluded that only a national "bank holiday" would restore the system. Soon thereafter Congress changed most of the banking laws. Banks could not have securities affiliates under the Glass-Steagall Act. The Federal Deposit Insurance Corporation (FDIC) was formed, although subsequent research has shown conclusively that the state deposit insurance schemes of the 1920s contributed to the banking problems in the agricultural states. The Insull securities empire also had held large amounts of tax-anticipation warrants, suggesting that the deteriorating condition of the municipalities themselves contributed to the weakness of the financial structure.

Chicago banks stabilized, but only after huge losses: Continental Illinois National Bank wrote off $110 million in a two-year period. Full recovery did not occur until after World War II. Between 1959 and 1968, 56 new banks were established in Cook County, with Chicago having 240 offices in 1960 and 295 by 1968. Deposit concentrations held by Chicago's banks as a share of all Illinois banks rose during that period from 43.9 percent to 45.1 percent. Gross loans doubled, and total assets increased by more than 70 percent.

The integrated financial market of the United States allowed Chicago banks to invest in Arizona real estate, lumbering in Maine, and businesses throughout the United States. One of the most important new sources of demand for loans was in oil and gas drilling and exploration. Ironically, oil and gas investments contributed to the downfall of what many insiders called Chicago's best-managed bank, Continental Illinois. In the late 1970s and early 1980s, a small Oklahoma City bank, Penn Square Bank, had begun offering "participations" in oil and gas loans that it originated. By 1982 Continental Illinois held $1.1 billion of Penn Square's "participations," which constituted 17 percent of Continental's energy loans. In mid-1982, however, the oil and gas loans went sour, and in May a run struck the bank. Continental Illinois threatened to collapse and had to be bailed out by loans from the federal government in 1989 because the bank had correspondent accounts from more than 175 banks, each of whom had at least half their capital in the struggling institution.

While Continental Illinois recovered temporarily, the importance of the integrated and international market was apparent: Chicago banks would no longer stand isolated as the "kings" of Midwest banking. Without branching, it was only a matter of time before Chicago's largest banks became relatively small and therefore takeover targets. During the merger waves of the 1980s and 1990s, Continental's many business interests were split; its commercial banking business became part of First National. The National Bank of Detroit (NBD) merged with First National to form First Chicago NBD, and the resulting firm then joined Banc One, a Columbus, Ohio, firm that moved its headquarters to Chicago. LaSalle Bank was purchased by ABN (later ABN-AMRO), a Dutch firm in 1979, and Harris Trust was acquired by the Bank of Montreal in 1984. This left Northern Trust as the only one of Chicago's major banks that retained Chicago ownership. These acquisitions effectively marked the end of Chicago's regional advantage as a financial center, due in large part to Illinois's long-standing limitations on branch banking. The rise of the Internet and electronic banking might have given Chicago's banks some advantages that the law denied them. For example, with electronic/Internet banking, branches became less important, and Chicago banks could have engaged in "interstate banking" without having physical branches. However, electronic banking remained in its infancy and did not mature fast enough to keep the large Chicago banks independent of outside interests.

Another wave of bank mergers brought further changes to Chicago banking when, in 2004, Banc One was acquired by New York–based JP-Morgan Chase. Three years later, Bank of America purchased LaSalle Bank. Those purchases, along with several others in the volatile banking environment of the first decade of the twenty-first century, not only helped them dominate the Chicago banking market; it also made those banks two of the Chicago area's largest employers.                    *Larry E. Schweikart*

**Breweries.** During the nineteenth century, beer making was transformed from a small-scale, seasonal activity for local consumers into a highly mechanized big business. Outside of New York City, Chicago became the nation's largest center of the malt liquor industry. In addition to its looming economic importance, brewing had several other major impacts on the city in the areas of science, technology, architecture, politics, and culture.

In 1833 German immigrants established the first brewery in Chicago. Soon renamed the Lill & Diversey Brewery, it made English-style ales and porters. In 1847, however, John A. Huck opened the first German-style or lager beer plant and an adjacent beer garden on the Near North Side. The city's swelling numbers of Irish as well as Germans preferred this lighter, more carbonated cold drink, relegating traditional brews to a small specialty market. The brewery's insatiable demand for ice in making and storing its highly perishable food product was largely responsible for creating the ice business in Chicago. In a similar way, its needs for strong animals to pull wagons laden with heavy barrels of beer to saloons and restaurants across the city on a weekly basis helped establish breeding farms for the biggest type of "city" horses.

From 1860 to 1890, brewing underwent a profound scientific and technological revolution. Louis Pasteur's work on beer yeast identified germs and other microorganisms as the main reason why such a large proportion of the beer went bad. The virtually complete domination of the industry in Chicago by German immigrants and their offspring meant that the city became a leading center of "scientific brewing," boasting a special school, the Siebel Institute of Technology. Successful businessmen such as Conrad Seipp, Peter Schoenhofen, Michael Brand, and Charles Wacker—giants in the brewing community—underwrote the inventions that helped bring refrigeration machines to a point of commercial practicality. They also replaced the traditional brewmaster with university-trained chemists. The malting business grew in tandem, branching off to form an important industry in its own right. Applying more and more energy in the form of heat, power, and cooling, beer making became one of the country's most highly automated and mechanized industries, complete with assembly lines in the bottling plant. By 1900 Chicago's 60 breweries were making over 100 million gallons a year.

At the same time, however, the half-century campaign for temperance was becoming a highly charged political issue, full of ethnocultural, gender, and class meaning. Concerns about new waves of European immigrants, women's changing roles, and working-class militancy fueled the attack on the neighborhood saloon as the city's greatest social evil. With the coming of World War I, the forces of reform won passage of the Eighteenth Amendment, marking the end of Chicago's role as a vibrant center of legal brewing innovation. After the repeal of Prohibition in 1933, the city's brewing industry did not recover in the face of competition from national brand names selling beer in cans. One by one, the city's breweries closed their doors.

Industrial beer making in Chicago languished until the 1980s. Attempts to reopen some of the old large-scale breweries ultimately failed, but microbreweries (small-scale brewing companies) and brewpubs (restaurants with attached breweries) kept the city's beer-making tradition alive. Some, like Fulton Street Brewery LLC (producers of Goose Island beers), expanded to market their brews nationally and internationally. Although their breweries remained elsewhere, in 2008 Chicago became home to the headquarters of MillerCoors, a joint venture of SABMiller and Molson Coors Brewing Company aimed at helping them to compete more effectively with Belgium-based Anheuser-Busch InBev. The latter company entered the Chicago brewery market in 2011 when it purchased Fulton Street Brewery LLC.                                    *Harold L. Platt*

**Broadcasting.** Chicago emerged as a broadcasting center because its first radio stations, thanks to geography, were heard from the eastern seaboard to the Rockies and beyond. Its broadcasting flourished when Chicago became a central switching point for transcontinental network lines, allowing the city's production facilities to refeed programming to the various time zones with relative economy in the days before audio- and videotape. It survived because three generations of broadcasters, both on-air and behind the scenes, were consistently able to retool the broadcast media and sell them to an evolving market.

Chicago's age of broadcasting began the evening of November 11, 1921, when KYW (licensed to Westinghouse Electric and Manufacturing Company and operated jointly with Commonwealth Edison) began regular scheduled programming. For the next two months, KYW aired live performances of the Chicago Grand Opera Company—and nothing else. Managers of a later era might cringe at the thought of an "opera-only" station. But in 1921, only a year after Westinghouse's pioneer KDKA went on the air in Pittsburgh, the content of programs was secondary to the novelty of the medium. Westinghouse claimed there were 200 radio receivers in Chicago when the 1921 opera season began, 25,000 when it ended. KYW's live opera broadcasts were a major factor in the spread of America's "radio craze" and the creation of a local radio boom.

By the spring of 1923, 20 Chicago radio stations cluttered the largely unregulated dial. Many (including WBU, licensed to the city of Chicago, and WHT, separately licensed to Mayor William Hale Thompson) did not last the decade. Most that made the cut were owned by established businesses with pockets deep enough to absorb the losses until radio could pay its own way. WMAQ survived thanks to the backing of the *Chicago Daily News* (as well as the skills of general manager Judith Waller); WBBM thanks to a collaboration between the brothers H. Leslie and Ralph Atlass and the Stewart-Warner Corporation; WGN thanks to its ownership by the *Chicago Tribune*; and WLS thanks to Sears, Roebuck (and, after 1928, Prairie Farmer Publishing) and its rural-oriented programming. KYW, meanwhile, forged an alliance with the Hearst papers that lasted until its license was transferred to Philadelphia in 1934. Two stations survived thanks to their institutional affiliations: WCFL (licensed to the Chicago Federation of Labor) and WMBI (licensed to the Moody Bible Institute). Lower-powered WCRW, WEDC, and WSBC thrived because of their foreign-language programming.

The extension of AT&T's network lines to the West Coast in November 1928 turned Chicago into a national radio production center. Both NBC and CBS were committed to an 18-hour broadcast day. The time couldn't be filled without Chicago's participation.

Locally produced prime-time shows like Freeman Gosden and Charles Correll's *Amos 'n' Andy* and Jim and Marian Jordan's *Fibber McGee and Molly* were among the nation's most popular. But Chicago's network output was most substantial during the daytime, beginning with Don McNeill's *Breakfast Club* (1933–68) and continuing with hours of soap operas, a genre pioneered in Chicago. For many, the highlight of the broadcast day was *Vic and Sade* (1932–46). Writer Paul Rhymer's low-key comedy with a distinct midwestern flair provided 15 minutes of welcome relief from the drama of the soaps.

Chicago rapidly lost its status as a network radio production center following the end of World War II. But the completion of the coaxial cable linking the East Coast and the Midwest in January 1949 turned it into the origination point of some of early television's most memorable programs. WBKB (licensed in 1939 to the Balaban and Katz theater chain) had already trained the medium's first generation of technicians and producers. Network radio's departure had left a substantial pool of underutilized talent. Critics called the programming that resulted the "Chicago School of Television." Technically innovative, on the one hand, simple and straightforward, on the other, the "Chicago School" was above all characterized by the belief of its proponents that television was a unique medium unto itself.

By the mid-1950s, most of Chicago's major network television talents had been lured to the East Coast or West Coast. Emerging videotape technology meant that Chicago's studios were no longer necessary for live network broadcasts. At WGN-TV in particular, children remained a key target of local programming. A generation of Chicago's youth grew up watching *Garfield Goose and Friends*, while at least two generations watched (and hoped they could acquire tickets for) *Bozo's Circus*. But increasingly Chicago's commercial stations directed their resources toward local news coverage. The quality of local television news in Chicago generally remained high, thanks to the city's strong newspaper tradition and seasoned radio journalists like Clifton Utley and Len O'Connor, who brought their skills to the video medium. Meanwhile, WTTW (licensed in 1955) evolved into the nation's most-watched public television station.

Chicago's radio stations searched for new identities in the post-network era. In 1960 WLS abandoned its rural audience and adopted a fast-paced Top 40 format. WCFL followed suit a few years later. WMAQ shifted from middle of the road to country and western. WBBM experimented with an all-talk format, then shifted to all news. Phil and Leonard Chess, owners of Chess Records, purchased suburban Cicero's WHFC and changed its call letters to WVON. For the first time, Chicago had a station that targeted African Americans around the clock (Chicago's pioneer black radio personalities—Jack L. Cooper, Al Benson, and Sam Evans—had settled for small slices of time on primarily foreign-language stations). WGN was the lone holdout as a "full-service" station.

In the 1970s, music, for the most part, moved to the FM band. Three decades after Zenith Radio's Eugene McDonald put experimental station W51C on the air, FM had become profitable. Popular music dominated the dial. But Chicago's audience still supported a fine-arts station, WFMT, and public radio station WBEZ. Until his death in 2009, Paul Harvey remained Chicago's lone network radio personality. His daily news and commentary broadcasts were almost as long-lived as the ABC network that carried them.

But long after satellite dishes supplanted the network lines that once made Chicago a broadcasting hub, tens of millions of Americans continued to watch Chicago-made programs, thanks to the growing popularity of syndicated daytime television talk shows. Phil Donahue pioneered the genre. Oprah Winfrey perfected it. Jenny Jones and Jerry Springer threw it (sometimes literally) into the arena of controversy. With the 2011 close of the *Oprah Winfrey Show*, the most famous of these talk shows, Chicago's talk show dominance seemed at an end.                                        *Rich Samuels*

**Chemicals.** Although the chemical industry has never represented one of the leading economic sectors in Chicago, the metropolitan region has been home to several significant chemical-making enterprises. A center for the production of soap and other basic chemical goods since its early years, the Chicago region became an important producer of industrial chemicals during the first half of the twentieth century. By the end of that century, several of the world's leading chemical-producing corporations were headquartered in the city.

During the first part of the city's history, the production of chemicals was not a particularly important part of the local economy. The city was home to a few chemical-making companies of some significance during this period. The factory of J. V. Z. Blaney, which employed about 15 Chicagoans during the 1850s to manufacture various chemicals, was reportedly one of the leading producers of chemicals in the western part of the United States. Two decades later, during the 1870s, the Chicago Union Lime Works employed about 200 local residents at its large factory. With the capacity to produce lime (calcium oxide) at the rate of 1,300 barrels a day, this establishment was a major supplier to the makers of lime-using products such as cement and bleach. By the 1880s, another basic chemical, sulfuric acid, was being produced down the Illinois & Michigan Canal, at the zinc works of Matthiessen & Hegeler in La Salle.

During the first half of the twentieth century, the local chemical industry grew rapidly. Several Chicago firms became leading suppliers of water-treatment products. The Dearborn Chemical Company, established in 1888 by chemist William H. Edgar, specialized in making water treatments that would reduce the formation of mineral deposits in boilers and other industrial equipment. The Chicago Chemical Company, founded in 1920 by H. A. Kern and Frederick Salathe (a chemist for the Standard Oil Company of Indiana), made water-treatment products such as sodium aluminate. In 1927 this company merged with a competitor to form the National Aluminate Corporation (later Nalco), which soon grew to encompass subsidiaries in Texas and New York. By the late 1940s, Nalco was producing 181 different chemicals, many of them for water treatment; by the late 1970s, it employed about 1,700 men and women in the Chicago area. At the beginning of the twentieth-first century, Nalco—still headquartered in Naperville—stood as one of the leading firms in the chemical industry.

Among the several large industrial chemical factories established in the area during the early twentieth century, only some were owned by local interests. One of the homegrown operations was the Victor Chemical Works, which was started by the German-born August Kochs in 1902. Kochs, who for several years had been experimenting with the manufacture of baking powder, directed the production of monocalcium phosphate at the Victor plant in Chicago Heights. By the 1910s, Victor was making ammonium phosphate and sulfuric acid. By the 1960s, the company (then controlled by the Stauffer Chemical Company) employed more than 1,000 Chicagoans.

Many of the chemical factories that sprang up in the metropolitan area during the early twentieth century were controlled by large corporations based outside the region. One of the largest of these establishments was the East Chicago plant of the Grasselli Chemical Company, which made acetic acid and other industrial chemicals. The Grasselli works (which was eventually taken over by DuPont) employed about 500 men by 1910 and more than 1,000 by the middle of the Great Depression. Other nonlocal firms with chemical factories in the Chicago region during this period included Union Carbide & Carbon Corporation, which owned plants that made industrial gases; Sherwin-Williams, which had dye-making operations in addition to its paint works; and the Interchemical Corporation, another maker of paints and inks.

Some of the most important parts of Chicago's chemical industry have been located not in firms that specialized in the production of chemicals but rather in divisions or subsidiaries of large companies better known for other products. Leading meatpacking firms such as Armour and Swift, for example, used waste from their slaughterhouses to manufacture soap, glue, and fertilizer. In the twentieth century, the Quaker Oats Company used by-products from its food-processing plants to manufacture furfural and other chemicals. And Standard Oil of Indiana (later known as Amoco and then BP) created a chemicals division to complement its petroleum business.

By the end of the twentieth century, the industrial production of chemicals in the Chicago area had declined and corporate reorganizations shifted ownership away from the city as well. Morton, an important Chicago company since Joy Morton began to expand the salt marketing firm he took over in the 1880s, became a producer of chemicals during the twentieth century. By the 1950s, Morton—which continued to be based in Chicago but had operations around the world—was making photographic chemicals, adhesives, dyes, and a variety of other goods. Morton, one of the world's leading makers of specialty chemicals and chemical preparations, was purchased first by Rohm and Haas and then Dow Chemical. Among the other leading chemical-making corporations previously headquartered in the Chicago area were IMC Global, a leading producer of phosphate fertilizers, which joined with Cargill to create Minnesota-based Mosaic; and CB&I Industries (a descendant of the Chicago Bridge & Iron Company), which produced carbon dioxide and other industrial gases and is now a Dutch corporation. By 2010 only Deerfield-based CF Industries, Northfield's Stepan Co., and Northbrook's Old World Industries were still headquartered in the area.                    *Mark R. Wilson*

**Clothing and Garment Manufacturing.** Clothing, traditionally made at home or by custom tailors, began to be commercially produced in the early nineteenth century. In Chicago, this industry developed rapidly after the Great Fire of 1871 and remained one of the most dynamic sectors until the Great Depression.

Starting from the 1860s, the city's men's clothing merchants employed tailors and had ready-to-wear clothes made at their shop. The industry expanded in the next decade, as merchant-manufacturers like Harry Hart and Bernard Kuppenheimer produced suits as well as work clothes and marketed them in the midwestern and southern states. Those years also saw women's clothing production added to the industry, when manufacturers like Joseph Beifeld began producing ready-made cloaks. Chicago was increasingly involved in nationwide competition, which led to the sweating system in the 1880s. Manufacturers sent out work to be done by contractors and subcontractors, who often opened tiny shops in poor districts, the Near West Side in particular, and hired immigrants for long hours at low wages. In the early 1890s, urban reformers engaged in an anti-sweatshop campaign in Chicago and across the country.

By that time, however, Chicago was already turning to the factory system. Trying to secure an edge against their New York and Philadelphia competitors, manufacturers began producing better grades of garment with fine material and workmanship. They established large factories, where each worker took up only one segment of the whole production process and dexterously performed it. They also endeavored to improve the public image of ready-made garments through national advertising. The pioneer in this arena was Joseph Schaffner of Hart Schaffner & Marx, a Chicago firm that was to grow into a giant, employing 8,000 workers and leading the U.S. clothing industry in the early twentieth century. These efforts, aimed at the emerging urban middle classes, led to industrial expansion. By the end of the century, Chicago became the second largest production center for men's clothing, with its output roughly amounting to 15 percent of the national total. As the center of fashion, New York dominated women's clothing, attracting numerous small shops and producing four-fifths of the national output. With only 4 percent of the women's market, Chicago concentrated on cloaks and suits and attempted to establish only a relatively few small factories.

Although the factory system never entirely replaced sweating, it led to modern labor relations. Ethnic diversity particularly characterized Chicago's workforce, which included a significant number of Swedes, Czechs, Poles, and Lithuanians, in addition to Jews and Italians. The workforce remained further fragmented by gender and skill. Women constituted the majority on the shop floor but had little access to high-paying jobs. Cutters, mostly of German or Irish descent, despised tailors. Yet factories—mainly located close to immigrant settlements in the Northwest, Near West, or Southwest districts in addition to the Loop—helped workers cultivate close social networks and resort to collective action. In men's clothing, a general strike involving over 40,000 workers and lasting for 14 weeks in 1910–11 prompted the formation of a local union of immigrant workers. This organization, chartered by the United Garment Workers, helped launch the Amalgamated Clothing Workers of America (ACWA) in 1914. Under the leadership of Sidney Hillman, the ACWA completely organized Chicago in 1919 and claimed a membership of 41,000 in the following year. The International Ladies' Garment Workers' Union (ILGWU) helped the small and unstable local women's clothing unions of the city to form a joint board in 1914. The joint board conducted unionization campaigns and soon secured a citywide agreement with employers. By 1920 the ILGWU claimed a membership of 6,000, two-thirds of Chicago's women's clothing workforce.

The mid-1920s turned out to be a high point. With a larger share of the national market than before and with labor relations stabilized through collective bargaining, Chicago's clothing industry was faced with new challenges. Men looked for lower-priced garments, spending more money on automobiles, radios, and other modern conveniences; women preferred the dress and waist to the coat and skirt. Manufacturers were less interested in technological innovations than in concessions to be made by the unions. When the ILGWU lost a major strike in 1924, the ACWA retreated without completely giving up high wage rates. Consequently, large men's clothing firms tried to maintain sales by integrating retail outlets, but small ones began to leave for non-union towns in the midwestern countryside.

By the late 1920s, Chicago's clothing industry was already on the decline, a tendency greatly accelerated by the Great Depression. The New Deal revived women's clothing; government contracts for military uniforms boosted men's; and postwar prosperity temporarily benefited both. Soon, however, manufacturers began to leave Chicago, many settling in the South, where labor expenses were lower. Lower production costs fit American preferences for spending less on clothing than on homes, home appliances, and automobiles, and for informal wear that accommodated increasing leisure time and the suburban lifestyle. Lower costs also made it easier to compete with imports, particularly those made in low-wage countries in northeast Asia, which were taking an expanding share of the American market. By the mid-1970s, Chicago had only 7,000 workers engaged in the clothing industry. The few manufacturers still remaining in the city have attempted to integrate the making of men's and women's clothing and to experiment with new technologies like laser cutting or programmed sewing.

By the 1990s, Hartmarx (as Hart Schaffner & Marx was then known) moved its clothes production outside the United States. The following decade, that firm, the last of Chicago's leading clothing manufacturers, filed for bankruptcy and was purchased by Emerisque Brands UK, SKNL North America.                                              *Youngsoo Bae*

**Commodities Markets.** Chicago's ascendant commodity markets were the result of the city's strategic position within the nation's transportation network and its close proximity to some of the most productive farmland in the world. The unprecedented production of corn, wheat, and hogs within Chicago's immediate environs plus the cattle and lumber shipped in from the upper Midwest and Canada filled the city's enormous mechanical grain elevators and vast stockyards. The immense volume of agricultural produce forced the city's commercial community to use their ingenuity (and state law) to temporarily store then ship these goods to domestic and international markets.

The completion of the Illinois & Michigan Canal in the fall of 1847 and its opening in the spring of 1848 inspired the formation of the Chicago Board of Trade, the city's first voluntary association of businessmen. The Board of Trade reorganized in 1850 to conform to a law governing boards of trade passed by the Illinois General Assembly in 1849.

The city's merchants adopted their procedures to handle grain in bulk, not in bags, as traditionally had been the case. The first small shipment of grain in bulk had occurred in 1839. Chicago's grain traders gained national recognition as a reliable and competitively priced source of grain during the 1850s.

The Board of Trade enhanced its role in the grain trade by implementing regulations for grading grain. The state legislature recognized its reg-

Board of Trade, interior, ca. 1900. This photograph captures the activity in the Chicago Board of Trade building designed by William W. Boyington, which opened in 1885 and was demolished in 1929 to make way for the current CBOT building. Courtesy of the Chicago History Museum (ICHi-18146).

ulations by granting it a special charter in 1859. The special charter gave the board the power to impose rules and regulations for the handling of grain and to arbitrate disputes between commodity merchants.

During the Civil War, the Union quartermaster procured supplies with contracts that postponed delivery of commodities until they were needed and payment was secured. These contracts created a market in "seller's" or "buyer's" options for the future delivery of commodities. Delivery before a date was "optional" because of the risks of transporting commodities to Chicago. Speculative purchases and sales of commodities were also inspired by these options. Regulations governing them were published by the Board of Trade in October 1865. These crude seller's or buyer's options evolved into "futures" contracts by the end of the 1870s.

Merchants bought and sold grain for cash, storage, or for future delivery. Elevator operators stored grain until it could be shipped after navigation opened on the Great Lakes or by railroad. Commission merchants received a fee for satisfying the demands of buyers and sellers of grain or provisions. Speculators bought and sold commodities when it was profitable.

The Illinois Constitution of 1870 placed railroads and elevators under the control of a Railroad and Warehouse Commission. The commission had the power to regulate rail and storage rates and to inspect public grain elevators. Ira Munn, an elevator operator in Chicago and a former president of the Board of Trade, challenged the legality of the commission in *Munn v. Illinois*. The case was appealed to the U.S. Supreme Court in 1876. In the spring of 1877, the Supreme Court affirmed the commission's power as being in "the public interest."

The Board of Trade sued to prevent the unauthorized use of its quotations in *Board of Trade v. Christie Grain & Stock Company* (1905). Justice Oliver Wendell Holmes Jr. wrote the brief for the majority affirming the board's ownership of its quotations and speculation as a means that an economy adjusts to changing conditions. By legitimating speculation, "hedging"— or shifting risk to speculators by merchants—was recognized.

Chicago's grain market became the world's preeminent commodity market by the end of the nineteenth century. Although the Board of Trade was the predominant market in membership and in trading volume, Chicago was also the location of smaller but influential markets. The Chicago Open Board of Trade was organized in 1880; it has continued on as the MidAmerica Commodity Exchange and is a subsidiary of the Chicago Board of Trade. A butter and egg exchange that traces its roots to the post–Civil War era was reorganized in 1919 as the Chicago Mercantile Exchange. The remnants of a local produce market are still visible at the intersection of Halsted and Randolph Streets.

During World War I, representatives of Chicago's commodity markets staffed the government agencies created to procure, handle, and distribute the nation's food supplies. The federal government established grades for wheat, corn, and oats while in control of the grain trade. The futures market was closed from September 1917 until May 1920.

After the armistice in November 1918, foreign governments were given access to the nation's grain supplies. Their activities disrupted the grain market and resulted in the federal regulation of commodity markets with the passage of the Grain Futures Act of 1922. The Federal Warehousing Act of 1931 extended federal oversight to grain elevators.

The viability of Chicago's commodity markets was challenged during the 1920s by the depression in farm prices, subsidized grain exports by foreign governments, and by competition for investors' capital from securities markets. The nation's farmers coped with the relentless decline in prices by seeking help from the federal government. The decade ended with the passage of the Agricultural Marketing Act of 1929, which created the Federal Farm Board and made the federal government a competitor in the private grain market.

Chicago's commodity markets entered the 1930s in a weakened condition. The Federal Farm Board began to intervene in the grain market, and the commodity markets started shifting to the South and West. The amount of grain received in the city declined in 1934 to a level unprecedented since the 1870s. Congressional suspicion that grain markets were responsible for the decade's low grain prices inspired a revision and enhancement of commodity market regulation, the Commodity Exchange Act of 1936.

The imposition of price controls and the appropriation of commodities by the federal government after the United States' entry into World War II in December 1941 postponed futures trading until the end of the war. But the federal government still retained a substantial and a continuing interest in the agricultural economy with the commencement of the Cold War.

As federal control over commodity prices and production began to recede in the 1960s, Chicago's exchanges began to diversify their trading out of agricultural commodity futures. The Board of Trade initiated trading in silver futures in 1969 and, along with the Mercantile Exchange, commenced trading in gold futures in 1974. The board opened the Chicago Board Options Exchange in 1973. A futures contract in government-insured mortgages began to trade on the board in 1975. The Mercantile Exchange began its futures market in financial instruments with contracts for foreign exchange in 1972, for Treasury bills in 1976, and for Standard & Poor's stock index futures in 1982. The Board of Trade's most successful contract, federal government bond futures, began trading in 1977. Innovations in Chicago and other commodity markets in futures contracts for financial instruments, metals, and other commodities led Congress to replace the obsolete Commodity Exchange Act of 1936 with the Commodity Futures Trading Act of 1974.

As the twentieth century ended, Chicago's commodity markets recast themselves as futures exchanges for financial instruments and other commodities. They moved into electronic trading, bringing an end to the pits that had been their iconic image. In 2007 the CME purchased the CBOT, recreating Chicago's dominance in futures markets that it enjoyed a century earlier. In 2008 the new CME Group purchased the New York Mercantile Exchange and now operates a common clearing link that includes trading rights and contracts of the CME, the CBOT, the NYMEX, and COMEX (formerly Commodities Exchange Inc. and a division of NYMEX). No longer tied to the industries that fueled their initial growth, the CME Group in 2011 considered moving from Chicago, taking with it the 2,000 jobs it provides and putting at risk some 60,000-plus jobs in other fields that support its activities. Tax-code revisions passed in December 2011 by the Illinois legislature helped convince the CME Group to stay.

*Owen K. Gregory*


**Construction.** One of the most remarkable aspects of the history of the Chicago region has been the rapid development of the built environment. In the early 1800s, the local landscape was not dominated by human settlements. Only a few decades later, Chicago stood as a thoroughly constructed place, in which buildings, roads, and other human creations filled the landscape. This tremendous growth rested upon the efforts of thousands of people—including carpenters, masons, contractors, developers, and regulators—who worked in the field of construction. Few of the city's industries have employed more people, and few have been so volatile or so closely connected to the activities of government. Virtually every piece of Chicago's modern landscape stands as a testament to decades of developments in the city's construction industry.

The extraordinary growth of Chicago's built environment has proceeded at an uneven pace. Among the city's building-boom periods, during which structures were erected at a rapid pace and construction workers were in high demand, have been the mid-1850s, 1864–73, the 1880s, 1901–16, the 1920s, the 1950s, the 1980s, and the late 1990s. The overall rate of expansion was greatest between the 1830s and the 1920s, when Chicago grew from a tiny settlement into one of the world's largest cities. In 1840 there were fewer than 1,000 structures in the Chicago area. This figure passed 10,000 around 1854 and 100,000 during the 1880s. By the end of the 1920s, the city contained roughly 400,000 buildings, most of them one- or two-family dwellings.

Chicago has long been associated with the development and construction of inexpensive residential buildings. In the early 1830s, Chicago carpenter Augustine D. Taylor became one of the pioneers of balloon-frame construction, which cheapened housing costs by avoiding the use of heavy posts and beams. During the latter part of the nineteenth century, Chicago developers such as Samuel E. Gross erected thousands of houses around the city and suburbs and offered prospective buyers innovative finance plans that allowed them to pay in periodic installments. Similar arrangements lay behind the city's bungalow boom of the 1920s, when as many as 100,000 one-story cottages went up in Cook County alone. Many of these bungalows were financed by local building and loan associations, often tied to particular ethnic groups. By this time, most new houses were made of brick and featured central heating, electricity, and indoor plumbing.

In commercial construction, Chicago became a world leader in building technologies and business organization. Starting in the 1880s, Chicago architects, engineers, and builders created structures with deep foundations and steel skeletons that allowed them to reach extraordinary heights. The construction of the world's first skyscrapers relied on the designs of leading Chicago architects such as William L. Jenney, Burnham & Root, and Holabird & Roche. Equally important was the role of a new kind of construction contractor. The building of the first skyscrapers went hand in hand with the rise of large general contracting firms that coordinated the activities of the dozens of building specialists and hundreds of workers involved in the creation of these huge structures. The pioneering general contracting firm was led by George A. Fuller, who came to Chicago in 1883. The rise of general contracting firms such as Fuller's, which responded to the complex problems associated with the building of large structures, was part of the ongoing industrialization of construction.

The late nineteenth-century revolution in construction methods—which affected the small dwellings of Chicago families as well as the city's huge skyscrapers—was partly a matter of technological innovations and the rise of a manufacturing sector that provided cheap, mass-produced building supplies. New construction materials, such as structural steel and reinforced concrete, were used in the early skyscrapers. In Chicago, with its wet and unstable soils, big buildings also depended upon innovations in foundation digging. Starting in the 1880s, Chicago engineers and construction workers used compressed air to create deep caissons that allowed them to anchor the tall buildings in bedrock. Other key building technologies introduced during this period were not as spectacular but were no less important. By the middle of the nineteenth century, a few buildings were starting to be outfitted with modern conveniences such as running water, gas, steam heating, and even indoor toilets. During the 1880s and 1890s, these conveniences were installed in larger numbers of new homes and buildings and became available to more of Chicago's residents. The considerable rise in the quality of the city's housing stock during this period was possible because manufacturers were producing large quantities of cheap building supplies such as plumbing fixtures, shingles, and pre-made doors and windows. Among the leaders in the late nineteenth-century American building supply industry were Chicago businesses like the plumbing and heating equipment companies of Richard T. Crane and Ludwig Wolff. By 1900 many of the technologies and conveniences that late twentieth-century residents would expect from buildings were already in place, including elevators and electric lights.

Throughout Chicago's history, the construction industry has seen considerable conflict between workers and employers. Construction workers have tended to be highly unionized and successful in retaining craft traditions. By the 1890s, the Chicago Building Trades Council included about 30,000 workers in 31 separate trade unions. This association was soon countered by Chicago's contractors, who in 1899 created the Building Contractors' Council. Between 1899 and 1901, the contractors won several disputes with their employees over the control of the workplace. The most severe labor disputes in the history of the Chicago construction industry occurred in the early 1920s. In 1921, when the local construction industry was still in a severe slump and unemployment was high, workers refused to accept wage cuts of about 25 percent, and employers locked them out. Even after official arbitrator Judge Kenesaw Mountain Landis endorsed proposed wage cuts, workers refused to accept them, provoking Chicago business leaders to form a "Citizen's Committee" to uphold the Landis award. In the end, and after two deaths, a new construction boom helped the workers to defeat the wage cut. By 1926 most leading contractors agreed to pay rates higher than the Landis ruling and to hire union workers for most tasks. The unions remained strong in the years that followed.

The construction industry in the Chicago area has long been subject to governmental regulations about materials, safety, and land use. As early as 1833, the city enacted municipal rules for construction, many of which were designed to prevent fires. By the 1850s, wooden structures were banned from the central business district. After the Great Fire of 1871, building codes became a major political issue. The next mayoral election was won by Joseph Medill, who ran on a "fireproof" ticket that fought for the extension of the brick-only district. A building code was enacted by Chicago in 1881, and the city's Board of Health soon set new standards for light, ventilation, and plumbing. By the time the city's building code underwent a major revision in 1910, the rules governing local construction covered the numbers of doors and sizes of vents, as well as fireproofing and fire escapes. In the 1910s, local ordinances began to govern not only construction practices but the kind of buildings that could be erected in certain areas. As early as the 1880s, real estate developers and local communities had begun to attach restrictions to real estate transactions in an attempt to control land use in certain areas. By the 1910s, these restrictions were increasingly upheld by the courts; meanwhile, local governments began to create their own land-use regulations. In 1919 the Illinois General Assembly passed a zoning law modeled on similar legislation created three years earlier in New York. The new law allowed Chicago and other localities to create geographical zones that carried restrictions on building height, area, and land use.

Government agencies were also the industry's leading customers. By 1890 Chicago had spent about $11 million on sewers. During the 1830s and 1840s, Illinois spent millions of dollars to complete the Illinois & Michigan Canal, and over $3 million more was paid to contractors during the late 1860s in order to deepen it. The 1890s saw the creation of another major waterway, the Chicago Sanitary and Ship Canal, a $60 million building project that employed as many as 8,500 men at once. From the city's early years, many of Chicago's construction contractors depended on government orders for a large fraction of their business. Government expenditures on building projects became even more important to the industry during the twentieth century. By the 1970s, between one-quarter and one-half of the value of all new construction in the Chicago region—which totaled roughly $2 billion a year—was paid for by public agencies in any given year. The construction of large numbers of public housing units, which responded in part to the decline in construction during the Great Depression, peaked between the 1940s and 1960s. By the 1970s, the Chicago Housing Authority (CHA) owned buildings that had cost over $560 million and were home to about 140,000 tenants. Even more government spending was devoted to the construction and maintenance of roads for automobiles. Chicago's expressway system, much of which was built during the 1950s, cost roughly $1.1 billion to create. By the end of the twentieth century, federal, state, and local governments were paying several hundred million dollars a year for the construction and maintenance of roads in the Chicago region.

Given that the construction industry has always involved large transactions between government agencies and contractors, it is hardly surprising that it has often been surrounded by rumors and allegations—some of them well-founded—about corruption and other illegitimate activity. During the 1880s, the *Chicago Tribune* ran a series of articles exposing corruption in the awarding of construction contracts by the Cook County commissioners. In 1922, when the Illinois legislature completed an extensive investigation of Chicago's construction industry, it concluded that bribery, graft, and extortion were widespread. Contractors and union officials, as well as government officers, were frequently accused of illegal activity. William Lorimer, a leading Republican politician in Chicago at turn of the twentieth century, was one of several local politicians of his generation who profited from public contracts to construction companies they owned. Ed Kelly, one of the city's leading Democrats, was involved in many questionable transactions when he served as chief engineer of the city's Sanitary District during the 1920s. After an investigation that ended in 1928, Kelly was charged with defrauding the Sanitary District by awarding inflated construction contracts—including some that went to close acquaintances—for sewage plants, roads, and Soldier Field. (These accusations did not prevent Kelly from being voted in as mayor in 1933.) During the latter part of the twentieth century, charges of cronyism and lack of competition in the awarding of government contracts still abounded.

As the twenty-first century began, the construction industry in the Chicago area was still mostly recognizable as the descendant of what it had been during the 1920s. Building techniques and tools were more sophisticated, but changes after 1920 were less radical than those that had transformed the industry between the Civil War and the Jazz Age. The geography of construction changed with the expansion of the suburbs and then, in the 1990s, the residential redevelopment of the city. But the organization of work in the building trades was relatively resistant to change. Compared to many sectors of the economy, the construction industry in the Chicago area featured relatively small firms and a workforce that remained highly unionized and at least somewhat connected to craft traditions. Several of the region's largest companies have national and even international operations, sometimes organized into different firms to operate in union and right-to-work states. Of the four companies with more than half a million dollars of local revenue in 2010, three—Walsh, Power, and Pepper—were headquartered in the Chicago area. The fourth, Turner, was the New York–based subsidiary of a German firm.

The pattern of relatively slow long-term change in the modern construction industry applied even to one of its most important developments during the second half of the twentieth century—the participation of women and minority ethnic groups as both workers and contractors. During the 1960s and 1970s, federal affirmative-action programs gave a small boost to the numbers of African Americans and other minorities in the skilled construction trades. Government contracting rules began requiring that a share of public business go to firms owned by women or members of certain ethnic minorities. As the twentieth century came to a close, however, men of European descent still dominated the local industry, and established contractors had begun to challenge affirmative-action measures.                                              *Mark R. Wilson*

**Consumer Credit.** From 1910 to 1940, household finance was transformed by a revolution in consumer credit. A credit system that had been disorganized, disreputable, and poorly capitalized was replaced by a new corporate system that was regulated by the state, widely promoted, and in such demand that living on credit became part of the American way of life. Chicagoans played an important role in this transformation.

Credit for consumption is as old as the city itself. Wages for late nineteenth-century workers were so low that the slightest upsets—from illness, injury, layoffs, or firings—left households in need of borrowed money. Before the credit revolution, borrowers obtained credit from a market that was highly stratified on the basis of social class.

Pawnbrokers served the needs of the poorest. In 1897, 68 pawnbrokers operated shops on State, Clark, and Halsted Streets. Small loan lenders lent money to wage-earners on security of chattel mortgages or wage assignments. The first professional small loan lenders in the country appeared in Chicago in 1870. By 1916 the city led all others in loan offices, with 139 offices lending to one out of five families. Operating illegally under the state's restrictive usury laws, most lenders were honest, but the few who were not gave the entire industry a reputation for remorseless extortion. A third source of credit was the city's retailers. Street peddlers and "borax" stores sold cheap goods on installments to low- and moderate-income customers, while thousands of neighborhood shopkeepers sold "on tic." At Marshall Field's, well-to-do customers were allowed charge accounts.

By 1906 Chicago's leading installment seller was the Spiegel House Furnishings Company. Spiegel boasted, "We Trust the People—Everywhere," and their mail-order department spread the gospel of small, easy payments from coast to coast. Spiegel's example prodded Sears and other

Loan store, northwest corner of Dearborn and Washington, 1962. City Hall is visible in the background. Photo: Bob Tobias. Courtesy of the Chicago History Museum (ICHi-27835).

retailers to follow suit. The result was a credit revolution marked by the "installment plan."

Another leader in the credit revolution was the Household Finance Corporation. Founder Frank Mackey opened a loan office on Madison Street in 1885, and in 1894 he moved his headquarters from St. Paul, Minnesota, to Chicago. In 1905 Household became the first cash lender to offer monthly installment terms. Household also pioneered in the fight for a Uniform Small Loan Law, a reform of the usury laws that ended the era of the "loan shark" and began the era of the personal finance company. Growth in the 1920s made Household the largest personal finance company in the nation. Other consumer finance companies, including Universal CIT Credit Corporation and General Finance Corporation, joined Household in making Chicago their home.

After 1930 consumer credit became more available from credit unions, commercial banks, and issuers of credit cards. Buying "on tic" and pawnbroking declined. But in the 1970s, the share of the population operating outside the mainstream financial system grew markedly. In the 1980s and 1990s, pawnbrokers returned in numbers, and Chicago led the way in another credit innovation: high-interest "payday" loans from check-cashing outlets, of which there were more than 560 in 1985.

Throughout the city's history, consumer credit has enabled Chicagoans both to survive financial emergencies and to improve their standard of living.                                                            *Lendol Calder*

**Cosmetics and Hair Care Products.** Chicago residents participated in the rise of the cosmetics industry during the twentieth century not only as consumers but also as producers and distributors. As they spent more time and money on personal grooming and so-called beauty products, the area's women—and men, to a lesser extent—participated in a development that was going on throughout much of the United States and the industrialized world. Chicago played a more distinctive role in the development of the cosmetics and hair care industries through the leadership of several of the area's business firms in this economic sector. At the same time, Chicago entrepreneurs built one of the most important of the industry's subsectors: hair care products and cosmetics designed for consumers of African descent.

Two leading cosmetics and hair care products makers, Helene Curtis and Alberto-Culver, grew into big businesses while they were headquartered in Chicago. In 1927 Gerald Gidwitz and Louis Stein started a cosmetics manufacturing company in Chicago. During the years following World War II, Stein named the company Helene Curtis, combining the names of his wife and son, and the company expanded with the success of products such as Suave, one of the first modern shampoos. By the 1950s, Helene Curtis was also selling hair spray and deodorant, and it had branches around the world. Meanwhile, a competitor arrived from California. In

1955 Leonard and Bernice Lavin moved the Alberto-Culver Company from Los Angeles (where it had started as a supplier of hair care products to the film industry) to Chicago; by 1960 the company was moving into a new headquarters and manufacturing facility in nearby Melrose Park. Like Helene Curtis, Alberto-Culver prospered by selling branded lines of products such as shampoo and deodorant—items that, although they were virtually unknown before the twentieth century, many consumers now regarded as indispensable.

The development, manufacture, and marketing of cosmetics and hair care products for African Americans was led by Chicago firms for much of the twentieth century. During the 1910s and 1920s, the Kashmir Chemical Company of Claude A. Barnett, a graduate of the Tuskegee Institute, manufactured specialty hair care products. In 1935 S. B. Fuller established the Fuller Products Company, a cosmetics company, on the city's South Side. Fuller, the first African American member of the National Association of Manufacturers, led the company through an expansion that peaked in the 1950s. By that time, an army of 5,000 salesmen sold nearly $20 million a year worth of various Fuller Products cosmetics—to European Americans as well as African Americans. One of Fuller's employees, George Johnson, left the company in 1954 to start his own business. Along with Chicago barber Orville Nelson, Johnson created the company that would soon become the most important of all manufacturers of African American hair care products: the Johnson Products Company. The company's Ultra Wave hair straightener proved popular, as did its Ultra Sheen and Afro Sheen lines, and by the end of the 1960s annual sales were over $10 million. During the 1970s, as sales expanded even further, Johnson Products ranked as the largest African American–owned manufacturing company in the nation. Johnson Products was not the only Chicago company engaged in the manufacture of beauty products for African American consumers. The Johnson Publishing Company, creator of *Ebony* magazine, entered the cosmetics business in the 1970s. And Johnson Products' leadership in the hair care sector was challenged by Chicago's own Soft Sheen Products Inc., a company established in the 1960s by Edward Gardner that found success with brands such as Care-Free Curl.

Chicago's status as a center of the hair care and cosmetics industry declined during the last years of the twentieth century. Johnson Products encountered declining profits and market share by the mid-1970s, when large cosmetics companies such as Revlon and Avon began to target African American consumers. In 1993 the company left local hands when it was sold to the Ivax Corporation, a Miami-based company. By 2000 it had become part of the French company L'Oréal. Soft Sheen, which had about 400 employees in the Chicago area and $100 million in annual sales by the mid-1990s, was also sold to L'Oréal in 1998. Helene Curtis, which had grown into a billion-dollar company, experienced declining growth after the 1980s and was bought in 1996 by Unilever, the huge British-Dutch corporation. Of the several Chicago companies that had been so prominent in the industry since the 1950s, only Alberto-Culver—with about $2 billion in annual sales and 16,000 employees worldwide—was still based in Chicago at the end of the century. In 2011 Unilever acquired it as well.

*Mark R. Wilson*

**Department Stores.** In the last two decades of the nineteenth century, Chicago established itself as a leader in the development of the department store, a central feature and symbol of the nation's emerging consumer culture. The most important figure in the rise of this local industry was Marshall Field, and his establishment has received credit for being one of the three that most influenced the nationwide development of the department store (the other two were in New York and Philadelphia). In the mid-1850s, the young Field moved to Chicago and worked his way through various retail establishments. Field's early partnerships with Potter Palmer and Levi Leiter were significant precursors to the establishment of Marshall Field & Company in 1881. Along with Marshall Field's, other establishments in the late nineteenth and early twentieth century also thrived in the Loop shopping district, including Carson Pirie Scott & Company, Mandel Brothers, the Fair, and Schlesinger & Mayer.

The development of the department store posed a serious threat to smaller retailers. Many small merchants tried to rally the public against the new behemoths, but they failed to gain much support. Rather than rally to the side of traditional merchants, Chicago shoppers embraced the new form of retail. The opening of the new Marshall Field's State Street store in 1902, only a few years after anti–department store protests, signaled that this newer type of institution had won the admiration of consumers. The opening was a sensational event, and the store decided not to start selling items on its first day of business so that more of the eager public would be able to pass through.

The new Marshall Field's store was more than a place for people to spend their money; the 12-story building became a public landmark and spectacle. The store's magnificent architecture alone was enough to inspire visitors' awe. The highlight of the Marshall Field store was the Tiffany Dome (1907), a glass mosaic covering 6,000 square feet, six floors high. Other stores, most notably Schlesinger & Mayer, also offered opulent buildings to house their goods. The Schlesinger & Mayer store, which Carson Pirie Scott later bought, was the last large commercial building designed by Louis Sullivan, and many of his admirers regard it as the culminating work in his career.

Service was yet another part of the department store allure. More than any other establishment, Marshall Field's gained a reputation for pampering its customers. Field's sent all of its elevator operators to charm school, was the first to offer a personal shopping service, and even maintained an information desk with personnel who spoke several languages and answered any question about the store or about the city in general.

In addition to affecting consumer habits, department stores had a significant impact on the city's labor force. In 1904 Marshall Field's alone employed between 8,000 and 10,000 people, but department stores' effect on labor was more than quantitative. Traditional retail stores needed employees who could be responsible for a variety of tasks, but department stores hired many more workers, which enabled them to specialize. As a result, many of the jobs in department store work required fewer skills, and the greater size of the stores meant that top executives could earn much greater salaries. Probably the most significant impact that the department store had on labor was that it brought women into the retail workforce. Traditional retail stores had believed that their work was too demanding for women, but department store managers reasoned that many of the specialized positions in their stores, especially in sales and clerical work, did not require manly characteristics and could be filled by a lower-paid female workforce.

With few other options available to them, many women coveted work in department stores, even though the industry paid them extremely low wages. As women came to dominate many of the sales and clerical positions, the department stores received increasing criticism for the way they treated these employees. In 1913 executives from Marshall Field and Carson Pirie Scott found themselves involved in state legislative hearings on a proposed minimum wage. The stores' labor practices gained even more notoriety as the executives testified that they could double the pay of their female employees and still make a profit, yet they still refused to pay women a living wage.

In the 1920s, Chicago's department stores expanded their reach and opened small branches elsewhere in the city and in the outlying metropolitan area, joining other local department stores like Wieboldt's and Goldblatt's. However, it was not until after World War II that suburban shopping centers, with full-size department stores, developed fully. In the 1950s, Field's was part of the group that developed one of the metro region's first suburban shopping centers, Old Orchard, in Skokie.

Along with continuing decentralization, the influx of stores based in other parts of the country has been one of the most noticeable recent developments in Chicago's department store industry. Many of the stores that have opened in Chicago have come from New York, such as Bloomingdale's and Saks Fifth Avenue, as well as from other parts of the country, such as Neiman-Marcus of Dallas, Nordstrom of Seattle, and, at the discount end, Walmart of Bentonville, Arkansas, and Target of Minneapolis. Another development has been the transfer of local ownership of even the most iconic of Chicago of stores. Since 2005, Marshall Field's has been rebranded with the name of its newest owner, Macy's. After over a century of development, department stores seem to have lost none of their popularity, but Chicago is no longer a leader in the industry as it was in the late nineteenth and early twentieth century.          *Jeffrey A. Brune*

**Drug Retailing.** Though one might have been able to find a patron of John Kinzie's retail establishment or of Mark Beaubien's hotel in frontier Chicago who would have touted the "medicinal benefits" of the cheap liquor both men dispensed over the counter, the business of drug retailing in early Chicago consisted primarily of odd elixirs, suspect folk remedies, and medicine-show potions.

The newspapers of the 1830s were filled with advertisements for "cures" such as Dr. William B. Egan's Sarsaparilla Panacea, "the most perfect restorative ever yet discovered for debilitated constitutions and diseases of the skin and bones." Small drugstores such as the one operated by Dr. Edmund S. Kimberly began to dot the frontier town and were in fierce competition with, of all places, bookstores, many of which held exclusive franchises to sell certain remedies.

The Civil War created a great new demand for drugs and furthered the growth of the drug retailing industry. Drugstores (often called apothecaries) began to operate in most city neighborhoods.

In the years following the Great Fire of 1871, the drug retailing business boomed because of two forces, industry and science. The Industrial Revolution, with its development of manufacturing methods that could be used to mass-produce drugs, coincided with such scientific developments as phytochemistry and synthetic chemistry, resulting in new derivatives of old drugs and new chemical entities.

Though European firms dominated the drug manufacturing industry and would until the 1920s, a late 1880s catalog for the Chicago-based G. D. Searle listed 400 fluid extracts, 150 elixirs, 100 syrups, 75 powdered extracts, and 25 tinctures and other drug forms.

Many of those were on display at the opening of the first Walgreen's drugstore at 4134 South Cottage Grove Avenue in 1901, an operation similar to most turn-of-the-century drugstores. Haphazardly arranged in the front windows were clusters of products like the "only genuine old-fashioned" Castile soap, Peerless tooth powder, vegetable tonics, perfumes, and tins and small jars of pills and tablets for ailments ranging from dyspepsia to bronchitis. Along the aisles were cabinets and shelving with medicinal and non-medicinal products (the latter called "sundries"). At the store's far end, from floor to ceiling, was a wooden grillwork partition behind which medicines were compounded out of the sight of customers. Back there were the tools of the trade: a mortar and pestle, a set of scales, a jar of leeches, a bottle capper, and rows of bottled drugs bearing Latin labels, plus small unfilled bottles and tiers of little drawers that contained various ingredients used in filling prescriptions. It was a dark and uninviting place, though one that played a central role in every neighborhood, as the corner druggist often referred to as "Doc" became the primary source of medical care, diagnosing illnesses and concocting remedies.

That role would diminish during the twentieth century, due largely to government regulations, primarily through the Pure Food and Drug Act, passed in 1906. In the early twentieth century there was much agitation and press clamor against nostrums that included tonics with alcohol, syrups that contained cocaine and morphine, ointments to enlarge or reduce bosoms, and lavishly advertised "cures" for cancer, alcoholism, impotence, rupture, and other ailments.

The pharmacist, with increasingly less time devoted to compounding drugs, supplemented his income by adding various elements to the drugstore. One of the most important and romanticized was the soda fountain, where the pharmacist dispensed ice-cream sodas and sundaes. They also began offering on their shelves a variety of other products not conveniently handled at any other stores: school supplies, personal grooming aids, baby food.

In the 1920s, 80 percent of the prescriptions dispensed in Chicago pharmacies required a knowledge of compounding. But by the 1940s, only 26 percent did. Further reducing the time that pharmacists spent making drugs was the 1951 passage of the Durham-Humphrey Amendment to the Federal Food, Drug and Cosmetic Act, which precluded dispensing a wide class of medications without a physician's prescription.

From that point, drugstores began to assume the look of small supermarkets, with pharmacies tucked into the back. Chains such as Osco and Walgreens grew as the number of independent drugstores decreased. Large supermarkets and retailers began including pharmacies within their stores. Deerfield-based Walgreens expanded nationally; by 2009 it had stores in all 50 states, the District of Columbia, and Puerto Rico, as well as online operations. Since most drugs are supplied by manufacturing firms, pharmacists today double-check physicians' orders and watch for contraindications to prescriptions. They must also keep track of new developments in drugs and drug manufacturing, have knowledge of shelf life and other storage issues, and be able to judge the reliability and reputations of the manufacturers.

Though buying drugs through the Internet might eventually prove a serious threat to the conventional (and increasingly computerized) pharmacy business in Chicago, it is still possible to find, tucked into the city's corners, practitioners of herbal or alternative medicine, whose stores charmingly resemble drugstores of the past.          *Rick Kogan*

**Electronics.** Chicago companies and their employees have long stood as leading players in the American electronics industry. For much of the twentieth century, the major consumer electronics products—that is, devices that manipulate the motion of electrons through such media as vacuum tubes and semiconductors—were radios and televisions, and the Chicago region was a major manufacturing center for these goods. During the latter part of the century, as the production of these devices moved overseas, Chicago's general preeminence in the American electronics industry faded, despite the importance of several area companies in the growing digital computer and telecommunications sectors.

By the time that tens of thousands of Chicago residents and visitors had examined the exhibits of machines and devices at the Electricity Building on the grounds of the World's Columbian Exposition in 1893, electric lighting and telephone technologies were already well established, and it was obvious that electrical devices would become an increasingly important part of modern life. But it was not until the 1920s that radios— the first major consumer electronics product—began to be produced (as well as purchased) in large numbers by Chicago-area residents. One of the leaders in the field of early radio technology was Western Electric, the huge manufacturing and research arm of AT&T, based in suburban Cicero. During the 1910s, Western Electric researchers pioneered the development of the high-vacuum electronic tube, the condenser microphone, and air-to-ground radio communication. Such technologies were quickly put to use in the new radio equipment industry.

During the 1920s and 1930s, the production of radios was a major economic activity in the Chicago area, which was one of the centers of this new industry. By the end of the 1920s, about a third of the radios being made in the United States were manufactured by Chicago-area companies. At the end of the 1930s, about 12,000 local residents worked in radio and phonograph factories, which had an annual output valued at about $75 million.

During World War II, many of Chicago's radio manufacturers turned to the production of electronics equipment for the military. The Zenith Radio Corporation, one of the city's leading radio makers since the 1920s, joined Western Electric and other firms in efforts to produce new radar equipment. Several of these manufacturers affiliated themselves into a trade organization called Radar-Radio Industries of Chicago Inc., an association of area companies that together employed over 40,000 people, who made over half of the electronics equipment manufactured in the United States during the war. Another local electronics manufacturer turned military contractor was the Galvin Manufacturing Corporation (which would become Motorola after the war), which had been specializing in the production of radios for automobiles. During the war, Galvin supplied the military with two-way portable radios known as walkie-talkies.

From the end of World War II through the beginning of the 1970s, Chicago-area companies and their workers continued to be leaders in the consumer electronics industry, which now entered the age of television. By 1949 local factories owned by Zenith and other companies employed about 40,000 people making televisions; roughly 40 percent of domestic output came from the Chicago area. By the early 1960s, the production of all kinds of electronics and communications equipment accounted for a total of about 140,000 area jobs—which made electronics the city's leading manufacturing sector. At that time, the Chicago area made nearly half of the consumer electronics goods produced in the United States, and area companies such as Zenith, Admiral, and Motorola were widely recognized as industry leaders.

As the electronics industry matured and moved into the computer age, Chicago's status as a leading manufacturing center declined. Competition from overseas cut into the profits of local makers of radios and televisions, forcing many of them to shrink or fold. One of the most dramatic chapters in this story was the fall of Zenith, the leading television manufacturer, which still employed over 12,000 area residents as late as the early 1970s. Zenith lobbied vigorously for protection from international competition but received little, forcing the company to cut jobs and move production out of the area. By the end of the twentieth century, a crippled Zenith had been purchased by a South Korean company, and its survival was uncertain. The fate of this one company was representative of the Chicago area's declining importance as a maker of consumer electronics products. By the early 1990s, there were still about 69,000 area residents with jobs making a wide range of electronic and other electric equipment, but area companies now only accounted for under 5 percent of national output—a far cry from the roughly 45 percent they had made a generation earlier.

In the late twentieth century, as the electronics industry began to use semiconductors to produce smaller and more sophisticated computing and communications equipment, a few Chicago-area companies and their workers played a part. Zenith, as it attempted to move into more profitable fields, became a major computer products maker during the 1980s. But the most important Chicago-area company in the new electronics industry was Motorola, which after changing its name from Galvin in 1947 had made a successful reconversion back from military to civilian production. As its headquarters moved from Chicago to suburban Franklin Park and then Schaumburg, Motorola was growing into a large corporation that stood as one of the leaders of the U.S. electronics industry. As the manufacture of car radios and televisions became less profitable, the company managed to find success with new products. In the early 1990s, Motorola stood as the world's third-leading producer of the semiconductors and microprocessors that were at the heart of the computing industry; it also sold nearly half of the world's cellular phones and dominated the market for electronic pagers. By the late 1990s, Motorola employed roughly 25,000 Chicago-area residents, making it one of the region's leading sources of jobs. In 2011 Motorola split into two separate companies— Motorola Solutions and Motorola Mobility. Soon thereafter, the latter was purchased by the Internet giant Google Inc.

At the beginning of the twenty-first century, Motorola and a few smaller firms in the area continued to represent Chicago in what had become a highly competitive and dynamic global industry.

*Emily Clark and Mark R. Wilson*

**Film.** From the beginning, the film industry in Chicago had many supporters. The inaugural June 1907 issue of the Chicago-based trade magazine *Show World* proclaimed that "Chicago leads the world in the rental of moving picture films and in the general patronage of the motion view." Both of these claims were probably true of Chicago at the time. In the early film era, Chicago very likely had more film theaters per capita than any other city in the United States, with five-cent theaters, or nickelodeons, opening early and often, as the Chicago Election Day expression goes. The number of new nickelodeons grew each year from 1905 through World War I, and the opening of new film venues continued to play a significant, even anchoring role in the commercial development in Chicago neighborhoods until the onset of the Great Depression.

The *Show World* commentator was also correct about the city's role in film distribution. Chicago was the home of the film exchange, or film rental house. The exchanges created a new niche in the industry, giving exhibitors access (through rentals) to a larger number of films than they could afford to purchase and allowing theaters to change their films frequently. By 1907 there were over 15 film exchanges in operation in Chicago, and they controlled 80 percent of the film distribution market for the whole United States.

Several film production companies were actively making moving pictures in Chicago and the suburbs during this time. William Selig, a former magician and theatrical troupe manager, was creating and exhibiting films in Chicago by 1897. In 1907 the Selig Polyscope Company built a production facility at Irving Park Road and Western Avenue that covered three acres and employed over 200 people. The other prominent production company with substantial Chicago facilities was Essanay Studios, founded by George Spoor and Gilbert Anderson. Spoor, a moving-picture exhibitor, and Anderson, a film actor, founded the company in 1907 and built a studio in Uptown on Argyle Street in 1908. Both Charlie Chaplin and Gloria Swanson worked at the Essanay Studios in Chicago for a time.

After the organization of major film interests into the Motion Picture Patents Company in 1908, Chicago became the center of the independent movement, the effort to make, import, and distribute films while avoiding the use of patents held by the trust—or avoiding litigation from those whose patents they had violated. Carl Laemmle's Independent Motion Picture Company and several independent antitrust importers and exchanges were located in the city. The films produced in Chicago and/or distributed by Chicago companies were increasingly important nationally and internationally as U.S. firms tried to compete with imported films for domination of film screens.

Several "race film" companies (companies run largely by African Americans who made films for black audiences) were formed during the silent-film era in Chicago as well. The Foster Photoplay Company, owned by William Foster, began producing films in 1912. The Ebony Pictures Corporation began production somewhat later and made films throughout World War I and for some years after. Many race-film production companies were founded and sought investors in Chicago but never actually made any films. All of the race-film firms were profoundly undercapitalized and suffered from the lack of strong distribution networks. However, it is clear that Chicago was a significant market for these films, on several occasions bringing in the highest grosses in the nation for them.

By the late teens, those production firms that had not fled to California to avoid patent litigation left seeking better weather and more consistent sunlight. Chicago remained, however, an important distribution market in spite of these departures and even after the rise of the talkies in the late 1920s. The 800 to 1500 blocks of South Wabash had high-profile distribution offices for MGM, Columbia, Warner Brothers, Republic, Universal, RKO, and Paramount. Other film-related businesses gravitated to this "Film Row" to be where the market was; companies that made theater seating, film posters, and concessions had offices there. According to legend, Hollywood studios sent their toughest negotiators to the Chicago market, where audiences often produced large grosses for the studios.

Chicago was the original home of the largest theater chain in the studio era (1919–52), the Balaban and Katz chain, started by two West Side exhibitors. Obtaining expansion capital in 1915 from Chicagoans in the retailing and taxi businesses, Balaban and Katz built increasingly large and elaborate "movie palaces" in which they showed movies and offered popular stage shows. The Chicago Theatre, the Oriental, and the Uptown were all Balaban and Katz movie theaters. Balaban and Katz affiliated with the Paramount studio to form one of the most powerful companies of the studio era, which ended after prolonged antitrust litigation forced movie studios to divest their theaters.

In the 1930s Chicago was the home of a regional branch of the Workers' Film and Photo League, which in Chicago was called the Film and Photo League. Nominally associated with the Workers' International Relief and the Communist Party, the Chicago Film and Photo League made several short films and newsreels that dealt with labor issues in Chicago and other locales as well as exposing slum conditions in Chicago. Extant films include *Halsted Street* (1934) by Conrad Friberg (often credited as C. O. Nelson) and Maurice Bailen's *The Great Depression* (1934), *Chicago May Day* (1936), and *Peace Parade and Workers' Picnic* (1936), each of which documents, at least in part, leftist demonstrations in the city as well as aspects of the cultural life of laborers.

In the 1980s, Chicago again became a center of moving-picture production. Illinois consistently ranked third or fourth among states in dollars spent in film production, much of it in Chicago. Several of the critical and popular successes of the 1980s were filmed in Chicago (*Ferris Bueller's Day Off*; *The Color of Money*; *The Untouchables*; *Planes, Trains and Automobiles*; *When Harry Met Sally*), and several feature-film directors and actors have returned to shoot films (either wholly or in part) in the Chicago area, including Dan Aykroyd and the Belushi family (*The Blues Brothers, About*

*Last Night, Blues Brothers 2000*), John Hughes (*Sixteen Candles, The Breakfast Club*), and Andrew Davis (*The Fugitive, Chain Reaction*). This film and television production activity fostered local boosterism and the hope that film production in the city would continue to increase.

In 2000 filmmaking began leaving Illinois for Canada and other states that provided financial incentives for filming there. In response, the state legislature passed the Illinois Film Tax Credit to attract filmmakers back to Illinois and Chicago. By 2007 film production brought $155 million in direct revenue to the state, up from $23 million in 2003. Indirect economic benefits were much higher. Anticipating even further growth, in 2011 Toronto-based Cinespace opened its Chicago Film Studios on the West Side in space formerly occupied by Ryerson Steel, joining Chicago's Studio City as a site for film and television production.     *J. A. Lindstrom*

**Food Processing, Local Market.** From its first days as a small settlement, Chicago has manufactured foodstuffs for its own and regional markets. The size and types of manufactories varied through time. Many small food producers have served Chicago's various ethnic communities with specialized products. Among the most important of these were alcoholic beverages, meat, baked goods, and candy.

Whiskey may have been the first manufactured "food" product. By 1812 members of the Kinzie clan had set up a still to sell their product from a shack. The first brewery was established in 1833, and German immigrants who arrived in midcentury brought forth many others. Names such as Berghoff, Gottfried, Schoenhofen, and Wacker were Chicago institutions. Like many other breweries throughout the country, all served the local populace. None became national brands like breweries in St. Louis and Milwaukee.

Given Americans' carnivorous propensities, meat processing was an important local industry. Archibald Clybourne's slaughterhouse, built in 1827 at the city limits, fed the immediate market. Clybourne sold his processed meat door-to-door in the 1830s, as did Sylvester Marsh. Food production was so localized that a contemporary claimed, "From 1832 to 1838 the incoming settlers consumed nearly all the products of those who had come before them."

George Dole's abattoir, begun around 1832, eventually not only served locals but began packing meat for the Lake Michigan shipping trade. The great national meatpacking industry thus was born. Nevertheless, sales to local customers by food manufacturers and processors who sold to wider markets would remain Chicago's pattern. Vienna Beef Company and many other packing companies located in the Randolph Street market area maintained retail outlet stores.

Candy companies followed a similar pattern. An 1857 survey shows 46 confectioners worked in the city, 7 of whom were large-scale manufacturers with wholesale markets. By the end of the century, Chicago would become the largest producer of candy in the United States, a position it retained into the twenty-first century. A number of firms became national, including the Wrigley Company (1891), Brach's (1904), and Curtiss Candy Company, maker of the Baby Ruth bar (1921). The Blommer Chocolate Company, a large regional wholesale chocolate manufacturer, maintains an outlet store to service local clientele. A number of other candy makers, such as Margie's Candies in the Logan Square neighborhood, remained small concerns dedicated to local clientele.

The manufacture and distribution of dairy products were always local. In 1911 there were 1,200 to 1,500 small dealers (most doing home deliveries with milk wagons) in the city, receiving the milk of perhaps 5,500 regional producers. James Kraft, whose cheese-processing plant was located on Water Street, was one of them. As larger dealers perfected on-site bottling and an efficient distribution system, and with new pasteurization laws, the number of small dealers dropped. In 1935 there were 236 in the city, over half of whom received their milk from an average of just 5.4 farms. Two dealers, Borden and Bowman, accounted for over 58 percent of total purchases. The rise of centralized dairy businesses and national distribution systems beginning in the 1950s left only large producers selling to food stores. Hawthorn Mellody and Dean Foods were preeminent, leaving only Oberweis Dairy of Aurora, revived in the last two decades of the twentieth century, as an artifact of the old home-delivery business.

As the number of Chicago's food producers grew with the rising population, their character changed according to ethnicity. German immigrants produced beer and pickles. By the mid-nineteenth century, Chicago had 4 "pickle warehouses," 3 pickle makers (all with German names), and 14 vinegar manufacturers who catered to this new clientele. B. Hyde manufactured "Vermicelli and Maccaroni," showing the city's increasingly diverse citizenry.

Bakeries are one of the best indicators of ethnic change. By 1861 there were 59 where a generation before none had existed. Many of the bakers had German surnames, an indication of the large influx of central Europeans. By the early twentieth century, bakers selling to the Chicago market included S. Rosen and Kaufmann's (Jewish), Mary Ann (Greek), and Baltic Bakery (Lithuanian) among many other small companies. Rosen's and Mary Ann transcended their neighborhood origins to achieve regional distribution. Italian bakeries followed a similar pattern. As interest in Italian food became widespread throughout Chicago in the 1960s, Italian bread followed suit. Gonnella Baking Company, founded as a neighborhood bakery in 1886, became Chicago's largest producer of Italian bread and rolls. Others, such as Fontana Brothers Bakery, remained in their ethnic enclaves. The cracker, sold from barrels in grocery stores, was a staple American snack food. Cracker makers sold products to regional markets, but they also supplied the city's growing numbers of neighborhood grocery stores. By the end of the century, snack foods would be prepackaged, with national brands such as Uneeda Biscuits beginning to dominate store shelves. Local snack food companies such as Jays Foods (founded in 1927 as Mrs. Japp's) followed suit. Jays Potato Chips remains a major Chicago regional brand.

The arrival of other ethnic groups brought new food products to the local market. Eastern European immigrants brought their food preferences with them—as did African Americans, Italians, and, later, Mexicans. Emblematic of eastern Europe were Vienna Beef and David Berg, both producing Chicago's singular all-beef hot dog; the Slotkowski Sausage Company, makers of Chicago's famous "Polish" sausages; Leon's Sausage Company (Ukrainian); Daisy Brand Meat Products (Bohemian); and many other small producers. Vienna Beef achieved national distribution. African Americans were served by Parker House Sausage Company's southern-style hot and mild links. Italian makers included Lucca Packing Company, Fabbri Sausage Manufacturing Company, and a host of neighborhood butcher shops.

Ethnicity remains a key to local food production. The Chinese population required more "authentic" Chinese products. The Hong Kong Noodle Company, established in 1914 in the "new" Chinatown on Wentworth Avenue, was one such supplier. By the 1970s, with immigration from mainland China, new companies such as the Wah King Noodle Company and bakeries producing almond cookies, fortune cookies, moon cakes, and other specialties appeared, servicing both retail and restaurant markets. In similar fashion, the newer Korean (Lawrence Avenue), Arabic (North Kedzie Avenue), Indian (Devon Avenue), and Southeast Asian (Argyle Street) communities have brought forth bakeries and spice and sauce packers geared to local consumption.

As members of these groups moved out of their original neighborhoods, these goods followed them. Although the process is old, there is no better example than Chicago's Latino communities. The Mexican population grew rapidly after 1960. Pilsen soon sprouted tortilla factories such as Del Rey, Atotonilco, and Sabinas. As native Mexicans and Mexican Americans spread across the Chicago and northern Illinois region, and as tastes for Mexican fare grew among many population segments, tortillas were to be found in many food stores, including chain supermarkets. Similarly, food processors and canners such as La Preferida Inc., once Hispanic-targeted, sold their beans, chiles, sauces, and other "Mexican" products to the general public while maintaining their ethnic customer base.

Local markets also mean food distribution systems. The oldest systems were open-air markets and door-to-door street peddling. A market at the corners of Lake and State Streets was superseded by a municipal market hall built in the middle of State Street in 1848. By 1850 population pressure led to three more market halls near the Loop area. However, continued dispersal of the citizenry spelled the end of central market halls. Except for the great Maxwell Street open-air market that flourished from the 1890s to the 1980s, they were replaced by neighborhood grocery stores. Such establishments could better address local ethnic communities and served as the main distribution system for locally manufactured foodstuffs. Neighborhood grocers and meat markets were, in their turn, mostly eliminated by the spread of large supermarkets beginning in the years after World War II. By 1990 multipurpose markets dominated the food retail business in Chicago. Dependent as they are on national and proprietary brands, these stores have provided venues for only a few locally produced, mainly fresh bread products and tortillas. Therefore, local manufacturers such as sausage makers have used smaller stores and factory outlet stores as their main distribution networks.

Ideas about food often move in cycles. New open-air retail markets replicated the city's earliest public markets. Rising interest in fresh foods led to the appearance of farmers' markets in the city in the late 1980s. During the growing season, local produce was trucked in and sold by farmers in various locations throughout the city. Daley Plaza in downtown Chicago became the scene of a weekly farmers' market, replicated on a smaller scale in other neighborhoods. In 1999 the popular Green City Market, selling only locally produced organic produce, was established in downtown Chicago. *Bruce Kraig*

**Food Processing, Regional and National Market.** As the leading city in one of the world's most productive agricultural regions, Chicago has long been a center for the conversion of raw farm products into edible goods. Best known for its dominance in meatpacking, Chicago has also been home to leading firms in other areas of the food-processing industry—including cereals, baked goods, and candy—since the 1880s. At the end of the twentieth century, during which most parts of the industry became concentrated under fewer firms, food processors stood among Chicago's largest companies.

In early Chicago, the most important food-processing activity was grain milling. Before 1800, Catherine and Jean Baptiste Point DuSable had a pair of millstones and had constructed a bake house just north of the Chicago River. By the 1830s, Chicago contained steam-powered flour mills and enjoyed a brief period of importance as a local milling center for spring wheat. But the great bulk of wheat handled by the city's booming grain trade was never milled locally: it was shipped east, to be processed in major U.S. cities such as Buffalo or in Europe. After the Civil War, as wheat farming moved north and west, the national center of wheat flour manufacture shifted to Minneapolis. Meanwhile, other kinds of milling operations settled within close reach of Chicago. In 1910 the town of Argo (Summit), southwest of Chicago, became the site of a new plant opened by the Corn Products Refining Company. By the 1930s, this plant, manufacturing products with the Argo brand name, had become the largest corn refinery in the world.

The milling of oats served as the foundation for another of Chicago's leading companies. By the 1880s and 1890s, oatmeal producers in Chicago and around the Midwest had begun to form industrial combinations. Between 1901 and 1911, many of the industry's leading producers, then operating under the umbrella of groups such as the American Cereal Company and the Great Western Cereal Company, were absorbed by the Quaker Oats Company. This Chicago-based giant grew steadily, making big business out of oatmeal. At the close of the twentieth century, when it sold over $5 billion annually of a diverse range of products—including cereals, pastas, and Gatorade sports drink—Quaker, with its corporate headquarters in Chicago until it was purchased by PepsiCo in 2001, was still an industry leader and one of the city's largest companies.

Compared to the highly industrialized milling and cereal business, bread in Chicago and elsewhere has been characterized by a more diverse range of producers. Even after the appearance of mechanized ovens, baking continued in the kitchens of individual households and in small shops. In 1880 most of Chicago's 280 bakeries were small neighborhood retailers, and the number of small bakeries continued to grow until the 1930s. With the rise of mechanized bread factories, chain grocery stores, and chain bakeries, more and more small bakers disappeared from the Chicago landscape.

Although bread baking saw significant consolidation over time, it was never as concentrated or industrialized as cracker and biscuit manufacturing, another business in which Chicago was a national leader. Between 1890 and 1898, Chicago lawyers A. W. Green and W. H. Moore led a series of cracker mergers that created the National Biscuit Company, which had its executive offices in Chicago until 1906. During its early years, this company (later known as Nabisco) controlled over 100 large bakeries—several of them in the Chicago area—which produced the company's well-known line of cracker and cookie brands, including Uneeda biscuits, Fig Newtons, and Oreos. In 1927 the Chicago region became home to another large cracker producer, the United Biscuit Company, based in Elmhurst. Renamed Keebler in 1966, this company has remained one of the region's largest. Another important baked-goods firm, the Sara Lee Corporation, takes its name from a Chicago bakery founded by Charles Lubin in 1949. By the end of the century, Sara Lee made clothing and meat products as well as frozen pies and cakes and had become an industry leader and one of Chicago's largest companies.

In the area of canned foods and processed meat and dairy products, Chicago firms have long been national leaders. By the 1880s, Libby, McNeill & Libby, a firm connected to Swift & Co., was packing 35 million cans annually, and several Chicago canners were filling large orders from European armies and navies. By 1918 Libby was the nation's second largest canner. In the dairy industry, Chicago's strength was generated by its proximity to Wisconsin, a leading dairy state. Major dairy companies located in the city during the twentieth century included Beatrice Foods, which moved from Nebraska to Chicago in 1913, and Dean Foods, founded in 1925 by Sam Dean, a local dealer in evaporated milk. In processed dairy foods, the industry leader was James L. Kraft, who began selling cheese in Chicago in 1904. By 1930 Kraft had taken over much of the cheese distribution business from Chicago's meatpackers, and by 1960 processed cheese, Kraft's specialty, accounted for half of U.S. cheese production.

Throughout the twentieth century, Chicago and Illinois dominated the American confectionery industry. William Wrigley Jr. founded his Chicago-based chewing gum company in 1891, and several of his brands, including Juicy Fruit and Wrigley's Spearmint, rapidly became big sellers. The well-known Cracker Jack brand of snacks, popular at the 1893 World's Columbian Exposition, were the creation of Chicago popcorn vendor F. W. Rueckheim. In the candy industry, some of America's best-known brands were produced in the Chicago area by companies such as M. J. Holloway (Milk Duds), and E. J. Brach. Another major candy firm, Tootsie Roll Industries, whose brands include Junior Mints and Tootsie Pop, has been located on Chicago's South Side since the 1960s.

For much of its history, Chicago has been an organizational center for workers in the food-processing industries. In the 1880s, German bakers in New York and Chicago created the first bakers' unions in the United States. From 1904 to 1955, Chicago served as the headquarters of the Bakery and Confectionery Workers International Union, which claimed 28,000 members in 1920 and 80,000 in 1940. From the 1880s through the 1920s, Chicago bakers and baked-good distributors went on strike frequently, but with mixed success, in attempts to gain some power over hours, working conditions, and production. A major defeat in Chicago in 1922 was symptomatic of labor groups' lack of success in their confrontations with large bakery owners, but unions continued to have some power in the smaller retail shops.

Since the earliest days of the city, Chicago food processors have been subject to a variety of government regulations concerning food quality and monopolistic business practices. Rules for flour grading and inspection were established in Illinois in the 1850s. By 1880 Chicago was licensing its bakeries. In the first decade of the twentieth century, the federal Pure Food and Drug Act, along with new state and municipal rules, placed broader controls over the food industry; and federal oversight increased significantly during World War I and World War II. During the 1920s, Kraft struggled with the state of Wisconsin over cream-skimming limits. In the realm of antitrust regulation, Quaker Oats was sued unsuccessfully in 1915 for alleged violations of the 1890 Sherman Act, and Beatrice was one of the companies investigated and regulated by the Federal Trade Commission between the 1930s and 1960s for alleged anti-competitive practices in the dairy industry.

As the twentieth century came to an end, Chicago-area companies continued to be important in the food-processing business, but the city's status as an industry headquarters had been shaken by a recent rash of corporate takeovers and acquisitions. In 1985 the Chicago-based food giant Beatrice, one of the largest companies in the United States, was dismantled by investment bankers in a leveraged buyout. And in the 1990s, Quaker Oats suffered a $1.4 billion loss on its Snapple drink brand. The massive capital flows involved in these kinds of transactions, combined with changing consumer preferences, suggest a volatile landscape of food processing. By the end of the first decade of the twenty-first century, Quaker, Dean, Keebler, and even Wrigley were owned by non-Chicago firms. Yet Kraft, Sara Lee, Tootsie Roll, and other firms maintained Chicago's important role in the industry.                *Mark R. Wilson*

**Furniture.** Chicago's furniture industry expanded in the mid-nineteenth century by serving a regional rural market. Farmers in the city's hinterland prospered by selling their products in Chicago, and they purchased manufactured goods, including furniture, with their profits. Such markets, along with Chicago's own demands, fueled the westward expansion of all kinds of manufacturing.

Railroad connections gave Chicago access to lumber and the market, which it combined with a skilled immigrant labor supply, primarily of German and Scandinavian workers. In 1870, 50 percent of Chicago's cabinetmakers had been born in Germany, 10 percent in Scandinavia, while another 16 percent came from a mixture of other European countries. Immigrants were almost as well represented among furniture manufacturers in an industry where small craft shops and medium-size firms still coexisted. Yankees, nevertheless, usually owned the very largest companies.

Many furniture manufacturers were located on the West Side along the North and South Branches of the Chicago River, near the neighborhoods of their workers and the lumber yards so well serviced by lake shipping and the railroads. They were also near industries producing by-products of the meatpacking industry that were of use in furniture manufacture—hair, leather, and glue.

Chicago's dense concentration of modest-size furniture plants made up an innovative center of specialty production, in which manufacturers made a wide variety of goods in response to changing and varied demand. In the 1880s, one Chicago firm advertised several thousand varieties of chairs, rockers, and cradles. Manufacturers depended on a core of skilled craftsmen to produce so wide a variety of goods, usually in small batches. Furniture makers were similar to other specialty producers—printers, foundries and machine shops, and millwork establishments.

The strong craft traditions and imported political values of the skilled furniture workers made them leaders in the labor movement. In the early 1870s, Chicago's German furniture workers founded the first local of what became a national American furniture workers' union. Rapid mechanization, using steam power and sophisticated new machines, stimulated labor organizing by changing, but not eliminating, the role of skilled workers in production. The concentration of the furniture workers in working-class neighborhoods near the factories contributed to labor's strength. Neighborhood organizations and communication networks supported the labor movement.

By the early twentieth century, the structure of the industry had changed significantly. The severe depression of the 1890s destroyed many smaller craft shops owned by the foreign-born; and, as in the rest of American industry, a merger movement increased the scale and influence of larger companies. In 1900 Chicago's more than 100 furniture plants averaged about 70 workers per firm, well beyond the scale of craft production. In 1910, 200 furniture manufacturers had a workforce of over 10,000. Nevertheless, medium-size firms still predominated, unlike the highly concentrated meatpackers or steel producers. Meanwhile, the extension of the railroad network and the growth of cities created a more integrated national market defined increasingly by urban tastes. Furniture manufacturers found it even more advantageous to be near urban centers of transportation, finance, and marketing.

Chicago's advantages in these areas made its furniture industry a national leader. In the early 1920s, Illinois ranked second only to New York in value of furniture produced, and Chicago dominated the state's furniture industry.

Taking advantage of Chicago's strengths in these areas, the city's furniture manufacturers became innovative leaders in national marketing. They published extensive catalogs, organized annual exhibitions for dealers, initiated installment buying, and sold extensively through Chicago preeminent mail-order houses, Sears and Montgomery Ward. Symbolizing Chicago's importance was the opening of the American Furniture Mart in 1924. This architecturally significant building at 666 North Lake Shore Drive housed the nation's most important furniture trade shows for decades. In 1928 almost 6,500 dealers from around the country visited the Mart. In the 1920s, manufacturers in the four states around Lake Michigan made the Midwest into America's largest producer of furniture by far. The region's furniture makers profited from a huge demand created by the housing boom of the decade.

Profound changes were, nevertheless, undermining the Midwest's primacy. After 1900, electricity powered ever more sophisticated tools, lessening the need for craft skills, while a decline of immigration shrank the supply of European craftsmen. Changing tastes increased the use of metal in furniture, and shaping metal required different kinds of workers and different machines. The Great Depression of the 1930s destroyed many firms. After World War II, when trucks challenged railroads, furniture makers discovered that they could manufacture and market furniture in states like North Carolina, where labor was cheaper, unions were absent, and raw materials were nearby. In the late 1970s, the Furniture Mart was sold for renovation into condominiums. By 1997 none of the top 25 manufacturers of household wood furniture were based in Illinois, whereas 15 of them were located in North Carolina and Virginia.

Chicago remains, however, a significant center of custom production and furniture design. Even before Frank Lloyd Wright, Chicago's architects, interior designers, and furniture makers worked together to define new styles. They still do today, drawing on Chicago's enduring significance as an innovative marketing and design center.          *John B. Jentz*

**Fur Trade.** The fur trade was the economic mainstay of Chicago during the first third of the nineteenth century. Fort Dearborn, which was established to protect U.S. interests in the fur trade, and the various trading posts formed the first stages of settlement preceding the land boom of the mid-1830s. Before that period, traders and travelers used Chicago mostly as a point of transit between the French and, later, the American settlements in the Mississippi Valley and the Straits of Mackinac. For a while, the wars between the Fox Indians and the French from the early 1700s to the 1740s closed access to the portage, and the line of communication shifted temporarily to the Wabash and Maumee Rivers south of Detroit. The flow of trade returned gradually to the more convenient location of Chicago, where the activity increased even more at the conclusion of the French and Indian War (1754–63).

English and Scottish merchants, now settled in Montreal, took over control of the fur trade and allied themselves with the remaining French traders. They imported goods from London for the Indian trade: flintlock guns, gunflints, awls, trade axes, knives, metal kettles, glass beads, liquor, and so on. They gave credit to the traders (*bourgeois*), a mixture of French, English, and Scots, who were stationed at various trading posts in the interior and who collected the furs from Indians and French Métis. The most-traded furs included beaver, bear, black fox, deer, marten, and otter. French *voyageurs* continued to transport the goods and the furs in their bark canoes.

A number of small and large companies competed for the fur trade in the Great Lakes region. The North West Company, organized in 1779, worked mostly west of Grand Portage on Lake Superior. The short-lived General Company of Lake Superior and the South, followed by the Michilimackinac Company with headquarters at Mackinac, included northern Illinois, the Mississippi River down to Cahokia, and the Wabash down to Vincennes in their operations.

The British monopoly thwarted efforts by the Americans to enter the fur trade in the Chicago area after the Treaty of Greenville of 1795, in which Indians ceded six square miles at the mouth of the Chicago River to the United States. In order to break the British hold on the region, the U.S. government established Fort Dearborn in 1803 and opened a factory, or trading post. The factory system had been enacted by Congress in order to protect Indians from unscrupulous private traders and to regulate prices. The operations of the Chicago factory were successful in its early years, attracting good-quality hatters' furs and shaved deerskins. The War of 1812 and the Fort Dearborn Massacre forced the closing of the factory. After it reopened in 1816, lack of financial support by the government and increased competition from the private sector gradually reduced its effectiveness until it was finally closed in 1822, when Congress abolished the system.

The American Fur Company, established in 1808 by John Jacob Astor to compete with the powerful Canadian North West and Hudson Bay Companies, practically took control of the fur trade in the United States following the War of 1812. It quickly became known for its ruthless practice of buying out or destroying the competition, as most private traders in Chicago soon found out. It appointed John Kinzie and Antoine Deschamps as its first agents in northern Illinois, and they reported to the company's headquarters on Mackinac Island. Their field of operations covered northeastern Illinois and the Illinois River. In 1819 Jean-Baptiste Beaubien was brought in to assist Kinzie and eventually became head of the outfit. Gurdon S. Hubbard replaced Deschamps in 1823 but soon went on his own by purchasing all interests of the company in Illinois.

Astor formed an alliance with the Chouteau family in St. Louis in 1822. By extending the trade of his company to the Missouri River region and eventually all the way into the Rocky Mountains, he consolidated commercial connections between St. Louis, Chicago, and Mackinac. By the mid-1820s, Astor's American Fur Company dominated the economy of Chicago and, in consequence, its social life as well.

The opening of the Erie Canal in 1825 enabled easterners to migrate in increasingly large numbers to the lands west of Lake Michigan. White settlements limited the supply of game for the Indians, who could no longer afford to pay their debts to the American Fur Company. By 1828, when Hubbard took over the business of the company in Illinois, the fur trade at Chicago was measured in hundreds instead of thousands of dollars. The Treaty of 1833, which extinguished all Indian land claims in Illinois, marked the end of the fur trade as a significant part of the Chicago economy. Diminishing profits convinced Astor in 1834 to sell his interest in the American Fur Company, which reorganized under Ramsay Crooks and moved its operations to the Far West. Fur trading disappeared from Chicago as the population boomed and land speculation became the rage.

*B. Pierre Lebeau*

**Gas and Electricity.** Gas and electric help supply the city's insatiable demand for energy. Until the 1930s, these two systems played a critical role in defining the urban environment. The "city lights" made Chicago distinctly different from more rural places. Its gas and electric services were developed as privately owned public utilities. To use the public streets for their networks of pipes and wires required a special franchise from city hall. The growth of utility companies took place within a context of government regulation and political conflict over the price, quality, and distribution of services.

Although gas lighting was introduced in the United States in 1816, Chicago had to wait until 1850 for this urban amenity. All of the gas supplied to the city was manufactured from coal. This cheap and abundant fuel was placed in retorts and heated until it gave off a gas that could be used for illumination. The coal gas was stored in huge tanks until the evening, when lamplighters would make the rounds of the streets, starting open burners that produced a relatively feeble 12–15 candlepower. Compared to the alternatives of tallow candles or whale oil, however, gaslights were brighter, more convenient, and less prone to ignite fires. By 1860 the Chicago Gas Light & Coke Company had hooked up 2,000 customers in the city center to its 50 miles of underground pipes. In 1862 the People's Gas Light & Coke Company started service, but a secret agreement established a duopoly that divided the city into noncompetitive zones. The result was high rates that kept gas lighting a luxury restricted to commercial and affluent residential districts. The cost of service—together with technological limitations such as dim illumination, excessive heat, and the risk of fire—continued to spur the search for better lighting.

In 1878 Chicago ushered in the electrical age with experimental demonstrations of arc lights, brilliant 2,000-candlepower devices that created a spark or arc of current across two carbon rods. While solving the problem of illuminating large public spaces, this technology was unsuitable for homes and shops. Two years later, Thomas A. Edison was the first to bring an incandescent lightbulb to a point of commercial practicality. This invention was a revolutionary breakthrough because it produced light without a flame inside a fire-safe container. Equally important, parallel improvements in motors quickly led street railways and rapid transit cars to become the largest consumers of electricity. Light and power systems were sold just like steam engines as self-contained systems to individual customers. However, Edison and many of his competitors also imitated the model of the gas company by building central stations that offered service to everyone within limited distribution areas. The Chicago Edison Company, for example, initially sold only hardware, but in 1888 it opened an electric station with a capacity to power 10,000 lights in the offices of the financial district around Adams and LaSalle Streets.

The years between 1878 and 1903 witnessed the "battle of the systems," a period marked not only by intense technological competition but by political conflict as well. In addition to the rapid growth of the electric industry, the gas business underwent a revolution of its own. New appliances and methods of making gas greatly improved its heating and illuminating qualities while dramatically cutting costs. As the expensive albeit preferred electric bulbs pushed gas lighting out of elite establishments and homes, the utility companies extended service pipes into working-class neighborhoods and began marketing energy for heating and cooking purposes. During this period, corruption and bribery of the city council became endemic as gas, electric, and transit promoters scrambled for the most advantageous franchises and lucrative service territories. In part, the reform movement known as urban progressivism was a response to this perversion of the political process. A wide range of women's and men's groups campaigned to clean up city hall and to impose a reasonable set of regulations on the utility companies that were providing what had truly become essential urban services.

The arrival of Samuel Insull in 1892 permanently changed the history of public utilities in Chicago. Within ten years, he established a virtual monopoly of central station electric service in the city under the corporate banner of the Commonwealth Edison Company. Insull used low rates and marketing schemes to undercut the competition. After gaining key power contracts with the transit companies, he took a risk in 1902 when he installed the world's first modern turbogenerator at the Fisk Street Station. Over the following decade, this success encouraged him to integrate and expand suburban utilities into a unified network of power. He also worked to stabilize government-business relations through the creation in 1913 of a state-level utility commission. When the gas companies fell into financial difficulty during World War I, Insull was called in to apply his business strategy of low rates, high technology, and metropolitan consolidation. In the late 1920s, he spearheaded efforts to lay a natural gas pipeline from Texas to the Midwest. The stock market crash brought about the collapse of Insull's securities empire. Energy demand briefly dipped during the ensuing Great Depression, but Chicago's utilities helped lead the way toward its economic recovery.

In the post–World War II period, demand for energy in the form of gas and electric continued to soar. The Commonwealth Edison Company took a leadership role in becoming the first privately owned utility to operate a nuclear power plant. In April 1960, the Dresden Station began generating electricity, inaugurating a building program that would eventually make Chicago the metropolitan area most dependent on this form of energy in the United States. In the gas business, deregulation at the national level has meant increased competition at the local level, as well as corporate consolidation at the regional and national levels. Similar trends in government-business relations are opening new markets for electricity. At the same time, however, mounting environmental problems resulting from ever-increasing energy use have engendered a new set of technological challenges and political controversies. This had led utilities like Exelon, the parent company of Commonwealth Edison since 2000, to experiment with alternative forms of energy production. It, for example, opened its first solar power plant on a former industrial site in West Pullman.

*Harold L. Platt*

**Grocery Stores and Supermarkets.** Supplying Chicagoans with a basic necessity, the retail food industry has not experienced the rise, decline, and renaissance that other industries in the area have seen; instead, it has steadily grown with the population. It has seen the passing of the public market, the decline of small family-owned neighborhood groceries and farmers' markets, the rise of large chain store companies, and the development of the supermarket.

During the early 1800s, general stores supplied food as well as manufactured items like tools, boots, glass, and medicines to the soldiers at Fort Dearborn and the several settlers who had come to trade with the Indians in the area. Baldwin & Parsons and Andrus & Doyle, among other merchants, also offered to exchange their manufactured goods for farmers' produce, most of which they then sold to the local market.

Most people got their daily food from a variety of sources. In 1839 the city council granted Joseph Blanchard the right to construct the city's first public market and to rent out stalls to local butchers, grocers, and produce dealers. The council prohibited the sale of retail proportions of meat, eggs, poultry, and vegetables anywhere else in the city during market hours. Such arrangements were a convenient way of assuring dealers of perishables that they would be able to find customers for their goods. The public market also provided customers with a central place to purchase food and to socialize. The city council authorized the construction of two more markets in the 1840s—one on the aptly named Market Street and another on State Street in the city's first municipal structure, the Market Building.

Mid-nineteenth-century wholesale and retail grocers typically handled only imported goods or those items that were impossible to manufacture or process cheaply at home. Flour, sugar, syrup, salt, tea, coffee, tobacco, spices, and dried fruit were some of the more popular articles they advertised.

The phenomenal growth of the city in the second half of the nineteenth century meant that city markets became less convenient to growing numbers of people. Rising real estate prices and the restrictive building codes in the city center following the Great Fire of 1871 forced residents and small retailers out of the old market areas. Large wholesalers and commission merchants remained. Rather than individual customers buying from stall merchants and nearby grocers, turn-of-the-century markets consisted of retailers and jobbers haggling with wholesalers for goods to stock the retail stores in the surrounding neighborhoods.

The late nineteenth and early twentieth century were the age of the independent mom-and-pop store. As residents moved into neighborhoods segregated by class and ethnicity and into the suburbs created by the new street railways and railroads, small family-run stores sprang up to meet their needs. These new groceries, meat markets, vegetable stands, and bakeries typically reflected the ethnic demographics of the neighborhood—Polish neighborhoods were served by Polish grocers, Jewish neighborhoods by Jewish grocers. Stores often carried ethnic foods that were hard to find elsewhere and conducted business in the native language of their customers. Workers followed this pattern as well. The bakers' union had separate locals for its German, Bohemian, Scandinavian, Polish, and English members, while the meat cutters had separate German, Bohemian, Jewish, and African American locals.

Thousands of small neighborhood stores dotted Chicago's urban landscape until the 1950s. Families rarely owned any sort of refrigeration besides an icebox, so housewives shopped for food almost daily. This put a premium on convenience; the store had to be within walking distance of home. By 1914 some 7,400 groceries, 1,800 meat markets, and several hundred fruit and vegetable stands served the city. Except for those stores located where streetcar lines crossed, proprietors could expect only a few hundred regular customers. To protect themselves from the fierce compe-

Grocery interior, Glen Ellyn, 1920. This view captures the environment of the small store that would, as the decade progressed, experience sharp competition from larger grocery chains. Courtesy of the Chicago History Museum (ICHi-37003).

tition that characterized their industry, Chicago's retail food store owners formed many associations over the years. Since the industry was notorious for its long hours, these associations often agitated for early closing and Sunday closing rules. As early as 1855, retailers formed an Early Closing Association to give themselves time off in the evening. The Chicago Grocer and Butcher Clerks Protective Association joined with the Retail Grocers and Butchers Association in 1900 to pressure employers who refused to join the Sunday closing crusade, but their successes were short-lived until union contracts introduced in the 1920s, 1930s, and 1940s effectively set the hours of operation for the industry.

The rise of chain store companies in the years after World War I seriously challenged the dominance of the independent grocers. The Great Atlantic & Pacific Tea Company (A&P) established its first branch in Chicago just after the Great Fire of 1871, but until the 1910s chain store companies sold mainly teas, coffees, and spices. In 1912 A&P introduced its "economy stores," which sold a full line of groceries at low prices on a cash-and-carry basis. Instead of maximizing the profit per item like the independent grocer, A&P and other chain stores sold a heavy volume for little above cost. With many stores in a single city, chains could afford newspaper space to advertise specials and encourage more trade. They also circumvented wholesalers by buying in bulk from manufacturers and purchasing facilities where they produced their own store brands. Chicago's large chain store companies—National Tea, A&P, and Kroger—acquired hundreds of stores during the 1920s. Chicago-based National Tea, for instance, grew from 41 stores in 1914 to more than 550 branches in the Chicago area in 1928, including 10 stores along just 12 blocks of North Clark Street. By 1933 chain stores accounted for only 20 percent of the grocery stores in the Chicago area, but they had 60 percent of the sales.

Independent grocers and wholesalers attempted to cripple the chain stores legislatively, but they ultimately failed. Independent store owners formed the Associated Food Dealers of Greater Chicago in 1936 to meet the chain threat through business education and political lobbying. Perhaps the most lasting legislative victory of the national movement against chain stores was the Robinson-Patman Act (1936), which attempted to outlaw wholesaler discounts and rebates to chains for bulk orders. The Federal Trade Commission prosecuted several large chains for violations of this act, but the suits did little to stop their growth. The most popular response of independents to the chain store threat was to form voluntary chains with Chicago's large wholesalers. This gave independents the bulk buying and advertising power of the chains while retaining individual ownership of the stores. The voluntary chains did not enjoy the benefits of the chains' centralized management, but, through affiliation, many found a way to compete with the major chains. The largest of these groups was the Independent Grocers Alliance (IGA). Other wholesaler-retailer voluntary chains included Royal Blue, Supreme, Centrella Stores, Certified

Grocers, and Grocerland Cooperative. By the 1950s, these voluntary chains counted more than 2,000 Chicago-area stores among their members.

In the late 1930s, large supermarkets challenged the dominance of the small neighborhood stores, whether they were independent or a member of a chain. The supermarket took advantage of several developments to become a viable method of marketing low-priced food. The availability of nationally branded packaged foods allowed supermarkets to replace full-service clerks with self-service aisles and counters staffed by "checkout girls." Increased use of the automobile and home refrigeration encouraged customers to abandon daily trips to neighborhood groceries, meat markets, vegetable stands, and bakeries for weekly trips to the supermarket, where all their food needs were met under one roof.

The shift from the family-owned neighborhood store to the corporate-run chain and supermarket occasioned a change in labor relations as well. Chicago's meat markets had been thoroughly organized by the Amalgamated Meat Cutters and Butcher Workmen since the 1920s, but Retail Clerks International was not able to organize the industry's clerks until the late 1930s, when chain stores and supermarkets with many employees broke the familial ties of the small neighborhood stores. The Retail Clerks Union flourished only after the supermarket industry began to dominate food retailing in the 1950s.

In Chicago, chain stores consolidated their neighborhood stores by opening supermarkets only after independents like Hillman's and Dawson's Trading Post proved supermarkets to be successful. After World War II, the industry shifted to fewer, larger stores. In 1933 the Chicago area had over 17,000 food stores. By 1954 the number had shrunk to 13,260 (the largest 700 stores accounting for half of the sales); in 1987 the number stood at a mere 3,638. National Tea was particularly slow in recognizing the importance of the supermarket trend, switching fully to self-service only in the 1950s. A recent arrival to the food store industry, Jewel Tea Company (an old door-to-door sales company), became a market leader in 1950s by remodeling the old Loblaw Groceterias chain and opening supermarkets in new suburban shopping centers. In the 1960s and 1970s, the once-dominant chains, A&P, Kroger, and National Tea—with their smaller, unprofitable supermarkets in the city center—failed to expand into the suburbs and ultimately left the Chicago market. Other smaller stores closed as well, creating what came to be known as food deserts—areas in which access to foods needed for a healthy diet is limited—in a number of city neighborhoods. The giant new 100,000-square-foot suburban stores of the 1980s and 1990s utilized computer scanners to control inventory and cut labor costs and sold everything from drugs and milk to meat and flowers. Newer companies and older independent chains that had successfully converted to supermarkets, like Jewel-Osco and Dominick's Finer Foods, dominated the industry by the late twentieth century.

The new century saw an increasing challenge to their dominance from discount groceries like Aldi, wholesale stores like Costco, and big-box stores like Walmart. On the other end of the price scale, gourmet markets proliferated in some regions of the city and suburbs. Although Jewel-Osco (now part of the SuperValu chain) and Dominick's (part of Safeway) remained among Chicagoland's biggest players in this volatile market, and Jewel-Osco remained one of the area's largest employers, the chains saw their number of stores drop in the first decade of the twenty-first century.                                                                      *Paul Gilmore*

**Hospitals.** The history of Chicago's hospitals begins with an almshouse established by Cook County as part of its responsibility to provide care for indigent or homeless county residents and for sick or needy travelers. Located at the corner of Clark and Randolph Streets, this public charity was in operation as early as 1835. It did provide medical attendance, but such places typically crowded the ill together with the healthy poor, the insane, and persons who were permanently incapacitated.

Unlike Cook County, the city of Chicago had no legal mandate to care for the sick poor, but its charter did charge it with guarding against "pestilential or infectious diseases." Cholera had hit the area in 1832, and smallpox and scarlet fever were familiar to many. By 1843 fear of epidemic prompted city officials to build the first institution devoted exclusively to medical care in Chicago, a small wooden structure located on the far northern border of the city. Ironically, it was built on land bought for a cemetery. This first "hospital," a frame structure at North Avenue and the lakeshore in what would become Lincoln Park, was designed to keep victims of contagious disease away from the center of population. Rebuilt after a fire, in 1852 it began to segregate smallpox cases from cholera cases, but when cholera threatened Chicago in 1854, the city council authorized a separate though only temporary hospital at 18th and LaSalle Streets. The city kept the smallpox hospital at North Avenue and even built a two-story building there, but it perished in the Great Fire of 1871. Beginning in 1874, a series of new hospitals to isolate contagious diseases was built on the Southwest Side of the city, near the courthouse at 26th and California.

Institutions like the smallpox hospital and the temporary cholera hospital were not meant to be locations of general medical care, and as early as 1837 citizens were suggesting that the city build a general hospital. It was not until a decade later, however, that both city and county officials worked with physicians from Rush Medical College to establish the first such hospital in the area, at North Water and Dearborn Streets. Newly opened and seeking students, Rush College wanted a hospital to fill a need for clinical education. Rush provided the doctors, the county supplied the medicine, and the city paid for the building rental. However, it soon became evident that the accommodations were inadequate for the large number and variety of patients, and the hospital went out of business.

Rush physicians soon incorporated another general hospital, called the Illinois General Hospital of the Lake, which opened in 1850 with 12 beds in the old Lake House Hotel at Rush and North Water Streets. The charge was three dollars per week per patient. The doctors asked the Sisters of Mercy, a Roman Catholic order, to provide nursing care, and in the spring of 1851 transferred control to the Sisters. With a new charter, the hospital was renamed Mercy Hospital. Cook County supervisors paid Mercy to care for county patients. The oldest continuously running hospital in Chicago, it moved in 1853 to a new building at Wabash and Van Buren, and in 1863 was relocated to its present campus at 26th and Calumet. Rush College retained the privilege of teaching medical students there until 1859, when Mercy switched affiliation to the Chicago Medical School (later known as Northwestern University Medical School).

Medical sectarians, some with unorthodox therapeutic practices, founded their own hospitals, such as the Hahnemann Hospital, which opened in the early 1850s. Popular despite unyielding criticism from "regular" physicians, homeopaths held that disease could be cured using very small doses of medicines rather than the typically large amounts of strong, even potentially lethal drugs that other doctors prescribed. Homeopathy had a large following in Chicago and elsewhere in the nineteenth century, and this was not surprising, since minimalist therapies such as theirs were usually easier on the body. Their support declined by the early twentieth century as scientific medicine became more accurate and effective; homeopathic medical colleges found improvement in medical education difficult to implement, and their hospitals closed or adopted traditional techniques. During the mid-nineteenth century, however, homeopaths in Chicago held a strong hand. Friction between them and regular medical practitioners became a political battle in 1857, when the former sought representation on the medical staff of what was to be the new city hospital at 18th and LaSalle Streets. The argument prevented the institution from opening until 1859, when Rush faculty members rented it for use as a private hospital. In 1862 the U.S. Army commandeered it for a military hospital, until the Civil War ended and the county leased it. Cook County finally had a relatively permanent hospital. As the number of charity cases grew, however, the old building proved too small, and County Hospital moved to new pavilions at the present site at Wood and Harrison Streets in 1876. Larger structures replaced these beginning in 1912, and these in turn were replaced in the first years of the twenty-first century.

In 1847 a Chicago physician built a private retreat for the insane just north of the city, and in 1854, when the county moved its almshouse to a site known as "Dunning" 12 miles northwest of the city, an asylum was among the buildings constructed. Authorities transferred this asylum, the Cook County Hospital for the Insane, to the care of the state of Illinois in 1912, and the name changed to Chicago State Hospital.

Institutional efforts against tuberculosis began with the Chicago Tuberculosis Institute, which established the Edward Sanatorium in 1907. The Municipal Tuberculosis Sanitarium, funded by the city, opened in 1915 at Crawford and Bryn Mawr Avenues. To care for sick and injured sailors who worked on the Great Lakes, the federal government set up a hospital in 1852 on the grounds of Fort Dearborn. It later moved north of the city to what became the Uptown neighborhood. After World War I, the United States Public Health Service established several large hospitals, forerunners of present-day veterans' hospitals. The Hines facility in Maywood was among the largest.

Seen as part of a church's mission, religious hospitals were shaped by a charitable imperative and a desire to save souls while caring for the sick. Religious symbols and the presence of religious nursing orders provided constant reminders of spirituality. St. Luke's Hospital, a charity of Grace Episcopal Church on the Near South Side, began in 1865 in a small frame structure at Eighth and State Streets, eventually moving into larger buildings on South Indiana and Michigan Avenues. The hospital remained at that site for almost a century, merging in 1956 with Presbyterian Hospital and Rush Medical College on the Near West Side. Lutheran pastor William Passavant established the 15-bed Deaconess Hospital at Dearborn and Ontario Streets in 1865. Destroyed by the 1871 fire, in 1884 it reopened at Dearborn and Superior as the Emergency Hospital, later named Passavant after its founder. In 1920 Northwestern University Medical School adopted Emergency as a site for clinical instruction. Methodist Wesley Memorial Hospital, established in 1888, joined Passavant as part of Northwestern's Chicago campus in 1941.

The Alexian Brothers, a Roman Catholic male nursing order originating during the bubonic plague of the thirteenth century, started a small hospital for men in 1866. Its first substantial building was at Dearborn and Schiller. After two years, Alexian moved to larger quarters at North and Franklin. It rebuilt after the fire, moving in 1896 to Belden and Racine and then to Elk Grove Village in 1966. The Sisters of Charity began St. Joseph's Hospital in Lakeview in 1868. It now serves the community from a modern high-rise building at Diversey Avenue near the lake. Other early Catholic hospitals were St. Elizabeth's, founded near Western and Division in 1887 by the Poor Handmaids of Jesus Christ, and St. Mary of Nazareth Hospital, established in 1894 by the Sisters of the Holy Family of Nazareth in the same neighborhood. St. Mary's served the Polish-speaking immigrant community.

Early Chicago Jews founded a hospital at LaSalle and Schiller in 1866. Like the nearby Alexian Brothers, this institution fell victim to the fire, but Jewish Hospital did not rebuild immediately. The family of philanthropist Michael Reese made large contributions, and the hospital bearing his name arose in 1882 at Ellis Avenue and 29th Street, becoming by 1950 the largest charity-sponsored hospital in Chicago, with 718 beds. The increasing population of Jews on Chicago's Near Southwest Side prompted the opening of Mount Sinai Hospital near Douglas Park in 1919.

The influx of German immigrants into the Chicago area led to the 1883 founding of the German Hospital. It was renamed Grant Hospital during World War I. Baptists established the Chicago Baptist Hospital in 1891, and Methodists founded Bethany Methodist. By 1897 Lutherans had built Augustana, Swedish Covenant, the Norwegian-American Hospital, and the Lutheran Deaconess Home and Hospital. Early twentieth-century Catholic groups started St. Anne's, St. Bernard's, and Columbus hospitals.

Several Chicago hospitals have specialized in treating specific types of patients. The Illinois Charitable Eye and Ear Infirmary began in 1858 under the direction of ophthalmologist Edward Lorenzo Holmes. In 1865 Mary Harris Thompson founded the Chicago Hospital for Women and Children, chiefly to serve widows and orphans of Civil War victims. Renamed the Mary Thompson Hospital when she died in 1895, it opened on Rush Street, then moved to West Adams Street. Julia F. Porter endowed the Maurice Porter Memorial Free Hospital for Children in 1882 in memory of her son. In 1903 it took the name Children's Memorial. Joseph B. De Lee founded the Chicago Lying-In Hospital and Dispensary in 1895 in a tenement house on Maxwell Street in an effort to lower the high neo-

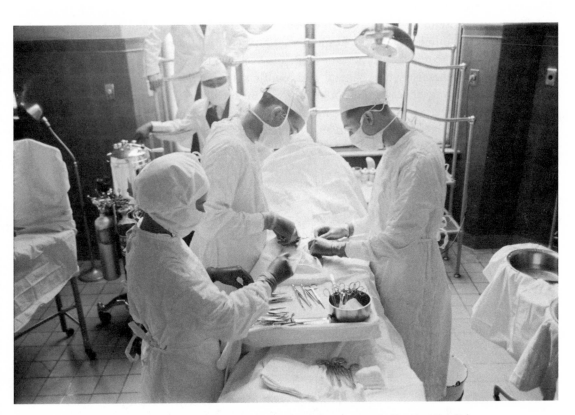

Operation at Provident Hospital, Chicago, Illinois, April 1941. From 1891 to 1987, Provident Hospital provided medical care and medical training to Chicago's African American community. Through the mid-twentieth century, segregation policies denied African Americans access to services at many other Chicago-area hospitals. Photo: Russell Lee. Courtesy of the Library of Congress.

natal mortality rates. The Martha Washington Hospital advertised itself as a haven for alcoholics, and the Frances E. Willard National Temperance Hospital, named after the famous temperance advocate from Evanston, was for nondrinkers. It was dedicated to proving that diseases could be cured without the use of alcohol or alcohol-based medicines.

Until the mid-twentieth century, many Chicago hospitals refused to treat African American patients or employ black doctors and nurses. Daniel Hale Williams, one of the first African American surgeons in Chicago, organized Provident Hospital in 1891 in an effort to ensure hospital services to African Americans in Chicago and to provide black health care workers a place to practice and learn.

Beginning in the last decade of the nineteenth century, groups of physicians and physician-entrepreneurs established for-profit hospitals such as the Lakeside Hospital, Garfield Park Hospital, Westside Hospital, and Jefferson Park Hospital. Later examples of this type included North Chicago, Washington Park, Ravenswood, South Shore, Washington Boulevard, Burnside, Chicago General, John B. Murphy, and Belmont hospitals. Most of these were small, and some lasted only a few years. Others became nonprofit institutions and continued to serve without investor ownership.

Reforms in nursing and a new understanding of the importance of cleanliness made the hospital a safer place for most patients by the end of the nineteenth century. Medicine began to incorporate developments in chemistry and biology, and aseptic surgery and clinical laboratories became effective tools in health care. Such changes in technology paralleled tremendous growth in population from immigration, which strained existing municipal services, including the provision of medical care. Hospital construction by both public and private agencies was one result. Tax-supported hospitals were built by the city, the county, the state, and federal government. Private hospitals included institutions owned or operated by medical schools, religious groups, individual doctors or groups of physicians, lay boards, and even companies such as railroads. Especially in a city filling with immigrants, a hospital could be a place of comfort to particular beliefs, customs, languages, and races, as well as a site of medical care.

Insurance programs beginning in the 1930s encouraged hospital development, and as the Hill-Burton plan took effect after World War II, hospitals all over the United States were built or expanded. As the number of available beds increased, so did competition for patients among neighboring institutions. By 1950, with a population of 3.6 million, Chicago had 84 hospitals, including public and private sanatoriums. The majority were nonprofit, receiving major funding from patient fees (often at least partly paid by insurance), donations, and endowments.

As government reimbursement programs initiated in the 1960s expanded to encompass so many patients that tax resources stretched thin, agencies demanded briefer hospital stays. New technologies allowed patients to be discharged earlier. Beds began to go unfilled, and hospitals faced declining revenues. Many closed or consolidated, and the number of hospitals in Chicago fell to approximately 50 by the late 1990s. The advent of health maintenance organizations (HMOs) and preferred provider organizations (PPO) was another factor in the loss of hospital income, since these organizations typically contracted for care at lower fees than traditional insurance paid or excluded particular hospitals from their networks.

Hospital ownership began to consolidate as large corporations or associations sought economies of scale by purchasing formerly independent institutions or locating nearby. By 2010 Oak Brook–based Advocate Health Care—originally created in a 1995 merger between EHS Health Care (associated with the United Church of Christ) and Lutheran General Health System—had become the largest integrated health care system in the state with 10 hospitals (9 in the Chicago area) and nearly 250 additional sites providing patient services. It had also become one of the area's largest employers. In 2012 Children's Memorial moved to Northwestern's downtown medical complex to take better advantage of the resources of the medical school and affiliated hospitals located there. This clustering of institutions is also visible on the West Side in the Rush/University of Illinois/Cook County medical complex.

The hospital landscape remains uncertain for the Chicago area's 121 hospitals. In 2011 the state of Illinois began to consider the tax-exempt status of nonprofit hospitals. National decisions regarding health care reform will have profound implications, especially for those hospitals often located in underserved areas that care for large numbers of Medicare patients.                                                              *Paul A. Buelow*

**Hotels.** When Chicago was a small village in 1830, the American palace hotel ideal was literally being cast in stone on the eastern seaboard. Therefore, the typical developmental pattern of traveler accommodations that proceeded elsewhere from tavern to city inn and then, beginning in the 1820s, to luxury hotel took place in Chicago rapidly and on a large scale. The first three taverns—Caldwell's Tavern (built by James Kinzie), the Miller House, and Mark Beaubien's tavern, soon known as the Sauganash Hotel—arose at Wolf's Point at the fork of the Chicago River during 1829 and 1830. In 1831 Beaubien added a frame addition to his log building, establishing Chicago's first hotel. Chicago's first Tremont House followed in 1833, and, though modest, it was no doubt named for Boston's remarkable Tremont House (1829). The Lake House opened in 1836 across the Chicago River from Fort Dearborn near where the Wrigley Building stands today. It was an elegant three-story brick building costing $90,000, and it served as a center for social and political activity.

During the mid-nineteenth century, the building, destruction, and rebuilding of hotels continued, fueled by fire and burgeoning development. The Tremont House, Briggs House, Palmer House, Sherman House, Adams House, Matteson House, Massasoit House, and Metropolitan House were among the pre-1871 hotels that served the city in luxurious style. These five-, six-, and seven-story block masonry buildings offered amenities such as steam heat, gas lighting, elevators, French chefs, and elegant surroundings. The Tremont House in particular, rebuilt for the third time in 1850, retained its position for many years as the city's leading hotel. Both Stephen A. Douglas and Abraham Lincoln spoke from its balcony to crowd-filled streets below, and in 1860 the hotel served as the headquarters for the Illinois Republican Party as it campaigned for Lincoln's presidential nomination. All of these hotels burned in the Great Fire of 1871. The Palmer House had been open only for a few months. Another hotel, the Grand Pacific, had been open only a few days.

The "Big Four" of the post-fire hotels included the Palmer House, the Grand Pacific, the Tremont, and the Sherman House. These buildings adopted the commercial palazzo style of architecture common to the grand hotel palaces of the East. All professed to be fireproof, above all, and boasted grand lobbies, monumental staircases, elegant parlors, cafés, barbershops, bridal suites, dining rooms, ballrooms, promenades, hundreds of private bedrooms and baths, and the latest luxuries. Typical room charges ranged from $3.50 to $7 per day and included three to four meals. Guests incurred extra charges for private parlors, room service, fires in private fireplaces, and desserts taken to one's room from the dinner table. Hotels like the Grand Pacific and the Palmer House not only served transient visitors but also appealed to wealthy permanent residents, who found in the palace hotel a convenient way to set up trouble-free elegant households. Hotels such as these served as models for other hotel construction, particularly in smaller American cities, where a luxury hotel symbolized and celebrated capitalist bourgeois values. Chicago also became a center for the hotel industry, with three of the major hotel trade journals being published in the city.

The architectural revolution that produced the skyscraper found its expression in Chicago's luxury hotels. First among these was Adler and Sullivan's Auditorium Building (1889), which featured a 400-room hotel in addition to the theater and 17-story office tower. A 400-room annex was added in anticipation of the 1893 World's Columbian Exhibition. The LaSalle Hotel (1908–9), one of the first of the new hotels to locate in the Loop, soared 22 stories into the Chicago skyline and claimed 1,000 bedrooms. A Michigan Avenue hotel strip anchored by the nationally renowned Blackstone (1910) included the Congress (formerly the Auditorium Annex) and the Auditorium. These were soon challenged by hotel development in the prosperous North Michigan Avenue region, where the Drake (1918–20) and the Allerton (1923–24) offered quiet, elegant alternatives with a view of the lake. The economic boom and population growth of the 1920s and Chicago's increasing attractiveness as a convention city led to a perceived shortfall in hotel rooms, remedied by the 2,000-room Morrison Hotel and the newest rendition of the Palmer House, a Holabird & Roche creation built in 1923–25 whose 25 stories housed 2,268 rooms and for a very short time held the record as the world's largest hotel.

This title soon passed to the Stevens Hotel (now the Chicago Hilton and Towers), developed by the Stevens family of the Illinois Life Insurance Company and owners of the LaSalle. Opened in 1927, the Stevens occupied an entire city block on Michigan Avenue between Seventh and Eighth Streets. Its 3,000 guest rooms and supporting facilities such as ballrooms, restaurants, retail shops, and meeting rooms were designed according to principles of mass production and retailing perfected for the hotel industry by E. M. Statler. The hotel's size and unsurpassed convention facilities depended on continuing national prosperity for economic viability. The Depression of the 1930s sent the Stevens into receivership, as it did for hundreds of other hotel properties across the nation. Chicago's hotel boom had temporarily come to a halt.

Chicago's hotel industry continued to expand during the second half of the twentieth century. After World War II, the growth of automobile travel led to the emergence of dozens of new "motels" in the suburbs. Meanwhile, the rise of airplane travel created new clusters of hotels near O'Hare Airport. By the end of the 1980s, the suburbs contained about 14,000 motel and hotel rooms. But the days of the large downtown hotels were far from over. Starting in the late 1980s, there was a new boom in luxury hotel construction and renovation in downtown Chicago. Huge new edifices such as the Hotel Nikko, the Four Seasons, and the 1,200-room Sheraton and Cityfront Center boosted the city's capacity to handle a large number of well-to-do business travelers and tourists. Chicago's ability to attract and retain large national conventions—many of which were held at its enormous McCormick Place facility—fueled this expansion and helped the business of all the area's hotels. As the twentieth century came to a close, there were roughly 75,000 hotel and motel rooms in the Chicago area, and more space was being added to handle the roughly 25 million people a year who stayed as guests in and around the city. By the time Chicago made its Olympic bid in 2010, it identified 700 hotels and more than 100,000 hotel rooms in the region.        *Molly W. Berger*

**Insurance.** Chicago is not an "insurance town" on a par with Hartford or New York City, but it still holds an important place in the history of the industry. While eastern cities were home to pioneering life insurance companies, Chicago insurers spurred historic growth and innovation in fire and automobile coverage, safety standards, and insurance for African Americans. The insurance industry also helped to shape and reshape the physical city and played a crucial role in the aftermath of the Great Fire of 1871.

The first insurance agent in Chicago was Gurdon Hubbard, a fur trader, investor, and speculator who arrived from Vermont in 1818. In 1834 Hubbard became the Chicago agent for the Aetna Insurance Company of Hartford, Connecticut, and this successful venture made him one of the city's most prominent midcentury businessmen. The Illinois Insurance Company, chartered in 1839, was the first insurance company to operate out of Chicago. The 1850s and 1860s were a period of growth for Chicago insurance, as more national companies opened midwestern offices and more Chicago-based firms were founded. By 1871 Chicago boasted 129 insurance companies, 14 of which were headquartered locally. Eighty-one were fire and marine insurers.

The Great Fire rocked the insurance world with the revelation that the industry was unprepared to meet such a massive calamity. Fifty-eight insurance companies were driven into bankruptcy by the fire. Even worse, thousands of policyholders were never compensated for their losses. While the venerable Gurdon Hubbard is said to have sold his own properties to meet the claims of some policyholders, in the end the industry paid the claims of only about half of the Chicagoans who had insurance policies.

The surviving insurance companies provided crucial capital for their policyholders to rebuild after the fire. But, by the most generous estimate, the insurance industry paid for less than a third of the total fire damage. Countless businesses and home owners were denied their insurance claims and were never able to start over. Still, some contemporaries argued that the fire was a boon to the insurance industry because it wiped out the most poorly managed insurance companies, and that the new barrage of fire regulations made Chicago "the safest insurance field in the world." This claim seemed verified in the 1870s, as the insurance industry rebounded dramatically. The terrible losses of the Great Fire led insurance companies to pioneer fire-safety procedures with an eye to protecting their reserves against similar disasters. The Chicago Board of Underwriters, the industry's trade organization, created new institutions of fire safety in Chicago, including a fire patrol (1871) and fire inspectors (1886). The insurance industry also spearheaded fire-safety improvements at the Union Stock Yard in the 1880s.

The Great Migration of African Americans to Chicago during the First World War spurred the next major development in Chicago insurance: the creation of insurance companies to serve the black community. In the 1890s, the life insurance industry's discriminatory practices had led to a proliferation of black-owned companies throughout the South. Chicago's Supreme Liberty Life Insurance Company, founded by Arkansas native Frank Gillespie in 1919, was the first northern black-owned insurance company. A tradition of saving for a dignified funeral made Chicago's black community an enthusiastic and stable market for life insurance, despite its poverty. Black-owned insurance companies were one of the few sources of white-collar jobs for Chicago's African Americans, and some firms, like the Chicago Metropolitan Assurance Company (founded in 1925), evoked nationalist sentiment by appealing to their policyholders' "race pride." However, the loss of African American customers to large insurers and the catastrophic black unemployment of the 1980s ended the age of the independent black insurance company. Supreme Life was purchased by a national white-owned insurer, but Metropolitan Assurance was acquired in 1990 by the black-owned Atlanta Life Insurance Company.

In 1931 the giant Sears, Roebuck & Co. leaped into the insurance business with the creation of Allstate Insurance Company, based on the novel idea of selling auto insurance policies by mail order. Recipients of the Sears catalog could simply clip a coupon from the book, mail it in, and receive an auto insurance policy by return post. After a few years, Allstate switched from mail to the more traditional agent sales and acquired a life insurance branch, but auto insurance remained its specialty. In 1939 Allstate was the first company to tailor its rates to the characteristics of automobiles and their owners, such as make, mileage, and age of driver. And, as with fire insurance companies in the previous century, Allstate's strategists realized that their best chance for steady profits lay in improving safety. The company introduced rate reductions for good drivers in 1939, and by the 1950s Allstate offered grants to improve the training of driving instructors and began to pressure automobile manufacturers to make safer cars. In partnership with other insurers, Allstate has worked to persuade Detroit to install safety features, from standardized bumpers to airbags, in all passenger vehicles. As Chicago's largest insurance company, Allstate contributed to the relocation of jobs to the suburbs by moving its headquarters out of downtown Chicago, first to Skokie in 1953 and then to Northbrook in 1967.

Kemper Insurance, Chicago's other major property and casualty company was founded in 1912 as Lumbermens Mutual Casualty Company to provide workmen's compensation for Chicago lumberyard workers. In health insurance, Chicago's best-known institution is the Blue Cross Blue Shield Association, headquarters for the federation of nationwide health and hospital insurance plans. The Chicago area is also home to the insurance industry's national research arm, Underwriters Laboratories Inc., which grew out of the old Chicago Board of Underwriters.

Chicago's skyline would not be the same without insurance companies. Insurers erected impressive Chicago landmarks like the Home Insurance Building (1884–85, by architect William Le Baron Jenney), the first skyscraper built using metal in its skeleton, and D. H. Burnham & Co.'s Insurance Exchange Building (1912). Two of Chicago's best-known (and most-criticized) skyscrapers, the Prudential Building and the John Hancock Center, bear the names of East Coast insurers. The landmark Standard Oil Building, currently Chicago's second tallest, in 2000 was renamed for the Aon Corporation. Aon, a giant insurance and brokerage company that adopted its name in 1987, resulted from the merger of Combined Insurance Corporation, founded by Chicagoan W. Clement Stone in 1919, and the

Ryan Insurance Group, founded by Patrick G. Ryan in 1964. By 2010 three insurance companies—Allstate, CNA Financial, and AON—were among Chicago's largest public corporations.                    *Beatrix Hoffman*

**Iron and Steel.** Iron and steel mills have ranked among the largest economic enterprises in the Chicago region since before the Civil War. During the second half of the nineteenth century, the area became one of the world's leading centers of steel production. For much of the twentieth century, tens of thousands of area residents worked to turn iron ore into steel and shape steel into a variety of products. Only after the U.S. steel industry suffered a sudden decline in the 1970s did Chicago-area mills begin to shut down and lay off thousands of workers.

The emergence of a large iron and steel industry in the Chicago region during the nineteenth century was a function of entrepreneurial effort and geographical advantage. Mills could obtain raw materials from the vast iron ore deposits in the Lake Superior region relatively cheaply and easily. Because most of the iron ore used by the American steel industry during its rise was mined in Minnesota and Michigan, mills located along the Great Lakes were well positioned to enjoy lower costs than their competitors elsewhere, especially after 1924, when U.S. government regulators ended the "Pittsburgh Plus" pricing system that had protected Pennsylvania mills from competition.

As Chicago grew from small town to world-class city between the 1840s and 1880s, the shape of the iron and steel industry was transformed completely. By the beginning of the 1850s, the city was home to several iron foundries, which melted preprocessed iron ingots and cast them into products such as stoves or boilers. But the first great iron-shaping enterprises in the Chicago area were mills that produced rails for the railroads. The local pioneer in this field was Eber B. Ward, who used part of a fortune made in the Great Lakes shipping business to build Chicago's first rail-rolling mill in 1857. Located on the North Branch of the Chicago River, Ward's plant was known as the North Chicago Rolling Mill Company. By 1860, when it employed about 200 men, it already ranked as one of the city's biggest enterprises; a decade later, it had expanded into a very large facility with 1,000 workers. In 1865 this mill experimented with rails made

Chicago's earliest metalworking industries were small in scale and located near the Chicago River in what is now central Chicago. The first steel mills and blast furnaces, supplying them with raw material, were not much farther out. As ironworks and steelworks grew enormously in size, companies moved to remote sites with abundant—and cheap—land and water, mostly on the southern metropolitan fringe, with its ample harbors for lakeborne iron ore imports and proximity to coal supplies. Large plants were built in southeast Chicago and northwestern Indiana, where lonely sand dunes and swamps were transformed into vast industrial areas. Joliet and Chicago Heights emerged as lesser steel centers, and early wire mills centered in nearby DeKalb (not shown) and Joliet. Small steelmaking operations, rolling mills, and pipe and wire works were somewhat more widely scattered along the region's railways. By 2000 most steelmaking in the city of Chicago had ceased.

# The Chicago Area's Iron and Steel Industry

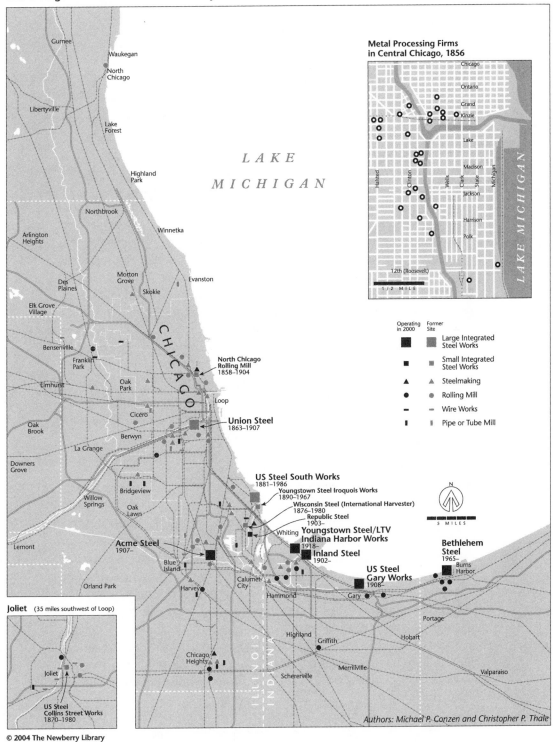

## Metal Processing Firms in Central Chicago, 1856

Chicago
Ontario
Grand
Kinzie
Lake
Madison
Jackson
Harrison
Polk
12th (Roosevelt)

Halsted
Clinton
Wells
Clark
State
Michigan

LAKE MICHIGAN

1/2 MILE

L A K E
M I C H I G A N

| Operating in 2000 | Former Site | |
|---|---|---|
| ■ | ▬ | Large Integrated Steel Works |
| ■ | ▪ | Small Integrated Steel Works |
| ▲ | ▲ | Steelmaking |
| ● | ● | Rolling Mill |
| ▬ | ▬ | Wire Works |
| ▮ | ▮ | Pipe or Tube Mill |

Gurnee
Waukegan
North Chicago
Libertyville
Lake Forest
Highland Park
Northbrook
Winnetka
Arlington Heights
Morton Grove
Evanston
Des Plaines
Skokie
Elk Grove Village
Bensenville
Franklin Park
Oak Park
Elmhurst
Cicero
Oak Brook
Berwyn
La Grange
Downers Grove
Bridgeview
Willow Springs
Oak Lawn
Lemont
Blue Island
Orland Park
Harvey
Calumet City
Hammond
Highland
Griffith
Hobart
Merrillville
Schererville
Valparaiso
Portage
Gary

C H I C A G O

Loop

North Chicago Rolling Mill 1858–1904

Union Steel 1863–1907

US Steel South Works 1881–1986
Youngstown Steel Iroquois Works 1890–1967
Wisconsin Steel (International Harvester) 1876–1980
Republic Steel 1903–
Whiting
Youngstown Steel/LTV Indiana Harbor Works 1918–
Inland Steel 1902–
Acme Steel 1907–

US Steel Gary Works 1908–

Bethlehem Steel 1965–
Burns Harbor

Chicago Heights

N

5 MILES

I L L I N O I S
I N D I A N A

Authors: Michael P. Conzen and Christopher P. Thale

## Joliet (35 miles southwest of Loop)

Joliet

US Steel Collins Street Works 1870–1980

© 2004 The Newberry Library

out of Bessemer steel ingots—the first such rails produced in the United States. At the beginning of the 1880s, Ward's company opened a sister mill at the mouth of the Calumet River on Chicago's South Side—the famous South Works. Meanwhile, several other mills had been established and became major rail producers. One of these was the Union Rolling Mill Company, built in 1863 on the South Branch of the Chicago River and employing about 600 workers by 1873. Another was the Joliet Iron and Steel Company, which employed about 1,500 men soon after it opened in 1871. By the 1880s, these three companies together accounted for nearly 30 percent of the total U.S. output of steel rails.

In the final years of the nineteenth century, the steel industry in Chicago and around the country was simultaneously expanding and consolidating. By this time, Chicago-area mills sold large quantities of iron and steel products to the railroads and companies that built skyscrapers and bridges, as well as to those that made goods such as pipe, containers, and wire. Dozens of area companies, from giants such as Pullman and Crane to much smaller firms, generated considerable local demand for steel. As local and national demand rose, mergers were thinning the numbers of steel producers. One of the first great mergers occurred in 1889, when most of the large Chicago-area mills—including North Chicago, South Works, Union, and Joliet—combined to form a huge new entity, the Illinois Steel Company. The world's largest steel company, Illinois Steel not only owned multiple mills employing a total of about 10,000 men but also controlled iron mines, coal mines, and transportation systems. By the end of the nineteenth century, workers at the various Chicago-area mills owned by this company were turning out about a million tons of finished steel per year.

During the first part of the twentieth century, even after many of Chicago's largest mills were absorbed into a giant national corporation, the area's importance within the American steel industry continued to rise. The most important single development in the history of the industry occurred in 1901, when New York banker J. P. Morgan engineered the creation of U.S. Steel, the world's largest business enterprise. Illinois Steel (by then also known as Federal Steel, a holding company created by Chicago lawyer Elbert H. Gary in 1898) became part of this giant entity. U.S. Steel closed some of the Chicago-area mills, but the South Works—which employed about 11,000 people in 1910—stood as one of its largest plants. And in 1906, U.S. Steel built a huge new mill on the south shore of Lake Michigan in what would become Gary, Indiana. By the 1920s, the Gary Works had 12 blast furnaces and over 16,000 employees, making it the largest steel plant in the country.

Although it dominated the industry, U.S. Steel was not the only important steel company in the Chicago area during the early twentieth century. Several local companies also operated large mills in the Calumet district and northern Indiana. Inland Steel, which was established in Chicago Heights in 1893, became a major player in the steel industry in 1901 when it decided to build a large new plant at Indiana Harbor. Inland Steel grew steadily through the 1930s, when the Indiana Harbor plant had four blast furnaces and over 9,000 employees. Another important local plant was the South Deering facility of Wisconsin Steel, which supplied metal to International Harvester, its Chicago-based corporate parent. Other important steel companies in the area during the early twentieth century included Republic Steel, Acme Steel, Youngstown Sheet & Tube, and Interlake Iron. Together with the U.S. Steel plants, all of these smaller companies made the Chicago area an increasingly important center of steel production.

The growth of the steel industry during the early twentieth century was accompanied by serious conflict between companies and their employees. Iron- and steelworkers in the Chicago area had been forming associations since the middle of the nineteenth century. Starting in the 1870s, hundreds of them became members of the Amalgamated Association of Iron and Steel Workers, a national group. During the first part of the twentieth century, Amalgamated and other groups led organized efforts designed to win higher wages, shorter hours, and safer working conditions. Many steelworkers at this time worked 12-hour shifts, six or seven days a week, in hazardous environments. For the most part, strikes at Chicago-area plants between 1900 and 1920 ended in defeat for workers. The largest of these strikes occurred in 1919, when 90,000 Chicago-area workers led an industry-wide, national protest coordinated by the American Federation of Labor (AFL) that sought union recognition and the eight-hour day. The strike temporarily halted steel production, but after state and federal troops were called in, workers returned to their plants. A nationwide collapse followed soon thereafter. When the steel industry agreed to an eight-hour day in 1923, the change resulted more from public pressure and the efforts of President Harding than from the strength of organized labor.

During the 1930s, in the midst of the Great Depression and the reforms of the New Deal, steelworkers in the Chicago area and across the nation finally won substantial gains through unionization. The successful unionization efforts of the 1930s brought together tens of thousands of workers of various ethnic backgrounds. At the turn of the century, most steelworkers in the Calumet and Indiana mills had been immigrants from southern and eastern Europe. During the 1910s and 1920s, large numbers of Mexican and African American men found work in the mills. Often area steel companies attempted to exploit ethnic differences among workers to fight unionization. For many years, steelworkers were divided by ethnicity and craft distinctions. But in the late 1930s, after New Deal legislation made unionization easier, workers were organized across the industry. In Chicago and elsewhere, Amalgamated joined the Steel Workers Organizing Committee of the Congress of Industrial Organizations (CIO) in launching a 1936 organization drive that won recognition by U.S. Steel in 1937. The most violent of the Chicago-area clashes accompanying this effort was the Memorial Day Massacre, in which ten people were killed by police gunfire during a strike outside the East Side plant of Republic Steel. But this incident did not prevent unionization, and in 1942 steelworkers formed a powerful national union, the United Steelworkers of America (USWA). By the beginning of the 1970s, when the USWA counted 130,000 members in the Chicago region, the predominant ethnic groups in the mills were Mexicans and African Americans.

From the 1940s until the 1970s, the steel industry remained one of the Chicago area's leading economic sectors. Immediately after World War II, the United States was making over half the world's steel, and mills in Indiana and Illinois accounted for about 20 percent of total U.S. production capacity. Many of the large open-hearth plants established in the early part of the century continued to make huge amounts of steel. Between 1959 and 1964, Interlake and Wisconsin Steel became two of the first U.S. mills to install basic oxygen furnaces, which were faster and cheaper than the older open-hearth equipment. Meanwhile, a large new plant was built by Bethlehem Steel at Burns Harbor, Indiana. The last giant mill constructed in the Chicago region, the Bethlehem plant helped make the Illinois-Indiana region the geographical center of the U.S. steel industry at the end of the 1960s.

During the Cold War, when most Chicago-area steelworkers were represented by the USWA, relatively high wage levels did not prevent labor conflict. Between 1945 and 1959, there were five industry-wide strikes. In 1952 about 80,000 Chicago-area steelworkers walked out for two months. An even more serious work stoppage occurred in 1959, when tens of thousands of workers in the Chicago area joined 500,000 steelworkers nationwide in a four-month strike to win changes in work rules, wage levels, and benefits.

During the 1970s and 1980s, the U.S. steel industry suffered a sudden collapse that threw thousands out of work. U.S. Steel and other American steel companies that still depended upon large numbers of older, inefficient plants failed to withstand the combination of a decline in demand and the rise of international competition in the 1970s. The sudden decline of American steel stunned the employees of mills across the Chicago area. Between 1979 and 1986, about 16,000 Chicago-area steelworkers lost their jobs. Wisconsin Steel closed abruptly in 1980 after attempts at a financial bailout failed. South Works endured a prolonged shutdown before closing its doors in 1992. Inland Steel cut thousands of workers. Republic Steel dismissed half its employees, and in 1984 it merged with LTV Steel, which declared bankruptcy in 1986. The closures left many steelworkers without jobs or health care and decimated communities in northwest Indiana and the Calumet district.

During the final years of the twentieth century, the Chicago region continued to be a leading center of production in an American steel industry that was much weaker and smaller than it had been before. By the mid-1980s, the area was home to several "mini-mills," small-scale plants that used sophisticated electric furnaces to recycle scrap metal. By the end of the 1980s, mills in northern Indiana were making about a quarter of all the steel produced in the United States. While the region remained a center of steel production, the industry was no longer the powerhouse that had been a crucial part of the Chicago-area economy for over a century.

The global reorganization of the steel industry at the beginning of the twenty-first century continued to reshape the remnants of the steel industry still in the Chicago area. Ispat International, which in 1998 purchased Inland Steel, merged in 2006 with ISG (International Steel Group), which owned both Acme and LTV, to create Netherlands-headquartered Mittal Steel. The following year, Mittal merged with Luxembourg-based Arcelor to create ArcelorMittal, the largest steel-producing company in the world. The new company located its North American headquarters in Chicago and continues to operate mills in northwestern Indiana.

*David Bensman and Mark R. Wilson*

**Law.** As Chicago's businesses grew in the late nineteenth century, so too did the city's need for a cadre of capable lawyers to handle the myriad problems caused by industrial expansion. Over the next century, solo practitioners and small partnerships gave way to large and powerful regional, national, and even international firms. The sheer number of lawyers practicing in the city grew rapidly, from some five dozen in 1850 to over 4,300 in 1900, about 14,000 in 1970, and 29,000 in the early 1990s. Moreover, the ranks of Chicago lawyers gradually, and sometimes grudgingly, opened to include Jews, African Americans, and women. Over this same period, the kind of law that lawyers practiced changed and evolved. Abraham Lincoln—who served a brief apprenticeship, later practicing in Chicago and other Illinois courts while the other partner in his firm tended to office matters—would have been hard-pressed to recognize the activities of twenty-first-century lawyers as having any connection to the practice of law as he knew it.

Perhaps the most revolutionary change in the practice of law in Chicago has been the emergence of the large firm as the most effective way to organize the day-to-day activities of lawyers. In the mid-nineteenth century, the practice of law was largely carried on by solo practitioners or small firms of fewer than five lawyers. The creation of the modern corporation and modern industry created new areas of legal concern, leading to changes in legal practice. Corporate and securities law emerged, and tort law developed in response to railroad accidents. Large firms could meet corporate clients' diverse and extensive legal needs under one roof, typically by distributing the work to specialists within the firm. Growth occurred gradually. For example, in 1906 Holt, Cutting & Sidley consisted of 4 lawyers, 4 clerks, and a non-lawyer staff of 10, but by 1957 the firm (then known as Sidley & Austin) had 29 partners and 20 associates, and over the next few decades it grew to include hundreds of lawyers. Such firms began adding departments to deal with new areas of the law, such as the administrative law revolution that the New Deal initiated. Large firms became dominant only after the middle of the twentieth century. In 1948, 6 of 10 Chicago lawyers were still solo practitioners, but only 1 in 5 was a solo practitioner by 1975; and almost as many worked in firms of more than 30 lawyers. Firms also expanded their client base from regional to national and even international. For example, after World War II, the Chicago-based firm of Baker & McKenzie undertook to serve an international market by opening an average of one new office each year. By 2000 the firm had 60 offices in 35 countries.

The other radical change in the legal profession that occurred between the mid-nineteenth century and the twenty-first century was the integration of groups other than white Anglo-Saxon Protestant males into the practitioners' ranks. The Illinois Supreme Court rejected Myra Bradwell's attempt to join the bar despite her passing the bar exam in 1869. However, in 1872 the Illinois legislature mandated that women be admitted to the bar. Members of other groups such as Jews, African Americans, and eastern European immigrants were allowed to get a license but were not hired by the firms that controlled the most lucrative business. The Chicago Bar Association was open only to invited members and did not admit African Americans until 1945, when, after a two-year battle, it admitted Earl B. Dickerson to membership. By the end of the twentieth century, although white males still predominated at the senior-partner level of elite law firms, the official policy of firms in hiring associates has evolved to value diversity of race, religion, national origin, and gender.

Lawyers also practice in different and more specialized areas of the law than did the general practitioner of the mid-nineteenth century, and, unlike most nineteenth-century lawyers, they are college educated and law school trained in these specialties. The New Deal inaugurated a new type of law practice in front of regulatory agencies such as the Securities and Exchange Commission. An entire segment of legal business grew out of the expansion of tort liability to allow recovery when manufacturers placed defective products into the stream of commerce. By the late twentieth century, the computer revolution and the Internet had created yet a new area of legal practice, information technology, and made intellectual property a new battleground in the fight to control the fruits of this revolution. Law firms with ties to Chicago were leaders in developing the expertise to deal with all of these changes in the law and many others.

*R. Ben Brown*

**Liquor Distribution.** The agricultural trade of the Midwest, particularly in grain and hops, made Chicago a natural choice for liquor manufacturing and retailing. The industry formed in close conjunction with Chicago's social evolution as it responded both to demand and to movements to limit the production, sale, and consumption of liquor.

Chicago's retail liquor trade began in 1827, when Samuel Miller and Archibald Clybourne established the Miller House, a store that doubled as the town's first tavern, serving a crude ale as well as some imported beer. By 1837 there were 10 taverns, 26 groceries—many of which sold liquor—and 1 brewery.

In 1860 Chicago had 8 distilleries, but by the 1890s Peoria had emerged as the center of distilling in Illinois. Beer production, however, grew enormously, particularly after 1870. By the turn of the century, the city had over 50 breweries, the great majority run by Germans. Because breweries depended on saloonkeepers for their livelihood, they tried to win the saloonkeepers' loyalty by such means as promising loans for remodeling or paying license fees. The brewers also became directly involved in the retail trade by opening their own saloons. By 1900 brewers dominated most of the barrooms of Chicago.

Ironically, organized efforts to restrict liquor spurred industry cooperation. In the early 1870s, the Liberty League, made up of both dealers and saloonkeepers, was the first organization of liquor dealers in Chicago. In 1880 the Illinois Liquor Dealers Protective Association, the industry's first statewide lobby, was organized. Local interest groups formed at the same time, some at the neighborhood level, including the South Side Saloon Keepers Association and the Hyde Park Liquor Dealers Association.

Even before Prohibition, the liquor industry faced problems. A 1907 act that allowed individual precincts and wards to enact their own prohibition laws led to the forced closure of saloons in two-thirds of the city. Grain conservation regulations during World War I restricted production of alcoholic beverages, and anti-German sentiment made beer drinking unpopular. After passage of the Eighteenth Amendment enacting Prohibition, brewery owners desperately searched for prospective buyers of their establishments. Some brewers, aided by mobsters, continued to produce alcohol illegally. Others turned to the manufacture of non-alcoholic drinks or made ends meet by selling the raw materials that went into liquor production.

After Prohibition, persistent gangster connections and incursions by stronger national corporations into the Chicago market dashed the hopes of local liquor manufacturers for an economic resurgence. A handful of national companies dominated the distilling industry, and wine and beer production eventually became concentrated as well. By 1984, 94 percent of American beer was produced by six companies, none in Chicago.

In the 1930s, aluminum beer cans and non-returnable bottles, coupled with widespread ownership of refrigerators, allowed consumers to drink cold beer at home. Packaged goods, sold in grocery and liquor stores, soon outstripped tavern sales. Drinking establishments remained but distanced themselves from the ethos of the old saloons. Federal and state legislation aimed to eliminate the "tied house." Wholesalers became the intermediary between beer, wine, and liquor producers and retailers (grocers, drugstores, taverns, liquor stores). In 1989 the Chicago Beer Wholesalers Association included some 30 wholesalers, each typically with a few dozen employees, each contracting with brewers to distribute exclusively in specified territories. Wine and liquor distribution became extremely concentrated in the 1980s and 1990s. Wirtz Beverage Group, with operations in Chicagoland and several other states, is the area's largest distributor.

*Sudhir Venkatesh*

**Lumber.** Lumber, along with grain and meatpacking, was one of the "big three" commodities of nineteenth-century Chicago commerce. Through the second half of the nineteenth century, Chicago was the world's greatest lumber market. The city owed its status to geography, transportation, and population. Geography placed Chicago in close proximity to the dense forests of the Upper Great Lakes, rail and water transportation links made Chicago the natural hub for moving forest products, and the city's phenomenal population growth made it one of the single largest markets for lumber.

The commercial lumber business began in Chicago in 1833 with the arrival of a shipload of cottonwood boards from St. Joseph, Michigan. During the 1830s and 1840s, the industry was largely focused on supplying the local market with building material. It was not unusual for farmers bringing a wagon of wheat across the prairie to Chicago to return home with a load of lumber for a frame house or outbuilding. The opening of the Illinois & Michigan Canal allowed Chicago to emerge as a national lumber distribution center. The amount of lumber flowing into Chicago in 1848, the year the canal opened, was nearly double that of the previous year.

The Illinois & Michigan Canal transformed the Lake Michigan basin into a funnel through which the forest products of Wisconsin and Michigan were deposited in Chicago for sale throughout the western United States. During the navigation season, a steady stream of logging schooners departed the mill towns of the north woods. During the 1860s and 1870s, a northerly wind could bring as many as 200 ships into the Chicago River on a single day. The crowd of ships in the river would force open the numerous swing bridges and bring downtown traffic to a maddening standstill. The destination of the lumber ships was the extensive lumber district that stretched out along the South Branch of the river all the way to the western margins of the city. "The timber yards are a considerable part of the city's surface," a British tourist remarked in 1887, "there appearing to be enough boards and planks piled up to supply a half-dozen States."

Numerous slips excavated into the banks of the river and extending for blocks into the district provided the lumber schooners with 12 miles of dockage space. Manpower in the form of burly lumber shovers unloaded the schooners. Working the docks of the district was a rite of passage for many immigrants to the nineteenth-century city. Lumber yards hired the fastest and cheapest workers they could find, so there was constant turnover among the stevedores. During the Civil War, labor gangs of Irish men not infrequently came to blows with African American lumber shovers over who had the right to unload a particular ship. In the Railroad Strike of 1877, Bohemian lumber shovers spearheaded the upheaval that resulted in pitched battles with police and a radicalization of workers in Chicago.

The decline of Chicago as the leading lumber market was tied to the exhaustion of the forests of the Upper Great Lakes region and changes in the economics of distribution. By 1900 Chicago lumber merchants, although heavily invested in the north woods, anticipated the decline and invested in southern pine lands. Into the 1920s, leading companies such as Edward Hines kept the city a major market by stocking their Chicago wholesale yard with trainloads of southern yellow pine. Hines and other lumber merchants also developed new northern hardwood products from their Michigan and Wisconsin forest operations. Yet the manufacture of lumber for specialized products such as flooring, furniture, and trim required new facilities that could be more cheaply built near the source of the supply than at a central distribution center. Railroad and communication networks that allowed Chicago to access southern pine also encouraged the distribution of lumber directly from the mill site, saving on the costly transshipment to, and storage at, Chicago. By the end of the 1920s, it was clear that the future of Chicago's lumber industry was in supplying the still considerable local market, the era of national significance having passed.                                                                *Theodore J. Karamanski*

**Mail Order.** Mail-order retailing became a big business in Chicago. During the half century that followed the establishment of a mail-order company by Aaron Montgomery Ward in 1872, Chicago companies dominated the business of selling directly to consumers across the country by using catalogs and deliveries through the mail. Montgomery Ward and Sears, Roebuck & Co., both based in Chicago, were the leaders of the early mail-order industry and became giant enterprises through catalog sales long before they began to open retail stores. Even after the 1920s, when the growth of the mail-order business slowed, Chicago companies continued to stand among its leaders. By the end of the twentieth century, when Montgomery Ward went out of business entirely and Sears no longer issued giant catalogs, the city's mail-order industry was no longer the precocious adolescent it had been in 1900. Nevertheless, Chicago remained home to several leading companies in an evolving but still important sector of the economy.

Montgomery Ward & Co., the world's first giant mail-order enterprise, started in Chicago just after the Great Fire of 1871. Aaron Montgomery

Ward, a native of New Jersey, arrived in the city following the Civil War. He soon found a job with Field, Palmer & Leiter, the dry-goods wholesaler and retailer that would become Marshall Field & Co. Ward left town to work as a salesman in St. Louis and the South, but he soon returned. In 1872, when he was twenty-eight, he opened his own business. Ward's company tried to convince rural consumers to buy a variety of goods (including clothing, furniture, and hardware) through the mail. It turned out that many farm families were willing and able to do so, especially after Ward initiated a policy of "satisfaction guaranteed or your money back" in 1875. Among Ward's first customers were members of the Patrons of Husbandry (or Grange), an agrarian organization that liked the idea of circumventing local mercantile middlemen by buying directly from Chicago. Ward advertised by sending out a catalog, which started as a single page but expanded quickly, growing to 32 pages in 1874, 152 pages in 1876, and nearly 1,000 pages by 1897. By the 1880s, the growing volume of orders from this catalog led Ward to employ over a 100 Chicagoans as clerks; by 1897 this workforce was up to over a 1,000. By that time, Ward's company had become Chicago's leading user of the U.S. mails, and annual sales had ballooned to about $7 million.

The heyday of the mail-order business occurred between the 1890s and the 1910s, when it was dominated by Montgomery Ward and Sears, Roebuck. During this period, these companies became two of the largest business enterprises in the United States. Montgomery Ward, which opened several mail-order branches across the country during the first part of the twentieth century, was employing over 7,000 men and women in the Chicago area by 1910. By 1913 Montgomery Ward was selling about $40 million worth of goods per year. Even more astounding than the rapid growth of Montgomery Ward was the rise of Sears. The firm of Sears, Roebuck & Co., which settled in Chicago in 1895, was the creation of a Minnesotan named Richard W. Sears. After getting his start in the 1880s by selling watches through the mail, Sears (whose partner Alvah C. Roebuck started as a watch repairman) established a general mail-order company along the lines of Montgomery Ward. Only a few years after its birth, Sears overtook Montgomery Ward as the leading mail-order company. Like Montgomery Ward, Sears issued giant catalogs and succeeded in attracting orders for a variety of goods from hundreds of thousands of rural consumers. By 1905 Sears had about 9,000 employees, and its annual sales approached $50 million. Much of its success was overseen by Julius Rosenwald, who became a partner in the company in 1895 and became its president after Richard Sears retired in 1909. By 1914, when Sears had branches in Dallas and Seattle in addition to its central operation in Chicago, the company's annual mail-order sales had surpassed $100 million.

By the early part of the twentieth century, the mail-order retailing business—led by the Chicago giants—had become a major sector of the American economy, through which millions of rural consumers purchased a variety of goods. This development—which was part of a general trend in which commodity consumption by individuals and households was taking on greater economic and cultural significance—was both embraced and resisted. By 1919 Americans were buying over $500 million worth of goods a year from mail-order companies (roughly half of this business went to Montgomery Ward and Sears alone). The millions of bulky mail-order catalogs sent from Chicago to points around the country had become important cultural documents, with significance that went beyond the purely economic. Particularly in rural areas, which were still home to half of the American population as late as 1920, the catalogs served not only as a marketing tool, but also as school readers, almanacs, symbols of abundance and progress, and objects of fantasy and desire. For many consumers, the kind of mail-order retailing pioneered by Montgomery Ward and Sears offered a wider variety of goods (which ranged from the smallest items to entire houses), more generous credit terms, and lower prices than they could get from local merchants. Farmers' groups, which tended to favor the bypassing of economic intermediaries, were supporters of the mail-order business from the beginning. Local merchants, on the other hand, fought the national mail-order houses in both the economic and political arenas. Between the 1890s and the 1910s, U.S. postal policy became a battleground for retailers. The adoption of rural free delivery in 1898 and parcel post in 1913, both of which were enacted by Congress over the objections of local retailers and their allies, represented victories for the mail-order business and for Chicago.

Montgomery Ward and Sears were not the only Chicago companies running successful mail-order enterprises during the early twentieth century. The Hartman Company, which sold furniture by mail out of its central depot on Wentworth Avenue, filled about $13 million in orders per year by the early 1920s. Another Chicago furniture dealer that would eventually become one of the most important firms in the mail-order industry was Spiegel. This company's founder, the German-born Joseph Spiegel, started a home furnishings company in Chicago just after the Civil War. In 1904 Joseph and his son Arthur decided to move into mail order. By 1929 the Spiegel family's company (which by then sold women's clothing as well as furniture) was selling over $20 million in goods per year through the mail. A strategy of generous consumer credit, low prices, and high volume allowed Spiegel to accomplish the remarkable feat of expanding its operations during the Great Depression.

During the 1920s, facing slower growth in sales, the Chicago mail-order giants decided to move into a new form of retailing by opening large numbers of stores around the country. Catalog sales continued, but Sears and Montgomery Ward soon ranked among the world's leading chain stores. Led by Sears chief Robert E. Wood, this change represented a massive transfer of capital from mail-order to brick-and-mortar retailing. By 1929, only five years after opening its first store, Sears had over 300 stores around the country; Wards had about 500. By the beginning of the 1930s, mail order was no longer the primary concern of the Chicago giants, which continued to grow and stand among the country's leading companies.

During the second half of the twentieth century, the original Chicago mail-order giants and their catalog operations faltered, but other local companies prospered in what continued to be a major industry. By the 1970s, when the mail-order business accounted for about a third of U.S. postal revenues, most catalog customers lived in urban areas. By this time, the volume of Sears's annual mail-order business was about $3 billion, and that of Montgomery Ward was close to $1 billion. But these mail-order sales (as well as those at the companies' stores) were no longer very profitable. During the 1980s and 1990s, both Montgomery Ward and Sears stopped issuing their big catalogs. The death of Montgomery Ward in 2000 was a final sign that the age of the Chicago mail-order giants was over. At the same time, however, the American mail-order business was expanding, and more specialized catalog firms in Chicago stood among its leaders. Spiegel—which in 1953 had chosen to pursue a different path from Sears and Montgomery Ward by abandoning its retail stores—continued to operate out of headquarters in the Chicago area, where it employed about 4,000 local residents during the 1970s. In 1988 Spiegel acquired the Eddie Bauer retail stores and mail-order brand. By the 1990s, the company had about 20,000 employees worldwide and did over $3 billion in annual sales. Other leading mail-order specialists based in the Chicago region during the late twentieth century included Hammacher Schlemmer, the Quill Corporation, and the Reliable Corporation, which together sold hundreds of millions of dollars' worth of office supplies and equipment. At the opening of the twenty-first century, as some old mail-order catalogs were being replaced or supplemented with electronic versions, the city continued to be a leading hub in the industry.        *Mark R. Wilson*

**Management Consulting.** Management consulting has a distinguished history in Chicago. Soon after Arthur Andersen, a professor of accounting at Northwestern University, founded his eponymous firm in 1913, Arthur Andersen & Co. began to specialize in "financial investigations," the forerunner of the modern consulting study. By 2001, when Andersen Consulting reorganized as an independent public corporation named Accenture, it was the largest consulting firm in the world, with its headquarters still in Chicago. In 1914 Edwin Booz, a recent graduate of Northwestern in psychology, founded his firm, Booz Surveys, which would eventually become the international consulting firm of Booz Allen Hamilton Inc. Chicago's early dominance in consulting culminated in 1926 when James O. McKinsey, a leading expert on cost accounting at the University of Chicago, founded James O. McKinsey & Co. In 1939, two years after McKinsey's death, the original firm split into McKinsey & Co., the New York office, and A. T. Kearney & Co., the Chicago office, managed by Andrew "Tom" Kearney. All four of these management consulting firms—Accenture, Booz Allen, McKinsey, and A. T. Kearney—remained among the largest and most influential consultancies in the world.

The historical success of Chicago's consulting firms can be explained, in large part, by Chicago's small investment banking community prior to World War II. Instead of employing local banking staff, New York and Boston financiers hired Chicago consultants to analyze the management of the midwestern companies in which they planned to invest. When New Deal banking legislation in the 1930s prohibited banks from performing internal investigations, Wall Street bankers turned instead to the Chicago consulting firms to investigate East Coast companies. By the 1940s, the consultancies from Chicago dominated the national market, and beginning in the late 1950s, these same firms expanded into Europe with remarkable success. Other nationally known Chicago consultants from the 1940s and 1950s included George Fry (a former partner of Booz, Fry Allen, & Hamilton) and George S. May, a notorious marketer who was investigated by the Kefauver Commission for his ties to Chicago gangsters.

By the early 1960s, the three leading consulting firms in the United States—McKinsey & Co., Booz Allen Hamilton, and Cresap, McCormick & Paget (a spin-off from Booz Allen)—did more business in New York than Chicago. Their Chicago roots, however, were memorialized in the Cresap Laboratory and the Allen Center at Northwestern University. Chicago's industrial strength and its distance from Wall Street nurtured the development of consulting expertise that came to dominate the international market for managerial advice.                    *Christopher McKenna*

**Meatpacking.** The preparation of beef and pork for human consumption has always been closely tied to livestock raising, technological change, government regulation, and urban market demand. From the Civil War until the 1920s, Chicago was the country's largest meatpacking center and the acknowledged headquarters of the industry.

Europeans brought cattle and hogs to North America, let them forage in the woods, and slaughtered them only as meat was needed. Commercial butchering began when population increased in the towns. Since beef was difficult to preserve, cattle were killed year-round and the meat sold and consumed while still fresh. Hogs were killed only in cold weather. Their fat was rendered into lard and their flesh carved into hams, shoulders, and sides, which were covered with salt and packed in wooden barrels. Packers utilized hides, but blood, bones, and entrails usually went into the nearest body of running water. City government, understandably, tried to confine these operations to the outskirts of town.

Americans took their cattle and hogs over the Appalachians after the Revolutionary War, and the volume of livestock in the Ohio River Valley increased rapidly. Cincinnati packers took advantage of this development and shipped barreled pork and lard throughout the valley and down the

Mississippi River. They devised better methods to cure pork and used lard components to make soap and candles. By 1840 Cincinnati led all other cities in pork processing and proclaimed itself Porkopolis.

Chicago won that title during the Civil War. It was able to do so because most midwestern farmers also raised livestock, and railroads tied Chicago to its midwestern hinterland and to the large urban markets on the East Coast. In addition, Union army contracts for processed pork and live cattle supported packinghouses on the branches of the Chicago River and the railroad stockyards that shipped cattle. To alleviate the problem of driving cattle and hogs through city streets, the leading packers and railroads incorporated the Union Stock Yard and Transit Company in 1865 and built an innovative facility south of the city limits. Accessible to all railroads serving Chicago, the huge stockyard received 3 million cattle and hogs in 1870 and 12 million just 20 years later.

Between the opening of the Union Stock Yard in 1865 and the end of the century, Chicago meatpackers transformed the industry. Pork packers such as Philip Armour built large plants west of the stockyards, developed ice-cooled rooms so they could pack year-round, and introduced steam hoists to elevate carcasses and an overhead assembly line to move them. Gustavus Swift, who came to Chicago to ship cattle, developed a way to send fresh-chilled beef in ice-cooled railroad cars all the way to the East Coast. By 1900 this dressed beef trade was as important as pork packing, and mechanical refrigeration increased the efficiency of both pork and beef operations. Moreover, Chicago packers were preserving meat in tin cans, manufacturing an inexpensive butter substitute called oleomargarine, and, with the help of chemists, turning previously discarded parts of the animals into glue, fertilizer, glycerin, ammonia, and gelatin.

The extension of railroads and livestock raising to the Great Plains prompted the largest Chicago packing companies to build branch plants in Kansas City, Omaha, Sioux City, Wichita, Denver, Fort Worth, and elsewhere. To promote their dressed beef in eastern cities, they built branch sales offices and cold storage warehouses. When railroads balked at investing in refrigerator cars, they purchased their own and leased them to the railroads. Thus, Chicago's Big Three packers—Philip Armour, Gustavus Swift, and Nelson Morris—were in a position to influence livestock prices at one end of this complex industrial chain and the price of meat products at the other end. In 1900 the Chicago packinghouses employed 25,000 of the country's 68,000 packinghouse employees. The city's lead was narrower at the end of World War I, but Chicago was still, in Carl Sandburg's words, "Hog Butcher for the World."

Government surveillance and regulation kept pace with the growth of the meatpacking industry. Even before Chicago annexed the Union Stock Yard and packinghouse district (Packingtown), city government tried to control smoke, odors, and waste disposal. Livestock raisers prevailed on state and federal government to investigate prices paid by the packers for cattle. At the behest of foreign governments, the U.S. Department of Agriculture started inspecting pork exports in the early 1890s. Upton Sinclair's sensational novel *The Jungle* (1906) led to the Meat Inspection Act, which put federal inspectors in all packinghouses whose products entered interstate or foreign commerce. Government inspectors began grading beef and pork in the 1920s; in 1967 Congress required states to perform the same inspection and grading duties in plants selling within state boundaries.

When the Armour, Swift, and Morris companies cooperated in a new National Packing Company and purchased some food-related firms, Charles Edward Russell warned about the existence of a "beef trust." His book *The Greatest Trust in the World* (1905) caused the federal government to start antitrust proceedings. Although the courts failed to indict, the National Packing Company voluntarily dissolved in 1912. In the Packer Consent Decree of 1920, the Big Three agreed to sell their holdings in stockyards, food-related companies, cold-storage facilities, and the retail meat business.

The packers faced challenges from their employees. First organized by the Knights of Labor, packinghouse workers in Chicago went on strike for the eight-hour day in 1886, but public reaction to violence in Haymarket Square ended that strike. The Amalgamated Meat Cutters and Butcher Workmen of North America, an affiliate of the American Federation of Labor, made impressive gains in all the packing centers at the turn of the century. In the summer of 1904, this union led a long, bitter contest for wage increases. Some 50,000 packinghouse workers walked off their jobs. But in the end, only Jane Addams's intervention with J. Ogden Armour saved the strikers from total defeat. In response to renewed organizing during World War I and a demand for collective bargaining, President Woodrow Wilson established a federal arbitration process, and workers won temporary wage increases and the eight-hour day. When packers cut wages at the end of 1921, the Amalgamated called a strike that it soon rescinded. Thanks to the New Deal's pro-labor policies, Amalgamated membership revived in the 1930s and the Congress of Industrial Organizations launched a new packinghouse union. At the end of the decade, the large packing companies finally signed their first labor contracts. Postwar changes in the industry, however, minimized the impact of this victory.

Railroads centralized meatpacking in the latter half of the nineteenth century; trucks and highways decentralized it during the last half of the twentieth. Instead of selling mature animals to urban stockyards, livestock raisers sold young animals to commercial feedlots, and new packing plants arose in the vicinity. Unlike the compact, multistory buildings in Chicago, Kansas City, or Omaha, these new plants were sprawling one-story structures with power saws, mechanical knives, and the capacity to quick-freeze meat packaged in vacuum bags. Large refrigerator trucks carried the products over interstate highways to supermarkets. Many of the new plants were in states with right-to-work laws that hampered unionization. Business in the older railroad stockyards and city packinghouses declined sharply in the 1960s. Chicago's Union Stock Yard closed in 1970, the same year that the Greyhound Corporation purchased Armour & Co.

At the end of the twentieth century, the meatpacking industry was widely dispersed but still under government regulation. Changing consumption patterns posed new challenges, as poultry and fish began to replace beef and pork in American diets.     *Louise Carroll Wade*

**Medical Manufacturing and Pharmaceuticals.** Chicago's preeminence in both medicine and industry has made the city a manufacturing center for medical products. Practitioners and patients throughout the world depend on a vast array of supplies and drugs produced in Chicago-area laboratories and factories. Chicago innovations read like a list of the twentieth century's greatest strides in medicine, including the development of antibiotics, blood transfusions, birth control, and AIDS drugs. While their products have saved or enhanced countless lives, the huge profitability of some Chicago medical and drug manufacturers has also embroiled them in controversies about the ethics of for-profit medicine.

## MEDICAL AND SURGICAL MANUFACTURING

For most of the nineteenth century, American physicians designed their own surgical instruments or imported them from Europe. Chicago's Charles Truax & Co. revolutionized surgical instrument making in the 1880s by establishing simplified standard designs and applying the techniques of mass production to what had formerly been an individual craft. Charles Truax (1852–1918), who had opened a physician's supply store in Iowa in 1878, relocated to Chicago in 1884 to be near the city's growing numbers of physicians and medical colleges. Within five years, his surgical instrument sales had increased 20-fold. Truax responded to the new importance of antisepsis in medicine by creating the first line of "aseptic" surgical instruments that could be easily sterilized. In addition to its design and manufacturing innovations, Charles Truax & Co. (later renamed Truax, Greene) was known for its aggressive patenting and marketing practices. The company's 1893 sales catalog was over 1,500 pages long, and its products were so well known that physicians attending the World's Columbian Exposition flocked to view Truax's Wabash Avenue headquarters. Charles Truax assured his place in medical history with the 1899 publication of his voluminous *The Mechanics of Surgery*, the first work to establish standard nomenclature for surgical devices.

By the time Truax & Co. dissolved in 1920, Chicago had become the leading center of medical manufacturing in the country. City directories listed a total of 74 surgical and dental instrument makers in Chicago at the turn of the century. The most important was V. Mueller & Co., manufacturer and retailer of medical devices, founded in 1898 by Vincenz Mueller, a German immigrant. V. Mueller was particularly renowned for its ear, nose, and throat instruments. In addition to surgeon's tools, Chicago manufacturers produced medical items as diverse as artificial limbs, druggists' scales, and hospital clothing. Medline Industries, founded in Chicago in 1910 as a manufacturer of nurses' gowns, is today the largest privately held manufacturer and distributor of health care supplies in the United States; its more than 70,000 products include bandages, gowns, and wheelchairs.

But the true Chicago-area giant in medical manufacturing has been Baxter International, the top-ranked medical products company in the nation. In 1929 California physician Donald E. Baxter developed a method to produce safer intravenous solutions, which hospitals had previously mixed themselves. With two partners, in 1931 he founded what would become Baxter Laboratories and soon opened a production site in a former garage in Glenview. Baxter Labs invented the "Transfuso-Vac" in 1939, a device that allowed blood to be stored for up to 21 days, making blood banking possible for the first time. Skyrocketing demand for blood devices and solutions during World War II forced Baxter to open temporary plants. Starting in 1953, Baxter enjoyed 24 consecutive years of more than 20 percent annual earnings growth as it introduced one revolutionary device after another, including the kidney dialysis machine, a blood oxygenator for open-heart surgery, and factor VIII blood products for hemophiliacs.

Baxter's success has been due to both its innovative research and development and its aggressive acquisition or elimination of competitors. The company's attempts to dominate the medical products industry began in the 1950s, when it purchased other major laboratories producing competitive plasma and blood products. Baxter presided over the largest health care industry merger of the 1980s, acquiring the Chicago-area distributor American Hospital Supply Corporation in 1985. This merger gave Baxter control over the distribution as well as development and manufacture of a huge array of medical supplies. In 1999, Baxter came under scrutiny for its role in the cancellation of an important cancer research trial by a small company, CellPro, that had developed bone marrow transplant technology to rival Baxter's. Baxter and partner's successful suit against CellPro for patent infringement forced the smaller company into bankruptcy and ended the trials of the rival technology, raising questions about contradictions between product monopoly and the needs of patients.

## PHARMACEUTICALS

Chicago's first druggist was Philo Carpenter, who arrived in 1832 and opened a drugstore on what is now Lake Street. Frederick Thomas, Chicago's first barber-surgeon, ran a retail drug business in the 1830s in addition to offering "bleeding, leeching and tooth-drawing." In 1844 the well-known homeopath David Sheppard Smith established a pharmacy in Chicago; his establishment soon became a national distributor of homeopathic medicines.

The founding of Rush Medical College in 1837 had made Chicago an important center of medical education, and by 1859 the city boasted its own pharmacy school, the Chicago College of Pharmacy on Dearborn Street. The College of Pharmacy fell on economic hard times and briefly closed during the 1860s, but it reopened its doors on October 3, 1871, to a "large and enthusiastic class." After barely a week of lectures, the college and all its supplies were destroyed by the Great Fire. A fund-raising drive enabled the college to open yet again in 1873 and to erect new headquarters on State Street. In 1896 it was absorbed by the University of Illinois. Another pharmacy school, the Illinois College of Pharmacy, opened in 1886 and five years later joined Northwestern University as its School of Pharmacy.

Pharmaceutical manufacturing also became an important part of Chicago's economy by the end of the nineteenth century. One of the nation's largest drug companies, Abbott Laboratories, originated in the city in 1888. That year Wallace C. Abbott began producing "domestic granules," precisely measured amounts of drugs, in his apartment on the North Side. First incorporated as Abbott Alkaloidal Company in 1900 and renamed Abbott Laboratories in 1915, the company opened a manufacturing plant in North Chicago in 1920. Abbott has been involved in some of the most important drug discoveries of the century. Abbott scientists developed the drug Pentothal in 1936, and in 1941 the company was one of five in the United States to begin commercial production of penicillin. During the second half of the century, Abbott's most important products have included new antibiotics, drugs for hypertension and epilepsy, and radio-pharmaceuticals. In 1996 Abbott began worldwide sales of Norvir, a protease inhibitor for AIDS patients. Abbott has also marketed a number of highly controversial products, including the barbiturate Nembutal (later found to be addictive) and the infant formula Similac (criticized for its nutritional deficiencies compared to breast milk). In 1996, under pressure from consumer groups and the Federal Trade Commission, Abbott agreed to cease making unsubstantiated claims about the benefits of its nutritional supplement Ensure.

In 1890 an Omaha druggist named Gideon Daniel Searle relocated to Chicago, where he began producing drugs for syphilis and amoebic dysentery. He incorporated G. D. Searle & Co. in 1908, which throughout the century has developed such well-known products as Metamucil (for constipation), Dramamine (for motion sickness), Aspartame (an artificial sweetener), and the first birth control pill. In 1985 Searle became the pharmaceutical sector of the chemical giant Monsanto Corporation.

At the beginning of the twenty-first century, the Chicago area's largest medical and pharmaceutical manufacturers were operating outside the city, with large campus headquarters and manufacturing facilities in the suburbs. Abbott, headquartered in suburban North Chicago and with 15,000 employees in Illinois, was named Chicago's number one company by the *Tribune* in 1999. Abbott, with over 90,000 employees worldwide, and Deerfield-based Baxter International, with over 48,000 employees, stand among Chicago's largest firms and as leaders in their industry.

*Beatrix Hoffman*

**Musical Instrument Manufacturing.** After the Great Fire of 1871, Chicago quickly became a national center in musical instrument manufacturing, especially organs and pianos. Indeed, by 1910 Chicago manufacturers were supplying about half of all pianos sold in the United States, and one firm, W. W. Kimball Company, became the largest single producer of pianos and organs in the world. Although most of the early technological innovations in piano design in the United States were by eastern manufacturers, they share credit with the rising midwestern firms for innovations developing the industrial magnitude of the trade. Significantly, the Chicago World's Columbian Exposition in 1893 sparked a national marketing competition over the "best" piano between eastern and midwestern manufacturers, generating valuable publicity for Chicago brands. By 1915 over 40 companies were producing pianos, organs, and other instruments; many had showrooms on Wabash Avenue, appropriately called "Music Row." Familiar brands included Bush & Gerts, Cable, Cable-Nelson, Conover, Hamilton (Baldwin), Kimball, Lyon & Healy (originally renowned for harps), Steger & Sons, and Story & Clark. Kimball, along with Baldwin, pioneered modern dealership organization and aggressive sales techniques, and they as well as Cable were among the strongest corporations in the industry.

In the era before radio and sound movies, self-playing instruments were a crucial part of the music industry. Chicago firms produced many brands associated with automatic pianos, notably Melville Clark, Kimball, and Gulbransen-Dickinson, whose famous "Gulbransen Baby" trademark rivaled Victor Talking Machine Company's "His Master's Voice" in familiarity. Furthermore, several Chicago companies specialized in manufacturing coin-operated, roll-activated electric music machines specifically designed for public entertainment. These "coin-pianos" and "orchestrions"—precursors of today's jukebox—often contained a variety of instrument sounds. Famous Chicago companies included Operators Piano Company, who made the Coinola, and the J. P. Seeburg Company, which, along with Wurlitzer, later dominated post–World War II jukebox production. Seeburg was also a leader in producing "theater photoplayers"—automatic instruments uniquely designed to provide music and sound effects for silent movies—until sound movies destroyed this market in the late 1920s. Not surprisingly, Chicago was a manufacturing center for the actions and perforated music rolls for all types of automatic instruments. Chief companies were Gulbransen-Dickinson and the Q-R-S Company, the largest manufacturer of music rolls in the world, producing 10 million rolls annually by 1926.

Chicago's historical prominence in musical instrument manufacturing also included Frank Holton Company brass winds (Holton had been first trombonist in Sousa's band), Lowry electronic organs, and Martin Band Instruments, one of the nation's oldest manufacturers. Chicago-based Montgomery Ward & Co. and Sears, Roebuck & Co. offered an impressive variety of musical instruments through their celebrated mail-order catalogs, including accordions, banjos, mandolins, guitars, violins, harps, harmonicas, drums, brass and woodwind instruments, even pianos and organs. For generations, Montgomery Ward and Sears provided Americans, especially in rural areas, with arguably the most important single source of instruments.

The music industry ceased to be dominated by the piano and organ trade after the Great Depression and World War II, and Chicago lost its leadership as the musical instruments trade struggled against a wider variety of entertainment choices available in the postwar culture. Many old Chicago trademarks still in production at that time—such as Gulbransen, Story & Clark, Q-R-S, Holton, and Martin—have long since been sold to corporations in other states. Nevertheless, present-day Chicago-area firms still produce a variety of instruments, including fifes and song whistles, guitars, banjos, basses, mandolins, band and orchestral instruments, digital pianos, and synthesizers. Historically prominent names include Lyon & Healy harps, Lowry electronic organs, and W. H. Lee & Co., the largest maker of handcrafted orchestral string instruments in the United States.

*Craig H. Roell*

**Music Publishing.** Chicago's music publishing has mirrored the cultural history of the city and the nation through music for the church, school, popular entertainment, and the home, from the first piece of music in 1854, "The Garden City Polka," by Christoph Plagge, published by B. K. Mould, to the rise of gospel music. The high point came during the Civil War, when patriotic songs like "The Battle Cry of Freedom" (1862) made Chicago a national center. Earlier, music had been issued primarily for a local market, but the Civil War songs made H. M. Higgins (1856) and Root & Cady (1858) nationally known. The Great Fire of 1871 ended this activity. For the next ten years, little music was published. Among the pre-fire firms, only Lyon & Healy (1864) survived.

In the 1880s inexpensive (five- to ten-cent) music began to be issued by the National Music Company (1882), Saalfield Brothers (1888), and McKinley Music Company (1891). Religious music became increasingly prominent, from publishers like Edwin O. Excell (1885), Hope Publishing Company (1894), and the Rodeheaver Company (1910). Clayton F. Summy was one of Chicago's longest-lived music publishers, specializing in teaching material, sacred music, and works by Chicago composers.

With the popularity of vaudeville in the 1890s, Chicago became a center for popular song publishers, like Will Rossiter (1891), publisher of "The Darktown Strutters' Ball" (1917), and the Melrose Brothers Music Company (1920), publisher of "King Porter Stomp" (1924) and "It's Tight Like That" (1928).

As Chicago became a center of gospel music, it also became a center for publishing that music. The most notable firms were established by musician/composers: Dorsey House (Thomas A. Dorsey) and the Martin and Morris Music Company (Kenneth Morris and Sallie Martin).

*Dena J. Epstein*

**Newspapers.** Chicago's newspapers have nurtured four traditions: combative partisanship, competitive journalism, handsome design, and noteworthy reporters and writers, especially columnists. Moreover, Chicago journalism has always been tamer than New York City's, as Rupert Murdoch learned when he unsuccessfully tried to import his *New York Post* sensationalism to the *Chicago Sun-Times*, which he owned briefly in the 1980s.

Chicago's first newspaper, the *Chicago Weekly Democrat*, was founded by John Calhoun in 1833 and bought by local politician "Long John" Wentworth three years later. It became a morning daily in 1840. Three Chicago businessmen founded the Whig (later Republican) morning *Chicago Daily Tribune* in 1847. Joseph Medill bought into the *Tribune* in 1855 and gradually became its chief editorial force, gaining control in 1874 and directing it until he died in 1899.

The roots of suburban journalism in metropolitan Chicago lie in the founding of the *Juliet Courier* (later the *Joliet Herald*) in 1939. The *Aurora Beacon* followed in 1846 and the *Waukegan Gazette* in 1851.

Chicago's city newspapers grew steadily in the 1840s and 1850s, reaching 11 dailies and 22 weeklies by 1860. Although most pre–Civil War Chicago papers were short-lived, the *Chicago Journal* (1844), an afternoon Republican paper founded by J. Young Scammon, and the *Chicago Times* (1854), a morning Democratic paper, survived the war and flourished. The *Journal* became Democratic and in 1897 acquired Finley Peter Dunne's satirical Mr. Dooley columns, written in Irish dialect.

The *Times* was sold in 1861 to Wilbur F. Storey, Chicago's most iconoclastic newspaper editor, who reasserted the paper's unpopular Democratic support for the Civil War. After the war, Storey, using the motto "to print the news and raise hell," turned the *Times* into an outspoken, eccentric reporter and critic of Chicago society. Storey edited the *Times* until his death in 1884; in 1895 the paper merged with the *Herald*, a daily founded in 1881, and became a Republican voice.

The morning *Chicago Republican* (1865), sporting the motto "Republican in everything, Independent in nothing," was edited briefly by Charles A. Dana and, in 1872, after passing through several hands, was renamed the *Chicago Inter Ocean*, an upper-class arbiter of cultural tastes. The *Inter Ocean* went into decline after 1895, when it became the property of Chicago traction boss Charles T. Yerkes, who used it as a tool in his political wars.

Melville E. Stone, believing that an evening penny paper could succeed in Chicago, founded the *Chicago Daily News*, on January 3, 1876. Although nonpartisan and specializing in bright, short news items, the paper was near death six months later, at which point Victor F. Lawson became its publisher and turned it around. In 1888 Stone left the paper to Lawson, who ran it with remarkable success until his death in 1925. The *Daily News* absorbed the *Journal* in 1929. A morning *Daily News*, started in 1881, was renamed the *Record* in 1893. It contained Eugene Field's humorous "Sharps and Flats" column, George Ade's "Stories of the Streets and of the Town" column, John T. McCutcheon's illustrations, and Ray Stannard Baker's stories about Chicago corruption.

In 1900 Chicago had nine general circulation newspapers when William Randolph Hearst's sensationalistic evening *Chicago American* appeared, followed by his morning *Chicago Examiner* (1902). The *American* upheld the raucous Hearstian/Chicago tradition of "The Front Page," even after it was sold to the *Chicago Tribune* in 1956, renamed *Chicago Today*, and turned into a tabloid. *Today* died in 1974. The morning *Examiner* became the *Herald-Examiner* in 1918 and died in 1939, never able to overtake the *Tribune*.

The *Chicago Defender*, *Tribune*, *Sun*, *Times*, and *Daily News* dominated twentieth-century Chicago journalism. The weekly *Chicago Defender*, founded by Robert S. Abbott in 1905, was the nation's most powerful African American newspaper in its first two decades, covering racism sensationally, advocating rights for blacks, and offering a beacon of hope for migrants from the South. More moderate after the 1920s and more local after 1940, when John H. Sengstacke became editor, the *Defender* became a daily in 1956.

The weekly *Southtown Economist* first appeared as a South Side community paper in 1906, became a daily in 1978, was renamed the *Daily Southtown* in 1993, and in 1994 was purchased by Hollinger International, which by 2000 also owned the *Sun-Times*, the Pioneer Press (with 48 Chicago suburban papers), and the Star Newspapers (with 23 Chicago suburban papers). Meanwhile, the *Herald*, founded in Arlington Heights as a weekly in 1872, was made a daily in 1969 and in 2000 published 27 localized editions for suburban communities.

The *Tribune*—which under conservative Robert R. McCormick from 1911 to his death in 1955 dominated Chicago's morning field and the Midwest—was a pioneer in four-color printing. Sportswriter Ring Lardner wrote the *Tribune*'s "In the Wake of the News" column from 1913 to 1919;

Bert Leston Taylor created and presided over the *Tribune*'s "Line o' Type or Two" from 1910 until his death in 1921.

Meanwhile, a second *Chicago Times* (1929) built Chicago's best news staff during its two decades. As World War II approached, Marshall Field III founded the *Chicago Sun*, a New Deal morning alternative to the isolationist *Tribune*. In 1947 the *Sun* acquired the *Times'* news staff and presses, creating the tabloid *Sun-Times* in 1948.

The *Daily News'* foreign news service began in 1898, carrying such noted interwar correspondents as Edward Price Bell, Paul Scott Mowrer, and Edgar Ansel Mowrer. The *Daily News'* staff included reporter and critic Carl Sandburg and columnists Ben Hecht (1914–22) and Mike Royko (1964–78). When the *Daily News* died in 1978, Royko moved to the *Daily News'* sister paper, the *Sun-Times*. He joined the *Tribune* in 1984, protesting Rupert Murdoch's purchase of the *Sun-Times*.

Technology and the economy have intervened over the last half century to change Chicago's daily press scene dramatically. The death of the afternoon *Daily News* was hastened by auto-based commuting patterns and television's early evening dominance of the news, leading to drops in circulation not only in Chicago but around the country. Competitive pressure from the expansion of the digital news and advertising environment grew as the last century ended and the new began. Each of Chicago's newspapers has struggled with the best ways to create online versions and business models to sustain them.

They have also been involved in the ongoing consolidation of newspapers. The *Sun-Times* was purchased in 2006 by Hollinger International and was renamed the Sun-Times Media Group following a scandal at the corporate level. After filing for bankruptcy in 2009, the company was purchased by an investor group and the Sun-Times Media Holding Company was formed. The previous year, the *Chicago Tribune*, purchased in 2007 by investor Sam Zell, also entered bankruptcy. The *Tribune* and the *Sun-Times* remain the two largest dailies in the metropolitan Chicago. The third largest by circulation in both Chicago and Illinois is the *Daily Herald*.

*Richard A. Schwarzlose*

**Oil Refining.** Chicago was not among the earliest locations of the petroleum industry, but when oil refining finally came to the area, it came with a bang. When the Standard Oil Company opened its new refinery in Whiting, Indiana, in 1890, the facility ranked as the largest refinery in the world. A century later, the Whiting facility still stood among the world's largest, and the Chicago region remained an important refining center.

Refining came to the Chicago area at a time when an already robust oil industry was devoted to the production of illuminating oils such as kerosene. By the end of the 1880s, when the Standard Oil Company of Indiana was created as a new subsidiary of the giant corporation built by John D. Rockefeller, nearly $80 million had been invested in the American refining industry, which already employed over 11,000 men and generated over $85 million in products annually. Given this context, the new Chicago-area refinery being planned by Standard of Indiana was a kind of second-generation production plant, one that would be larger and more modern than its predecessors in Pennsylvania and Ohio. Initially, Standard of Indiana planned on building its new refinery at South Chicago, the terminus of a pipeline originating in the oil fields of Ohio and Indiana. But land costs, tax rates, and local opposition were high enough to lead the company to look elsewhere. It soon decided to begin construction at Whiting, located in northwestern Indiana along the shore of Lake Michigan. A little over a year after construction started in May 1889, the Whiting refinery went on line, and it began to turn crude oil into kerosene and other products.

The relative importance of the Chicago area within the oil industry was never greater than in the 1890s, immediately after the Whiting refinery began to operate. By the middle of that decade, the Whiting plant could process as much as 36,000 barrels of crude oil per day and accounted for nearly a fifth of total refining capacity in the United States. By the end of the 1890s, about $6 million had been invested in the Whiting facility, which employed about 3,000 people, most of them European-born men.

During the early part of the twentieth century, as the oil industry began to focus upon the production of gasoline, the Whiting facility pioneered new refining technologies. In 1911, after the U.S. Supreme Court ordered the breakup of Rockefeller's oil trust, Standard of Indiana (based in Chicago) become an independent company. At the same time, the explosive growth of the automobile industry was causing the oil industry to expand quickly. During the 1910s, the value of the output of U.S. refineries increased by a factor of almost seven, and the number of workers in the industry quadrupled. Part of the industry's boom during the 1910s was attributable to technological innovations made at the Whiting refinery (which was now connected by pipeline to oil fields in Kansas and Oklahoma, as well as the older eastern fields). During the early 1910s, Standard of Indiana chemist and executive William M. Burton directed experiments at the Whiting plant that attempted to increase gasoline yields by processing (or "cracking") the crude oil at higher temperatures and higher pressures. These experiments proved successful, and Standard of Indiana collected $15 million in patent royalties between 1913 and 1920, as it and other oil companies used the new process to get more gasoline out of every barrel of crude.

By the middle part of the twentieth century, the Chicago region was home to several large refineries, and the employees of some of these plants took part in a national effort by oil industry workers to exert more influence over wages and the workplace. By the middle of the Depression, when Standard of Indiana employed about 7,000 residents of the Chicago area, the Sinclair Refining Company had about 1,000 workers in its East Chicago refinery. During World War II, more refineries sprang up around

Chicago, and the local industry responded to a labor shortage by hiring hundreds of women. (At the Whiting refinery, about 15 percent of wartime employees were women.) In late 1945, just after the end of the war, refinery workers throughout the United States—many of them members of the Oil Workers International Union—were part of a major strike that was intended to help workers achieve wage increases, industry-wide bargaining rights, and a closed-shop agreement. Within the Chicago area, there were over 4,000 employees on strike at Calumet-area refineries such as the one owned by the Socony-Vacuum Oil Company. Eventually, after President Truman authorized the U.S. Navy to seize some plants and the U.S. Department of Labor became involved in the dispute, many refinery workers in Chicago and the rest of the country were awarded a pay raise of about 18 percent.

During the second half of the twentieth century, as the U.S. refining industry became more concentrated in Texas, Louisiana, and California, the Chicago region became less important as an oil-processing center than it had been during the previous 60 years. Still, the area remained home to some large refineries. During the 1950s, refineries in the Chicago region were using about 175 million barrels of crude per year, which made the area the third largest refining center in the United States. The Whiting plant, which used more water than the entire city of Chicago, had a capacity of 200,000 barrels per day and employed over 7,000 local residents. Other large refineries in the area included the Sinclair plant in East Chicago; a Cities Service Oil Company refinery in East Chicago; a plant owned by the Pure Oil Company in Lemont; and a Texas Company refinery at Lockport (closed in 1981). By the end of the twentieth century, when the Chicago region's share of total U.S. refining capacity had declined to about 5 percent, there were still large refineries on the metropolis's southern edges. Four local refineries—in Blue Island (closed in 2001), Lemont (Citgo), Joliet (ExxonMobil), and Whiting (BP). The Whiting facility, which was extensively modernized in 2011, was still among the largest oil refineries in the United States.                                              *Mark R. Wilson*

**Printing.** In the late nineteenth century, Chicago became a center for commercial printing in the United States second only to New York. Chicago printers worked closely with magazine and catalog publishers; they had easy access to rail transportation; and they achieved a competitive position because Chicago was the point at which zoned shipping rates for bulky printed products increased. In the years after World War I, Chicago's centrality in the industry developed into a regional industrial concentration greater even than that of the big eastern cities. By the end of the twentieth century, four of the ten largest printing companies in the world were headquartered within 100 miles of Chicago. The internationalization of their operations since the 1970s, however, has included the exportation of the actual printing.

Before the widespread introduction of large power presses (ca. 1860), small printing houses were to be found in almost every American town. Markets outside major publishing centers were local or at most regional. Chicago was no exception. The city's earliest printer was John Calhoun, whose single press operated from 1833 to 1836 in printing the *Chicago Democrat* and a variety of occasional publications. There was nothing to distinguish Calhoun from hundreds of other printers in frontier towns. The early, rapid growth of Chicago, however, meant that already in 1846 there were 8 printing offices and 4 newspapers, making it the region's printing center. From 1850 to 1870, Chicago developed a fully integrated printing industry. Newspapers in 1860 reported 29 printing offices; the 1871 census listed 79 job printers in addition to the major newspaper offices. Numerous print distributors, 17 binderies, 68 bookstores, and 5 manufacturers of printing supplies and machinery, served the industry on a regional basis. Publishing houses fed the presses, led by A. C. McClurg, a general publisher, and by a variety of specialized publishers of textbooks, religious and trade literature, and catalogs. Magazines were particularly important, even in these early years: some 20 new titles per year started in Chicago between 1860 and 1880. From the 1850s onward, railroad printing became important because so many lines established headquarters or regional offices in the city. One early specialized railroad printer was Rand McNally & Co., founded in 1868. Another Chicago specialty that began during this period was the printing of mail-order catalogs.

The Great Fire of 1871 allowed printers to concentrate their works in the new central commercial district and on the Near South Side. Coinciding as this new construction did with technological advances in power presses, it also led to the creation of large-scale printing plants with skilled workforces and to the development of a characteristic tall and narrow loft-style building to house rows of presses in rooms with good natural light. Rand McNally, M. A. Donohue & Co. (1861), R. R. Donnelley & Sons (1864), and the W. F. Hall Printing Company (1892) were among the large firms that grew up to exploit such economies of scale for large print runs of textbooks, magazines, and catalogs. Simultaneously, type foundries and printing-press manufacturers opened in Chicago, although the great size and rapid growth of the industry meant that most machinery and type continued to be imported from the East. Barnhart Bros. & Spindler was for many years one of the largest midwestern type founders. Two Chicago press manufacturers became leaders in their respective fields. The Miehle Company (1890) made fine, high-speed sheet-fed presses, and the Goss Company (1885) developed web presses for newspaper work. The final pieces in Chicago's complex printing industry were added just before World War I with the invention of new proofing presses by Robert Vandercook and the founding of the Ludlow Typograph Company, the city's only manufacturer of typesetting machinery. Theodore Regensteiner of the Regensteiner Printing Company pioneered in the introduction of color offset presses.

The mature Chicago printing industry consisted of a fully integrated regional complex of suppliers and producers with extensive out-shipping to other regions and even worldwide. It was symbolized by the huge printing plants built at the south end of Dearborn Street and Plymouth Court near Polk Street for the Donohue (1883), the Donnelley (1897), and the Franklin Printing (1914) companies. Architectural gems of the present Printing House Row Historic District, these buildings are decorated flamboyantly with bas-reliefs and mosaics that portray the history and processes of printing from Gutenberg to Chicago.

Chicago's printing industry was a major field for labor and management organization. A price war broke out as early as 1840 and led to disputes about compositors' pay. The first printer's union in the city was founded in 1850 as a response to such wage concerns, and in 1852 the national union had recognized the Chicago Typographical Union as Local 16. Early organizing efforts achieved major wage-rate increases in the boom years of the 1860s, but these eroded in the slump after 1873. A union drive for a nine-hour day (part of a national effort) led the employing printers to form their own association in 1887, the Chicago Typothetae. Later in the same year, these employers were instrumental in founding the United Typothetae of America at a convention held in Chicago.

The industry expanded well beyond the printing house district even before World War I. Printing supply and press manufacturing companies did not need to be as close to each other or to the shipping hubs as the printing plants at first did. Miehle and Goss put early plants west of the river; Ludlow's was in the Clybourn Avenue industrial corridor. Printers also located elsewhere as the need for larger plants developed. The Henneberry Printing Company opened a large plant at 22nd and Clinton near the river in the mid-1890s, and it was vastly enlarged in the 1920s after the company was taken over by John Cuneo, becoming the city's second largest printer as Cuneo Press. But the symbolic leader of the industry was again the Donnelley Company, which built a vast printing plant designed by Howard Van Doren Shaw on 22nd Street near the lake between 1912 and 1929. Donnelley also opened one of the first regional printing plants of a Chicago firm at Crawfordsville, Indiana, in 1921.

The pace of regionalization quickened after World War II, when the need to arrange large new offset presses on single floors led the industry giants to build plants in suburban Skokie (Rand McNally, 1952) and even farther afield (e.g., Miehle-Goss-Dexter in Rockford; Rand McNally in Kentucky; Donnelley in Indiana and downstate Illinois, and later in Kentucky and Tennessee). Smaller companies also multiplied within the region. The process of regionalization has continued into the twenty-first century. In 1927 almost all the region's printing was in the city; some 1,500 production facilities employed over 30,000 workers. In 1960 there were 2,100 printing establishments in the city (including the world's three largest at the time: Donnelley, W. F. Hall, and Cuneo), but another 1,550 plants were located in the metropolitan area. Total employment in the sector was close to 100,000. Further erosion of the urban concentration occurred in the late twentieth century, with the most rapid changes from the late 1970s onward. From 1977 to 1984, for example, the total number of firms in prepress and press work (excluding newspapers) in the city dropped from 1,380 to 1,116, while jobs declined from 24,047 to 19,342.

Although Chicago has never been a major center for literary publishing, it was important in trade publishing and particularly in trade magazines and direct-mail sales from the 1860s onward. Starting in the 1920s, Chicago's large, versatile plants and edge in shipping rates lured major magazine accounts away from other regions. This aspect of its economy has continued to dominate the printing industry in Chicago. Industry giants like Donnelley and Rand McNally built their success on printing catalogs, magazines, maps, phone books, and textbooks, some published locally but most printed here for publishers outside the region. These Chicago companies have continued to serve huge bulk accounts, even though the printing is now done with cheaper labor in their plants elsewhere in the region, in other regions, or abroad.          *Paul F. Gehl*

**Publishing, Book.** Book publishing in Chicago, a business almost as old as the city itself, established its basic nature early on. Its initial growth and source of strength for a full century afterward was tied to the city's rapid development as the nation's rail center—Rand McNally got its start printing timetables, and the railroads also made possible Chicago's early emergence as a distribution point for subscription titles, reference books, and school texts. Though for brief periods Chicago flourished as a writers' town, the trade book and magazine publishers they needed to support their efforts were never sufficiently numerous to keep them here. Nevertheless, the distinguished University of Chicago Press has maintained its position as the nation's largest university press, and the metropolitan area's several specialty publishers have remained strong. By the 1990s, consolidation and technological changes in the book industry nationwide meant that the metropolitan area was no longer a center for any particular kind of publishing; on the other hand, changes in book distribution nationwide have enabled writers and small publishers in Chicago to compete with others around the country on an equal basis.

Chicago's first two publishers were printer Robert Fergus and bookseller S. C. Griggs. In 1839 Fergus issued the city's first regular directory, and in 1876 he began publishing the remarkable Fergus Historical Series, 35 titles chronicling the city's past. Griggs arrived in 1846, two years before the first railroad; a few years later his Literary Emporium on the Prairies had become the nation's largest domestic book agent. In 1872 he sold that business to concentrate on book publishing.

Rand McNally started in 1856 and soon began printing railroad tickets and timetables, which eventually led to guidebooks and maps, in which the firm pioneered both technologically and conceptually. Throughout its long history, Rand McNally often developed a substantial line of textbooks and occasionally a trade list; the latter included paperbacks for travelers in the 1870s and Thor Heyerdahl's *Kon-Tiki* in 1950. In the 1990s, it sold its printing business to confine its efforts to geography-related products.

When R. R. Donnelley & Sons was formally established in 1882, Richard Donnelley had been in both the printing and publishing businesses in Chicago for nearly 20 years. One of his first ventures was the Lakeside Library, an 1870s series of inexpensive paperbacks. Though the name has been continued in the annual Lakeside Classics gift books, the firm has followed its founder's dictum that publishing and printing are separate activities, dedicating itself to being North America's largest commercial printer.

However, with some help from these giants, Chicago had become the largest publishing center west of New York City by the 1880s. In addition to the "dime novel" and subscription book publishers—Belford, Clarke was a major one—publishers of county histories like Benjamin F. Lewis flourished here. Chicago's significance as a literary center began at the same time. In 1880 the *Dial* was established in cooperation with A. C. McClurg (originally Jansen, McClurg & Company), successor to Griggs and still a leading wholesaler and retailer. While the *Dial* was becoming the nation's leading literary magazine, the city's newspapers were drawing talents such as Eugene Field, George Ade, Theodore Dreiser, Floyd Dell, and Finley Peter Dunne, many of whom were attracted to the "Saints & Sinners Corner" in McClurg's Wabash Avenue bookstore. McClurg also published some Chicago writers, but his firm's most lucrative publishing venture came after his death, when in 1914 Oak Park native Edgar Rice Burroughs brought them his *Tarzan of the Apes*. By 1933 the Griggs and McClurg bookselling operation had evolved into Kroch's & Brentano's.

Stone & Kimball, another noted venture, began in 1893 and quickly distinguished itself not only for the graphic and literary quality of its books but the elegance and enthusiasm with which it promoted them. Essential to this was the noted *Chap-Book*, a combination sales piece and literary journal. Contemporaneous were Way & Williams, which followed the tradition of fine printing, and a firm eventually known as Reilly & Lee, which in 1904 began publishing L. Frank Baum's Oz books and later Edgar Guest's popular poetry. In 1918 the P. F. Volland Company brought out the first of Johnny Gruelle's phenomenal Raggedy Ann and Andy series and other books for children.

A. N. Marquis was the city's first major reference book publisher; his *Who's Who in America* appeared in 1899. The *World Book Encyclopedia*, an easy-to-read general reference, was first published in Chicago in 1917. *Compton's Pictured Encyclopedia*, compiled by innovator Frank Compton, first appeared to considerable acclaim in 1922. Sometime earlier, Sears, Roebuck had begun selling the *Encyclopaedia Britannica* through its catalog; in the 1930s, Sears moved *EB*'s editorial offices from New York to Chicago, where it became a major employer of editorial talent. After a few changes in ownership, it began evolving into an electronic information source in the 1990s.

The textbook business was led for nearly a century by Scott, Foresman & Co. In 1896 the company acquired *Robert's Rules of Order* from Griggs's firm and soon assumed national leadership through series such as the Elston Readers, first introduced in 1909, which evolved into the phenomenal Dick and Jane primers by the 1940s. In the 1920s, Row, Peterson published one of the first U.S. history texts to be used on both sides of the Mason-Dixon Line, and in 1939 Science Research Associates became a pioneer in the field of testing and guidance materials. Children's publishers included Albert Whitman & Company, which acquired its famed Boxcar Children series in 1942.

Evangelical publishing began in 1869 when Fleming H. Revell established a firm that could extend the ministry of evangelist Dwight L. Moody, his brother-in-law; one of the nation's premier religious houses for decades, it moved to the East Coast around 1910. Later, the Moody Bible Institute established its own press. One of its directors translated parts of the Bible into a version he called *The Living Bible* and in 1962 established Tyndale House Publishers to publish it. The firm later became the area's major evangelical publisher. In 1972 KAZI Publications was established to distribute and publish Islamic materials.

While the city's larger specialty publishers (Playboy Enterprises, Crain Communications, and Johnson Publishing Company) have published few books, some smaller specialty houses have been successful. By the 1990s, Third World Press had established itself as one of the nation's leading African American book publishers. The socialist Charles H. Kerr & Company was still around to observe its centennial in 1986; and Open Court, in nearby LaSalle, established in 1887 to publish scientific and religious books, also became a prominent publisher of textbooks and magazines for children.

More representative of late twentieth-century trends is the trade publishing firm established in 1947 by Henry Regnery; however distinctive, its nonfiction list was never very profitable, and 25 years later it became Contemporary Books, a publisher of sports titles and adult education material. In the early 1990s, it was acquired by the Tribune Company, which a few years later merged it into another acquisition, textbook house NTC Publishing. NTC/Contemporary was sold in 2000 to New York–based McGraw-Hill.

So although in 1900 it had looked as though trade publishing in Chicago could assume national leadership, this potential was ephemeral. By century's end, book publishing in Chicago was no longer even a major employer. The text and reference houses had moved or substantially contracted. Chicago's publishers were small-scale and specialized: Ivan R. Dee's nonfiction list, a revived Northwestern University Press, and Sourcebooks' popular compilations among them. Distributors such as the Independent Publishers Group capitalized on the growth of small independent publishers around the country. Various associations and a local book review tried to create a missing sense of community among Chicago-area publishers, but their dissimilar interests and geographic dispersion made that difficult. Chicago's various pieces of the book business may have been healthy, but its whole has never become greater than a sum of its parts.

*Connie Goddard*

**Publishing, Trade Publications.** The story of the Chicago trade press is a complicated one. It is a yarn of free enterprise—with entrepreneurs launching magazines, newspapers, and newsletters because an industry, profession, or business needed information. Yet it is also a tale of closed associations, far removed from capitalism—with organizations starting their own periodicals to offer news, features, and research to their memberships.

Chicago has long been a major center for the publication of specialized business periodicals; more than 200 were still published in the city in 2000. The majority were published by independently run corporations, large and small, such as Crain Communications, Real Estate News Corporation, Talcott Communications, Trend Publishing, Luby Publishing, and Jacobsen Publishing. But a large minority are published by associations headquartered in Chicago, including the American Medical Association, the American Bar Association, the American Library Association, and the American Marketing Association. Indeed, some of the most widely circulated specialized business periodicals are published by these organizations.

On the entrepreneurial side, the story of Crain Communications Inc. illustrates many important principles of Chicago trade publishing in both the nineteenth and twentieth century. G. D. Crain Jr.—who moved his small company to Chicago from Louisville, Kentucky, in 1916—was a master of launching publications and acquiring magazines. *Advertising Age*, the best known of the publications that he launched, started in Chicago in 1930 but has since moved to New York City. Many of the properties that Crain acquired were and continue to be based in Chicago. In 1967 Crain Communications purchased American Trade Magazines, publishers of *American Drycleaner* and the *American Laundry Digest*; those publications remain in the city. But Crain—like a number of trade publishers—discovered that Chicago alone could not be its sole base of operations. The acquisition of the Detroit-based *Automotive News* in 1970 signals this move.

In 2010 Crain remained a privately owned company with nearly all stock owned by family or active employees; the family also controlled the management of the company. The company itself was on strong financial footing, with some 30 business, trade, and consumer publications and websites. Headquartered in Detroit, it ran its operations out of 14 different offices in the United States and abroad, including Chicago. The Chicago office is home to *Business Insurance, Crain's Chicago Business, Modern Healthcare, American Trade Magazines, Workforce Management,* and editorial and sales staff for several other publications.

The other segment of trade publishing in Chicago is based in associations. Chicago is home to many professional and trade associations. Most organizations only publish one or two periodicals, but some of the larger associations—such as the American Library Association (ALA), the American Medical Association (AMA), and the American Bar Association (ABA)—each publish a variety of journals, magazines, and newsletters. One of the largest and best known is the *ABA Journal* (established in 1915, published since 1920 in Chicago), a slick monthly designed to cover law and the practice of it. With a circulation of almost 400,000, it is the most widely read magazine on law in the nation.

Chicago's trade publishing picture differs considerably from many other cities. Because of the diversity of the economic base of Chicago, the trade press has never been dominated by a single industry, business, or association. The *Chicago Daily Hide & Tallow Bulletin, Bowling Center Management,* and *JAMA* have all called Chicago home.          *Kathleen L. Endres*

**Railroads.** Chicago is the most important railroad center in North America. More lines of track radiate in more directions from Chicago than from any other city. Chicago has long been the most important interchange point for freight traffic between the nation's major railroads, and it is the hub of Amtrak, the intercity rail passenger system. Chicago ranks second (behind New York City) in terms of the volume of commuter rail passengers carried each day.

The first railroad in Chicago was the Galena & Chicago Union, which was chartered in 1836 to build tracks to the lead mines at Galena in northwestern Illinois. The first tracks were laid in 1848, and then not to Galena but to a point known as Oak Ridge (now Oak Park). The Galena & Chicago Union's terminal stood near the corner of Canal and Kinzie Streets.

Other railroads soon completed lines of track linking Chicago with the wheat fields of northern Illinois and southern Wisconsin. Later lines connected the city with Detroit, Cleveland, Cincinnati, New Orleans, St. Louis, Kansas City, Omaha, and St. Paul. Railroads were especially important as haulers of grain and livestock, which helped Chicago gain a primary role in the grain marketing and meatpacking industries.

Many of the railroads built west of Chicago had their corporate headquarters in the city, as well as yards and shops. Chicago became a center for the manufacture of freight cars, passenger cars (Pullman Company), and later diesel locomotives (Electro-Motive Division of General Motors, in La Grange).

Freight moving across the country is funneled through the railroad yards of Chicago, where it is classified and then transferred to the yards of other railroads within the metropolitan area. The largest of these yards include Proviso and Bensenville on the western edge of the city, Clearing

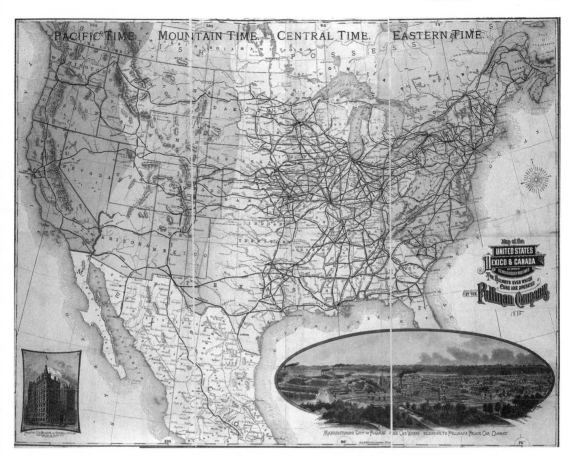

Map of Pullman Company Rail Network, 1885. By 1885 the Pullman Company had already become one of America's largest and best-known firms. As this map, an advertisement for the company, shows, Pullman cars carried passengers from coast to coast and from Canada to Mexico. As a manufacturer of passenger and freight railroad cars, the Pullman Company was closely involved—financially and managerially—with most of the nation's railroads. The company had also begun to expand into Europe. By the end of the century, Pullman was one of America's largest companies as well as the country's single largest employer of African Americans, almost all of whom worked as Pullman porters, the most familiar symbol of the company and its service. Courtesy of the Chicago History Museum (ICHi-34811).

Yard in Bedford Park, Barr and Blue Island Yards on the Far South Side, and Corwith Yard near the Stevenson Expressway. Although the nation's railroads now have been merged into just a few large systems, Chicago remains the hub where the tracks of one company end and those of another begin.

Until the 1960s, the Chicago Loop contained six major railroad terminals for intercity rail passenger traffic. Passengers traveling between the East and West Coasts often had half a day to spend in Chicago between trains and took advantage of the time by sightseeing. Journalists sometimes met trains arriving from New York or Los Angeles to spot the celebrities. The decline of intercity rail passenger travel brought about by the advent of jet airlines led to the decline of the passenger train and the eventual consolidation of remaining services under Amtrak in 1971.

Hundreds of thousands of Chicago-area residents still commute to the Loop by train each day, now under the auspices of Metra, the publicly owned regional rail transportation authority. Twelve such commuter-train services extend outward along the radiating routes of Chicago's rail network. The Burlington Northern Santa Fe line to Naperville and Aurora carries the heaviest volume of passengers.                    *John C. Hudson*

**Railroad Supply Industry.** It is often said that the railroads made Chicago, in the sense that the city's explosive growth was made possible by its position as a center of the national transportation network. What is observed less frequently is that Chicago made the railroads. Starting in the 1850s, the area was home to many manufacturers of railroad, track, and railcars. Not only the well-known Pullman Company, but several other of the area's leading economic enterprises made a big business out of providing railroads with the cars and supplies they needed to keep running. For much of the city's history, tens of thousands of local residents were employed in the industry, which ranked as one of the area's largest. Even after the rise of the automobile and the airplane, the railway supply business remained an important part of Chicago's economy; but, like the railroads, it declined considerably by the end of the twentieth century.

The manufacture and repair of railroad equipment and supplies became one of Chicago's leading industries during the decade before the Civil War, when the first lines began to reach the city. Both the railroads and independent companies operated major shops. By the 1850s, Chicago was home to several large railroad car makers, including the Eagle Works, the American Car Company, and the Union Car Works, each of which employed about 300 men. At the same time, the railroad companies started to operate large production and repair shops in and around the city. In 1855 the Illinois Central established shops along the lakeshore at the south end of the city; these works employed about 300 men in the 1850s. Another large establishment was the works of the Chicago, Burlington & Quincy, located in Aurora. By the 1870s, when the Aurora shops employed nearly 1,300 men, this might have been the region's largest single work site. Among the other large manufacturing sites in the area that supplied the railroad industry were the iron and steel mills, which started to make rails in the late 1850s. By the 1880s, Chicago-area steel mills were rolling nearly a third of all the rails made in the United States.

By the late nineteenth century, the railroad equipment and supply business was one of Chicago's leading industries. In 1880 four of the area's top eight manufacturing establishments in terms of wages paid were railroad company shops: a total of about 3,600 men were then employed at the shops of the Illinois Central; the Chicago & Northwestern; the Chicago, Rock Island & Pacific; and the Chicago, Burlington & Quincy. But it was the independent railcar makers that made Chicago the center of the U.S.

rail supply industry. By 1890 the 12,000 men working in the metropolitan area on car construction and repair were evenly divided among the railroad companies and independents. By that time, the manufacturing operations of the independents alone constituted the area's sixth largest industry. By 1900 two of the area's top 20 employers were independent railcar manufacturers: American Car & Foundry, which had about 1,500 workers in the Chicago area; and Pullman, which by that time employed about 6,000.

One of the world's leading manufacturers of railcars during the late nineteenth and early twentieth century, Pullman was the most important single company in the history of the railway supply business in America. This well-known enterprise was the creation of George M. Pullman, who began to experiment with the manufacture of specialty sleeper cars in Chicago during the 1850s and 1860s. In 1867, when there were already several dozen of Pullman's sleepers on the nation's railways, he formed the Pullman Palace Car Company. Although the new company was chartered in Illinois, it made most of its cars in New York and Michigan until the 1880s, when Pullman created a new company town a few miles south of Chicago. By the early 1890s, about 5,500 workers at the company's shops in the town of Pullman were making railcars at the rate of about 12,500 freight cars and 1,800 passenger cars per year. In 1894, after the company laid off hundreds of workers, Pullman became the center of a nationwide strike that would become one of best-known labor disputes in American history. In the years after the strike, Pullman workers continued to turn out huge numbers of railcars. By the 1920s, the Pullman-Standard Car Manufacturing Company was the leading U.S. manufacturer of railcars, with an annual production capacity of close to 100,000 freight cars and hundreds of passenger cars.

Pullman was not the only important railcar manufacturer in the Chicago area. There were dozens of area firms in the railcar business during the late nineteenth and early twentieth century. After the all-steel freight car was introduced in the 1890s, several Chicago companies became leaders in this field. The American Car & Foundry Company was formed in 1899 in a merger of 13 companies, including Chicago's own Wells, French & Co. During the first part of the twentieth century, American Car & Foundry employed about 1,500 area residents. Even more worked for the Western Steel Car & Foundry Company, a major freight car producer based in Hegewisch, which was making about 100 cars a day by 1905, when its annual sales came to over $7.5 million. This level of output was matched by the Standard Steel Car Company, which built a new plant in Hammond in 1906 and became part of Pullman-Standard in the 1920s. Another leading firm during this period was the Hicks Locomotive & Car Company, which ran two large plants in Chicago Heights.

Several Chicago-area firms specialized in supplying railroad companies and other firms in the industry with goods other than finished railcars. One such company was Crerar, Adams & Co., a firm led by John Crerar and

J. McGregor Adams, which during the late nineteenth century was one of
the Midwest's leading suppliers of specialty railroad goods such as lamps
and lanterns. Another important firm was Pettibone Mulliken Corporation, a Chicago company founded in 1880 that by the early twentieth century stood as a leading supplier of railroad track equipment such as frogs
(common crossings), crossings, and switches. Railroad cars across the nation stood on wheels manufactured by workers at the West Pullman plant
of the Griffin Wheel Company, which made as many as 500 wheels a day in
the 1900s and 1,000 a day in the 1920s. Other specialty manufacturers included Edward B. Leigh's Chicago Railway Equipment Company, a descendant of the National Hollow Brake Beam Company, founded in Chicago in
1887. During its first 20 years, this firm sold over 6 million brake beams.

Starting in the late nineteenth century, privately owned fleets of specialty cars—including sleepers, refrigerator cars, and tank cars—became
an increasingly important feature of the U.S. rail system. Chicago-area
companies were leaders in the production and operation of such cars. The
fleet of luxury sleepers built and run by the Pullman Company—8,000
of which were being used across the country by the 1930s—was particularly well known. No less important were refrigerator cars, which transformed the meatpacking industry. Introduced in the 1870s, these cars allowed packers to ship fresh meat to distant locations, giving them access
to larger markets. Many of the larger packers owned and operated their
own fleets of these cars: by the beginning of the twentieth century, Swift
& Co. owned nearly 6,000 cars and Armour & Co., nearly 14,000. Some
refrigerator cars were manufactured by the packers themselves; others by
specialty firms; and still others by large freight car makers such as Pullman and American Car & Foundry. Another important specialty car was
the tank car, which was used to transport oil or other liquids. During the
early twentieth century, local manufacturers such as the General American Tank Car Company of East Chicago were among the leading American
producers of tank cars.

By the early twentieth century, firms that leased freight cars to the railroads ranked among the most important kinds of enterprises in the U.S.
rail transport industry. Chicago-based companies led the field. The Union
Tank Car Company, a descendant of the Union Tank Line, created by John
D. Rockefeller's Standard Oil Company of Ohio, moved its headquarters to
Chicago in the 1920s. The first giant private car line in the United States,
this company increased the size of its fleet from about 10,000 tank cars in
1904 to over 30,000 during the 1920s. Another large Chicago-based company that leased huge numbers of freight cars was the General American
Transportation Corporation (later known as GATX). This company was
founded in Chicago in 1898 by Max Epstein as the Atlantic Seaboard Dispatch Company, which started with 28 used cars. Although it specialized
in leasing, General American soon began to manufacture some of its own
cars—including innovative specialty cars such as glass-lined milk tank
cars and nickel-lined compartments for holding acids—at its large shops

in East Chicago, Indiana. By the 1930s, General American had passed Union Tank Car as the owner of the nation's largest private freight car fleet; in 1948 it owned and operated about 55,000 cars, including tank, refrigerator, and other freight cars.

The railroad equipment and supply industry continued to employ thousands of Chicago-area residents through the middle part of the twentieth century, but it declined sharply (like many other manufacturing sectors in the Midwest) after the 1960s. By the early 1990s, the production of railroad equipment employed fewer than 5,000 area residents—a small fraction of the numbers of Chicagoans who had been working in the industry a century earlier. What caused this shrinkage? As the railroad industry became less dominant within the transportation field and less profitable over the course of the twentieth century, several leading companies shut down their Chicago-area factories, along with many other plants across the country. By the 1980s, Pullman, American Car & Foundry, and GATX had all closed their Chicago-area manufacturing operations.

Because the late twentieth-century decline of the railroad equipment manufacturing business in Chicago was part of a national trend, the importance of local firms within the national industry remained relatively high. In the early 1990s, workers at Chicago-area plants still accounted for about a fifth of the entire U.S. output of new railroad equipment. By that time, the leading local railcar maker was the Thrall Car Manufacturing Company of Chicago Heights, a division of the Elmhurst-based Duchossois Industries Inc. Another area firm that continued to make cars was the Union Tank Car Company, by then part of the Marmon Group, a Chicago-based conglomerate. And ABC Rail Products Inc., another firm based in the city, was selling about $240 million a year worth of railroad equipment such as wheels and track. Meanwhile, an Idaho-based company briefly used the old Pullman plant to make modest numbers of passenger cars, and GATX continued to be the leading U.S. lessor of tank cars. All of this activity amounted to a reasonably large economic chunk; but it was not comparable to what it had been at the height of the railway age, when Chicago was at the center of the railroad equipment and supply business, then one of the world's leading industries.          *Mark R. Wilson*

**Real Estate.** Few industries have been so closely connected to the development of the Chicago metropolitan region and the daily lives of its citizens as has real estate. In conjunction with governmental policies, regulations, and interventions, the real estate industry has exerted enormous influence on the sociogeographical contours of the entire metropolitan area.

Chicago's real estate activities divide into several branches, each with its trade, industry, or professional association. These include land assembly and subdivision platting, building, brokerage, property management, mortgage lending, land title insurance, and appraisal and land-value monitoring and research.

## NINETEENTH-CENTURY SUBDIVISION AND DEVELOPMENT

Chicago's early real estate enterprise was marked by large-scale development and land speculation attending one of the world's fastest-growing cities. In less than the life span of one of Chicago's earliest residents, Emily Beaubien Le Beau (1825–1919), Chicago grew from fewer than 100 people into being the fourth largest city in the world.

Most of Chicago's early builders and investors were attracted by the possibilities offered by canal building, the city's rapid growth after the Civil War, or its resurgence after the Great Fire of 1871. No other large city experienced such extensive and excessive subdivision platting and such volatile boom-and-bust cycles in land values. Fortunes were made and lost with each new cycle.

Subdividers fell into several categories of ownership and control: individuals, manufacturing companies, harbor and canal companies, improvement companies, land associations, syndicates, real estate corporations, and real estate companies. These early investors and developers shaped Chicago in many different ways. William B. Ogden, the first mayor of Chicago, was active in land sales connected with the Illinois & Michigan Canal, the Galena & Chicago Union Railroad, the Chicago Union Stock Yard, and the McCormick Reaper Company. John Wentworth, twice mayor of Chicago and three times congressman, facilitated the entry of the Illinois Central Railroad into Chicago and speculated in land in the Calumet region and Garfield Ridge. Senator Stephen A. Douglas also speculated in Calumet land in the late 1840s, bought 70 acres of lakefront between 33rd and 35th Streets in 1852, and helped arrange a federal land grant to the Illinois Central in 1853. Potter Palmer bought three-quarters of a mile of State Street in 1867, built a score of buildings there, and bought land on the Near North lakefront in 1882 for his mansion.

In the 1870s, the Pullman Palace Car Company and the Pullman Land Association bought nearly 4,000 acres for a factory and company town in Pullman, and Brown Steel Company built a company town in Irondale, now South Deering. During the same decade, the Calumet and Chicago Canal and Dock Company platted 6,000 acres in South Chicago, Calumet Heights, and the East Side. The firm of S. E. Gross targeted German buyers in bilingual ads for lots near horsecar and rail lines in the 1880s and near elevated lines in the 1890s, selling up to 500 lots a week in the land boom in the early years of that decade. In 1911, during another boom era, Bartlett Realty platted 600 acres in Archer Heights, Clearing, Gage Park, and Garfield Ridge. In 1918 the company created Greater Chicago, the city's largest single subdivision, in Roseland. Nine years later, it purchased 3,600 acres in what is now Beverly Shores, Indiana, to create a development that would rival Atlantic City.

This frenetic platting by individuals, land associations, and real estate corporations resulted in excessive subdivision. Riverside was platted in

1871 for a population of 10,000, a target reached only briefly a century later. Harvey was subdivided in 1890 to shelter a population of 25,000, a figure achieved 70 years later. The subdivision boom lasted until 1926. Only when the Great Depression slowed population growth to a standstill did the extent to which the Chicago area was over-subdivided become clear. By 1935 there were enough lots in the region to accommodate a population of 15 million, about three times the population at the time and almost 40 percent more than the population at the end of the century.

## RESIDENTIAL FINANCE

The success of subdivisions also depended on the highly interdependent building and mortgage lending industries. Before the introduction of long-term mortgages in 1934, a response to the crisis of the Great Depression, other lending instruments facilitated building. Cyclical building booms were sustained by state banks before 1970. Eastern insurance companies financed the post–Great Fire boom of 1889–92. "Shoestring" financing through the sale of real estate bonds fueled the building boom of 1922–28.

The Great Depression and World War II put the brake on building until 1945. Housing legislation under the New Deal replaced the familiar five-year balloon loan with the long-term mortgage loan. New housing programs sponsored by the Federal Housing Authority (FHA) and the Veterans' Administration (VA) were welcomed by the National Association of Home Builders, formed in 1942 to plan for postwar housing needs. The Mortgage Bankers Association of America (MBAA), created in 1914, was less receptive, fearful of competition from commercial banks and savings and loans to serve the greatly expanded market for home loans. The MBAA relented with the advent of VA loans in 1944 and expanded its membership to commercial banks and savings and loans.

FHA housing programs also had another significant effect on the metropolitan area. Adopting the evaluations of the Home Owners' Loan Corporation (HOLC) and the best practices of the National Association of Real Estate Boards, FHA mortgage insurance was readily available only in areas where both the housing stock and population mix met well-defined standards. As a result, postwar housing development and expansion occurred predominantly in newer suburban communities and in more affluent white neighborhoods.

## LAND TITLE SYSTEM

Several land title abstractors met in Chicago in 1907 to form the American Association of Title Men, renamed the American Title Association in 1923 and the American Land Title Association in 1962.

Ownership of real estate is conveyed by title. In Cook County, title is sometimes certified by the Torrens system of land registration, but more often by title insurance, which guarantees against title defects and liens. Illinois is one of a few states that allow title to be held in a "blind" trust, where title is held by a trustee for the benefit of the holder. Chicago Title and Trust Company is Chicago's largest title insurer and trustee of blind trusts.

## APPRAISAL AND RESEARCH

Inaugurating what would become the most reliable historical index of land values in the nation, George C. Olcott began his annual "Blue Book" of land values in 1910, establishing Chicago as a land-value laboratory. Foremost of the resulting surveys is Homer Hoyt's *One Hundred Years of Land Values in Chicago* (1933). Hoyt documented the highly volatile boom-and-bust cycles, determining that peak land values had occurred in 1836, 1856, 1869, 1891, and 1925, and that troughs had occurred in 1842, 1865, 1878, 1898, 1920, and 1933.

Recent advances in computerizing data on asking and selling prices on house sales reported in Multiple Listing Services maintained by local Boards of Realtors greatly facilitate the task of monitoring changes in housing values. Continuously updated data on asking and selling prices for different types of houses and locations allow the broker to identify housing suitable for buyers and the appraiser to determine the selling price of units comparable to the unit being appraised.

## POST–WORLD WAR II DEVELOPMENTS

Large subdivision building resumed after World War II, with plans that included two "new towns" of the British model. In 1949 Philip M. Klutznick assembled 3,000 acres of cornfield on the southern edge of Cook County to build the planned new town of Park Forest. In 1967 Lewis Manilow built the sister town of Park Forest South, now University Park.

Other large postwar subdividers have included Sam and Jack Hoffman, who bought a 160-acre farm in 1954 to build Hoffman Estates; the central Texas Centex Corporation, which assembled 1,500 acres for the planned residential/industrial complex of Elk Grove Village and Centex; and Hanover Builders and Three-H, who built several subdivisions in Hanover Park between 1961 and 1971.

Recovering from a 20-year moratorium on office-building construction took longer. The completion of the Prudential Building in 1955 opened a new era of skyscraper building in the Loop, topped out at the time by three of the world's tallest buildings.

In the 1970s, mortgage lenders in Chicago were accused of racial bias, as mortgage redlining—a term derived from the HOLC maps of the 1930s classifying certain neighborhoods as inappropriate for loans—became a big issue in the high-interest-rate era of the mid-1970s. Chicago's anti-redlining activists were in the forefront of protests and lobbying that culminated in passage of the Home Mortgage Disclosure Act of 1975 and the Community Reinvestment Act of 1977.

## REALTORS, URBAN RENEWAL, AND OPEN HOUSING

Chicago serves as national headquarters for the National Association of Realtors (NAR), the Institute of Real Estate Management (IREM), and five other real estate associations. Local brokers were prime movers in the founding of the National Association of Real Estate Exchanges in 1908, renamed the National Association of Real Estate Boards (NAREB) in 1916. The next year NAREB adopted "Realtor" as the title for its members. Among its activities was the creation of ethical practices for Realtors, including a commitment to not selling properties that would change the racial makeup of a community. NAREB took the name of National Association of Realtors in 1972. The Chicago affiliate changed its name from the Chicago Real Estate Board to the Chicago Association of Realtors at the same time.

NAREB's 1941 report "Housing and Blighted Areas" outlined a plan of federal-aided slum clearance that later inspired the National Housing Acts of 1949 and 1954. Local NAREB and IREM leaders including Holman Pettibone, Ferd Kramer, and Newton Farr helped guide Chicago's early renewal efforts. Pettibone worked hard to promote the "write down" formula, which was later incorporated in the Illinois Redevelopment Act of 1947. Kramer, president of the Metropolitan Housing and Planning Council, managed Lake Meadows, a project funded by New York Life, and developed Prairie Shores. Farr, a past president of NAREB, served on the Committee of Six that oversaw the Hyde Park–Kenwood Urban Renewal Project.

Urban Renewal legislation in the 1950s gave Chicago hospitals, universities, and community boards the power of eminent domain to clear slums and build Sandburg Village, Lake Meadows, Prairie Shores, Hyde Park A & B, and Lincoln Park I & II. New public buildings included the Dirksen, Daley, and Thompson Centers, the University of Illinois at Chicago, McCormick Place, and the Harold Washington Library.

Both NAR and IREM and its members were hard hit by steering/anti-steering lawsuits brought by local open housing groups, culminating in the Supreme Court decision in *Gladstone, Realtors v. Village of Bellwood* (1979). The Chicago Housing Authority was found guilty of operating a racially discriminatory housing program and ordered to desist in the *Gautreaux v. Chicago Housing Authority* decision of 1969, expanded by the Supreme Court in its *Gautreaux* opinion of 1976.

## RECENT TRENDS

Population growth in the Chicago region slowed in the 1970s before climbing again, especially in suburban areas. As it did, the real estate boom-and-bust cycles that punctuated Chicago's first century of rapid growth eased, until the first decade of the twenty-first century.

Overbuilding has persisted in some sectors, particularly in office space, resulting in double-digit vacancy rates both downtown and in the suburbs as new communications environments allowed for greater decentralization of business operations. Residential vacancy rates fluctuated around a low 3 percent in the 1990s in both the city and the suburbs. Spurred by the region's prosperity, low interest rates, and the desirability of real estate for investment, the closing years of the century witnessed a boom in the Chicago housing market. Developers converted downtown office buildings into residential units and built high-rise apartment buildings, condominiums, town houses, and single-family homes throughout the city, and whole areas were transformed. A new South Loop emerged, and most of the Chicago Housing Authority's high-rises were torn down. The suburban real estate market expanded to accommodate the sometimes dramatic population growth in the collar counties. Farmland was transformed into subdivisions of substantial homes. Properties like the former Glenview Naval Air Station became new communities, seemingly overnight.

Although Chicago was spared the worst of the sharp boom-and-bust real estate cycles experienced in California, Texas, and New England between 1983 and 1991 that resulted in the closing of hundreds of S&Ls in those regions, the easy credit of the early 2000s made Chicago's home real estate market vulnerable following the subprime mortgage crisis at the end of that decade. Falling housing prices put many mortgage holders "underwater" with loan amounts greater than the depressed market value of their homes.

The long-term impact of the housing crisis remains unclear. What is clear, however, is that the real estate industry will continue to shape the metropolitan region as it has since the early years of land speculation.

*Pierre deVise*

**Record Publishing.** Chicago's performers drive its record industry. While major labels maintain regional distribution offices in Chicago, their studios are in New York or Los Angeles. This vacuum creates opportunities for hundreds of independent labels run by local entrepreneurs. Many "indies" struggle, but some succeed.

Beginning in 1922, Brunswick (Iowa), Gennett (Indiana), Okeh (New York), and Paramount (Wisconsin)—largely offshoots of Midwest piano manufacturers—recorded Chicago's leading blues and jazz talents, making the city a pioneer in "race records." In 1924 Marsh Recording Laboratories, based in Chicago, released the first electric recordings, on its Autograph label. By 1930 most jazz activity had moved to New York. Between August 1942 and November 1944, Chicago's James C. Petrillo, president of the American Federation of Musicians, enforced a wartime national recording ban.

After World War II, Chicago-based companies such as Chance (1950), Chess (1950), J.O.B. (1949), Delmark (1953), Parrot (1952), United (1952), and Vee-Jay (1953)—the largest black-owned label before Motown—mined the city's talent (especially blues, doo-wop, gospel, jazz, and soul), forming the core of Record Row on South Michigan Avenue (1960s). Chicago's psychedelic bands appeared on Dunwich and USA, and Curtis Mayfield founded soul label Curtom (1968). Mercury, the city's last major label, closed in 1964. The 1970s welcomed blues and folk staples Alligator (1971), Flying Fish (1974), and Earwig Blues (1978), while Trax and D.J. International featured Chicago house music (1980s). Since then, indies such as Cedille (1989) and Cajual (1994) have continued to accompany Chicago's performance scene.                                                       *Mark Clague*

**Restaurants.** Public dining has an important role in Chicago's social, cultural, and economic history. Types and numbers of eating establishments are tied to Chicago's growth from village to city. Dining outside the home may be divided into three broad categories: sit-down restaurants (from fine dining to "cheap" eateries); street food (including dining at public events such as ball games and fairs); and a combination of these two, fast-food stands. Within these groups are varied establishments such as saloons of the pre-Prohibition era, beer gardens, taverns, and cafeterias. All are or have been critical segments of the dining industry.

Because dining enterprises mirror the city's economic growth, their histories might be considered in two ways: pull and push. Restaurants represent the centripetal forces that made the city the economic hub of the Midwest. Chicago's famed steakhouses testified to its hegemony in cattle shipping and meat processing. The city's historical core business area, the Loop, has been an economic catchment center. Visitors to the Midwest's capital city and the necessity of feeding incoming hordes of workers made Chicago's eating places elements of a major industry. By 2000 the Chicago area's dining establishments did an estimated $10 billion in sales, second among U.S. metropolitan areas only to Los Angeles.

Types of prepared-food retailing businesses in the city followed this pulling-in pattern on three levels. Traditional sit-down, white-tablecloth restaurants became featured attractions for locals and visitors alike. The dining room of the Lake House Hotel on Kinzie Street set the pattern in 1835. It used menu cards, napkins, and toothpicks and served oysters brought in from the East Coast. The many others that followed in the nineteenth century, from Henrici's to Rector's, made Chicago a destination restaurant city.

Interior of a restaurant with a primarily working-class male clientele, ca. 1895. Courtesy of the Chicago History Museum (ICHi-30447).

City shoppers and workers who packed downtown offices led to a boom in eating places. "Cheap eats" restaurants first appeared in the 1880s, and many upscale restaurants and hotels served inexpensive lunches. Beginning in 1880 with H. H. Kohlsaat's "dairy lunch room," quick-service restaurants for midday meals sprang up. John Kruger began a small chain in the 1890s, dubbing them "Cafeterias." Soon major chains such as Thompson's (with more than one hundred outlets), B/G Foods, Pixley & Ehlers, and many others were so numerous that the area around Madison and Clark Streets became known as "Toothpick Alley." Through proximity to work and shopping, city restaurants became magnets for urban populations.

Food stands and street vendors fall into the category of petty consumption. Though important parts of the food economy, some have historically operated as cash businesses and therefore have been underreported and are an aspect of the underground economy. Stands selling one of Chicago's paradigmatic foods, hot dogs, dot the city: an estimated 3,000 in present-day Chicago. None of the places are destination dining spots, but they are significant economic players by sheer numbers alone. By the end of the twentieth century, the major purveyor of hot dogs in Chicago, the Vienna Sausage Manufacturing Company, was a business with some $98 million in annual sales. In neighborhoods where immigrants lived and did business, ethnic restaurants and fast-food stands specializing in national cuisines flourished. More recently, despite more restrictive licensing regulations than in many other cities, updated versions of food trucks began, at the end of the first decade of the twenty-first century, to offer Chicagoans a wide variety of ethnic and upscale cuisines at locations throughout the city.

Cafeterias and lunch counters were some of many innovations in dining that pushed out across the country. Lunch counters, the ancestors of fast-food establishments, began in 1858 at Chicago's Rock Island Railroad Station. By 1900 the name "cafeteria" had spread across the country, carried along the transportation lines that flowed through the Chicago hub. Latter-day versions of this process are corporate fast-food dining places such as Chicago-area-based McDonald's, which in 2008 had sales of more than $70 billion worldwide.

Fast-food stands and cafeterias were not the only restaurant innovations that became national trends. Fred Mann opened a Chicago seafood restaurant in 1923 with a maritime decor that include fishnets, portholes, and waitresses dressed as sailors. An instant hit, other theme restaurants quickly sprang up across the country. The pattern was updated in the 1970s when Richard Melman and partners opened a series of casual dining restaurants in the Chicago area beginning with R. J. Grunts in 1971. The idea was quickly copied by national chains. In its 40 years of operation, the company Melman founded, Lettuce Entertain You Enterprises Inc., has owned or licensed many well-known restaurants across the United States and Japan. Like McDonald's, this and other dining enterprises have extended outward, thus enriching Chicago's economy and its reputation for dining. By the beginning of the new century, Chicago-based celebrity chefs and their restaurants expanded the city's reputation for fine dining, a reputation acknowledged in 2010 when Michelin's introduced its first 2011 Guide to Chicago Restaurants. Its starred restaurants showcased the city's internationally famous restaurants, and the guide demonstrated the wide range of restaurants that made the Chicago region such a good place to dine.                                                                         *Bruce Kraig*

**Savings and Loans.** Chicago's first building and loan association (called savings and loans after the 1930s) was established in 1849. Building and loan associations originated as part of the cooperative movement that began in England in the eighteenth century and came to the United States in the early nineteenth century. Building and loans originally were established for working-class people who wanted to buy homes but did not have access to banks. A group of people would deposit their savings into an association, then as the association gained enough money, it would finance mortgages for its members. Unlike banks, building and loan associations made their investments based primarily on the interests of their members, rather than investing for the greatest return and security. Associations also tended to serve small groups or communities and did not offer many of the services that banks did.

Chicago's small associations flourished in the 1880s, and by 1893—largely because of Chicago—Illinois ranked third in the nation in the number of building and loan associations, with 518. The impressive growth of Chicago's building and loan associations was steady between roughly 1880 and 1930, except for a portion of the 1890s. The 1890s was a period of depression and of "national" building and loan associations, many of which were based in Minnesota and Illinois. Because many nationals were fraudulent, associations across the country formed strong local, state, and national organizations that ran publicity campaigns and lobbied for legislation to ban nationals. Illinois passed such legislation in 1896.

Building and loan associations were most important to Chicago's working class, especially those who were members of ethnic communities. Commercial banks were rare in working-class neighborhoods. Although there were private ethnic banks, these often failed, did not receive as much public confidence as building and loans, and were banned in Illinois in 1917. Building and loan associations were especially popular among the ethnic groups that were hungriest for home ownership, namely, the Czechs, Poles, and Italians. Even when commercial banking became more widely accessible after World War I, many ethnic community leaders endorsed the local building and loan associations instead of non-ethnic commercial banks, because they thought the associations promoted ethnic solidarity. By the end of 1918, there were 255 building and loan associations in Chicago, and the majority of them were part of ethnic working-class communities.

There was, however, tension between the ethnic and non-ethnic associations, as the latter looked askance at the business practices of smaller and more community-oriented ethnic associations. Efforts to get ethnic associations to change their business practices and join industry organizations met with mixed success. Many of the ethnic associations formed their own organizations, such as the American Czecho-Slovak, Polish American, Swedish, and Lithuanian Building and Loan Leagues, some of which eventually joined the Illinois League.

The Great Depression of the 1930s had a tremendous impact upon building and loan associations. Part of the reason they fared poorly, especially the ethnic ones, was that they had made many of their investments in the best interests of the community rather than profit. Many Chicago associations folded or were bailed out by the federal government. As a result of this crisis, the government took a much stronger role in the industry, both through regulation and by insuring customers' deposits.

Associations that survived had to follow more stringent business rules and as a result became more similar to commercial banks. This was also the period when the associations came to be called savings and loans. The operation of S&Ls was still distinguishable from banks, but associations after World War II made greater efforts to replicate the services of commercial banks.

In the post–World War II era, savings and loans continued to grow until the crisis of the 1980s. In an effort to make ailing S&Ls more competitive with banks and to allow them to deal with high inflation rates, the Ford, Carter, and Reagan administrations substantially deregulated the industry. To bolster their business, many associations began making high-risk/high-yield loans, but as these ventures often failed, the industry came crashing down. Deregulation had also made it easier for banking officials to engage in corrupt practices, which worsened the crash.

Although Chicago's institutions fared much better than those in the South and West, most savings and loans were in trouble, and publicity from the crash discouraged patronage. In its effort to save the industry, the federal government forced many of Chicago's associations to close or merge, producing fewer and larger S&Ls. The largest association to come out of this era was Talman Home Federal, which was forced to merge with two other institutions and emerged as the third largest savings and loan in the nation.

Talman's history is illustrative of the major changes that affected Chicago's S&Ls. It began as a Bohemian ethnic association, became more similar to a bank in the postwar era, merged with other S&Ls during the crisis of the 1980s, then merged with the LaSalle Bank, which in turn was purchased by Dutch giant ABN-AMRO and subsequently by Bank of America. At the end of the twentieth century, approximately 14 savings and loans still existed in the Chicago metropolitan area, but there were far fewer than before the 1980s, and their character was more similar to that of banks than was the case before the Great Depression.     *Jeffrey A. Brune*

**Sporting Goods Manufacturing.** Sports are played for recreation and personal fitness, while sporting events are prominent entertainment and business enterprises. Sports and sporting activities consistently attracted Chicagoans, and the types of sporting goods manufactured and activities pursued by the residents of Chicago provide insight into shifting social and economic conditions. In the late nineteenth and early twentieth century, as income levels began to rise, the citizens of Chicago and the nation experienced expanding levels of prosperity, which allowed them to turn to sporting activities in their leisure time. Time away from work helped create and expand the market for sporting goods manufacturers. With companies like Spalding, Wilson, Brunswick, Schwinn, and Kiefer, Chicago has been home to many of the most recognizable brands in sporting goods manufacturing.

Chicago's physical expansion and demographic dynamism have stimulated demand for an increasingly wide range of sports equipment. German American immigrants pushed the Chicago School Board to initiate a gymnastics program in 1885. By 1914 every one of the city's public high schools had gymnasiums and physical fitness programs. The popularity of archery, handball and racquetball, swimming, tennis, golf, bowling, weightlifting, roller-skating, and bicycling all depended upon the availability of space as well as affordable equipment. Space became more available as public parks began to be not merely public gardens but also locations that increasingly encouraged recreational and fitness activities. In 1895 the city of Chicago opened its first public beach, in Lincoln Park. Five years later, there were 26 golf courses and a number of public outdoor swimming pools in the metropolitan area. Equipment became more affordable as escalating industrialization encouraged mass production, resulting in falling prices in this industry as in others.

The emergence of the sporting goods industry is closely linked with the growth of organized sport teams, especially professional baseball. Although early sporting goods equipment was crudely fabricated and locally supplied, one Chicago-based manufacturer shaped and redefined the industry with its aggressive marketing strategy. Chicago had the economic advantage in the manufacture of balls and gloves with its plentiful supply of hides and leathers, a by-product of the meatpacking industry. After opening a sporting goods store in 1876, Albert Goodwill Spalding (1850–1915), in partnership with his brother and brother-in-law, manufactured baseball gloves and, beginning in 1878 and for the next hundred years, was the exclusive supplier of the "official baseball of the National League." While still an early star player of professional baseball, Spalding was one of the first players to wear a baseball glove, which was, of course, manufactured and sold by A. G. Spalding & Brothers. Soon professionals and amateurs alike were using the equipment made and distributed by Spalding, and his name became synonymous with baseball and other sporting activities. As a player, manager, promoter, and manufacturer, Albert Spalding helped establish baseball as a national pastime. By the time the press began referring to Spalding as baseball's "Big Mogul," he had branded himself the "father of American baseball." By the late nineteenth century, Spalding had a virtual monopoly on sporting goods equipment.

Another sporting goods manufacturer that profited from the proximity of the by-products of Chicago's stockyards was the Ashland Manufacturing Company, founded in 1913. In 1914 Thomas Wilson was named the new president of Ashland. In 1916 the company was renamed the Thomas E. Wilson Company and in 1931 became the Wilson Sporting Goods Company. Even though Thomas Wilson left the firm in 1918, as a brand name Wilson has remained one of the most familiar trade names in sporting goods manufacturing. From its origins on the South Side of Chicago, Wilson manufactured a diverse line of balls, racquets, athletic footwear, golf clubs, and other sporting goods and, with its early acquisition of knitting mills, significantly expanded its product line into the production of jerseys and uniforms. Wilson has been innovative and aggressive in both its manufacturing activities and in its marketing campaigns. It was among the first American manufacturers to rely on celebrity consultants and had endorsements from such prominent sporting figures as Knute Rockne in football, Gene Sarazen and Sam Snead in golf, "Lefty" Gomez and Ted Williams in baseball, and Jack Kramer in tennis.

Along with baseball, another emerging national pastime in the late nineteenth century was cycling. The popularity of bicycles can be understood by their use not only in sporting events but also for recreational activity and as a means of basic transportation. By the late 1880s, bicycle races had become familiar events in Chicago and helped to promote the general use of bicycles. By the late nineteenth century, there were approximately 300 firms manufacturing bicycles in the United States, and even though many of these manufacturers were based in New England's Connecticut Valley, there were 101 Chicago-based manufacturers by the mid-1890s. The popularity of cycling allowed Spalding to diversify its product line to include bicycle manufacturing in 1894. In 1895 German immigrant Ignaz Schwinn (1860–1948) founded a bicycle manufacturing partnership with Adolph Arnold, as Arnold, Schwinn & Co. The firm became Schwinn & Co. in 1908. From its first production facility in downtown Chicago, it became one of the most recognizable names in the industry and for decades accounted for at least a quarter of bicycle manufacturing in the United States.

The oldest manufacturer of recreational and leisure-time products in the United States is the Brunswick Corporation. Brunswick originated in the 1840s as a Cincinnati-based carriage and cabinetry maker that manufactured billiard tables. The company moved to Chicago in 1848; by the 1880s, when the firm had diversified its product line to include bowling pins and bowling balls, Brunswick was one of Chicago's most well-known and successful manufacturers. Another prominent sporting figure and sporting goods manufacturer from Chicago is Adolph Kiefer. In 1946 the former Olympic swimmer and spokesman established Adolph Kiefer & Associates, which has over the years not only designed and manufactured sporting goods but also promoted and enhanced aquatic sports and safety.                                                               *Timothy E. Sullivan*

**Tourism and Conventions.** Always a place of commerce and spectacle, Chicago from its infancy played host to major conventions and to individual travelers. As early as 1847, Chicago hosted a meeting of American business and political leaders that brought 20,000 to a city whose population was only 16,000.

The city's central location in the United States, access, large meeting areas, and ample hotel rooms over the years created a spot unequaled for efficient gatherings, and by the 1990s industry-specific conventions such as the hardware or housewares show generated $5 billion annually for the local economy. While conventioneers or businesspeople come for a reason—to meet or to study an innovation—such visitors typically branch out and enjoy the city's shopping, cultural, entertainment, or sports offerings.

From 1850 on, political, industrial, commercial, religious, and sports conventions have been held regularly in Chicago. Even in the beginning, business leaders underwrote infrastructure costs for such events, knowing that upfront spending brought even greater returns when visitors arrived and opened their wallets and purses for the city's plentiful goods and services. Local and federal funds were used as well, and by the 1960s, under the guidance of Mayor Richard J. Daley, convention halls, highways, and the airports had been built, expanded, or modernized, creating one of the world's most modern and functional meeting centers.

Temporary outdoor stages were among the first structures built to accommodate conventions. Permanent structures followed: the Wigwam was built to attract the 1860 Republican Convention, and by the turn of the century the vast, turreted Coliseum became home to large gatherings and political conventions. The Republican Party chose the Coliseum for its gathering three times from 1908 through 1916.

In 1960 the McCormick Place Convention Center was opened. While the hall was not an instant success, when it burned seven years later, it was quickly rebuilt and expanded. Two more halls were added in later years, creating 2.1 million feet of space. By 2011 a fourth building had been built increasing exhibition space to 2.67 million square feet and adding a ballroom and 250,000 square feet of meeting rooms. Owned by the Metropolitan Pier and Exposition Authority, McCormick Place hosted over 2 million visitors for conventions, meetings, and other events in 2010. The United Center opened as a sport (Chicago Bulls and Blackhawks) and entertainment showcase in 1994; it was also home to the 1996 Democratic National Convention.

While conventions typically have been a boon to the city, some have proved to be a public relations disaster (e.g., television cameras captured Chicago police beating students protesting the Vietnam War during the 1968 Democratic National Convention).

For decades Chicago tourism was limited to domestic travelers, typically honeymooners, businesspeople, or residents from smaller midwestern cities and rural towns who came to shop and marvel at the city's manifestations of power and wealth: Prairie Avenue mansions, grand European-style hotels, massive grain elevators, and endless train yards. Later, Gold Coast homes, the Willis (Sears) Tower and other skyscrapers, and the trading floors of the Chicago Board of Exchange provided the same power to awe.

But before 1900, writers and visitors from Europe either praised the city for its rapid growth or dismissed it as a mishmash of wealth and poverty. The World's Columbian Exposition of 1893 boosted the city's image, but some observers noted that the magnificent and orderly fairgrounds were temporary, while the city's problems with grime and poverty appeared to be permanent. Domestic visitors were not put off by the city's extremes, however, and before its close, 12 million total attendees had come for the fair. In a single day set aside to celebrate Illinois, more than 540,000 came.

The Century of Progress Exposition in 1933 provided a similar occasion for visiting Chicago, as well as a bright glimmer of hope in the midst of the Great Depression. Again, observers noted how the forward-looking fairgrounds compared with the grim reality of Chicago's slums. Even so, visitors flocked to the fair: more than 39 million attended over the course of a year.

By the 1950s, most tourists came from a 500-mile radius and were friends or family of area residents. It wasn't until the late 1980s that Chicago blossomed as a world-class destination, its image fueled by top-flight retail stores lining North Michigan Avenue, major one-of-a-kind shows at the Art Institute of Chicago and other museums, blues and jazz clubs, dazzling architecture, lake and river cruises, fine dining, gallery districts, discount shopping in the suburbs, historic Wrigley Field, as well as the opportunity to see in action basketball legend Michael Jordan. By 1995 tours of ethnic neighborhoods and their cultural institutions were added to many itineraries. Certain neighborhoods such as Pilsen, with a large Mexican population, began courting tourists with walking maps and periodic festivals and ethnic fare timed with cultural holidays. More recently, the summer music festival Lollapalooza has attracted hundreds of thousands of tourists to Chicago.

The increase in domestic and international tourists had a major economic impact on Chicago in the 1990s, causing a boom in hotel building, restaurant openings, and services geared to travelers, both in the city and the suburbs. The city's efforts to host the 2016 Olympics, although unsuccessful, demonstrated how important tourist dollars have become for the local economy. In 2010 Chicago hosted some 39 million domestic and foreign visitors who spent over $11 billion in the city and contributed over $600 million in tax revenues. That year the tourism industry contributed some 124,000 jobs.                                                  *Anne Moore*

**Toy Manufacturing.** Throughout the twentieth century, Chicago was home to the leading manufacturers of toys, from Lincoln Logs and Tinkertoys to Pac-Man machines and Beanie Babies. Toy manufacturers thrived in Chicago for the same reasons makers of other products did: rail, water, and air transport provided a cheap means to receive raw goods and to ship finished products to wholesalers and retailers worldwide. The city's abundant labor supply also contributed to the area's attractiveness as a manufacturing base.

By 1900 manufactured toys were designed to be smaller versions of the machinery, conveniences, or building materials used by adults: cars, trains, cabs, and tractors were molded from cast iron, fitted with clockwork engines, and stamped with a real brand name at such firms as Hafner Manufacturing Company, whose plant was on the Near West Side. By 1907 Hafner was handling huge orders for the look-alike mechanical toys—especially their model trains, the American Flyer line—pouring in from New York wholesalers and local merchants such as Montgomery Ward & Co.

So great was the demand for realistic toy cars that in 1923 Freeport-based Structo Manufacturing Company turned from making Erector Set–style building toys to making model-kit vehicles such as a toy Model T, which came with a real hand crank and shifting gears. Similarly constructed trucks and tractors filled out the Structo line, which flourished for decades.

A special variety of miniature toy got its start in Chicago, when publisher Charles O. Dowst saw a Linotype machine at the World's Columbian Exposition and lit on the idea that such a machine could be modified to stamp out tiny metal charms. From there, Dowst founded Tootsietoys, the company that made tiny charms and novelties, including the prizes found in boxes of Cracker Jack. Dowst was the first to create a die-cast miniature car; he later made a replica of the Model T Ford, then General Motors cars and Mack trucks. Makers of those cars and trucks often requested a look-alike by Tootsietoys and used the miniatures as marketing gimmicks.

Chicago was also the birthplace of some famous wooden toys. Tinkertoys—still a popular building toy—were created in Evanston by Charles H. Pajeau, who poked holes on the rim of a wooden sewing spool and created an ingenious building joint, allowing wooden spokes to be connected in a variety of directions. Pajeau first exhibited his invention—as a windmill—in a storefront during a New York toy fair in 1914 and never lacked for buyers after that time. By the 1960s, 2 million Tinkertoy sets sold annually. The product was then owned by another company, but Pajeau ran the Toy Tinkers Company from Evanston until 1952.

Lincoln Logs, first made out of notched redwood in 1918, were invented by John Lloyd Wright, the architect's son, and marketed along with other sturdy, functional wood toys under the Red Square Toy Company name. The company was bought in 1943 by Playskool Corporation, another toy giant with roots in Chicago, which still markets Lincoln Logs.

Metal toy makers were caught in a squeeze for raw goods during World War II—when certain materials were rationed or became exorbitantly expensive—and an industry-wide consolidation over several decades left Chicago with few local toy manufacturers by the 1960s. Also, toy makers turned to plastic by the 1950s, rendering much of the Chicago manufacturers' equipment obsolete.

Some toy makers live on in the area. Chicago-based Radio Flyer Inc., for example, markets a toy-size version of its distinctive red wagon, though the manufacturing of that toy is done overseas.

The making of coin-operated amusements took off just as toys made from metal and wood began their decline. In 1932 Chicago-based Lion Manufacturing Corporation created the first pinball machine, the Bally-hoo—which sold 50,000 in less than a year—and spawned a new company, Bally Manufacturing Company, which is still based here.

While Bally was the biggest, two other Chicago-area companies—Williams Electronics and D. Gottlieb & Co.—were also major makers of hand-operated games, and once again Chicago became a major center for the manufacture of goods for amusement.

Of the three, Bally reigned supreme because of steady innovation. Bally created the first electric slot machine in the 1960s, and only ten years later, it embraced a variety of the newest technologies to create the best-selling arcade games of the late twentieth century: Space Invaders and Pac-Man.

By 1994 miniatures came back into fashion with the arrival of Beanie Babies, made by Oak Brook–based Ty Inc. The beanbag animals came tagged with amusing names like Cubbie the Bear, Patti the Platypus, or Bronty the Brontosaurus. Such was the craze for the little limited-edition creatures that collectors bid as high as $5,000 for $5.95 items.     *Anne Moore*

**Underground Economy.** The underground economy involves the exchange of goods and services that are hidden from official view. Examples of such activities range from babysitting "off the books" to selling narcotics. Over time the underground economy has changed as lawmakers redefine what is legal or what is to be taxed. How far "underground" an activity is depends not only on its legal status but also on the capacity of government to enforce laws and/or collect taxes. The underground economy serves willing customers. However, the fact that it is hidden from official view may impose unique costs on participants (e.g., bribes), create opportunities for monopoly, reward a sub-optimal scale of operations, or even encourage violence.

Early Chicago's underground economy was limited, for relatively few economic activities were licensed or regulated. Social and economic change led Americans to demand tighter regulation of personal behavior and, later, economic activity. Shortly after the city's founding, some Chicagoans, especially affluent ones of native stock, expressed worry over gambling, vice, and alcohol; the first temperance society was founded in 1833. Nineteenth-century Chicago also attracted disproportionate numbers of young men, many unattached, and many business travelers. In conditions of urban anonymity, commercial gambling, sex, and drinking thrived, despite the law. City officials were reluctant to alienate voters, visitors, or underground entrepreneurs who cultivated them with political support and outright bribery. There were sporadic raids and arrests but no serious attempt to close illegal businesses until the turn of the twentieth century, when the old Levee vice district was closed. However, proposals for legal, regulated prostitution made no headway.

By the late nineteenth century, the illegal sector of the underground

economy consisted of hundreds of small, mostly owner-operated businesses, primarily brothels and gambling houses. Prostitution was a multi-
million-dollar business, and gambling was even more lucrative. Gambling
houses thrived in and near the downtown, and specialized vice districts
radiated out from rail stations at the edges of the Loop, making little effort at secrecy. Protection from police raids was absolutely essential, and
a handful of politicians arranged this.

Meanwhile, the underground economy broadened as businesses whose
products were legal evaded new regulations aimed at controlling the
emerging industrial economy. For example, despite the enactment of an
ambitious building code by the 1870s, vast numbers of small contractors
and landlords continued to erect structures and operate them in violation
of the code. An 1893 state law prohibited employment of children under
the age of 14 in manufacturing, and the law was soon extended to other
industries. Authorities claimed that 8,543 underage children worked in
industry in Illinois cities in 1900. Enforcement was difficult because enforcement agencies were understaffed. Child labor declined most rapidly
in large enterprises targeted by inspectors, such as meatpacking. Compulsory schooling helped as well, though smaller businesses such as garment
makers continued to hire children.

Other products, once legal, became illegal. In 1897 state law restricted
the sale of opiates, which had previously been available in ordinary drugstores. Subsequent legislation tightened up access to narcotics, and druggists, drug companies, and doctors gradually conformed to the law. The
demand for these drugs was intense, and new entrepreneurs appeared.
By the 1920s, illegal drug importers and wholesalers were well organized.
Small-scale retailers sold to friends and acquaintances, often in established vice areas.

A similar process drove the manufacture and sale of alcoholic beverages underground during national Prohibition (1920–33). Prohibition was
the greatest achievement of the constellation of movements to regulate
personal behavior that was deemed immoral. Bootlegging quickly became
the largest source of illegal income and jobs. Gross receipts from Chicago
breweries, beer distributorships, and liquor importing were estimated at
$60 million in 1927.

Bootlegging shows how a business's illegal status could transform its
character. The absence of legal property rights to most illegal businesses,
and the participants' unwillingness to rely on the police, led to violence.
At first bootlegging in Chicago was conducted by numerous independent
operators, but it was eventually organized into a cartel that divided sales
territories, raised prices, and reduced consumer choice and product quality. Illegal entrepreneurs devoted extraordinary energy and ingenuity to
arranging political protection, guarding against hijacking, and murder-
ing rivals. While great wealth was possible, imprisonment was likely and
a violent death was not uncommon.

Ordinary jobs in this sector were relatively undesirable. Employees were drawn from impoverished neighborhoods, and, in spite of earning above-average incomes for those neighborhoods, they suffered from violence and arrest, enjoyed few benefits, and (with a few exceptions) had low status. Women recruited by cheap brothels daily risked becoming infected with sexually transmitted diseases.

Class, race, and ethnicity helped determine where illegal businesses located. For instance, when the old vice areas were forced out of the Loop in the 1910s, sex businesses moved into immigrant and African American neighborhoods. Because they were politically weak or represented by politicians linked to vice interests, these areas had difficulty keeping out vice. Some illegal businesses were more welcome than others. "Policy" (known elsewhere as the numbers game) was a major source of jobs and of investment capital in African American neighborhoods. Similarly, some less affluent suburbs welcomed or at least tolerated illegal enterprises because they contributed to local tax revenues and created jobs. By contrast, residents of well-to-do areas were more vigilant in enforcing the law, especially Prohibition.

Since the 1930s, the underground economy continued to change as taxation and government regulation grew, while its illegal sector began emphasizing new activities. During World War II, the federal government rationed hundreds of items and controlled prices. In Chicago and elsewhere, a black market quickly emerged to sell goods in limited supply. More important, the federal government paid for the war by taxing the incomes of most wage and salary earners. After the war, extensive taxation remained, to pay for the war debt and the enlarged size of the federal government, including the military. In the 1970s, the IRS estimated that Americans failed to report at least $100 billion in income, most of it legal income. Other taxes were evaded as well.

Tens of thousands of Chicagoans work for cash that they may not report—babysitters, lawn-care workers, even garment workers. Typically they work in small-scale businesses or are self-employed. Some are moonlighting; some are seriously exploited. Tax evasion peaked in the early 1980s, diminishing as the federal government cut tax rates.

Some workers and businesses operate underground to avoid government regulations. For instance, when licensed taxi cabs failed to provide adequate service to South Side African American neighborhoods in the 1930s and 1940s, unlicensed jitney cab operators filled the gap, plying their trade openly on the streets until Mayor Martin Kennelly ordered a crackdown. In 1980 an estimated half of all Chicago home-remodeling jobs were completed without required permits. Unlicensed child-care providers have met a growing demand for services, evading official requirements concerning facilities.

Beginning in the 1930s, the illegal sector changed as the syndicate formerly headed by Al Capone declined and a new syndicate arose. After

Prohibition this syndicate, with its centralized organization and substantial capital, expanded its suburban gambling operations and in the late 1940s muscled its way into the independent "policy" gambling operations, dominated by African American entrepreneurs. This "traditional" syndicate lost ground, however. Demand for prostitutes' services diminished, competition from the state lottery and legalized casinos cut into gambling and policy revenues, and courts imprisoned mobsters for tax and other violations.

Even as this syndicate wound down, the demand for narcotics and other controlled substances rose, and the illegal drug business expanded. In the 1950s and 1960s, street gangs such as the Blackstone Rangers began selling illegal drugs. Despite aggressive and successful federal prosecutions beginning in the 1970s, large street gangs remained in the drug business. Their activities spread throughout poor neighborhoods, where legitimate jobs are scarce. Some customers are local, but many came from elsewhere. In more affluent city neighborhoods and suburbs, drug dealing takes different forms, off the street, embedded in social networks where it is very difficult to police.

Perhaps the most unusual part of the underground economy was Jane, a group founded in 1969 by feminists in Hyde Park to provide abortions. Illinois had banned abortions in 1867, but initially recognized broad exceptions to the ban. As definitions of legal "therapeutic" abortion narrowed and official surveillance increased, abortion providers dwindled in number. Jane was a loosely organized group, operating out of conviction rather than a profit motive. Four years after its founding, the U.S. Supreme Court decriminalized abortion, making it again officially part of the regular economy.

Government enforcement capacity grew substantially in the twentieth century, but the underground economy will likely continue to exist. Even with strong public support for law, some enterprises will always engage in illegal activity to meet demand and make a profit. Enforcement is especially difficult when politically effective constituencies are divided over what to define as illegal.                                        *Christopher Thale*

**Wholesaling.** Given that Chicago long ranked as America's "Second City," it is not surprising that it has served since the mid-nineteenth century as a major wholesaling center. Like most cities, Chicago has been a place for the exchange and distribution of commodities and information. Some of the most important actors in this urban economy have been wholesalers—that is, merchants who specialize in connecting the producers of commodities with the retailers who sell them to final users. Chicago wholesalers have been among the leading distributors and marketers of all sorts of goods, including lumber, grain, dry goods, hardware, and metals. Although the power of merchant middlemen has declined in many industries during the years since Chicago was founded, at the beginning of the twenty-first century, the city remained a wholesaling capital.

Chicago's wholesale trade grew rapidly after the Illinois & Michigan Canal was completed in 1848, and this growth was boosted even further by the completion of major railroad links to the city during the 1850s. By the eve of the Civil War, when the volume of the city's annual wholesale trade was estimated at no less than $32 million, Chicago had become one of the most important centers in North America for the distribution and marketing of lumber and grain. Leading Chicago lumber merchants like Charles Mears built fortunes during the city's early years by serving as wholesalers of forest products, sorting and grading lumber, and collecting commissions by connecting producers and consumers. Meanwhile, grain-elevator owners and merchants were making the city into one of the world's most important sites for the marketing of corn and wheat. The Chicago Board of Trade, one of the city's most important institutions, served as a regulator and promoter of the wholesale trade in grain.

During the latter part of the nineteenth century, when Chicago continued to serve as a major center for the distribution of farm products, the city's merchants became some of the world's leading wholesalers of manufactured goods. By 1900 there were nearly 3,400 wholesale dealers in the city, and the volume of the annual wholesale trade handled by Chicago firms stood at about $1 billion. The city's greatest wholesalers at this time were the companies led by Marshall Field and John V. Farwell, both of which sold dry goods such as textiles and clothing. Marshall Field & Co., which by the later twentieth century would be known only as a department store retailer, was once one of the world's leading wholesalers. By the early 1880s, when Field's partner Levi Leiter left the company, its annual sales totaled about $4 million in the retail department and $22 million in wholesale. The company's wholesale division, headed by John G. Shedd, purchased most of its goods from dealers in New York City and sold them to retailers throughout the Midwest by sending out catalogs and traveling salesmen. In 1887 Shedd's division moved into an enormous new Chicago wholesale store, designed by the architect H. H. Richardson and containing about 12 acres of floor space and 1,800 employees. Only slightly smaller than the wholesale operations of Marshall Field & Co. were those of the company owned by John V. Farwell, a veteran of the Chicago dry-goods trade. By the 1880s, when Field and Farwell reportedly ranked as two of the three leading wholesalers in the United States, the latter company was selling $20 million worth of goods a year to retailers around the country.

Field and Farwell were not the only important firms during the wholesaling heyday that was occurring in Chicago during the late nineteenth and early twentieth century. In the field of dry goods, other major Chicago wholesalers included Mandel Brothers and Carson Pirie Scott. Among the city's leading dealers in groceries were Henry Horner & Co., which started wholesale operations in 1856, and William M. Hoyt & Co., which also started before the Civil War and was selling over $5 million worth of groceries a year by the early 1890s. The city's leading jewel merchant at this time was Henry A. Spaulding, who opened a business in Chicago in 1888. One of the most important firms in the drug industry was headed by Robert Morrison and Jonathan Plummer, who moved their business from Richmond, Indiana, to Chicago in 1876. By the 1910s, when it became the Fuller-Morrison Company, it employed 38 traveling salesmen and ranked as one of the largest drug wholesalers in the United States. No Chicago wholesaling company during this period was more prominent within its industry than the hardware-dealing firm of Hibbard, Spencer, Bartlett & Co., which grew out of a business established in the city during the 1850s by William G. Hibbard. By 1903, when the company moved into a new 11-story building at the foot of State Street Bridge, it was one of the leading hardware wholesalers in the country, a position it retained through the first half of the twentieth century.

Although the aggregate volume of the city's wholesale trade has grown considerably over the years (from virtually zero before 1848 to $6 billion by 1929 to nearly $200 billion a year by the end of the twentieth century), the history of wholesaling in Chicago is not one of steady expansion across all industries. In fact, for a variety of reasons, wholesalers of certain kinds of commodities have lost economic power over time. In several industries, the growth in the size of manufacturers on the one side and retailers on the other squeezed out independent wholesalers. The urbanization of the American population, which reduced the geographical scope of large markets, boosted the rise of department stores and chain stores that could bypass middlemen by buying in bulk directly from manufacturers. Meanwhile, many of the merchants who served rural markets were being pushed out by large mail-order firms, including Chicago's own Montgomery Ward and Sears, Roebuck. At the other side of the supply chain, some of the large industrial corporations that began to appear in the late nineteenth century (including Chicago meatpackers such as Swift & Co.) began to dispense with wholesalers by creating their own distribution and marketing departments.

In Chicago one of the most notable transformations of the commercial sector during the early twentieth century was the decline of the great dry-goods wholesalers. At Marshall Field & Co. as late as 1906, about two-thirds of the annual sales volume of $73 million came from the wholesale department. Over the next two decades (when the company was headed by John Shedd, the former wholesale division chief), Field's continued to attempt to make money from the wholesale trade. In an effort to gain a steady supply source for its wholesale operations, Field's bought about 30 textile mills during this period; and during the late 1920s, it began to build the Merchandise Mart, the huge Chicago structure—intended as a wholesaling center—that became the world's largest building when it was completed in 1931. But despite these considerable efforts, Field's was unable to keep its wholesaling operations profitable, and they ended entirely during the Great Depression. At John V. Farwell & Co., wholesaling ended even earlier, in 1925. Carson Pirie Scott & Co., which (like Field's) had a growing retail business, closed its wholesale department in 1941.

Although some of Chicago's leading wholesale dealers were pushed out of business before World War II, wholesaling remained an important part of the city's economy during the latter part of the twentieth century. The numbers of wholesaling firms in the Chicago area and the aggregate volume of their business continued to grow, and the city remained home to leading wholesalers of commodities such as hardware, groceries, paper products, and metals. During the Depression, the number of Chicagoans employed in various aspects of wholesale commerce declined from about 140,000 to about 120,000. But by the 1950s, about 175,000 local residents worked for roughly 11,000 Chicago-area wholesaling firms, which did a total of about $20 billion in annual sales. Only New York City was a more important American wholesaling center. By the early 1990s, when the Chicago area's roughly $190 billion in annual wholesale trade accounted for about 6 percent of the national total (down from 8 percent in 1929), the metropolitan area was home to about 18,000 wholesaling firms with 260,000 employees.

During the latter part of the twentieth century, one of the city's leading wholesalers was Ryerson Tull Inc., the descendant of an old Chicago firm founded by Joseph T. Ryerson before the Civil War. During the Depression, the Ryerson company merged with Inland Steel and served as the processing and distribution arm of that leading Chicago metals producer. By the end of the twentieth century, this operation had evolved into Ryerson Tull, a processor and distributor of metals with about 5,000 employees worldwide and $3 billion in annual sales. An even bigger Chicago wholesaler with deep roots in the city was the Truserv Corporation, an enormous dealer-owned cooperative hardware company that was a descendant of the old firm of Hibbard, Spencer & Bartlett. Truserv's leading competitor, the Ace Hardware Corporation, was also a homegrown Chicago company. Among the most important of the other wholesaling firms headquartered in the Chicago region at the beginning of the twenty-first century were W. W. Grainger Inc., a dealer in machinery; Anixter International, which specialized in wire; Boise Cascade Office Products and United Stationers Inc. (both sellers of paper products); Topco, a distributor of groceries; and the Chas. Levy Company, one of a handful of magazine wholesalers remaining in the United States.                    *Mark R. Wilson*

# III. Chicago's Businesses

**Abbott Laboratories.** Chicago physician Wallace C. Abbott founded the Abbott Alkoloidal Co. in 1900. Abbott's experiments with the manufacture of alkaloid drugs and antiseptics proved successful, and the company's annual sales rose from about $200,000 in 1905 to $2 million by 1923. Renamed Abbott Laboratories in 1915, in 1920 the company moved to a new headquarters in North Chicago. In the mid-1930s, Abbott employed about 750 men and women in the Chicago area. Sales of anesthetics such as Nembutal and Pentothal drove annual sales up to $12 million by 1939. The company continued to grow during World War II, when it was one of the first mass producers of penicillin. After the war, annual sales grew from about $100 million in the mid-1950s to $1 billion in the 1970s. The company built new headquarters in Abbott Park (in Lake County) during the 1960s. As Abbott continued to expand, the number of its Chicago-area employees grew from about 1,400 in the mid-1970s to roughly 10,000 by the late 1980s. During the 1980s and 1990s, the company pioneered blood tests for HIV, as well as drugs designed to combat AIDS; it also made a variety of other drugs and products, including infant formula. By 2002 Abbott's annual sales exceeded $16 billion, and it employed roughly 17,000 Chicago-area residents, accounting for slightly less than a quarter of its global workforce. Abbott continued to expand its worldwide operations in the twenty-first century. In 2010 it had more than 100 facilities on 6 continents and nearly 90,000 employees, including some 13,000 in the Chicago area. With its products being sold in more than 130 countries, its revenues exceeded $35.2 billion.

**Ace Hardware Corp.** Ace was created 1924 in Chicago by Richard Hesse and other Chicago hardware dealers who wanted to provide a centralized purchasing organization to supply their stores and others. The company was incorporated in 1928 as Ace Stores Inc. Its retail network expanded to hundreds of dealers by 1949, when annual sales reached about $10 million.

After Hesse retired in 1973, Ace was sold to its retail dealers, and the headquarters moved to suburban Oak Brook. By 2010 the dealer-owned cooperative cleared over $3.5 billion in annual revenue, supplied a network of over 5,000 retail stores in all 50 states and more than 70 countries, and employed about 1,000 Chicago-area residents.

**Alberto-Culver Co.** In 1955 Leonard and Bernice Lavin bought Alberto-Culver Co. from Blaine Culver and moved it from Los Angeles to Chicago. Before the move, Alberto-Culver already had become a leading supplier of hair care products to the entertainment industry. The company built a new plant and headquarters in Melrose Park in 1960, and annual sales of products such as shampoos and deodorants rose from $25 million in 1961 to $100 million in 1964. In 1969 the company bought a 10-store retail chain called Sally Beauty, which would grow over the next 30 years to a network of over 2,000 stores. Sally Beauty became an independent company in 2006. At the beginning of the twenty-first century, still based in Melrose Park and led by a second generation of the Lavin family, Alberto-Culver grossed about $2.6 billion in annual sales and employed about 1,400 people in the Chicago area and almost 17,000 worldwide. In 2010 British-Dutch multinational Unilever purchased Alberto-Culver, which that year had $1.6 billion in sales and 26,000 employees worldwide.

**Allstate Corp.** The Allstate Insurance Co. was created by Sears, Roebuck & Co. in 1931 after a friend suggested to Sears head Robert Wood that his company should sell auto insurance. It quickly became one of its parent company's fastest growing and most profitable divisions. In its first year, the company had a staff of about 20 people. Fifty years later, still a part of Sears, Allstate employed over 40,000 people around the world. The widely recognized slogan "You're in good hands with Allstate" was first used in 1950. The company began to offer life insurance during the 1950s, and the auto insurance business continued to boom. In 1967 Allstate's headquarters moved to suburban Northbrook. During the 1970s and 1980s, when many of Sears's operations faltered, Allstate remained profitable. In 1995 Allstate finally spun off from Sears. At the beginning of the twenty-first century, Allstate continued to be a U.S. insurance industry leader. With nearly $100 billion in assets, Allstate employed close to 10,000 people in the Chicago area and over 40,000 nationwide. In 2010 the Northbrook-based company enjoyed revenues of over $31 billion and employed 8,600 in the Chicago area and almost 36,000 nationwide. Late in 2011, Allstate expanded its operations with the purchase of Esurance Insurance Services Inc., a firm that offers car insurance direct to consumers online and over the phone in 31 states, as well as well as home, renters, health, and life insurance coverage.

**American Steel Foundries.** This company was created in 1902 by the merger of eight separate foundries, including the American Steel Foundry

Co. of Granite City, Illinois (near St. Louis), and the business of George M. Sargent, then based in the Chicago suburb of Englewood. The company's headquarters moved to Chicago in 1905. Over the next several decades, it operated large plants at East Chicago and Hammond, Indiana; the latter facility had about 2,600 workers during the 1930s. During World War II, the company produced about a quarter of the cast armor made in the United States. In 1962, when its name became Amsted Industries, the privately held company bested $100 million in annual sales and ranked as the leading manufacturer of steel castings in the United States. Amsted Industries continued to grow into the 1970s, when it employed about 2,500 Chicago-area residents. By 2002 Amsted reached about $1.4 billion in annual sales and employed fewer than 1,000 Chicago-area residents but over 9,000 people nationwide. Eight years later the company, with almost $2 billion in revenue, remained headquartered in Chicago but employed fewer than 500 persons locally.

**Andersen (Arthur) & Co.** This pioneering accounting services firm was founded in Chicago in 1913 by a young Northwestern University professor, Arthur Andersen, and Clarence DeLany. The firm started with two partners and six employees, and offered customers help with new federal income taxes and other accounting problems. During the 1920s, Andersen opened six new offices across the country, and annual billings rose to $2 million. The firm weathered the Great Depression and continued to expand after the founder's death in 1947. Between 1947 and 1973, Andersen's client base rose from 2,300 to 50,000, and the Chicago office increased from about 250 to more than 1,500 employees. Expansion continued during the late twentieth century, as the company became increasingly international and created a fast-growing management consulting division. In 1989 Arthur Andersen and Andersen Consulting became separate units, which were controlled by Arthur Andersen & Co., SC; this multibillion-dollar parent company soon became known as Andersen Worldwide. At the beginning of the twenty-first century, Andersen Consulting changed its name to Accenture Ltd.; and Arthur Andersen became simply Andersen. At that time, the consulting and accounting groups together employed nearly 8,500 Chicago-area residents. In the wake of the Enron scandal and the firm's indictment for obstruction of justice in 2002, Andersen ceased auditing clients in 2002 and began selling its overseas assets to other firms. Accenture, now headquartered in Dublin, Ireland, continues to have some 5,000 of its 220,000-plus employees in Chicago.

**Anixter International Inc.** Founded in 1957 as Anixter Bros. Inc. by brothers Alan and William Anixter, this Skokie-based company grew into one of the country's leading wholesalers of electrical wire and cable. In 1986, when annual sales stood at about $600 million, Anixter was purchased for about $500 million by the Itel Corp., a large holding company controlled by Chicago financier Sam Zell. Itel soon sold many of its businesses but retained Anixter. In 1995 Itel became Anixter International Inc. At the end of the first decade of the twenty-first century, the company, headquartered in Glenview, sold close to $5.5 billion annually in 50 countries and employed almost 8,000 employees worldwide and about 1,000 Chicago-area residents.

**Aon.** Founded in Chicago by W. Clement Stone, Combined Insurance Co. of America would become the nation's largest door-to-door accident and health insurance company. Stone, who worked with his mother in the insurance business when he was still a teenager, opened his own small agency, the Combined Registry Co., in Chicago in 1922. Twenty-five years later, after his business had expanded considerably, Stone created the Combined Insurance Co. of America. By the beginning of the 1960s, Combined Insurance employed about 1,500 people and collected nearly $100 million in annual premiums. During the final decades of the twentieth century, Stone's company continued to expand, particularly after merging with the Ryan Insurance Group in 1982. By 1987, when Combined Insurance changed its name to Aon Corp., annual revenues stood at roughly $2.5 billion. The number of Chicago-area residents employed by the company rose from 1,500 in the mid-1970s to about 6,000 by the end of the 1990s. By 2010 Aon was a large international corporation with over 59,000 employees in 500 offices in 120 countries around the world and one of Chicago's 25 largest public companies ranked by revenue.

**Armour & Co.** New York–born Philip D. Armour began working in the pork-packing business in Milwaukee, where he made a substantial fortune in the immediate aftermath of the Civil War. In 1875 he moved to Chicago to take charge of Armour & Co. (a firm owned by Philip and his brothers), which had started its move to Chicago in 1867. During the late nineteenth century, when Chicago and its Union Stock Yard stood at the center of the meatpacking industry, Armour became a national operation and one of the country's largest businesses. By 1880, with an average of over 1,500 men on the payroll at any given time and as many as 4,000 during the peak season to process $17.5 million worth of meat, Armour was Chicago's leading industrial enterprise and employer. By the late 1880s, Armour slaughtered more than 1.5 million animals each year and reached about $60 million in annual sales to its worldwide market. Many of those sales derived from the processing of all the parts of the animal—"everything but the squeal"—making such products as glue, lard, gelatin, and fertilizer. When Philip died in 1901, the company employed about 7,000 Chicago residents and had a total workforce of 50,000 nationwide. By the early 1920s, financial troubles led the Armour family to cede control of its operations, but Armour remained a leading Chicago employer. During the worst years of the Great Depression in the early 1930s, over 9,000 men and nearly 2,000 women worked for Armour at the Union Stock Yard, and another 1,400 men and 400 women worked for its Chicago-area auxiliaries, which produced soap, glue, and other goods made from packing plant waste. Armour remained one of the nation's largest companies at the end of World War II, when annual sales stood at $1 billion, but its fortunes declined in the postwar period. In 1959 Armour stopped slaughtering in Chicago. In 1970 Armour was bought by the Greyhound Corp., which relocated the company to Arizona.

**Associated Negro Press.** The Associated Negro Press (ANP), a national and international news agency, was established in Chicago in 1919 by Claude Barnett. A graduate of Tuskegee Institute, Barnett was deeply influenced by the self-help/service-to-the-race philosophy of Tuskegee's founder, Booker T. Washington, and served on the governing boards of such organizations as Supreme Liberty Life Insurance, the American Negro Exposition in Chicago of 1940, and Tuskegee. With correspondents and stringers in all major centers of black population, ANP provided its member papers—the vast majority of black newspapers—with a twice-weekly packet of general and feature news that gave African American newspapers a critical, comprehensive coverage of personalities, events, and institutions relevant to the lives of black Americans. After 1945 ANP established a significant presence in Africa. By the late 1950s, some 75 African papers subscribed to the service's weekly news packets in French as well as English. Beset by climbing debts and Barnett's failing health, ANP ceased operation in midsummer 1964. His Associated Negro Press provided a vital service to one of black America's most important institutions during an era when African American newspapers realized record circulations, profits, and influence.     *Lawrence Daniel Hogan*

**Baker & McKenzie.** Soon after leaving the University of Chicago Law School in 1925, Russell Baker, a native of New Mexico, and friend Dana Simpson opened a small practice, Simpson & Baker. During the firm's early years, Baker frequently represented people from the city's growing Mexican American community. After Simpson retired in 1932, Baker formed a new firm, Freyberger, Baker & Rice; it soon represented major Chicago companies such as Abbott Laboratories. In 1949 Baker found a new partner in litigator John McKenzie; they started Baker & McKenzie, which began as a four-lawyer operation. This enterprise became the world's first multinational law firm when it began to open overseas offices in the late 1950s. By the late 1980s, the firm's franchises around the world had a total of about 1,000 lawyers. By the end of the first decade of the twenty-first century, that figure had climbed to almost 4,000 attorneys worldwide, just over 200 of whom worked in Chicago.

**Bankers Life and Casualty Co.** Bankers Life and Casualty Co. was small and nearly bankrupt when Chicago insurance salesman John D. MacArthur purchased it in 1935. The new owner used the company to sell insurance by mail, which proved to be a profitable business. By the 1950s, Bankers Life and Casualty was the nation's largest privately owned insurance company. By the mid-1970s, the company had nearly 5,000 Chicago-area employees. In 1978, after the death of MacArthur, his holdings in the company were transferred to the John D. and Catherine T. MacArthur Foundation, a large nonprofit organization based in Chicago. In 1992 Bankers Life was acquired by Conseco Inc. of Indiana.

**Baxter International Inc.** In 1931 physicians Donald Baxter of Los Angeles and Ralph Falk of Boise, Idaho, started the Don Baxter Intravenous Products Corp., which made supplies for IV systems in hospitals. In 1933 Baxter started a manufacturing plant in Glenview. A pioneer in blood-preservation methods as well as IV supplies, Baxter grew steadily. In 1947 it moved its headquarters to Morton Grove; the company soon employed over 500 people in the Chicago area, including those in its Travenol (in-TRAVENous sOLutions) Division. Annual sales grew from about $10 million in the mid-1950s to more than $100 million by 1967, when the company was making dialysis equipment, heart-lung machines, and many other equipment items for hospitals. In 1975, when it employed about 2,200 people in the Chicago area, the company moved its headquarters to suburban Glenview. The company, now Baxter Travenol Laboratories, grew rapidly thereafter. In 1985, when annual sales stood at about $2 billion, Baxter bought the American Hospital Supply Corp., an even larger Chicago-area medical supply company. The new company, which in 1988 became Baxter International Inc., was an enormous entity that soon approached $10 billion in annual sales; about 10,000 of its 50,000 employees worldwide were in the Chicago area. During the 1990s, however, Baxter sold off several divisions, including many of the old American Hospital Supply Corp. operations. At the beginning of the twenty-first century, Baxter again began buying firms such as ESI Lederle. By 2010 Deerfield-based Baxter's annual worldwide sales exceeded $12 billion, and it had 48,000 employees worldwide.

**Beatrice Foods Co.** The Beatrice Creamery Co. was founded in Nebraska in the 1890s by partners George Everett Haskell and William W. Bosworth. By the time Beatrice moved its headquarters to Chicago in 1913 (settling in a large facility on South State Street in 1917), it was already a leading seller of dairy equipment and operator of dairies. By the early 1930s, its national network of 32 plants produced about 27 million gallons of milk and 9.5 million gallons of ice cream per year; its Meadow Gold brand of dairy products was particularly successful. In 1946, when the company became Beatrice Foods Co., annual sales stood at about $170 million; sales doubled over the next decade. Starting in the 1960s, the company expanded rapidly by purchasing other food firms, and annual sales jumped to $12 billion by 1984. During the 1970s, Beatrice employed as many as 8,000 Chicago-area residents. After the company changed hands in 1986, however, it was dismantled with stunning speed. By 1990 the last of Beatrice was sold off, and the company that had once been one of Chicago's largest was gone.

**Bell & Howell Co.** Bell & Howell Co. was incorporated in 1907 by Albert Howell, a film projector inventor, and Donald Bell, a movie projectionist working in northern Illinois. From its headquarters in suburban Skokie, Bell & Howell made equipment used in the motion picture industry. It introduced an innovative all-metal camera in 1912 and a home movie camera in the 1920s, helped to make 35-millimeter film the industry standard, and served as a leading supplier to Hollywood. By 1925, when Bell & Howell had about 500 employees at its Larchmont Avenue plant, annual sales had reached $1 million. During World War II, a workforce of 2,000 made gun cameras and other optical equipment for the military. After the war, the company expanded into microfilm equipment and other products; annual sales passed $50 million in 1957. In 1966 Bell & Howell took over the DeVry Technical Institute (which it would sell in 1987), a for-profit school that offered electronics education. During the mid-1970s, when the company's annual sales approached $500 million, it employed about 4,000 people in the Chicago area. During the 1980s and 1990s, the company expanded its efforts in electronic imaging and information with the purchase of University Microfilms Inc. and the creation of ProQuest Information service. In January 2000 the company, with sales nearing $1 billion, announced plans to create separate companies reflecting the firm's different interests. Eighteen months later, ProQuest Co., headquartered in Ann Arbor, Michigan, was launched as a separate company. In December 2002, Bell & Howell merged with Böwe Systec Inc. to form Böwe Bell & Howell. In 2011 the Wheeling-based corporation filed for bankruptcy and made plans to be purchased by Philadelphia-based Versa Capital Management Inc.

**Booz Allen Hamilton Inc.** One of the world's first management consulting firms originated in Chicago in 1914 under the leadership of Edwin G. Booz. In 1916 Booz formed the Business Research & Development Co., which became Business Surveys in 1924. As late as 1929, Booz's three consultants advised many Chicago companies. In 1936 Booz, Fry, Allen & Hamilton was established. The following year, the firm moved into offices in the Field Building. In 1943, when the firm's name became Booz Allen & Hamilton, it had about 400 clients. During the 1950s, Booz Allen & Hamilton became the world leader in the consulting field, and the firm employed over 500 people; at the end of the 1960s, when Booz Allen was still the largest American consulting firm, annual revenues were about $55 million. Starting in the 1970s, the firm fell behind its competitors and left the city in which it had grown up. After seven decades as a Chicago company, the firm moved to New York, where it remained during the 1980s. In 2008 the now McLean, Virginia–based firm split into two firms, one retaining the Booz Allen Hamilton name and the other named Booz and Company.

**BorgWarner Inc.** In 1918, after 14 years in Moline, Illinois, Charles W. Borg and Marshall Beck moved their automobile clutch manufacturing business to Chicago. In 1928 Borg & Beck merged with three other midwestern auto parts makers—Warner Gear of Muncie, Indiana; Mechanics Universal Joint of Rockford, Illinois; and Marvel Carburetor of Flint, Michigan—to form Borg-Warner Corp., headquartered on Michigan Avenue in Chicago. This new company expanded quickly. In 1929 the Ingersoll Steel Disc Co. of Galesburg, Illinois, joined Borg-Warner; in 1935 the company bought the re-rolling mill of the Calumet Steel Co. in Chicago Heights. Annual sales rose from about $50 million in 1929 to over $600 million by the late 1950s, when Borg-Warner became a leading manufacturer of automatic transmissions. Meanwhile, Borg-Warner entered the industrial plastics business and opened offices and plants overseas. In the early 1970s, the company employed more than 5,000 people in the Chicago area, along with tens of thousands around the world. In 1978 Borg-Warner began to build a large security services business; during the 1990s this operation—known as Borg-Warner Security and later as Burns International Services—spun off and was soon bought by a Swedish corporation. Meanwhile, Borg-Warner sold its plastics and chemicals operations to General Electric. By the late 1990s, BorgWarner Inc. had again become an auto parts specialist, with about $2.5 billion in annual sales and about 1,300 employees in the Chicago area. In 2005 BorgWarner moved its headquarters to the Detroit suburbs but maintained several plants in the Chicago area.

**Brach's Confections.** In 1904 Emil J. Brach opened his Palace of Sweets at North Avenue and Towne Street in Chicago. The output of this candy factory grew quickly, producing more than 25 tons a week by 1911 and 1,000 tons a week by 1918. In 1922 E. J. Brach & Sons built a large new plant on the city's West Side; this facility, the largest candy factory in the United States, soon employed hundreds of men and women. Brach's annual sales grew from about $8 million in 1925 to $22 million in 1945 and $62 million in 1961. Between 1966 and 1986, Brach was owned by the American Home Products Corp. of New York; it was then purchased by Jacobs Suchard, a Swiss company. By the end of the 1980s, Brach was still the clear leader in the bulk candy market, and the company's 3,500 workers made it the leading employer on the city's West Side. But Brach performed poorly under Suchard, which cut jobs and moved the executive offices to suburban Oakbrook Terrace. In 1994 Brach merged with the Brock Candy Co., creating a new company called Brach & Brock Confections Inc., based in Chattanooga, Tennessee. In 2007 Brach's Confections was sold to Minnesota-based Farley's & Sathers Candy Company.

**Brunswick Corp.** By the beginning of the 1850s, Swiss-born John M. Brunswick and his half-brothers David and Emanuel had begun to make billiard tables in Cincinnati, Chicago, and other cities. In 1874, when J. M. Brunswick & Bros. became the J. M. Brunswick and Balke Co., the company operated a factory on Lake Street, where about 60 workers turned out two billiard tables a day. By the mid-1880s, now called Brunswick-Balke-Collender Co., the company was the world's leading billiards equipment manufacturer. Its large Chicago production facility at Huron and Sedgwick Streets, which was housed in a building designed by Louis Sullivan, employed about 700 men by the beginning of the twentieth century. In 1908 Chicago became the official headquarters of the company, then led by Benjamin E. Bensinger, a grandson of John Brunswick. In the 1910s, Brunswick manufactured phonographs and automobile tires; these businesses helped push annual sales up to about $30 million by the end of the 1920s. Revenues collapsed during the Great Depression, but the company began to recover during World War II; after the war, it enjoyed great success as a supplier of bowling equipment. During the bowling craze of the 1950s, Brunswick (along with rival AMF) sold thousands of automatic pin-setting machines and other bowling supplies. Annual sales skyrocketed from about $30 million in the early 1950s to about $400 million by 1960, when the company changed its name to Brunswick Corp. During the 1960s, when the company made many kinds of recreational equipment, the decline of the bowling craze meant losses for Brunswick; but it recovered somewhat in the 1970s, when annual sales reached $1 billion and it employed over 1,200 people in the Chicago area and about 25,000 worldwide. During the last decades of the twentieth century, Brunswick's main business was making boats and boat engines. In 1993 it moved its headquarters to suburban Lake Forest. As the new century began, Brunswick had approximately $3.4 billion in annual sales and 15,000 employees worldwide.

**Burnett (Leo) Co.** After years working in the advertising business in cities around the Midwest, including a stint as a vice president at the Chicago ad firm of Erwin, Wasey & Co., 44-year-old Leo Burnett started his own firm in Chicago in 1935. His venture soon became one of the world's leading advertising agencies. As Burnett took on more clients, billings rose from about $200,000 in 1935 to about $10 million by 1948 and $100 million by 1958. Among the most prominent of the company's ad campaigns were the Jolly Green Giant for Minnesota Valley Canning Co.; the Doughboy for Pillsbury; the Marlboro Man for Philip Morris; Charlie the Tuna for Star-Kist; Tony the Tiger for Kellogg's; and the lonely Maytag repairman. Burnett was known for the relatively conservative, midwestern flavor of its ads. By the early 1970s, when billings stood at about $400 million and it employed about 1,200 people in the Chicago area, Burnett was the world's fifth largest advertising firm. In 1989, when Burnett had dozens of offices around the world, the firm's headquarters moved into a new Chicago skyscraper, the Leo Burnett Building, located on Wacker Drive. The firm struggled against stiff competition in the 1990s, losing several major clients, including large Chicago-based companies United Airlines and McDonald's. At the end of the 1990s, when Burnett employed over 2,000 people in the Chicago area, it merged with a rival firm in New York and became part of the Bcom3 Group, a Chicago-based advertising giant that then ranked as the world's seventh largest ad agency. In 2002 Bcom3 Group was bought out by the French Publicis Groupe SA. As part of that firm, Leo Burnett Worldwide, still headquartered in Chicago, operates a network of 96 agencies in 85 countries.

**Burnham & Root.** This famous partnership was formed in 1873 by Daniel H. Burnham and John W. Root, two young men who had been working for the Chicago architects Carter, Drake & Wight. The new firm's first major commission came in 1874, when Root and Burnham designed a Prairie Avenue mansion for Chicago stockyards boss John B. Sherman. Over the next few decades, the firm designed dozens of large homes and commercial buildings in Chicago. Their 10-story Montauk Building (1882) was the first of their contributions to the new field of skyscraper design. Among the partners' many contributions to the Chicago landscape were the Rookery; the original Art Institute; the Monadnock Building; the offices of the *Chicago Daily News*, then the city's leading newspaper; and the Masonic Temple, which became Chicago's first 20-story building when it was completed in 1892. After Root died in 1891, D. H. Burnham & Company's Burnham continued to design many notable Chicago buildings, including the Reliance Building; the offices of the city's two leading banks (First National and Commercial & Continental); a department store for Marshall Field & Co.; and the Field Museum, completed in 1920. Outside Chicago, major works of the Burnham firm included the Flatiron Building in New York City and Union Station in Washington, D.C. At the time of Burnham's death in 1912, the firm had nearly 200 employees, making it one of the largest architectural businesses in the United States.

**Capsonic Group LLC.** As a young engineer in the mid-1960s, Jim Liautaud conceived a process that bound plastic to metal to create parts for use in the electronics industry. In 1968 he started Capsonic Inc. and began applying his innovation to manufacture injection-molded parts in a small building in Elgin, Illinois. The company grew quickly, employing 40 workers in a new plant that it occupied in 1970. By the mid-1990s, it had expanded beyond the electronics field and was supplying parts to the automotive, computer, appliance, and telecommunication industries, reaping over $40 million in sales a year. The company was called Capsonic Group LLC by the early 2000s and had spun off several related subsidiaries. Still owned by Liautaud and headquartered in Elgin, it had operations in Michigan and Mexico. With over 450 employees—over a third in the Chicago area—and revenues in excess of $60 million in 2009, Capsonic Group ranked among Chicago's largest minority-owned firms.

**Carson Pirie Scott & Co.** This leading Chicago department store originated with a business founded in Amboy, Illinois, in 1854 by Samuel Carson and John T. Pirie, two Scotch-Irish immigrants. By the end of the Civil War, Carson & Pirie was based on Lake Street in Chicago; during the late 1860s, annual sales (wholesale and retail) reached $800,000. In 1890 the entry of Robert Scott as a partner led the growing firm to change its name to Carson Pirie Scott & Co. By 1900 its two downtown Chicago stores on State and Washington and Franklin and Adams each employed about 1,000 men and women. In 1904 the company moved into a new Louis Sullivan–designed building at State and Madison. During the twentieth century, the retail operations of Carson's (as it came to be known) continued to grow; by the beginning of the 1960s, it operated 11 stores around the Chicago region, where it employed about 8,000 people and did about $150 million in annual sales. In 1989 Carson Pirie Scott was bought by P. A. Bergner & Co., a Milwaukee-based subsidiary of a Swiss company. After going through bankruptcy in 1991, this department store chain reemerged as Carson Pirie Scott & Co.; but this entity was acquired in 1997 by Proffitt's Inc. of Knoxville, Tennessee. In 2005 ownership shifted to the Bon-Ton Stores Inc. which closed the Sullivan-designed flagship store on State Street early in 2007. In 2010 Carson's was still the name of 34 department stores in Illinois and Indiana.

**CDW LLC.** This direct marketer of computers, originally named Computer Discount Warehouse, was established in Chicago in 1983 by Michael Krasny after he found it surprisingly easy to sell his own computer. Krasny soon started to buy and sell wholesale and publish a mail-order catalog; he opened a retail showroom in Chicago in 1989. The company became CDW in 1993, when it started to sell stock to the public. After acquisition in 2007 by Chicago-based Madison Dearborn Partners LLC, the company again became privately held. In 2010 CDW, based in suburban Vernon Hills, had $8.8 billion in annual sales and employed almost 3,800 Chicago-area residents.

***Chicago Defender.*** Robert Sengstacke Abbott produced the first issue of the *Chicago Defender* on May 6, 1905. What began as a four-page handbill quickly became the most important black metropolitan newspaper in America. Flaming headlines and indignant editorials chronicled the plight of African Americans in sensational detail. Its commitment to safeguarding civil liberties opened a new space for blacks to air their views and to voice their discontent. Abbott's conviction that "American Race Prejudice must be destroyed" led the *Defender* to fight against racial, economic, and social discrimination, baldly reporting on lynching, rape, mob violence, and black disfranchisement. It championed fair housing and equal employment, and was a chief proponent of the "spend your money where you can work" campaign. The *Defender* remains most sig-

Newsboy selling the *Chicago Defender*, April 1942. Newsboys were common sights on Chicago's streets as Chicago's newspapers competed with one another for headlines and readers. Here a newsboy sells the *Chicago Defender* near the Supreme Liberty Life Insurance Building at 3501 South Parkway (later Martin Luther King Drive). Photo: Jack Delano. Courtesy of the Library of Congress.

nificant for the active part it played in the Great Migration. Most southern migrants got their first glimpse of life in Chicago in the pages of the *Defender*, glimpses that made the city a striking symbol of the migration even for those moving elsewhere. Setting departure dates and showing pictures of the best schools, parks, and houses in Chicago next to pictures of the worst conditions in the South, the *Defender* stirred migration fever across much of the South. Southern cities banned the newspaper and exacted serious penalties on anyone found distributing or reading it.

The "World's Greatest Weekly" also constituted a revolutionary departure for black newspapers and set new standards for African American journalism. The *Defender* devoted columns to editorials, society news, culture, and local politics, printing what many black southerners were afraid to whisper among themselves. The *Defender*'s circulation of approximately 50,000 in 1916 was an important factor in the Great Migration of black southerners to northern cities. By 1919 the *Defender*'s advocacy of migration had won new subscribers, especially in the South, which contributed three-fourths of its approximately 130,000-copy circulation that year. In 1956 publisher John H. Sengstacke, Abbott's nephew, began publishing the paper as the *Chicago Daily Defender*, America's first African American daily newspaper.                                                *Wallace Best*

**Chicago Title and Trust Co.** The Chicago Title and Trust Company was born of disaster and grew from unrivaled opportunity. The Great Fire of October 8, 1871, which destroyed a substantial portion of the city of Chicago, might have also prevented its orderly and timely rebuilding had it not been for the "abstract men" who had prepared meticulous indices and abstracts of all land transactions in Cook County since 1847. Official property records prepared and stored in the courthouse were turned to dust in the flames. Fortunately for the city, three abstract firms, using a system of indexing and summarizing land trading pioneered by Edward A. Rucker, independently salvaged their records. With a minimum of legal challenge and political wrangling, clear title to property was maintained after the fire. The state of Illinois gave the abstracted land titles the status of law in all courts by passing the Burnt Records Act of 1872. Chase Brothers & Co., Jones & Sellars, and Shortall & Hoard consolidated their records and earned for their efforts a legal monopoly on all land dealings in Cook County. The Illinois General Trust Company Act of 1887 allowed the company (renamed Chicago Title and Trust in 1891) to act as executor, administrator, guardian, and trustee for corporations and individuals. With its archive of land tracts and roster of "blind trusts," CT&T remained the only legal title company operating in Cook County until the 1960s, when the franchise was first opened to out-of-state companies. With their unique inside view of city land dealing, the officers of Chicago Title often found themselves at the critical boundary between politics and business. Under the leadership of men like Holman Pettibone, the company had a discreet and nearly invisible role in the planning and development of modern Chicago. In 1969 CT&T was purchased by Fort Wayne, Indiana–based Lincoln National Corp., and it operated as a subsidiary of that company until 1985, when it was purchased New York–based Allegheny Corp. While part of Allegheny, the company purchased California-based SAFECO (renamed Security Union Title Insurance Co.) and Ticor Title Insurance Co. and New York–based Ticor Title Guarantee Co. Spun off as an independent entity in 1998, Chicago Title Corp. was one of largest title insurance company in the United States. In 2000 it merged with the smaller California-based Fidelity National Financial Inc. to create the Fidelity National Title Group, which, in 2011, issued over a third of residential and commercial title insurance policies in the United States. Chicago Title Insurance Company, the descendent of Chicago Title and Trust, is still headquartered in Chicago.                                          *Ross Miller*

**CNA Financial Corp.** The Continental Assurance Co. of North America, founded in Detroit in 1897, soon changed its name to the Continental Casualty Co. In 1900 Continental Casualty merged with a Chicago insurer, the Metropolitan Accident Co., creating a new Chicago-based Continental Casualty that then ranked as the fifth largest accident insurer in the United States. Six years later, it became an international firm when it began selling industrial health and accident policies in London. In 1911, when it began to offer automobile insurance, Continental Casualty created a new subsidiary, Continental Assurance, which sold life insurance. By the mid-1960s, Continental Casualty and Continental Assurance, which shared the same headquarters on Michigan Avenue, together collected roughly $850 million in annual premiums and employed nearly 8,000 people nationwide. In 1967 these two operations became part of a new parent company, the CNA Financial Corp. By the mid-1970s, when it was acquired by the Loews Corp., CNA employed about 5,000 Chicago-area residents. At the end of the 1990s, following a 1995 merger with the Continental Corp., CNA employed about 4,500 people in the Chicago area and another 20,000 around the world, and its annual revenues reached about $16 billion, making it one of the ten largest insurance companies in the United States.

**Commonwealth Edison Co.** The Western Edison Light Co. was founded in Chicago in 1882, three years after Thomas Edison developed a practical lightbulb. In 1887 Western Edison became the Chicago Edison Co. Samuel L. Insull became president of Chicago Edison in 1892; in 1897 Insull incorporated another electric utility, the Commonwealth Electric Light & Power Co. In 1907 Insull's two companies formally merged to create the Commonwealth Edison Co. As more people became connected to the electric grid, Insull's company, which had an exclusive franchise from the city, grew steadily. By 1920, when it used more than 2 million tons of coal annually, the company's 6,000 employees served about 500,000 custom-ers; annual revenues had reached nearly $40 million. During the 1920s, its largest generating stations included one on Fisk Street and West 22nd and one on Crawford Avenue and the Sanitary Canal. Although Insull went bankrupt and fled the country during the Great Depression, Com-monwealth Edison survived; after World War II, it received a new 42-year franchise from the city. During the second half of the twentieth century, the company became a world leader in nuclear power. In 1959 it opened the Dresden nuclear generating plant near Morris, Illinois, southwest of Chicago. Over the next three decades, the company known as "ComEd" opened several plants around the region and became the largest operator of nuclear power facilities in the United States. Although the company re-ceived several warnings from federal regulators about safety problems at these plants, most of them continued to operate, and by the 1990s nuclear power accounted for well over half of the company's output. Meanwhile, the company employed a workforce of more than 15,000 men and women in the Chicago area. With its rates subject to approval by state regulators, the company saw its annual revenues rise to roughly $7 billion by the late 1990s, when it had about 3.4 million customers in the northern Illinois region. In 1994, ComEd became part of a parent company named Unicom; in 1999, after merging with the Philadelphia-based PECO Energy Co., the new parent company took the name of Exelon. In 2011 Exelon, headquar-tered in Chicago, announced merger plans with Baltimore-based Constel-lation Energy, creating the second largest regulated distributor and gas in the United States. Through Commonwealth Edison, it supplied electricity to over 3.8 million customers in northern Illinois and employed nearly 6,200 workers in the Chicago area.

**Container Corporation of America.** In 1926 Walter P. Paepcke led the formation of Container Corporation of America, which united sev-eral smaller manufacturers of paper boxes and containers and included 14 plants around the country. The enterprise had its national headquar-ters in Chicago, and by 1928 it operated four plants around the city, includ-ing those formerly owned by the Chicago Mill & Lumber Co., the Robert Gair Co., and the Sefton Manufacturing Co. By the mid-1930s, Container Corp. employed about 1,300 area residents. As the company grew, annual sales rose from about $20 million in 1936 to over $400 million by 1965, when Container Corp. employed over 20,000 people nationwide. In 1968 the company merged with Montgomery Ward & Co., the giant Chicago-based retailer; the new parent company was called Marcor. In 1976, when Container Corp. had 150 plants around the world, Marcor was purchased by Mobil, the giant oil company. In 1986 Mobil sold Container Corp. to Jefferson Smurfit Corp., another box manufacturer. This company's 1998 merger with the Chicago-based Stone Container Corp., which created the Smurfit-Stone Container Corp., meant that the remnants of Container

Corp. were again managed from Chicago. In 2011 Smurfit-Stone was purchased by Georgia-based RockTenn Company.

**Continental Illinois National Bank and Trust Co.** One of the city's two largest banks for most of the twentieth century, Continental was the product of a 1910 merger of two Chicago enterprises, the Commercial National Bank and the Continental National Bank. The older of the two was the Commercial National Bank, formed during the Civil War and led by Henry F. Eames. Commercial National Bank had become one of the city's leading banks by the early 1870s. The Continental National Bank, chartered in 1883, was led during its early years by John C. Black. By the turn of the century, both banks had grown by absorbing several competitors. In 1910 the merger of Commercial and Continental created a new entity, the Continental & Commercial National Bank of Chicago, which had $175 million in deposits, making it one of the largest banks in the United States. It continued to grow during the 1920s. In 1929 it merged with Illinois Merchants Trust Co.; three years later, the bank's name became Continental Illinois National Bank and Trust Co. During the Great Depression, the bank required a $50 million loan from the Reconstruction Finance Corp. (a federal government agency) to stay afloat. After World War II, the bank grew: by the beginning of the 1960s, Continental had over $3 billion in deposits and employed 5,000 people. By the early 1970s, when it had 60 branches and affiliates around the world, the bank employed about 8,200 Chicago-area residents, many of whom worked at Continental's main offices on LaSalle Street in Chicago's Loop. During the early 1980s, after many of its large loans to companies in the oil and gas industries went bad, the bank experienced a sudden and unexpected crisis. Continental's Great Depression–era experience was repeated as the Federal Deposit Insurance Corp. came to the rescue. In 1994 a diminished Continental was acquired by BankAmerica Corp. of San Francisco.

**Corn Products Refining Co.** This company, created in 1902 by E. T. Bedford, had its executive offices in New York for most of the century, but its main manufacturing operation was located just outside of Chicago. In 1910 Corn Products built a new $5 million plant at Summit, southwest of Chicago; the site of the plant was known as Argo, and the company sold cornstarch and other products under the Argo brand name. The company employed more than 1,000 Chicago-area residents at its Summit plant. In 1960 the Argo facility still ranked as the world's largest corn wet-milling plant. During the early 1970s, the plant employed as many as 4,000 people, but its workforce declined to about 1,000 by the 1990s. In the late 1990s, the general offices of the company finally came to the Chicago area when Corn Products International Inc. was spun off from Bestfoods Inc., a larger conglomerate. The new company, now based in suburban Westchester, achieved in excess of $4.3 billion in annual sales in 2010 and boasted 37 plants in 24 countries employing 10,700.

**Cracker Jack Co.** F. W. Rueckheim emigrated from Germany to Chicago in 1869. In 1872 Rueckheim and his brother Louis formed F. W. Rueckheim & Bro., a small candy and popcorn shop. Business grew steadily, and by the 1880s the brothers had relocated to a three-story plant on South Clinton Street. In 1896 the company began to sell its caramel-coated popcorn under the Cracker Jack brand name, a name that would be made famous by Jack Norworth's 1908 song "Take Me Out to the Ball Game." In 1912, when the company employed about 450 women and girls and 250 men and boys at its large new factory on South Peoria and Harrison Streets, it began to insert small toys into the packages with the popcorn. This "prize in every box" marketing strategy proved successful. In 1922 the name of the company, which made marshmallows and candies as well as its signature popcorn product, became Cracker Jack Co. During the 1950s, the company employed over 1,000 Chicago-area residents. During the last decades of the twentieth century, Cracker Jack was purchased by a number of large international food companies. After being held for many years by Borden Foods Inc., the Cracker Jack brand was purchased in 1997 by the Frito-Lay division of PepsiCo, the food giant based in Purchase, New York.

**Crane Co.** Richard Teller Crane, a nephew of Chicago lumber dealer Martin Ryerson, moved to Chicago from New Jersey in 1855. Richard and his brother Charles soon formed R. T. Crane & Bro., which manufactured and sold brass goods and plumbing supplies. The new company won contracts to supply pipe and steam-heating equipment in large public buildings such as the Cook County courthouse and the state prison at Joliet. By 1865, when the name of the company was changed to the Northwestern Manufacturing Co., it ran a large pipe mill and manufactured engines and steam pumps; by 1870, when it employed about 160 people, it was making elevators as well. After the Chicago Great Fire of 1871, the company decided to expand its operations. Just after the firm became Crane Bros. Manufacturing Co. in 1872, it employed as many as 700 men and boys and manufactured over $1 million worth of products per year. In 1890, when it had sales branches in Omaha, Kansas City, Los Angeles, and Philadelphia, the company changed its name to Crane Co. By this time, Crane was supplying much of the pipe used for the large central heating systems in Chicago's new skyscrapers, and it was also selling the enameled cast-iron products that were soon found in bathrooms in residences across the country. In 1910, when Crane had begun to manufacture at a plant in Bridgeport, Connecticut, its Chicago plants employed more than 5,000 people. A large new Chicago plant on South Kedzie Avenue was built in the 1910s. During the 1920s, when Crane expanded overseas, the company was the world's leading manufacturer of valves and fittings. During the next few decades, Crane continued to employ thousands of Chicago-area residents at its Kedzie Avenue plant, and the company's annual sales rose to over $300 million by the mid-1950s. In 1959 the company was acquired by Thomas M. Evans, its first owner who was not a member of the Crane family. Evans proceeded to turn Crane into a global conglomerate that made aerospace equipment as well as plumbing supplies; the headquarters eventually moved from Chicago to Bridgeport. By the mid-1970s, Crane employed only about 1,000 people in the Chicago area. By the end of the century, Crane was doing annual sales of about $2 billion, but it was no longer a leading company in the city in which it was born.

**Crate & Barrel.** This house furnishings retail chain was created in 1962 by two young Chicago residents, Gordon and Carole Segal. The Segals began with a small store in the city's Old Town neighborhood; they began to issue catalogs in 1967. Between 1968 and 1975, they added new locations in Wilmette, Oak Brook, and downtown Chicago on Michigan Avenue. In 1983, soon after it started selling furniture, the company built a new warehouse and headquarters in suburban Northbrook. By the mid-1990s, when annual sales had climbed to roughly $300 million, the company already had 46 stores and was opening about 5 new stores each year. In 1998 Gordon Segal sold a controlling interest in the company to Otto Versand GmbH & Co., a German catalog company. The company launched its CB2 stores in 2000 and partnered the following year with the Land of Nod, a Wheeling-based catalog retailer for children's furnishings, the following year. In 2010 Crate & Barrel had over $1.3 billion in revenues from its 160-plus stores in the United States, as well as stores in Canada and Dubai, and through its catalog and Internet sales.

**Dean Milk Co.** Sam Dean, an evaporated milk dealer who sold to Chicago-area customers, founded the Dean Evaporated Milk Co. in Pecatonica, Illinois (west of Rockford), in 1925. During the 1930s, Dean began to sell fresh dairy products, including fluid milk; it entered the ice-cream business in 1947. During the 1950s and 1960s, Dean's business—then based in suburban Franklin Park—began buying smaller dairy companies. By 1961, when it went public, the firm employed about 1,300 people and did over $60 million in annual sales. Five years later, Dean doubled in size by purchasing the Bowman Dairy Co., another large Chicago-area food company. By 1985, when the company's annual sales hit $1 billion, it sold pickles and other foods, but dairy products still accounted for about two-thirds of its business. During the 1990s, with many dairy facilities around the Midwest, Dean became the largest milk processor in the United States, as well as diversifying to buy such brands as Birds Eye. By the end of the century, Dean had reached nearly $4 billion in annual sales, but only a few hundred of the company's some 14,000 employees worldwide were based in the Chicago area. In December 2001, Dean Foods was purchased by the Suiza Foods Corp., a rival company based in Dallas, Texas, which took the Dean name.

**Dick (A. B.) Co.** Albert B. Dick, who started a lumber business in Chicago in 1883, abandoned that field to pioneer the manufacture of mimeograph machines based on a design by Thomas Edison. The first of these primitive copiers were cranked by hand; eventually, Dick introduced larger and more automated models. In 1918 the company established the Ditto trademark. By the mid-1930s, Dick employed about 900 people in the Chicago area. In 1949 the company moved its headquarters to suburban Niles, where it opened a new plant. During the 1960s, Dick's mimeograph technology lost out to the new copy methods pioneered by Haloid Xerox. By the mid-1970s, when Dick's annual sales approached $300 million, it had about 3,000 workers in the Chicago area. In 1979 the company was purchased by General Electric Co. of Great Britain. In the late 1990s, A. B. Dick, as a division of Nesco Inc. of Cleveland, still called Chicago home. In 2004 New Hampshire–based Presstek Inc. purchased the firm and ended its 121-year history in Chicago.

**Dominick's Finer Foods Inc.** This retail grocery business was founded in Chicago by Dominick DiMatteo. In 1968, when it had grown to a chain of 18 stores, the company was purchased by Fisher Foods of Cleveland, Ohio. During the mid-1970s, the Dominick's chain employed about 6,000 Chicago-area residents. In 1981, when there were 71 stores in the chain, the DiMatteo family bought it back for $80 million. The chain proceeded to expand; its share of the retail grocery market in Chicago grew from about 13 percent in 1984 to about 25 percent by 1993. By the late 1980s, it had close to 18,000 workers in the Chicago area. In 1995 Oak Brook–based Dominick's was purchased by the Yucaipa Cos., a grocery company based in Los Angeles; three years later, when it boasted 112 stores, it was acquired by a different California-based national chain, Safeway Inc. In 2011, with nearly 80 stores in the Chicago area, the Safeway-owned Dominick's remained a leading grocery chain and an important area employer.

**Donnelley (R. R.) & Sons Co.** In 1882 Richard R. Donnelley, a veteran of the printing and publishing business in Chicago, started his own printing company, R. R. Donnelley & Sons. Under the leadership of his son Thomas, the company grew quickly during the first decades of the twentieth century, when it printed the Montgomery Ward and Sears catalogs and launched efforts such as Lakeside Classics. It continued to expand by winning contracts to print major national magazines such as *Time* (introduced in 1927) and *Life* (1936). By the mid-1930s, Donnelley employed about 1,800 men and 700 women at its plant on East Cermak Avenue. By the beginning of the 1960s, as the number-one company in the commercial printing industry, R. R. Donnelley grossed about $150 million in annual sales and employed nearly 10,000 people. A Los Angeles division was opened in 1978. In 1993, after Sears canceled its catalog, Donnelley closed its large plant on the city's South Side. By the end of the 1990s, when it was moving into electronic publishing and was printing paper manuals for computer industry companies such as Microsoft, annual sales stood at over $5 billion. Donnelley—which operated more than 50 plants in the United States, Mexico, South America, the United Kingdom, Central Europe, and Asia—ranked as the world's third largest commercial printer. Of its some 34,000 employees, about 2,500 worked in the Chicago area. A decade later, having expanded its operations particularly in the area of electronic publishing, Donnelley's annual sales reached $10 billion and it employed 55,000 individuals worldwide.

**Duchossois Industries Inc.** The Thrall Car Manufacturing Co. was founded in Chicago Heights in 1917. In 1946 Thrall was a small railroad equipment maker, with about 35 employees and $200,000 in annual sales. Richard L. Duchossois, a native of Chicago's South Side, joined the company after serving in World War II and marrying Beverly Thrall, daughter of the head of the firm. By the 1970s, the company was making as many as 90,000 railcars a year; but annual production dropped to about 10,000 cars during the 1980s, when annual sales were around $750 million. Meanwhile, Duchossois—who created a parent company named after himself that expanded into electronic consumer products, national defense supplies, and various capital goods—moved into the horse-racing business by purchasing facilities in suburban Arlington Heights. By the mid-1990s, when railcar production reached 50,000 per year, annual revenues from horse racing approached $600 million. In 2001 Thrall was purchased by Trinity Industries of Dallas, Texas, a leading railcar manufacturer. At the beginning of the twenty-first century, the privately held company led by Craig Duchossois (Richard's son) still employed about 1,500 people in the Chicago area and grossed about $1 billion in annual sales. By 2010, as the Duchossois Group, the company's full-time Chicago-area employment had fallen to 450.

**Elgin National Watch Co.** This enterprise, initially named the National Watch Co., was founded in Chicago during the Civil War by a group of investors that included former mayor Benjamin W. Raymond; John C. Adams, a Chicago watchmaker; and Ira G. Blake and P. S. Bartlett, both of whom had been involved with the famous Waltham Watch Co. By 1867 the company had begun to manufacture watches at a new plant in Elgin. By 1870 the plant employed nearly 300 men and 200 women and produced some 30,000 watches a year. In 1874 the name of the company was changed to the Elgin National Watch Co. Under the leadership of company president T. M. Avery, annual output rose to about 500,000 watches by the late 1880s, when the company employed nearly 2,500 people at its Elgin plant. By the early twentieth century, Elgin had surpassed its old rival Waltham and stood as the world's greatest mass producer of watches. The company built the Elgin Observatory in 1909; it opened the Elgin Watchmakers College in 1920. By the late 1920s, Elgin National Watch was making about 2 million watches each year. After World War II, the company struggled against overseas competition. By the beginning of the 1960s, when the company was doing about $30 million in annual sales and still employed nearly 3,000 people, it had begun to fail. The Watchmakers College closed in 1960; the Elgin plant closed in 1965, and the company's few remaining assets were transferred to Downers Grove–based Elgin National Industries in 1969.

**Evans Food Products.** Chicago attorney Lester W. Olin entered the pork rind business in 1947 when he purchased a large oil vat from a Mr. Evans, who had been renting a small office in the State Street building that Olin owned. Olin quickly patented his pork rind manufacturing process, and Evans Food Products was born. In the beginning, Olin sold his pork rinds, and soon corn chips, door-to-door to area homes and businesses. In 1955 Evans Food Products moved to a much larger manufacturing plant on South Halsted Street, about the same time that the company began selling to overseas markets. Evans continued to grow over the next several decades, employing several dozen people by the mid-1970s. Olin sold Evans Food Products to a subsidiary of Milwaukee-based Northwestern Mutual Life Insurance Co. in 1981. The next year, the company discontinued its corn chip line, focusing exclusively on pork rinds. Mexican pork rind manufacturers Alejandro Silva, Carlos Silva, and Jose Garza purchased Evans in 1985. By 2010 Evans Food Products was still headquartered at its plant on South Halsted, with manufacturing facilities in Texas, Ohio, and Mexico. Boasting annual revenues near $90 million, Evans was the world's top pork rind business and one of Chicago's largest minority-owned firms. It employed about 80 people in Chicago and an additional 150 in its other locations.

**Federal Signal Corp.** The Federal Electric Co., a manufacturer of electric signs, was incorporated in Illinois in 1901 by John Goehst and brothers John and James Gilchrist. In 1915 the company started making sirens. After spending a few years under the control of Chicago utilities titan Samuel Insull, the company became independent again in the 1930s, when it became the Federal Sign & Signal Corp. In 1958 Federal moved its main plant from 87th and State Streets on Chicago's South Side to Blue Island. By the middle of the 1960s, the company—a leader in the field of electric signs—was doing about $30 million in annual sales and had about 1,500 employees. After changing its name to the Federal Signal Corp. in 1975, the company moved its general offices to suburban Oak Brook and expanded its operations in the areas of safety and security systems, environmental solution, signal technologies, and fire rescue. In 2010 Federal Signal reported over $725 million in revenues and 2,800 employees in its various plants and offices worldwide.

Children's Day at Marshall Field & Company's Store as seen by McCutcheon
October 9 and 10, 1903

*Cartoons drawn especially for this event by John T. McCutcheon.*

Children's Day at Marshall Field, October 9 and 10, 1903. This 1903 cartoon by John T. McCutcheon captured the excitement of shopping at Marshall Field's on the special Children's Day and for shoppers coming downtown on other days as well. Courtesy of the John M. Wing Collection, the Newberry Library.

**Field (Marshall) & Co.** In 1856, 21-year-old Marshall Field moved to Chicago from Massachusetts. He immediately began working at Cooley, Wadsworth & Co. By the Civil War, Field was a partner in the company, then led by John V. Farwell. Not satisfied as the junior partner in Farwell, Field & Co., Field left in 1865. That year he joined Levi Leiter and Potter Palmer to create a new dry-goods house, Field, Palmer, Leiter & Co.; after Palmer sold out in 1867, this became Field, Leiter & Co. This new company operated on a very large scale, with about $9 million in wholesale and retail sales in 1867. Although two of its stores burned during the 1870s, the company continued to do an immense business. After Leiter retired in 1881, the name of the enterprise became Marshall Field & Co. By the late 1880s, when annual sales rose to over $30 million (about $5 million retail and $25 million wholesale), the company employed a total of nearly 3,000 people at its retail store on State and Washington Streets and its massive seven-story wholesale building at Quincy and Adams. The wholesale division, managed by John Shedd, made most of its purchases in New York City; meanwhile, by the 1890s, retail division chief Harry Selfridge was helping to create the modern department store by adding features such as a tearoom and large display windows. After Field died in 1906 (leaving $8 million for a natural history museum in Chicago that would bear his name), Shedd became president of a company that employed 12,000 people in Chicago (two-thirds of them in retail) and was doing about $25 million in yearly retail sales in addition to nearly $50 million wholesale. A new State Street store, completed in 1907, ranked as one of the largest retail establishments in the world. Under the leadership of Shedd and his successor James Simpson, Field & Co. expanded beyond Chicago during the 1920s. Shedd bought textile mills in North America and Asia; Simpson, who took over in 1923, concentrated on retail sales, opening branches in suburban Oak Park, Evanston, and Lake Forest, and acquiring a Seattle store at the end of the 1920s. Meanwhile, the company built the Merchandise Mart, a building in downtown Chicago that became the world's largest commercial structure when it was completed in 1931. Field & Co. would sell it in 1945. The expansion of the 1920s ended during the Great Depression, when the company closed its wholesale operations. At the end of World War II, Field & Co. ranked as one of the 20 largest retail enterprises in the United States. By the beginning of the 1960s, the company operated 10 stores, employed about 13,000 people, and did nearly $250 million in annual sales. In 1975, when it was adding stores across the country, Field opened a large new downtown Chicago store at Water Tower Place. In 1982, when it was purchased by BAT Industries of London, Field ceased to be an independent Chicago-based company. This continued to be the case after 1990, when Field (by then a 24-store chain) was purchased for about $1 billion by the Dayton Hudson Corp. of Minneapolis. By the end of the century, when Dayton Hudson became the Target Corp., it employed nearly 16,000 Chicago-area residents, who worked at Target discount stores as well as the department stores that retained the Marshall Field name. In 2004 May Co. purchased Marshall Field's only to be purchased itself by Federated Department Stores Inc. in 2005. The following year, Federated decided to rename all of its Field's stores Macy's. The decision generated still ongoing protests by those who felt that the name Marshall Field should remain. It remains now only on the State Street store, which was declared a National Historic Landmark in 1978 and a Chicago landmark in 2005.

**Field Enterprises Inc.** In 1940 Marshall Field III, a wealthy grandson of Chicago retailer Marshall Field, entered the publishing business by backing *PM*, a left-leaning newspaper published in New York City. In 1941 Field launched the *Chicago Sun*, conceived as a liberal alternative to the conservative *Tribune*. Three years later, Field Enterprises Inc. was created with the *Sun* as its largest asset. In 1947 Field bought the *Chicago Daily Times*, founded in 1929 as the city's first tabloid, and merged it into the *Sun*.

This created the *Chicago Sun-Times*, which during the second half of the twentieth century became the primary rival of the *Tribune*. By the 1950s, when it was led by Marshall Field IV, Field Enterprises was a major media company that owned not only the *Sun-Times* but also the *World Book Encyclopedia*, book publisher Simon & Schuster, paper manufacturers, and several radio and, in the 1960s, television stations around the country. In 1959 Field Enterprises bought the *Chicago Daily News*, which had long been one of the city's leading newspapers, and in 1978 it was folded into the *Sun-Times*. In the early 1980s, the Field family decided to leave the media business, and Field Enterprises was dismantled and its assets sold, the largest of which, the *Sun-Times*, to international media titan Rupert Murdoch.

**First National Bank of Chicago.** In 1863 a group of Chicago investors led by Edmund Aiken pooled $250,000 to establish a new bank under the guidelines established by new federal banking legislation. By 1876 First National ranked as the city's largest bank; it (and its descendants) would continue to be either Chicago's biggest or second biggest bank through the end of the twentieth century. By 1902, after it absorbed Union National Bank and Metropolitan National Bank, the $100 million in assets held temporarily by First National made it the nation's second largest bank. In 1913 it became one of the original members of the Federal Reserve System. Surviving the Great Depression, its assets passed $1 billion in 1938. By the beginning of the 1960s, when it opened an office in Tokyo, First National had over $3 billion in deposits and employed about 3,600 people. In 1969, when First National moved into a new skyscraper in Chicago's Loop, it became part of the First Chicago Corp., a holding company for the bank. During the 1970s, when it employed more than 5,000 people in the Chicago area, the bank saw its assets rise from $8 billion to $30 billion. First Chicago continued to grow during the 1980s and early 1990s, when it was the city's largest bank. In comparison to many of the giant banking enterprises around the world, however, First Chicago was a relatively small, regional operation. This changed in 1995, when First Chicago merged with NBD of Detroit to create the First Chicago NBD Corp., which became the seventh largest bank in the United States. Three years later, First Chicago NBD merged with the Banc One Corp. of Ohio to form Bank One, which had about $260 billion in assets, making it at that time the nation's fifth largest bank. At the beginning of the century, the Chicago-based Bank One employed about 14,000 Chicago-area residents and more than 70,000 people worldwide. In 2004 New York–based JPMorgan Chase purchased Bank One. In 2010 Chase, one of America's two largest banks, employed over 13,000 people locally and over 242,000 worldwide.

**Florsheim Shoe Co.** In 1892 Milton Florsheim, the son of a Chicago shoemaker, started a small shoe store. Florsheim soon moved into manufacturing, and by 1910 the company had 600 workers at its factory at Adams and Clinton Streets. By the end of the 1920s, when annual sales stood at $3 million, there were five Chicago-area factories, employing a total of 2,500 men and women. Business slowed during the Great Depression, but Florsheim emerged at the end of World War II as one of the top ten firms in the industry, with nearly $18 million in annual sales. Control of the company left the Chicago area in 1953, when Florsheim was purchased by the International Shoe Co. (later Interco Inc.) of St. Louis. Florsheim became International Shoe's most profitable unit, leading the market for high-quality men's shoes. At the beginning of the 1970s, still a subsidiary, the Florsheim division consisted of 14 factories and 500 retail stores nationwide. During the 1980s, many of its manufacturing operations were moved overseas. In 1994, soon after Interco entered bankruptcy, Florsheim was spun off as an independent company with its headquarters in Chicago. By the end of the 1990s, Florsheim Shoe Group Inc. had about 10 percent of the market for men's dress shoes, making it the leading company in the trade. By that time, when it was doing close to $250 million in annual sales, only about 10 percent of its 2,000-plus employees worldwide worked in the Chicago area. In 2002 Florsheim was purchased by the Weyco Group of Glendale, Wisconsin.

**Flying Food Group Inc.** In 1983 real estate developer, bakery owner, and former Chinese restaurant worker Sue Ling Gin decided to start an airline catering business shortly after eating a particularly unsatisfying breakfast aboard a Midway Airlines flight. She founded Flying Food Group Inc. that same year and made Midway Airlines her first client. The company's airline kitchen in Midway Airport was soon making 10,000 meals a day for air travelers. In subsequent years, Flying Food opened kitchens in several more airports around the country, including O'Hare, and began focusing on foreign-owned airlines flying internationally. By 2000 Flying Food produced meals for 80 airlines, employed over 2,000 people, and had $125 million in revenues. It had kitchens in nine U.S. airports and a joint catering venture at Hongqiao Airport in Shanghai. The September 11, 2001, terrorist attacks devastated the American air travel industry and the air catering business along with it. While Flying Food's heavy reliance on non-American air carriers helped to insulate it partially from the industry downturn, it nevertheless laid off hundreds of its employees, and sales slumped. Gin quickly diversified Flying Food Group's operations, expanding into gourmet prepackaged foods that the company sold to grocery stores. By mid-2003 the Chicago-based company had begun to grow back to its pre-9/11 levels, ranking a distant third among the world's largest airline caterers. With over 3,200 employees worldwide—including over 400 in Chicago—and $300 million in revenues, Flying Food Group was one of Chicago's largest minority-owned firms.

**FMC Corp.** This company traces its origins to the Food Machinery Corp., a California maker of agricultural and industrial pumps that was itself a successor to the John Bean Spray Pump Co., founded in 1904. During World War II, the California-based company made landing craft for the American military. Its name became FMC in 1961, when it had over $400 million in annual sales and employed nearly 19,000 people nationwide. In 1972, soon after it purchased the Link-Belt Corp. of Chicago, FMC moved its headquarters from San Jose to the Windy City. As the owner of Link-Belt, which had a Chicago-history reaching back to 1875, FMC became a major local employer, with about 10,000 workers in the Chicago area during the mid-1970s. By this time, the company was already operating in several fields, including machinery and chemicals; annual sales stood at about $2 billion. By the late 1980s, FMC, which was now a leading producer of agricultural chemicals, was one of the nation's leading exporters; its Defense Systems unit, which produced the Bradley Fighting Vehicle for the U.S. Army, accounted for nearly one-third of sales. In the 1990s, FMC shed its military contracting division to concentrate on chemicals and products and services for the oil and gas industries. In 2001 FMC split into two companies: FMC Corporation, the chemical division, moved its headquarters to Philadelphia; FMC Technologies, the machinery division, remained headquartered in Chicago until 2004, when it moved officially to Houston.

**Follett Corp.** In 1873 Charles Barnes started running a bookstore out of his home in Wheaton, Illinois. In 1917, after Barnes's son William moved to New York to create the company that became Barnes & Noble, the Illinois business changed hands. The new owners were John Wilcox and C. W. Follett, who had worked for many years as a salesman in the Barnes organization; the new enterprise was called the J. W. Wilcox & Follett Co. By 1923 Follett took charge; after his death in 1952, his son Dwight Follett became head of the company, then a leading wholesaler of textbooks. The company became the Follett Corp. in 1957, with headquarters in downtown Chicago. By the mid-1970s, Follett had about 800 employees in the Chicago area, and annual sales were around $50 million. Robert Follett, a son of Dwight, took over in 1977 and led a considerable expansion. The company bought dozens of college and university bookstores around the country, becoming a leading retailer of textbooks. Having expanded into digital resources and into international markets, in 2010 Follett—based in River Grove—exceeded $2.7 billion in annual sales and employed about 2,500 people in the Chicago area and some 10,000 worldwide.

**Foote, Cone & Belding.** This company was the descendant of one of the original American advertising firms, Lord & Thomas, which was founded in 1873 and became a national enterprise based in New York City. When Lord & Thomas chief Albert Lasker retired in 1942, several of the company's executives came together to create Foote, Cone & Belding, which was based in Chicago. By 1965 annual billings stood at nearly $230 million, and the firm had over 2,000 employees around the country. By this time, the firm was a leading producer of advertisements for television. Among the ad campaigns launched by the company were those that promoted Levi Strauss clothing, Coors beer, and the Kleenex and Kotex brands of Kimberly-Clark. Among Chicago-based ad agencies, Foote, Cone & Belding trailed only Leo Burnett. During the 1990s, Foote, Cone & Belding became part of True North Communications Inc., a new global ad firm headquartered in Chicago. At the end of the century, True North had nearly $1.5 billion in annual revenues and employed about 1,200 people in the Chicago area. In 2001 Interpublic purchased True North. Five years later, Foote, Cone & Belding merged with Draft to create Draftfcb. Headquartered in Chicago, Draftfcb North America employed 1,200 people in the Chicago area and over 9,300 worldwide.

**Fuller (George A.) Co.** This construction company was founded in Chicago in 1882 as Clark & Fuller by C. E. Clark and George A. Fuller, a Boston architect and engineer. The company soon became the leading builder of the world's first skyscrapers going up around Chicago. By 1890, when Fuller's company became one of the first construction firms to be organized as a corporation (capitalized at $750,000), it had already built several skyscrapers, including the Tacoma Building designed by Holabird & Roche. Fuller was one of the first true general contractors: it completed large structures by coordinating the work of hundreds of men working under several subcontractors. The company opened a New York office during the 1890s and built several large structures in that city, including the New York Times Building and Daniel Burnham's Flatiron Building, which was known briefly as the Fuller Building because the company was headquartered there. By the time George Fuller died in 1900, his company—which between 1903 and 1922 was led by Paul Starrett—had started to serve as the general contractor for large commercial buildings around the country. Between 1900 and 1914 alone, Fuller Co. erected 600 buildings. In addition to the Tacoma Building, among the many structures the company built in Chicago were the Marquette, Pontiac, and Rand-McNally buildings; the Tribune Tower; and large department stores such as the Fair, Carson Pirie Scott, Marshall Field, and Montgomery Ward. Although headquartered in New York, the company still employed hundreds of people in the Chicago area through the 1960s. In the 1970s, the firm was sold and liquidated.

**GATX Corp.** In 1898 Max Epstein founded a Chicago-based railcar leasing firm called the Atlantic Seaboard Dispatch. One of the first companies to lease specialty railcars to railroads, Epstein's operation started with only 28 used railcars. In 1902 the name was changed to German-American Car Co. In 1907, when the company owned a fleet of 400 railcars, it opened repair and maintenance shops in East Chicago, Indiana; it then began to manufacture new steel tank railcars in addition to leasing used ones. By 1916, when the company began to sell stock to the public and changed its name to General American Tank Car Corp., it had a fleet of 2,300 railcars and annual revenues of about $3 million. By the 1920s, General American had become a leading producer of tank railcars, including specialty railcars lined with glass or nickel for the transportation of milk, acids, and other liquids. By the early 1920s, the company's plants at East Chicago and Warren, Ohio, were turning out 10,000 new railcars a year, worth about $20 million. In 1933, when it owned a fleet of nearly 50,000 railcars, the company changed its name to the General American Transportation Corp. By the 1940s, when about 3,000 men worked at the East Chicago plant, General American was the nation's leading lessor of railcars. By the beginning of the 1960s, annual revenues approached $250 million. In 1973 it purchased the American Steamship Company, which continues to operate in the Great Lakes. Soon after changing its name to GATX Corp. in 1975, the company began to exit the railcar-manufacturing business. But GATX Corp. added to its traditional operations by expanding its water-based fleet, leasing aircraft, and setting up a large financial services division. In 2010 GATX, still headquartered in Chicago, owned a worldwide fleet of nearly 132,000 railcars, employed about 2,000 people around the country, and had annual revenues over $1.1 billion.

**Grainger (W. W.) Inc.** William W. Grainger, an engineering graduate from the University of Illinois, started an electric motor wholesaling business on West Cermak Avenue in Chicago in 1927. With his sister Margaret, Grainger built a business based on mail-order catalog sales. By 1937, when annual sales hit $1 million, the company had sales offices around the country. In 1968 sales passed $100 million, and the company began to sell stock to the public. During the 1970s, led by Grainger's son David, the company bought electric motor factories and moved its headquarters to suburban Skokie. By the end of the 1990s, when its headquarters moved to suburban Lake Forest, Grainger's annual sales of motors and other industrial machines stood at $4.5 billion. In 2010, with revenues exceeding $7 billion, the company employed about 18,500 people in North America and Asia. In 2011 it expanded into the European market with the purchase of the Netherlands-based Fabory Group.

**Hammond Organ Co.** In 1928 Evanston resident Laurens Hammond founded the Hammond Clock Co. His enterprise had little success until 1934, when Hammond patented an electric organ and began to manufacture the instruments. In 1936 he sold more than 1,750 of the 275-pound organs, mainly to churches and households. During the 1950s, when the company employed over 1,000 people in the Chicago area, it changed its name from Hammond Musical Instrument Co. to Hammond Organ Co. By the early 1970s, with annual sales approaching $100 million, Hammond had four plants in the Chicago area and employed a total of 4,500 people nationwide. During the late 1970s, when organ sales declined, the company was purchased by the Marmon Group, a conglomerate owned by the Pritzker family of Chicago. By the 1990s, Hammond was owned by the Suzuki Group of Japan.

**Harpo Productions Inc.** Talk-show host Oprah Winfrey, who worked in radio and television in Nashville and Baltimore during the 1970s and early 1980s, arrived in Chicago in 1984. Her *Oprah Winfrey Show*, which started in 1985, became one of the most popular talk shows on American television. In 1986 Winfrey founded Harpo Productions Inc., a production company that used her first name spelled backward. In 1988 the company took full charge of Winfrey's show, which was produced in new facilities on the city's Near West Side. By the late 1990s, Winfrey's show had about 20 million regular viewers, and Harpo Productions had annual revenues of about $150 million with about 200 Chicago employees. Although the *Oprah Winfrey Show* was broadcast for the last time in May 2011, Harpo Productions remained headquartered in Chicago. With its 350 local employees and revenues of almost $290 million, it was part of a larger constellation of organizations associated with Winfrey involved in television and film production, publishing, and new media.

**Harris Trust & Savings Bank.** In 1883, 35-year-old Norman Wait Harris founded N. W. Harris & Co., a small Chicago-based investment banking firm. By 1890, when Harris opened an office in New York, the company had nearly $2 million in assets and specialized in marketing of municipal bonds. In 1907, when it was selling about $70 million worth of bonds a year, the company was incorporated as the Harris Trust & Savings Bank. By 1922 it employed about 440 people; by 1929 it had over $100 million in assets. After World War II, the company grew to become one of Chicago's leading banks. During the 1970s, when assets passed $4 billion, the institution was restructured as Harris Bankcorp Inc. and employed about 3,500 people in the Chicago area. In 1984, when Harris ranked as the third largest bank in Chicago, it was purchased by the Bank of Montreal. By early 2011, before its merger with Milwaukee-based Marshall & Isley and its renaming as BMO Harris Bank, Harris (still a division of its Canadian parent the BMO Financial Group) was Chicago's second largest bank, boasting assets of almost $50 billion and some 700 branches in Illinois, Indiana, Arizona, Missouri, Minnesota, Kansas, Nevada, Florida and Wisconsin.

**Hart Schaffner & Marx.** In 1872 Harry and Max Hart, German immigrants to Chicago, founded Harry Hart & Bro., a small men's clothing store on State Street. In 1879, along with brothers-in-law Levi Abt and Marcus Marx, the Harts formed Hart, Abt & Marx. The company not only sold

Garment workers' strike, December 12, 1910. A parade of women support strikers on West Jackson Boulevard near Morgan Street, 1910. The United Garment Workers strike began in September of that year and continued until early February 1911, shortly after an agreement was signed with Hart, Schaffner & Marx but while over 20,000 garment workers were still on strike against their employers. Photo: *Chicago Daily News*. Courtesy of the Chicago History Museum (DN-0056264).

clothing but also employed dozens of women around the city to manufacture close to $1 million worth of garments a year. In 1887, when Joseph Schaffner joined the firm, its name was changed to Hart Schaffner & Marx. By the beginning of the twentieth century, it owned dozens of small garment factories—identified by many observers as "sweatshops"— around the city; about two-thirds of its several thousand employees were foreign-born men and women. In 1910, when its annual sales were roughly $15 million, the company became a target of one of the biggest strikes in Chicago. Hannah Shapiro, an 18-year-old Russian-born worker at one of the Hart Schaffner & Marx shops, led a walkout in response to a wage cut. Within three weeks, about 40,000 Chicago garment workers went on strike. In 1911 Hart Schaffner & Marx became one of the first companies to settle with the workers when it signed a collective bargaining agreement that was one of the most comprehensive ever to occur in the clothing industry; by 1915 the majority of the company's employees were members of the Amalgamated Clothing Workers of America, a new union that was an outgrowth of the Chicago strikes. Hart Schaffner & Marx continued to be a leading employer in the Chicago area, and it became the largest of all U.S. men's clothing companies. By the beginning of the 1970s, it had 38 factories and 250 retail stores nationally and over 5,000 workers in the Chicago area. During the 1970s, when the company was banned by U.S. Justice Department regulators from buying any more men's clothing stores, its sales grew from $360 million a year to $630 million a year. In 1983, after buying Chicago rival Kuppenheimer Manufacturing Co., a producer and retailer of inexpensive men's clothing, the company changed its name to Hartmarx Corp. At the beginning of the 1990s, the company endured its worst losses since the Great Depression; it responded by selling its retail businesses and manufacturing facilities and refashioning itself as a men's clothing wholesaler, with over $600 million in annual sales to department stores, catalog companies, and other retailers. Its headquarters remained in Chicago, where it employed about 1,000 people. In 2009 Hartmarx filed for bankruptcy and, after workers fought its liquidation, was sold to Emerisque Brands UK and India-based SKNL North America.

**Helene Curtis Industries Inc.** In 1927 Gerald Gidwitz and Louis Stein formed the National Mineral Co., which made the Peach Bloom Facial Mask and other beauty products. During the 1930s, the company had success selling shampoos, Lanolin Creme, and Suave brands. After World War II, the company changed its name to Helene Curtis, which combined the names of Stein's wife and son. By the early 1960s, when it employed more than 1,000 people in Chicago, the company's annual sales of shampoo, hairspray, deodorant, and other products topped $50 million. During the 1970s and 1980s, when its Suave and Finesse brands were among the best-selling shampoos in the United States, Helene Curtis continued to grow. Annual sales reached $600 million during the 1980s, when the company's plant on North Avenue in Chicago employed nearly 1,000 people. In 1996, one year after Helene Curtis moved its headquarters to suburban Rolling Meadows, it was purchased by Unilever, the giant British-Dutch corporation. By the end of the century, Unilever announced that it would close the old North Avenue plant and soon thereafter moved the company's headquarters to New Jersey, leaving the company with little presence in the Chicago area.

**Hewitt Associates.** In 1940 Ted Hewitt founded an insurance brokerage company in suburban Lake Forest providing financial planning for business executives and professionals. Hewitt Associates began offering compensation and benefit plan consulting services to area employers in the 1950s. With the opening of its Minneapolis branch office in 1959, He-witt expanded nationally and then globally with its Toronto office in 1974. After a half century of astonishing growth, Chicago's largest management consulting business went public in 2002. Worldwide, it boasted 86 offices in 37 countries, 15,000 employees, and revenues of nearly $2 billion. Its headquarters, located in the Chicago suburb of Lincolnshire, employed 3,400 full-time consultants. In 2010 Aon purchased the firm to form a subsidiary known as Aon Hewitt.

**Hibbard, Spencer, Bartlett & Co.** This leading hardware dealership was the descendant of a Chicago store called Tuttle, Hibbard & Co., which took that name in 1855 when William G. Hibbard became a partner. In 1865 Hibbard was joined by Franklin F. Spencer, and the enterprise was renamed Hibbard & Spencer. By 1867 the company's annual sales of hard-ware had reached $1 million. When longtime company employee A. C. Bartlett became a partner in 1882, the company's name became Hibbard, Spencer, Bartlett & Co. When Spencer died in 1890, the company was al-ready among the leading wholesalers of hardware in the United States. In 1903, the year Hibbard died, the company opened a 10-story warehouse next to the State Street Bridge in downtown Chicago. In 1932 the company introduced a new line of hand tools under the brand name True Value. By 1948 Hibbard's annual sales reached nearly $30 million. Business slowed and profits were shrunk, however, as new hardware cooperatives began to bypass traditional wholesalers. In 1962 the company's owners, who wanted to move into the real estate business, sold the hardware opera-tions and the True Value brand to John Cotter for $2.5 million.

**Household Finance Corp.** The Household Finance Corp., the descen-dant of a business founded in the late 1870s by Frank Mackey, moved from Minneapolis–St. Paul to Chicago in 1894. In 1905 Mackey's company added to its pioneering efforts in the field of consumer credit by introduc-ing installment payment systems. By 1908 it had several dozen offices na-tionwide, with total loan accounts of $1.5 million. The Household Finance Corp. came into being in 1925 when Mackey merged 33 of his company's branch offices across the country into a single entity. At the end of the 1920s, Household Finance ranked as the largest personal finance company in the United States, with about $30 million in loans to tens of thousands of people. The company grew more slowly during the Great Depression and World War II, but during the postwar years Household Finance expanded quickly. By the early 1960s, when it employed about 7,000 people around the country, the company had about 1,200 offices with about $1.1 billion in outstanding loans. In 1965 Household Finance entered the retailing busi-ness on a large scale when it purchased the City Products Corp., owners of the Ben Franklin retail chain, which had long been operated by Butler Bros. of Chicago. In 1981 Household Finance changed its name to Household International Inc. By 1985, just before it sold the Ben Franklin stores, Household had 28,000 employees worldwide and had about $3.4 billion in annual revenues. At the end of the 1990s, when it was based in suburban Prospect Heights, Household International employed about 4,700 people in the Chicago area. In 2003 Household International was bought out by British banking giant HSBC Holdings PLC, making it the largest subprime lender in the United States at that time. In 2009 HSBC announced the closing of Household International Inc. and all of its offices.

**Hyatt Hotels Corp.** In 1957 the Hyatt House hotel near the Los Angeles Airport was purchased by Jay Pritzker, a member of the wealthy Chicago family descended from Nicholas Pritzker, who emigrated from Kiev to the Windy City in 1881. By 1961 Jay Pritzker had created a six-hotel chain. During the late 1960s, Hyatt spun off a separate entity, Hyatt International. By the end of the 1970s, Hyatt operated a 52-hotel chain with nearly $300 million in annual sales, placing it among the top 15 hotel chains in the United States. At the end of the century, still owned by the Pritzker family and still based in Chicago, Hyatt and Hyatt International together operated or licensed about 200 hotels and employed about 80,000 people around the world. In the Chicago area, the companies had about 3,500 workers. In 2009 Hyatt became a publicly traded corporation. By 2011 Hyatt, with 45,000 employees worldwide, had expanded its portfolio of properties to 456 located in 44 countries. including the Hyatt Regency, Chicago's largest hotel.

**IC Industries Inc.** Illinois Central Industries was created in 1962 as a holding company for the Illinois Central Railroad. In 1965 the company's annual revenues approached $300 million. William Johnson, who became president in 1966, transformed the company. In 1968 it purchased the Abex Corp. (formerly known as American Brake Shoe & Foundry), a manufacturer of automobile and railroad products that had been employing hundreds of workers in the Chicago area. During the early 1970s, the company bought Pepsi-Cola General Bottlers Inc. of Chicago, as well Midas International Corp., the Chicago-based chain of automobile maintenance shops. The company changed its name to IC Industries in 1975, and it employed about 8,000 people in the Chicago area. By that time, railroad transportation no longer constituted the larger part of its business. By the mid-1980s, when IC Industries sold food, aerospace equipment, and a variety of other goods and services, annual revenues were over $4 billion. At this point, the huge conglomerate stopped growing and began to sell off some of its operations. During the late 1980s, IC changed its name to Whitman Corp. and rid itself of the Illinois Central, the railroad that had once been the foundation of the company. By the end of the 1990s, Whitman was primarily a bottler of soft drinks, with about $2.6 billion in annual sales; it employed about 1,700 people in the Chicago area and another 10,000 around the country. In early 2001, the company substantially expanded its share of the soft drink bottling market by acquiring Minneapolis-based PepsiAmericas Inc. and adopting its onetime rival's name. The company moved its headquarters to Minneapolis but maintained most of its operations in Chicago. In 2011 Chicago-based operations of this segment of PepsiCo Inc. (which in 2010 acquired PepsiAmericas) were headquartered in Schaumberg

**IGA Inc.** The Independent Grocers Alliance was created in 1926 by a group led by Chicago accountant J. Frank Grimes. It was designed as a network for independent grocers who sought to use the purchasing power of the association to compete with the rising chain grocery companies. The enterprise was a success and lasted through the end of the century. By the 1980s, when it was known as IGA, the combined sales of its 3,000 affiliated stores made it the fourth largest food retailer in the United States. The 1990s saw operations expand into China, Singapore, Malaysia, and the Caribbean. At the end of the century, with annual sales of $18 billion, IGA was a wholesaling operation supplying the world's largest voluntary network of 4,000 supermarkets in 30 countries. By 2010 IGA's network included 5,000 stores in 46 states and 5 continents.

**Illinois Bell Telephone Co.** The Bell Telephone Co. of Illinois was chartered in 1878; three years later, it became part of the Chicago Telephone Co. By the beginning of the twentieth century, Chicago Telephone was associated with the Bell network of American Telephone & Telegraph Co. (AT&T), the largest phone company in the United States. The number of Chicago-area telephones served by this company grew from 34,000 in 1900 to roughly 1 million by 1930. By the early 1920s, Chicago Telephone employed about 16,000 people in the Chicago area; many of these employees were female operators. Illinois Bell continued to grow in the decades that followed, until it had roughly 36,000 Chicago-area employees by the early 1970s. After federal courts dismantled AT&T's Bell system in 1984, Illinois Bell became the largest division of Ameritech, the new leading telecommunications company in the Midwest. At the end of the 1990s, when it employed about 20,000 people in the Chicago area and collected nearly $20 billion in annual revenues, Ameritech was purchased by SBC Communications Inc., another giant phone company and former "Baby Bell." In 2005 SBC acquired AT&T and adopted the name AT&T Inc. In 2010 just over 12,000 of AT&T's 267,000 employees worked in the Chicago area.

**Illinois Central Railroad.** The first U.S. railroad promoted by a large (2.6-million-acre) federal land grant, the Illinois Central cost about $25 million to build; as many as 10,000 workers at a time were engaged in building the railroad between 1851 and 1856. British and Dutch investors provided much of the capital required for construction. At its name suggested, the 700-mile railroad—the longest in the world at the time it was completed—ran down the length of the state, from Chicago and other northern towns all the way to the southern tip of Illinois, at the meeting of the Ohio and Mississippi Rivers. In Chicago, the principal terminus, the Illinois Central (which would become known as the IC), operated out of the Great Central Depot, located just south of the Chicago River near Lake Michigan. By the end of the 1850s, the railroad's annual revenues had reached $2 million a year. After the Civil War (when it transported troops and military supplies at a discount because of its land-grant status), under the leadership of William H. Osborn, the railroad expanded outside of Illinois. It reached Sioux City, Iowa, in 1867 and extended all the way to New Orleans by 1882. In 1887, when Stuyvesant Fish became president of the railroad, the Illinois Central owned 2,300 miles of track, had $12 million in annual revenues, and employed about 8,500 people. It continued to grow, and by the first years of the twentieth century, it owned 5,000 miles of track in 13 states, as well as 800 locomotives, 700 passenger cars, and 33,000 freight cars. By this time, the IC employed more than 30,000 people nationwide, including about 5,000 men at its repair and maintenance shops at 95th and Cottage Grove on the South Side of Chicago. In the 1890s, the railroad opened a large new Chicago depot near Roosevelt Road called Central Station, which was torn down in the early 1970s. The IC's annual revenues stood at about $150 million by the 1920s, when it employed over 70,000 people around the country; but it was forced to cut back during the Great Depression. By the beginning of the 1960s, when it retired the last of its old steam locomotives, the IC had annual revenues of about $250 million; its national workforce had declined to about 20,000 people. In 1962 ownership of the company was transferred to a holding company called Illinois Central Industries, which proceeded to enter a variety of businesses; it became IC Industries in 1975. In 1971 IC Industries sold its passenger service to Amtrak; the following year, it merged with the Gulf, Mobile & Ohio Railroad to become the Illinois Central Gulf Railroad, which had nearly 10,000 miles of track. During the 1980s, it sold much of this track to concentrate the Chicago–New Orleans corridor, its primary route since the nineteenth century. In 1988 the IC sold its Chicago commuter lines to the Metropolitan Rail (Metra). One year later, the railroad left IC Industries and became an independent railway company, called Illinois Central Corp. In 1998 the railroad was purchased by the Canadian National Railway Co. for more than $2.4 billion.                                   *John P. Hankey*

**Illinois Tool Works Inc.** In 1912 Byron L. Smith, along with his sons and several veterans of the tool-and-die industry from Rockford, Illinois, started a small company at Huron and Franklin Streets in Chicago. After Byron Smith died in 1914, his son Harold guided the firm, which specialized at first in the production of metal-cutting tools. During the 1920s, the company became a leading producer of metal fasteners. By the mid-1930s, Illinois Tool had about 500 workers in Chicago. After World War II, the company began to make plastic fasteners. Annual sales rose from about $30 million in 1960 to nearly $300 million by the mid-1970s, when the company had about 3,000 workers in the Chicago area. During the 1980s, under the leadership of John Nichols, Illinois Tool doubled in size by buying other companies, including Signode, another old Chicago-based fastener company. At the end of the 1990s, Illinois Tool bought Premark, a Chicago-area company that made kitchen appliances and plastics. By that time, Illinois Tool grossed over $9 billion in annual sales and employed nearly 5,000 people in the Chicago area, which the company still called home. In 2010 Glenview-based Illinois Tool Works had revenues of almost $16 billion and employed over 60,000 people in 52 countries working on 6 continents.

**Inland Steel Co.** Chicago's leading homegrown steel company, Inland was founded in 1893 in Chicago Heights by Joseph Block and his son Philip. The Blocks' company started small after Philip had purchased the plant of the defunct Chicago Steel Works, a maker of farm equipment. In 1897 it had about 250 workers and only about $350,000 in sales. But in 1902, when it built a large new open-hearth steel mill at Indiana Harbor (in East Chicago, Indiana, 27 miles southeast of downtown Chicago), Inland Steel suddenly became a big business. By 1910 the Indiana Harbor facility had about 2,600 workers; by 1917 annual output passed 1 million tons. During the 1920s, when Inland made about 2 percent of all the steel produced in the United States, its workforce grew to about 7,000 people. In 1935, when annual output stood at 2 million tons, Inland purchased Joseph T. Ryerson & Son, an old Chicago wholesaler of steel products. Inland, like other steel companies, had all the business it could handle during World War II; annual output passed 3.5 million tons. During the 1950s, when Inland was among the ten largest steel companies in the United States, annual sales grew to nearly $700 million. A new Chicago headquarters, the Inland Steel Building on Monroe Street, was built in 1957. During the 1960s and 1970s, about 25,000 people worked at the Indiana Harbor plant. Like most American steel companies, Inland went into decline and laid off thousands of workers during the 1980s. In 1998 it was purchased by Ispat International, a large corporation based in the Netherlands that specialized in acquiring underperforming companies to make them more profitable. Operating under a new name, Ispat Inland Inc., the company cut almost one-fifth of its workforce by 2002, to 7,800 employees. At that time, as the sixth largest integrated steel producer in the United States, it produced about 5 percent of the country's steel. In 2011, as part of the ArcelorMittal Indiana Harbor mill—which brought together the former Inland works and the former Youngstown plant across the canal—was one the largest steel mills in the United States.                                    *Jonathan Keyes*

**International Harvester Co.** Cyrus Hall McCormick, a Virginia inventor of plows and reapers, decided to move to Chicago in 1847, when he and his partner Charles M. Gray built a reaper factory on the North Bank of the Chicago River. McCormick's mechanical reapers (which required horses to pull them) proved to be popular with farmers, and the enterprise expanded steadily. By the middle of the 1850s, the Chicago plant had 250 workers, who made more than 2,500 reapers a year, worth over $300,000. After the original plant burned in the 1871 Great Fire, McCormick built a larger factory along the South Branch of the Chicago River. This facility soon employed about 800 men; annual sales well exceeded $1 million. After Cyrus died in 1884, his wife, Nettie, and his son Charles took over the business. Hostile toward labor unions and their demands for an eight-hour workday, the McCormicks faced strikes by their workers in 1885 and 1886; the second of these, often regarded as one of the more important events in American labor history, was associated with the explosion of a bomb at Haymarket Square in Chicago. Meanwhile, William Deering—a veteran dry-goods wholesaler who had been doing business in Maine and New York—had established a rival harvester factory at Plano, Illinois, southwest of the big city; in 1880 Deering moved his factory to Chicago. Weary of competition, the Deering and McCormick families began to talk about a merger of their companies during the late 1890s. By this time, McCormick had a plant at Blue Island and Western Avenues that employed over 5,000 people; the Deering Harvester works on Fullerton Avenue on the city's North Side employed about 7,000. In 1902 McCormick and Deering—along with the Plano Manufacturing Co. (which had about 1,400 workers at its West Pullman plant) and two smaller farm equipment makers—merged to form International Harvester. The new company was capitalized at $120 million and dominated the American market; and, as its name suggested, it played an important role in world markets as well. For most of the twentieth century, International Harvester (IH) was one of the leading industrial corporations in the United States; its operations were concentrated in Chicago and its suburbs. By 1910, when IH grossed about $100 million in annual sales, it had over 17,000 workers in the Chicago area, making it the leading employer in the region. By that time, IH had established its own steel mill on the city's far South Side, which it named Wisconsin Steel, as well as manufacturing plants in Sweden, Russia, and Germany. A manufacturer of trucks as well as tractors, during the first years of the twentieth century, the company moved away from animal-powered equipment and toward motorized vehicles. In the 1930s, as the nation's leading manufacturer of trucks, IH had a sales network of about 11,000 dealers across the country. During the 1940s, when the company's national workforce grew to about 70,000 people, many IH workers joined one of two rival unions, the Farm Equipment Workers and United Auto Workers (UAW). In the 1950s, their annual sales were over $1 billion, and yet John Deere surpassed IH as the nation's leading maker of agricultural equipment. IH still employed about 20,000 people in the Chicago area and tens of thousands more around the world in the 1970s. But the company was beginning to struggle. Between 1977 and 1979, the company sold Wisconsin Steel to Envirodyne Inc. IH then endured a five-month UAW strike from 1979 to 1980. The company was losing huge amounts of money in the early 1980s, and it chose to sell its farm equipment business (as well as the International Harvester name) to Tenneco Inc., a competitor. By 1986 most of what had been International Harvester became Navistar International Corp. Navistar, headquartered in suburban Warrenville, had become the nation's leading manufacturer of large trucks by the end of the 1990s. It employed about 2,500 people in the Chicago area, one-tenth of the number who once worked in and around the city for International Harvester. Its total revenues in 2002 stood at almost $7 billion. In 2010 Navistar's facilities on six continents earned it more than $12 billion in revenues.

**Jewel-Osco.** The Jewel Tea Co. was founded in 1899 by Frank V. Skiff and Frank Ross, who sold coffee, tea, and other groceries to Chicagoans from their wagons. By 1915 the company had 850 routes and $8 million in annual sales. In 1930, when the company had traded in its old horse-drawn vehicles for motorized ones, it moved its headquarters from Chicago to suburban Barrington. Threatened by local ordinances that prohibited uninvited door-to-door sales, the company started to open retail stores around Chicago. By 1936 it owned 100 stores, which together grossed about $20 million in annual sales. By the end of World War II, Jewel was among the ten largest retail grocery chains in the United States. At the beginning of the 1960s, when it purchased the 30-store Osco drug chain (founded in the late 1930s by L. L. Skaggs) and changed its own name to Jewel Companies Inc., the company had over $500 million in annual sales and nearly 300 grocery stores. By the late 1960s, Jewel owned more than 600 supermarkets in 9 states and employed close to 20,000 people; it was the leading retail grocery chain in the Chicago area. In 1984, when its share of the Chicago-area grocery market was about 30 percent, Jewel was purchased by American Stores Inc. of Salt Lake City. By the end of the 1990s, when it was acquired by Albertson's Inc. (based in Boise, Idaho), Jewel had nearly 40,000 workers in the Chicago area, making it one of the leading employers in the region. Jewel-Osco became part of the Minnesota-based Supervalu organization in 2006 when Supervalu purchased Albertson's to create America's third largest grocery retailing company. In 2010 Jewel-Osco, headquartered in Itasca, continued to be one of the Chicago area's largest employers, with some 8,000 employees in its 182 stores.

**Johnson Products Co.** George Johnson, a former door-to-door cosmetics salesman, formed this company in Chicago in 1954. At a plant on the city's

South Side, Johnson manufactured hair care products for African Americans. The company's first product was a hair straightener called Ultra Wave; in 1957 it introduced its successful Ultra Sheen brand. Johnson responded to cultural shifts in the 1960s by creating a new line of products called Afro Sheen. Meanwhile, Johnson Products was becoming one of the largest African American–owned manufacturing companies. Annual sales grew from about $4 million in 1967 to $40 million in 1976. By that time, Johnson had about 500 employees in Chicago, and it invested in a factory in Nigeria. But the company's profits declined in the late 1970s, as large cosmetics companies such as Revlon and Avon began to target African American consumers. In 1993 Johnson Products was purchased by the Ivax Corp. of Florida, a large drug and personal-care products company. At the end of the 1990s, Johnson became part of Carson Inc. of Georgia, a smaller company that specialized in cosmetics for African Americans. In 2000 Carson became part of L'Oréal USA, a company that had purchased Chicago's SoftSheen corporation two years earlier. Joining the two former Chicago firms into the SoftSheen/Carson division headquartered in Chicago, L'Oréal also opened its Institute for Ethnic Hair & Skin Research on the Near South Side. In 2004 SoftSheen/Carson headquarters left Chicago for New York City

**Johnson Publishing Co.** John H. Johnson moved with his family from Arkansas City to Chicago in 1933, when he was a teenager. In 1942, after working for the Supreme Liberty Life Insurance Co., the 24-year-old Johnson began to publish *Negro Digest,* a weekly publication covering the nation's African American community. *Negro Digest* used a format similar to that of the mass-market weekly *Reader's Digest.* In 1945 Johnson introduced *Ebony* magazine, the large-format glossy magazine that became the company's flagship publication. By the 1950s, *Ebony*'s circulation had climbed to 500,000; it would reach 1 million during the 1970s. Another magazine intended for African American readers, *Jet,* was introduced in 1951. The company launched its annual Ebony Fashion Fair in 1958, a traveling fashion show that had raised $48 million for scholarships and charities by the early twenty-first century. By the 1970s, when it moved into the cosmetics business with Fashion Fair Cosmetics, Johnson Publishing ranked as the second largest African American–owned company in the United States. Annual revenues passed $100 million in the early 1980s, when the company employed about 1,000 people in the Chicago area. By the end of the century, Johnson Publishing had added several more cosmetic lines, radio and television production, and a book division that published African American authors to its family-owned business. John Johnson continued to lead the company, which posted over $400 million a year in revenues and employed 2,600 people nationwide. Changes in the publishing environment fueled by the expansion of online outlets hit Johnson Publishing hard, as did the founder's death in 2005. By 2009

Johnson Publishing, headed by the founder's daughter Linda Johnson Rice, had $200 million in revenues and some 250 employees.

*Adam Green*

**Kemper Corp.** In 1912, after the state of Illinois passed a workers' compensation law, James S. Kemper founded the Lumbermens Mutual Casualty Co., which sold accident insurance. Kemper's firm soon became one of the first to offer automobile insurance. By 1919 Lumbermens had offices around the country. The company continued to operate through World War II and changed its name to James S. Kemper & Co. During the late 1960s, when annual revenues neared $150 million, the company moved its headquarters from Chicago to suburban Long Grove and became part of Kemperco Inc., a holding company. By the late 1970s, when the company was known as Kemper Corp., annual revenues had jumped to nearly $1 billion. Kemper expanded during the 1980s by moving into financial services. While Kemper would continue in the insurance business into the twenty-first century, its foray into the securities arena was short-lived. In 1995 Zurich Insurance of Switzerland acquired Kemper Corp. and promptly sold off the securities division to Kemper employees as a separate company named Everen Securities Inc. Kemper Insurance Companies, as it came to be called, dramatically downsized in the early 2000s, laying off thousands of employees in Chicago and nationwide and selling off its service organization in 2003. In 2010 the Chicago-based insurance and financial services firm Unitrin purchased the Kemper name from Lumbermens (its principal subsidiary). The following year, Unitrin—which in 2010 had revenues of $2.7 billion and employed over 7,000 nationwide—took the Kemper Corp. name.

**Kirkland & Ellis.** This law firm descended from a partnership formed in Chicago in 1908 by Stewart G. Shepard and Robert R. McCormick. (McCormick soon left to take charge of the *Chicago Tribune* newspaper, the family business.) In 1915 both Weymouth Kirkland and Howard Ellis started to work for the Shepard firm; their names eventually became those that identified the business. Among the firm's major clients were Chicago companies such as International Harvester, Inland Steel, Marshall Field, Motorola, and McCormick's own Tribune Co. The firm remained one of the city's largest into the twenty-first century, with revenues above $500 million and a workforce that included over 400 attorneys in Chicago and scores more at offices in New York and other cities around the world. By 2010 Kirkland & Ellis had more than 600 attorneys in Chicago and more than 1,400 in its worldwide offices.

**Kraft Inc.** James L. Kraft, born in Ontario, Canada, started a cheese-delivery business in Chicago in 1903. Within a few years, Kraft was producing cheese as well as distributing it, and the company grew. During the

1920s, it began operations in Australia and Europe. In 1928 a merger with Phenix Cheese created Kraft-Phenix, a large food company that supplied about 40 percent of all the cheese consumed in the United States. In 1930 Kraft-Phenix became a subsidiary of the National Dairy Products Corp., which was founded in 1923 by the Chicago pharmacist Thomas H. McInnerney. By the early 1930s, when National Dairy's annual sales of nearly $400 million made it one of the largest companies in the United States, Kraft-Phenix employed about 700 people in the Chicago area. In 1969 Kraft and National Dairy became known as Kraftco; in 1976, when annual sales stood at about $5 billion, the name changed to Kraft Inc. By this time, the company employed nearly 50,000 people around the world, including about 3,000 in the Chicago area. Kraft merged with Dart Industries in 1980, creating Dart & Kraft Inc.; the two companies split in 1986. In 1988, when it was based in suburban Glenview, Kraft was purchased by Philip Morris, the tobacco and food giant. The following year, it was merged with General Foods, another Philip Morris acquisition, and renamed Kraft General Foods. The new company had a much larger product offering, which it expanded in the 1990s, when the company again took the name Kraft Foods, through the purchase of international corporations. In 2001 Philip Morris (renamed the Altria Group in 2003) sold a large portion of Kraft stock to the public but maintained a controlling interest in the company. Four years later it spun off Kraft Foods, creating a publicly held independent company. In 2010 Kraft purchased UK-based confectioner Cadbury; with $49.2 billion in net revenues and 127,000 employees, as well as earlier international purchases, this made Kraft the second largest global food company. Reflecting market developments, Kraft announced in 2011 that it would split into a global snack company and a company targeting U.S. grocery businesses.

**LaSalle National Bank.** National Builders Bank was chartered in downtown Chicago in 1927 and managed to weather the Great Depression that followed shortly thereafter. It moved to the recently constructed Art Deco building on the northeast corner of Adams and LaSalle in 1940, changing its name to LaSalle National Bank and maintaining its headquarters there through the early twenty-first century. LaSalle soon grew to become one of Chicago's largest banks, boasting over $100 million in deposits by the early 1950s. By 1965 deposits exceeded $300 million, and the bank employed over 500 people. In 1979 LaSalle became a division of Algemene Bank Nederland (ABN), a giant Dutch bank. LaSalle continued to grow after this acquisition, purchasing numerous banks on its own throughout the Midwest over the next two decades. In the early years of the new century, LaSalle was Chicago's second largest bank, with more than 100 branches in the Midwest, over $50 billion in assets, and 10,000 employees in the Chicago area. In 2007 ABN AMRO, as the Dutch bank was then known, sold LaSalle NA to Bank of America; the following year, the LaSalle name was changed to Bank of America.

**Lettuce Entertain You Enterprises Inc.** In 1971 Richard Melman opened a restaurant in the Lincoln Park neighborhood of Chicago that he called R.J. Grunts. Over the next five years, Melman opened four more restaurants in the Chicago area. By the mid-1980s, his network of restaurants employed about 2,000 people in the Chicago area, and annual revenues stood at about $40 million. Among the restaurants at some time in the Lettuce empire were Ed Debevic's, Maggiano's, Corner Bakery, and Big Bowl. By the end of the 1990s, the company had over $200 million in annual revenues and owned a total of 75 restaurants worldwide. Most of these were in the Chicago area, where Lettuce employed about 4,000 people. In 2010, with 60-plus restaurants in Illinois, Nevada, California, Minnesota, Arizona, Georgia, and the Washington, D.C., metro area, the company employed 3,200 people locally and 5,700 nationally.

**Levy (Chas.) Circulating Co.** In 1893 the 15-year-old Charles Levy won a horse and wagon in a raffle and began to haul newspapers around Chicago's West Side. By the 1920s, his company was distributing newspapers to the suburbs as well. In 1949, when the company was distributing not only newspapers but also magazines and paperback books, the center of operations moved to Goose Island, in the middle of the Chicago River. By the early 1950s, the company owned a fleet of over 60 trucks and amassed annual sales of about $5 million. Over time the company began to increase its business outside the Chicago region. By the end of the 1980s, when Barbara Levy Kipper headed the company, over half of its some $360 million in annual sales occurred outside the Chicago area, where it still employed as many as 1,600 people. By the end of the 1990s, the Chas. Levy Co. was the largest distributor of periodicals in the Midwest and one of the largest in the nation; it continued to call Chicago home and employed several hundred people in the area. In 2005, when it was distributing magazines from California to Pennsylvania, the company sold its magazine division. When plans were announced in 2011 to sell Levy Home Entertainment LLC, as it was then called, to Readerlink Distribution Services LLC, the company was still overseen by the granddaughter of the founder and one of the nation's largest distributors of book product to mass-market retailers.

**Marmon Group Inc.** This large conglomerate, a creation of Chicago's Pritzker family, was the descendant of Pritzker & Pritzker, a law firm founded at the beginning of the twentieth century. By 1940 the firm had evolved into an investment company. In 1963 Jay and Robert Pritzker bought a large part of the Marmon-Herrington Co., a descendant of an automobile manufacturer. During the 1970s, the Pritzkers acquired the Cerro Corp., which had mining, trucking, and real estate operations; their company was known for a time as the Cerro-Marmon Corp. The Marmon Group continued to grow during the 1980s, when annual revenues passed

$3 billion. Among its holdings were the Trans Union Corp., a lessor of rail-road cars; Braniff International Airways; and the Ticketmaster chain. By the early 2000s, Marmon owned about 150 companies—mostly in the service and manufacturing industries—had nearly $7 billion in assets, and employed 30,000 people worldwide, with over 2,500 in the Chicago area. In 2002 Robert Pritzker retired from Marmon after spending 48 years at the company's helm in its Chicago headquarters. Soon thereafter, efforts were launched to liquidate large portions of the immense assets of what was still Chicago's largest privately held company. In 2008 Berkshire Hathaway acquired the Marmon Group, which still operates as an international association of some 140 units worldwide headquartered in Chicago.

**Material Service Corp.** The Material Service Corp. (MSC) was formed with $10,000 by brothers Henry, Irving, and Sol Crown in 1919. Henry Crown became president after Sol died in 1921. Originally a brokerage that bought and resold sand and gravel, MSC expanded rapidly by purchasing pits, mines, quarries, and factories to produce lime, pipe, stone, coal, and cement. Starting in 1938, the company operated the Thornton Quarry, one of the world's largest limestone quarries, in Thornton, just south of Chicago. The company soon benefited from large war-related contracts, enabling it to acquire coal mines and more limestone quarries, and to become one of the city's most prominent builders of commercial property. Among the major Chicago structures that MSC helped to build were the Merchandise Mart, the Loop Railway, and the Civic Opera House. In a stock-for-stock merger in 1959, MSC became part of the General Dynamics Corp. (GD), a leading military contractor. The Crown family obtained a major interest in GD through the deal. GD's bad financial health forced the Crowns to sell one of their prized possessions, the Empire State Building in New York City, in 1961. In 1965 the Crown family was forced to sell their interest in GD, and thus MSC. Within five years, however, the Crowns had reaccumulated enough General Dynamics stock to gain control of the company, including the Material Service division. Around this time, the Crowns created Henry Crown & Co., a holding company that would eventually form the massive core of the Crown family investments nationwide, including its stake in GD, major real estate and resort properties, Maytag Corp., and a 10 percent share of the New York Yankees. By the early 1980s, Material Service had become the leading distributor and producer of building materials in the Midwest; it employed more than 3,000 people. In 2006 Material Service Corp., still a subsidiary of General Dynamics, was sold to UK-based Hanson PLC. The following year HeidelbergCement AG, a German firm, purchased Hanson and with it MSC.

*Andrew W. Cohen*

**Mayer (Oscar) & Co.** In 1883 German immigrants Oscar F. Mayer and Gottfried Mayer started a small sausage-making operation on Chicago's

North Side. They opened a meatpacking plant in 1888; by 1909 the plant employed about 70 people. Starting in the 1910s, the company expanded more quickly. Annual sales rose from about $3 million in 1913 to $11 million by 1918. By the early 1930s, when a son of the founder named Oscar G. Mayer was running the company, it employed over 400 people in the Chicago area. Annual sales rose to about $275 million by the early 1960s, when the company had about 8,000 workers nationwide, including many in Madison, Wisconsin, as well as Chicago. By the 1970s, the company had moved its headquarters to Madison, and annual sales reached $1 billion. In the 1980s, Oscar Mayer became part of Philip Morris (Altria Group since 2003) and its Kraft Foods division.

**McDonald's Corp.** McDonald's was founded in 1955 by Oak Park native Ray Kroc, who worked as a salesman of milk shake machines. In 1954 Kroc encountered the hamburger stand of the McDonald brothers in San Bernardino, California, which used Kroc's mixers. After convincing the McDonalds to name him their exclusive franchising agent, Kroc opened a restaurant in Des Plaines; it was the first McDonald's in the Chicago area. The chain grew at an extraordinary rate: there were 14 restaurants in 1957 and 100 by 1959. In 1961, when there were 250 restaurants in the chain, Kroc purchased the interest of the McDonald brothers for $2.7 million. By 1968, three years after it started to advertise on television, Kroc's company oversaw 1,000 McDonald's franchises. The remarkable growth continued during the 1970s, when McDonald's—now based in Oak Brook—added 500 new restaurants each year in locations around the world. With this rapid expansion, annual revenues passed $1 billion. The company had become one of the world's largest users of beef, potatoes, ketchup, and other foods; its distinctive golden arches had become a familiar part of the landscape. By the beginning of the century, there were about 25,000 McDonald's restaurants around the world, annual revenues stood at about $15 billion, and over 400,000 employees worked for the company, which had become a symbol of America around the world. In the Chicago area, the company employed about 6,000 people. By 2010 McDonald's global revenues stood about $24 billion as an average of 64 million customers ate in one of the company's more than 32,000 owned or franchised restaurants.

**Molex Inc.** In 1938 Frederick Krehbiel founded a company in Brookfield that made plastic goods. In the 1940s, led by John Krehbiel, the company moved into electric and electronics products at its Brookfield factory. Annual sales passed $1 million in 1962. Molex became a leading manufacturer of electrical switches and connectors. At the beginning of the twenty-first century, Molex, based in Lisle, grossed about $1.7 billion in annual sales and ranked as the world's second leading maker of connectors, with factories and sales offices throughout the world. At the beginning of the century, approximately 1,600 of its 16,000 employees worldwide worked in the Chicago area. In 2006 Molex, in one of its key acquisitions, purchased Deerfield-based Woodfield Industries with its 21 locations in 10 countries. By 2010 the much-expanded company had revenues in excess of $3 billion and more than 35,000 employees worldwide.

**Morton Salt Co.** In 1880 a 25-year-old Nebraskan named Joy Morton arrived in Chicago to become a new partner in E. I. Wheeler & Co., a salt-marketing firm. Wheeler & Co. originated as a Chicago firm called Richmond & Co., which in 1848 had become a sales agent of the New York State Salt Manufacturing Co. After Wheeler died in 1895, the firm became Joy Morton & Co. Morton soon began to invest in salt evaporation plants in Michigan, and the company grew. The Morton Salt Co. was incorporated in 1910, and the company's "Umbrella Girl" logo and its "When It Rains It Pours" slogan soon became familiar to consumers across the United States. During the mid-1930s, the company had about 250 employees in the Chicago area. After World War II, Morton expanded into new regions and new products, including chemicals, drugs, and adhesives. Between 1961 and 1967, annual sales grew from $50 million to $250 million. A merger with a drug company in 1969 led the company to adopt the name Morton-Norwich. By the end of the 1970s, this company grossed $700 million in annual sales and had more than 10,000 workers around the world. In 1982 the company sold its drug business and purchased Thiokol Inc., a maker of cleaners, chemicals, and rockets; the new entity was named Morton-Thiokol Inc. In 1989, soon after the company's work was connected to the 1986 explosion of the U.S. space shuttle *Challenger*, Morton separated from Thiokol to focus on making chemicals. At the same time, it moved quickly into the production of safety airbags for automobiles and soon became a leader in the airbag business. By the 1990s, Morton International was still based in Chicago, where it employed about 1,500 people. Morton continued to earn profits from its market-leading salt brand, but most of its $3 billion in annual revenues came from sales of airbags and specialty chemicals. Two years after selling its airbag division in 1997, Morton was purchased by Rohm and Haas, a Philadelphia chemical company. In 2009 K+S purchased Morton Salt, making that German firm the world's largest producer of salt. As a subsidiary of K+S, Morton is still headquartered in Chicago.

**Motorola Inc.** In 1928 brothers Paul V. Galvin and Joseph E. Galvin purchased a battery eliminator business from the bankrupt Stewart Storage Battery Co. of Chicago. The brothers' new company, located on the West Side of Chicago, was called the Galvin Manufacturing Corp. and started out with five employees. The company began to make car radios in 1930 and manufactured larger radio sets for homes starting in 1937. During World War II, Galvin made hand-held, two-way FM portable radios—

which became known as "walkie-talkies"—for the use of the U.S. military. Although the company experienced a severe decline immediately after the war—with the end of large military contracts pushing its annual sales down from $68 million in 1945 to $23 million in 1946—it soon recovered in spectacular fashion. In 1947 the company changed its name to Motorola Inc. Six years later, it opened a large television assembly plant in the Chicago suburb of Franklin Park, where Motorola made the first television sets to sell for under $200. Motorola introduced new electronics products year after year. An all-transistor car radio appeared 1959; later the company pioneered eight-track tape players for automobiles and began to sell an all-transistor television set, the Quasar. In 1958, two years after Robert W. Galvin succeeded his father, Paul, as company president, Motorola started a semiconductors division, based in Phoenix, Arizona. By the middle of the 1960s, the company grossed $500 million in annual sales and employed some 30,000 people nationwide. One of Motorola's customers was NASA, which bought communications for its space missions. In 1974, the year it stopped making televisions, Motorola introduced its first microprocessor. By 1976, when the company moved its headquarters to a 325-acre campus in the Chicago suburb of Schaumburg, it employed over 7,500 people around the Chicago area. Expansion continued during the 1980s, when Motorola began to sell pagers and cellular telephones, boosting annual sales past $10 billion and the total number of employees (worldwide) beyond 100,000. Meanwhile, the company had become the nation's fourth largest manufacturer of semiconductors for the booming computer industry. In 1993 Robert Galvin's son Christopher was named company president. By the end of the 1990s, annual sales had passed $30 billion, and there were over 20,000 Motorola employees working in the Chicago area. Strong telecommunications competition with new rivals such as Nokia (a giant cellular phone manufacturer based in Finland) and slumping semiconductor markets in the early 2000s hit Motorola hard. Three-quarters of a century of rapid growth came to an end, as Motorola slashed tens of thousands of jobs in Chicago and worldwide. Christopher Galvin was replaced by the first non-Galvin to head Motorola in its storied history, a former executive at General Electric with a reputation for instituting relentless cost-cutting measures. By 2002, however, Motorola remained one of Chicago's largest corporations, with net revenues of almost $27 billion and 97,000 employees worldwide. The rapidly changing communications environment in the twenty-first century had significant ramifications for Motorola. In 2011 the company split into two separate companies: Motorola Solutions and Motorola Mobility. The former was composed of the Enterprise Mobility Solutions, Public Safety, and Networks divisions (the latter sold to Nokia Siemens Network later that year). Motorola Mobility's life as an independent company was short-lived. In August 2011, Google announced that it would purchase the company, which had created the smart phone that used Google's Android operating system.                                      *Timothy J. Gilfoyle*

**Nalco Chemical Co.** In 1920 Herbert A. Kern founded the Chicago Chemical Co., which sold water-treatment chemicals such as sodium aluminate. Two years later, P. Wilson Evans started the Aluminate Sales Corp. In 1928 a merger between these two companies created the National Aluminate Corp., based in Chicago. Annual sales neared $4 million by the end of the 1930s, and the company continued to grow thereafter. By 1959, when the company's name changed to Nalco Chemical, annual sales approached $50 million. Sales rose to $400 million by the mid-1970s, when Nalco—now a Fortune 500 company operating on a global scale—had about 1,700 workers in the Chicago area. In the 1980s, still specializing in the production of water-treatment chemicals, the company built a large new technical center in the Chicago suburb of Naperville. At the end of the 1990s, Nalco was purchased by Suez Lyonnaise des Eaux, a French company. Shortly thereafter, the company's name was changed to Ondeo Nalco, reflecting the name for its parent company's water-treatment divisions. In 2003 a group of American corporate investors purchased Ondeo Nalco, and in 2004 Nalco, through an IPO, returned to the New York Stock Exchange. Nalco Holding Co., with over $4 billion in revenues and 12,000 employees worldwide, is still headquartered in Naperville.

**Nicor Inc.** This company traces its origins to the gas companies founded in northern Illinois during the 1850s, such as the Ottawa Gas Light & Coke Co. The first steps toward the formation of the large company that eventually became Nicor occurred during the early 1910s. In 1911 a group of investors including Chicago utilities titan Samuel Insull created the Public Service Co. of Northern Illinois; one year later, a different merger of small gas companies in the region created the Illinois Northern Utilities Co. These two entities were united in 1954 as Northern Illinois Gas, which had about $60 million in sales during its first year. By the early 1960s, the company employed about 3,600 people around the region. In 1976 Northern Illinois Gas became a subsidiary of Nicor Inc., a holding company. In 2010 Naperville-based Nicor had revenues of $2.7 billion and employed some 3,800 people.

**Nielsen (A. C.) Co.** In 1923 Arthur C. Nielsen opened a statistical consulting firm in Chicago. During the 1930s, he added a service that provided radio ratings, which allowed advertisers to estimate the size of the audiences of particular stations and programs. The company soon introduced machines that recorded consumers' selection of radio and television programs; for many years, Nielsen dominated the market for television ratings information, much of which came from some 1,200 of these machines placed in homes around the country. By the middle of the 1960s, the company's annual revenues were about $60 million, and it employed nearly 7,000 people around the country. At the end of the 1970s, the company had become the nation's leading market-research firm, with $400 million in annual sales and 17,000 employees nationwide. Between 1984 and 1996, the company was a division of the Dun & Bradstreet Corp. of New York City. In 1999 VNU NV, a Dutch media company, bought Nielsen Media Research (television ratings), and two years later purchased ACNielsen (consumer shopping trends), reuniting the company that Dun & Bradstreet had split into separate entities in 1996. VNU was renamed the Nielsen Company in 2007 after being purchased by a group of private-equity firms. In 2011 Nielsen Holdings' initial public offering was at $1.89 billion, America's largest IPO to date. The firm has expanded into Internet and mobile ratings and other forms of market analytics. The North American Nielsen headquarters are located in Schaumburg.

**Northern Trust Co.** In 1889 Byron L. Smith collected about $1 million from leading Chicago businessmen, including Marshall Field and Philip D. Armour, to start a banking enterprise. Buoyed by the exposure it gained from opening a branch at the 1893 World's Columbian Exposition, the company's deposits grew to $10 million by the mid-1890s. From 1914 to 1963, the bank—which made its home on LaSalle Street in the Loop—was led by Solomon A. Smith, a son of the founder. Unlike many banks, Northern Trust grew during the Great Depression: deposits increased from about $50 million in 1929 to $300 million in 1935. By the beginning of the 1960s, when deposits totaled nearly $1 billion, Northern Trust was Chicago's fourth largest bank. After opening a branch in London and expanding to a new building at Wacker and Adams in 1974, the bank employed about 3,000 people in the Chicago area; its fortunes were boosted by a new federal law requiring that the assets in corporate benefit and pension funds be overseen by independent custodians. In 1982 it added banking operations in Florida. In 1998 Northern Trust Global Investments was formed to offer focused investment management for its customers. Despite the bear stock market of the early 2000s, Northern had become Chicago's third largest bank, with over $1.3 trillion in assets under custody and over 9,300 employees worldwide and almost 6,000 in the Chicago area. By 2010 Northern Trust had expanded to 18 states and had international offices in North America, South America, Europe, Asia, and Australia.

**Nuveen (John) Co.** John Nuveen emigrated from Germany to Chicago with his family in 1866, when he was two years old. After working for several of the city's merchant houses and real estate companies as a young man, Nuveen founded his own investment banking firm in Chicago in 1898. The company specialized in the marketing of municipal bonds issued by towns around the Midwest, as well as in Puerto Rico. In 1917 the annual revenues of this small firm passed $300,000. Nuveen expanded during the Great Depression by handling financial instruments issued by new public utilities, and it continued to grow after World War II. By the 1950s, with more than 100 employees, Nuveen had become a national leader in the municipal bond and public finance business. A downturn in the bond market in 1969 caused the company to suffer huge losses, and Nuveen was purchased by Investors Diversified Services (IDS) of Minneapolis. In 1974 it was acquired by another Minnesota business, an insurance group known as the St. Paul Companies of Minnesota. During the 1990s, as a Chicago-based division of St. Paul, Nuveen began to specialize in the management of assets. At the end of the century, it employed over 400 people in the Chicago area and had annual revenues close to $350 million. Purchased by Chicago's Madison Dearborn Partners LLC in 2007, by 2010 Nuveen Investments LLC had revenues of more than $790 million.

**Peoples Gas Light & Coke Co.** Chicago's first gas company, the Chicago Gas Light & Coke Co., was organized in 1849 and began to sell gas (used for lighting) in 1850. Peoples Gas Light & Coke Co. was chartered in 1855 and started delivering gas to Chicago customers in 1862. In 1897, after the Illinois legislature authorized gas company mergers, Peoples Gas merged with seven other firms. By this time, the company was a leading seller of gas stoves: it sold over 20,000 stoves to Chicago customers in 1898 alone. By 1907 Peoples Gas had a local monopoly, and it struggled with the city to establish fair rates. In 1913 Illinois created a Public Utilities Commission (which became the Illinois Commerce Commission in 1921) to regulate gas companies. By the beginning of the 1920s, Peoples Gas was delivering about 22 billion cubic feet of gas a year to Chicago customers via 3,100 miles of street mains. At this time, the company still manufactured gas out of coal and oil; in 1921 it used over 700,000 tons of coal and coke and 77 million gallons of oil. A critical shift in the company's operations occurred at the end of the 1920s, when it invested in long pipelines that connected Chicago to natural gas fields in Texas. By 1950 Peoples Gas had annual sales of over $80 million and employed over 4,500 people. The company changed its name to Peoples Gas Co. in 1968; twelve years later, it became part of Peoples Energy Corp. This entity controlled both Peoples Gas and the North Shore Gas Co., which operated in northeastern Illinois. By the early 2000s, Peoples Energy grossed more than $2 billion and had employed over 3,000 workers in the Chicago area. In 2007 the company merged with WPA Resources creating Integrys Energy Group Inc. and restored the name Peoples Gas to the company serving Chicago's 800,000 plus natural gas customers. Chicago-based Integrys, through its subsidiaries, provides energy (both gas and electricity) in Illinois, Wisconsin, Minnesota, and Michigan.

**Pepper Construction Co.** During the first years of the twentieth century, Frederick Pepper headed the carpentry shop at Marshall Field & Co. In 1927 his son, Stanley Pepper, started his own construction company. Subsequently, Pepper Construction would be led by successive generations of Frederick Pepper's sons, grandsons, and great-grandsons. Richard S. Pepper took over the business from his father in 1957 and continued to establish Pepper Construction as one of the region's leading general contractors for the next three and a half decades. Richard's son, J. Stanley Pepper, claimed the company reins in the early 1990s. Over the next decade, he expanded Pepper Construction to Texas, Ohio, and Indiana, eventually placing all business operations under a newly formed holding company headquartered in Chicago, Pepper Construction Group LLC. In 2003 J. Stanley's brother J. David Pepper took charge of the firm, the annual revenues of which exceed $1 billion.

**Perkins & Will.** This architecture firm was founded in 1935 by Lawrence B. Perkins and Philip Will Jr., who began his career designing houses. By 1950 the firm had a staff of 50, and it specialized in designing schools and colleges. A New York office opened in 1952. By 1970 the firm was nationally prominent, designing large office buildings and a variety of other structures. By the 1980s, when it employed about 250 people around the country, Perkins & Will ranked as Chicago's leading architecture firm in terms of local construction volume. At the beginning of the century, it employed about 100 architects in Chicago, working on such projects as the Chicago Park District Headquarters and the Halsted Street Sky Bridge downtown. With more than 1,600 professionals working in 23 offices around the world, Perkins & Will's architectural revenue in 2010 was third highest among U.S. firms.

**Pinkerton National Detective Agency.** Twenty-three-year-old Allan Pinkerton emigrated from Scotland to the United States in 1842, settling in the town of Dundee, northwest of Chicago. By the beginning of the 1850s, Pinkerton and a partner had established the North-Western Police Agency, which had its offices at Washington and Dearborn Streets in Chicago. One of the first private detective agencies in the United States, this company's 15 operatives worked for the Illinois Central and other railroads. During the Civil War, the company provided often questionable intelligence to the Union army. After the war, promoting itself with the slogan "We never sleep," the company opened offices in New York City and Philadelphia. Much of its business came from banks and express companies, who wanted to deter robberies. Starting in the 1870s, Pinkerton detectives also began to work for industrial companies as spies and strikebreakers, and they quickly became despised by American labor. The company's most infamous strike-busting operation came in 1892, when 300 Pinkerton employees fought with workers at the Homestead, Pennsylvania, steel plant owned by Andrew Carnegie. When the two sides exchanged gunfire, nine strikers and seven Pinkerton agents were killed. By the time Allan Pinkerton died in 1884, his sons William and Robert Pinkerton were leading the company, which had about 2,000 full-time employees and several thousand "reservists." During the 1920s, annual revenues approached

$2 million. In 1937 Robert Pinkerton II, a great-grandson of the founder, ended the firm's anti-union operations. By the late 1960s, just after the name of the enterprise became Pinkerton's Inc. and the corporate head-quarters moved to California, it had 70 branch offices (including central offices in Chicago and New York), about $75 million in annual revenues, and some 13,000 full-time employees worldwide. In the mid-1970s, the company had about 800 employees in the Chicago area. By the end of the century, the enterprise founded a century and a half earlier had become a subsidiary of a large Swedish corporation called Securitas AB.

**Playboy Enterprises Inc.** Twenty-seven-year-old Hugh Hefner, a former sociology student at Northwestern University, started *Playboy* magazine in Chicago in 1953. The first printing of 50,000 copies, which featured Marilyn Monroe on the cover, sold out quickly. By publishing photo-graphs of nude women and promoting the concept of sex as recreation, the magazine became a much-discussed phenomenon of American popu-lar culture. Annual sales of *Playboy* grew from $4 million in 1960 to about $175 million at the end of the 1970s, when it had a circulation of about 6 million and ranked among the top ten magazines (in terms of circula-tion as well as sales) in the United States. Meanwhile, from 1960 to 1986, Hefner's company operated the Playboy Club chain of nightclubs. By the late 1970s, Playboy employed about 4,000 people around the country. In 1982 Christie Hefner, the 29-year-old daughter of the founder, took charge of the company, which was moving into television and video products. By the end of the century, annual revenues stood at about $350 million, and Playboy employed about 500 people in the Chicago area. *Playboy*'s rev-enues and circulation fell in the early 2000s as it faced tough competition from a series of new so-called men's magazines, such as *Maxim* and *FHM*. It soon began to offset these losses, however, by emulating the graphics and photograph-heavy pages of its new competitors and expanding into the Internet market with Playboy.com.          *Max Grinnell*

**Prairie Farmer.** One of the leading farm papers of the Midwest, *Prairie Farmer* was the most influential force in the commercialization of Illinois agriculture. Headquartered in Chicago, the paper not only promoted sci-entific farming practices but also was dedicated to improving rural life through education, recreation, and better health practices. First pub-lished in 1841 by the Union Agricultural Society, *Prairie Farmer* was the brainchild of founding editor John S. Wright. After a succession of own-ers, newspaperman Burridge D. Butler bought the paper in 1909. By 1931 Butler had absorbed *Prairie Farmer*'s competitors and expanded circula-tion to Indiana, Wisconsin, and Michigan by offering premiums, staging corn-husking contests, and landing the company plane in cow pastures. Butler purchased radio station WLS from Sears in 1928 to offer farm pro-gramming and produced the popular *Barn Dance* show. Butler saw his paper as the voice of the common farmer, and he conducted editorial campaigns against crime and deceptive marketing practices. The paper agitated for pro-farm legislation, and editor Clifford Gregory strongly supported the New Deal. From a peak of 370,000 subscribers in 1950, circulation dwindled below 60,000 at the end of the century, a sign of the declining importance of farming as a way of life. Claiming the distinction of being America's oldest continuously published magazine, the *Prairie Farmer* is part of suburban St. Charles–based Farm Progress Companies Inc., an agriculture-focused media firm that is part of Fairfax Media Ltd., an Australian media firm.                              *Susan Sessions Rugh*

**Pullman Inc.** Toward the end of the 1850s, George M. Pullman of Chicago began to remodel passenger coach railroad cars. The Pullman Palace Car Co. was incorporated in Illinois in 1867; its first manufacturing shops were located in Detroit and Elmira, New York. By 1877 it operated about 460 luxury passenger cars, service on which was supervised by white conductors and African American porters. In 1880 Pullman began building a new manufacturing plant and a company town on a site about 14 miles south of downtown Chicago. By 1885 the town's population stood at nearly 9,000. In the early 1890s, nearly 6,000 of the company's 14,000 employees nationwide worked in Pullman, where annual output stood at about 12,000 freight cars and 1,000 passenger cars. After an economic downturn in 1893, the company laid off thousands of workers; Pullman employees responded in 1894 by going on strike. This strike soon had national effects, because tens of thousands of American Railway Union members showed their support for Pullman workers by launching a boycott of trains pulling Pullman cars. In 1898 the Illinois courts ordered the company to sell its non-factory lands in the town. The company, however, continued to grow. By 1900, when the company changed its name to Pullman Co. after acquiring the assets of its only real competitor, the main plant had nearly 6,000 employees and produced about $14 million worth of railroad cars per year. Ten years later, when the company completed its transition from wooden cars to steel cars, there were about 10,000 workers at the Pullman plant. Meanwhile, the company operated about 7,500 passenger cars, which it leased—complete with porters and other workers—to railroad companies around the world. During the 1920s, when the workforce at Pullman reached a peak of about 20,000 people, the company was reorganized. In 1927, a holding company called Pullman Inc. was established to oversee two separate divisions: the Pullman Car & Manufacturing Corp., the company's manufacturing division, and the Pullman Co., which operated the world-famous passenger cars. The latter company's racial policies gave birth to the Brotherhood of Sleeping Car Porters. In 1929 Pullman Car merged with the Standard Steel Car Co., creating the Pullman-Standard Car Manufacturing Co., which had plants in Hammond and Michigan City, Indiana, as well as other U.S. locations. During the 1930s, Pullman-Standard was the nation's largest manufacturer of freight cars and passenger cars. After World War II, the U.S. Department of Justice forced Pullman Inc. to sell one of its two divisions. The operating company, which kept the Pullman Co. name, was purchased by a group of railroad companies. Pullman Inc. kept Pullman-Standard, which declined steadily through the 1970s, by which time it was no longer an important manufacturer of railcars. In 1977 Pullman Inc., still based in Chicago, had annual revenues of $2 billion and employed 32,000 people nationwide. In 1980 Pullman Inc. was purchased by Wheelabrator-Frye Inc., a New Hampshire–based conglomerate. Two years later, the Pullman Car Works closed. Most of its rail-car manufacturing assets and its remaining freight car plants were subsequently sold to Dallas-based Trinity Industries.                            *Martha T. Briggs and Cynthia H. Peters*

**Quaker Oats Co.** In 1879 a group of investors that included John and Robert Stuart built the Imperial Mill at 16th and Dearborn Streets in Chicago. At the end of the 1880s, this and several other leading mills around the Midwest became part of the American Cereal Co., a grain-milling giant headquartered in Chicago. In 1901 American Cereal became the Quaker Oats Co. (The Quaker brand name came from an Ohio mill owned by Henry P. Crowell.) By 1907 Quaker's annual sales of oatmeal, flour, and feed amounted to $20 million. In 1909 the company used new machines to produce its popular Puffed Rice and Puffed Wheat ready-to-eat cereals. By 1918 annual sales exceeded $120 million. In 1925 the company bought the "Aunt Jemima" mills of St. Joseph, Missouri. By that time, Quaker had begun to use oat hulls to produce the chemical furfural, which was soon used by industry to manufacture nylon and synthetic rubber. The company also became a leading maker of pet foods. In 1942 Quaker purchased Ken-L-Ration Dog Foods of Rockford, Illinois. By the middle of the 1960s, annual sales approached $500 million, and the company employed about 12,000 people nationwide, although only a few hundred worked in Chicago. The company proceeded to introduce new lines of ready-to-eat breakfast cereals, including its popular Life and Cap'n Crunch brands, as well as Quaker instant oatmeal. By the middle of the 1970s, when the company employed about 1,800 people in the Chicago area, annual sales were about $1.5 billion. Over the last decades of the century, Quaker continued to make cereals, but its greatest success and greatest failure came with beverages. Its Gatorade sports drink brand became an immensely popular and profitable product and helped push Quaker's global workforce up to 32,000 by 1989. The company suffered in 1994, however, after paying $1.7 billion to acquire the Snapple drink brand, which it dumped in 1997 at a huge loss. At the beginning of the twenty-first century, when Quaker grossed nearly $5 billion in annual sales and had about 1,200 workers in the Chicago area and another 10,000 worldwide, the company was acquired by PepsiCo Inc. of New York. The Quaker Foods and

Snacks N.A. Division of the larger corporation remains headquartered in Chicago.

**Rand McNally & Co.** In 1856 William H. Rand arrived in Chicago from Boston and set up a printing shop. Rand soon hired Andrew McNally, an Irish immigrant and a trained printer. In 1859 the two men started managing the printing shop of the *Chicago Tribune* newspaper. Rand, McNally & Co. was created in 1868, when it began to publish business directories and railroad guides. After publishing its first map in an 1872 railroad guide, the company became a pioneer in the field of mapmaking. Applying a wax engraving method, which made it possible to mass-produce maps at low cost, Rand McNally became the largest maker of maps in the United States. In 1880, when the company employed about 200 men and 50 women at its shops, its annual sales were about $500,000. The company soon moved into atlas and textbook publishing. Rand sold his interest in the company to McNally in 1899; both of the founders died in 1904–5. For most of the twentieth century, McNally's descendants ran the company. Annual sales reached $2 million in 1913, soon after the company began to make road maps to serve the growing numbers of automobile users. Rand McNally published its first road atlas, the *Auto Chum*, in 1924. In 1952, when it employed over 1,000 people in the Chicago area, the company moved its headquarters from downtown Chicago to nearby Skokie. Annual sales passed $100 million in the 1970s, when there were about 750 employees in the Chicago area. In 1989 Rand McNally started to open retail stores; ten years later, it owned about 30 stores around the country. Meanwhile, it moved quickly into electronic map products, including its Streetfinder brand. In 1998 the McNally family sold the company, by then divested of most of its non-map groups, to a private investment group, AEA Investors Inc. of New York, for $500 million. The 30-year-old AEA, whose founders included the Mellon and Rockefeller families, had hoped to transform Rand into a high-tech multimedia company. A series of financial and strategic missteps and competition from other Internet-based map providers dimmed those hopes. Rand McNally filed for Chapter 11 bankruptcy protection in 2003, emerging later that year with a new majority owner, Los Angeles–based acquisitions company Leonard Green & Partners LP. In 2007 New York–based Patriarch Partners LLC became the sole owner of Rand McNally, which still operates from Skokie.

**Ryerson (Joseph T.) & Son.** Soon after he arrived in Chicago in 1842 as an agent for a Pittsburgh iron manufacturer, Joseph T. Ryerson opened his own store, which sold boilers and other iron products. Over the next few decades, Ryerson's company became one of the leading American processors and wholesalers of steel products. In 1926 the company was one of the first to offer stainless-steel goods. When the founder's grandson Edward L. Ryerson Jr. became president of the company in 1929, it operated ten distribution centers across the United States. In 1935 Ryerson was acquired by Inland Steel, the Chicago steel producer, which used Ryerson as its processing and distribution arm. By the late 1960s, the Ryerson division remained a major distributor of steel products; it was also the nation's leading aluminum distributor and a major dealer of plastics. Inland Steel acquired another distributor, the Atlanta-based J. M. Tull, in 1986. During the early 1990s, Inland spun off its distribution wing, creating an independent company called Ryerson Tull Inc. By the end of the twentieth century, this company had become the leading processor and distributor of metals in North America, with close to $3 billion in annual sales and about 1,600 employees in the Chicago area. The company restored the Ryerson name in 2006; the following year, it was purchased by California-based Platinum Equities. With 2010 revenues in excess of $3.9 billion, Ryerson, with its 400 local and 4,500 worldwide employees, is one of Chicago's largest privately held firms ranked by revenue.

**S&C Electric Co.** This manufacturer of electrical fuses and switches, first called Schweitzer & Conrad Inc., was founded in 1911 by Nicholas J. Conrad and Edmund O. Schweitzer, who were then employees of Commonwealth Edison, Chicago's electric utility. The company served as a military contractor during World War II and grew during the 1950s. It opened a large Chicago facility called the Conrad Laboratory in 1961. By the mid-1970s, S&C employed about 1,400 people in the Chicago area. By the early 2000s, S&C was still a leading manufacturer of electric switches, grossing more than $100 million in annual sales and employing 1,700 workers at its Chicago headquarters. At that time, the company had a handful of manufacturing, engineering, and research and development operations in the United States, Canada, Brazil, China, and Mexico. The company became employee-owned in 2007. Three years later, it opened a new Advanced Technology Center on its Rogers Park campus. At the beginning of its centenary year, the global firm boasted revenues of $600 million, 1,800 Chicago area employees, and 2,500 employees worldwide.

**Sara Lee Corp.** The giant food company that was known by the end of the twentieth century as Sara Lee Corp. was the descendant of a Chicago grocery store called Sprague, Warner & Co. This enterprise, which started on State Street, was founded during the Civil War by Albert A. Sprague and Ezra J. Warner. When it moved into a large new facility on Erie and Roberts Streets in 1909, Sprague, Warner & Co. was one of the leading wholesale grocery companies in the United States, famous for house brands such as Richelieu and Batavia. In 1942 this company was acquired by Nathan Cummings, the Canadian-born owner of C. D. Kenny Co., a large grocery enterprise based in Baltimore. The new Chicago-based company, at first called Sprague Warner-Kenny Corp., ranked as the largest grocery wholesaler in the United States. Annual sales grew from about

Outdoor advertising for Sara Lee under the Palmolive Building, 1954. Sara Lee marketed its pastries on this giant billboard at North Michigan and Walton. © Chicago Historical Society. Photo: Hedrich-Blessing. Courtesy of the Chicago History Museum (HB-17280).

$20 million in 1942 to $120 million by 1946. After changing its name in 1945 to Consolidated Grocers, Cummings's company became the Consolidated Foods Corp. in 1953. In 1956 the company bought the Kitchens of Sara Lee, a five-year-old Chicago bakery named after the daughter of founder Charles Lubin; as a division of Consolidated, this became the world's leading producer of frozen pastries. The company opened a large new automated bakery in suburban Deerfield in 1964. The company grew rapidly. Annual sales rose from $500 million in the early 1960s to nearly $5 billion by the late 1970s, when the company employed over 2,000 people in the Chicago area and about 75,000 more worldwide. By this time, Consolidated was selling not only food but also underwear and other products. In 1985 the company changed its name from Consolidated Foods to the Sara Lee Corp., with headquarters in Deerfield. By the mid-2000s, Sara Lee, with its relocated headquartered in Downers Grove, was a huge international food and clothing company, amassing over $17 billion in annual sales, over one-third of which were made overseas. At the same time, its Deerfield bakery had closed, and only about 2,000 of the company's some 150,000 employees worldwide were Chicago-area residents. Having divested itself of many of its divisions, in 2011 Sara Lee announced plans to split into two companies. Accomplished in 2012, the American-based food division took the name Hillshire Brands Co., and the European-based beverage division, D.E Master Blenders 1753.

**Sayers Group LLC.** In 1984 former Chicago Bears Hall of Fame running back Gale Sayers and his wife, Ardythe Sayers, founded the Sayers Group LLC in the Chicago suburb of Mount Prospect. In the beginning, the small company sold computer-related supplies such as printer cartridges and fax machines. By the mid-1990s, the Sayers Group had expanded to establish itself as a national leader in selling used and refurbished computers to households and businesses. The Sayers Group took advantage of the technology sector bust of the early 2000s by acquiring devalued computer and Internet-related companies. By 2003 the company was still involved in its earlier operations but had diversified into the fields of Internet consultancy and asset management, with offices in several states. At that time, the Sayers Group employed about 100 people nationwide, 60 of whom worked at its Mount Prospect headquarters. With annual revenues around $300 million, the Sayers Group was one of the Chicago's largest minority-owned firms. Reorganized in 2003 as Sayers 40 Inc., the company has offices in suburban Vernon Hills, Massachusetts, Florida, Georgia, and Tennessee, and is one of the country's largest black-owned businesses.

**Schwinn Bicycle.** In 1895, during the midst of a national bicycle craze, Ignaz Schwinn (who arrived in Chicago from Germany in 1891) and partner Adolph Arnold (a Chicago meat industry veteran) founded a bicycle manufacturing company. They joined a competitive industry: by 1900, when the Chicago region made more than half of all the bicycles and bicycle equipment produced in the United States, about 30 different bicycle makers were concentrated along Chicago's Lake Street. In 1901 Arnold, Schwinn & Co. moved its offices to North Kostner Avenue, where it stayed until 1986. By 1905 the company had become one of the leading firms in the industry. Many of its bicycles were sold by Sears, Roebuck & Co., the giant Chicago-based retailer. In 1908 Arnold sold his interest in the company, and a new factory was built on North Kildare Avenue in Chicago. Even during the Great Depression, the company still managed to build more than 100,000 bicycles each year; annual output rose to nearly 350,000 by 1941. After World War II, the company was led by Frank W. Schwinn, a son of Ignaz Schwinn, who died in 1948. By the 1950s, the company, still known as Arnold, Schwinn & Co., sold about one-quarter of all bicycles in

Lake View Cycling Club, 1890s. The Lake View Cycling Club in front of its clubhouse at 401–403 Orchard Street (old numbering). Courtesy of the Chicago History Museum (ICHi-22247).

the United States. Sales reached $20 million in 1961, when the company employed about 1,000 people in the Chicago area. From the 1950s through the 1970s, a third generation of Schwinn family members led the company and changed its name to Schwinn Bicycle. The "Phantom," "Sting Ray," and "Varsity" models were Schwinn's best sellers. The Schwinn factory on the city's West Side, which made 1 million bicycles in 1968, still employed as many as 1,800 people during the 1970s. But the company's share of the national bicycle market began to shrink. In 1980 there was a strike at the West Side factory; three years later, it closed for good. By this time, Edward Schwinn Jr., a great-grandson of the founder, led the company. In 1992, when Schwinn's market share had declined to about 5 percent, it entered bankruptcy and was sold by the Schwinn family to a group of investors led by Chicago's Sam Zell. In 1993 Schwinn's general offices moved to Colorado.

**Sears, Roebuck & Co.** The business that would become Chicago's leading company and America's leading retailer for much of the twentieth century was founded in 1893 by Richard W. Sears. In 1887 Sears moved his watch-selling business from Minneapolis to Chicago and hired watch-maker Alvah C. Roebuck to assist him. While Roebuck's name would remain with the company for decades, ill health forced his retirement around the turn of the century. Sears soon sold the watch business and returned to Minneapolis for a time, but by 1895 he returned to Chicago to head a general mail-order firm. This enterprise expanded at an extraordi-nary pace and soon surpassed Montgomery Ward, the Chicago firm that had pioneered large-scale mail-order retailing. Like Montgomery Ward, Sears, Roebuck issued thick catalogs and sold all sorts of goods, including clothing, appliances, and furniture. By 1906, when it first issued stock to the public, the company was capitalized at $40 million, had about 9,000 employees, and was approaching $50 million in annual sales. Mail-order branch houses soon opened in Dallas and Seattle. In 1908 Sears retired, and Julius Rosenwald, a partner since 1895, took charge of the company. Although the company was successful with its "No Money Down" pol-icy of generous consumer credit, which helped to push annual sales to $235 million by 1920, the tremendous growth of the mail-order industry was slowing. In 1924 the company made a significant change in its opera-tions by opening its first retail store. By 1929 there were over 300 Sears stores across the country. The move into retail stores was engineered by Robert E. Wood, a former U.S. Army supply officer who joined Sears af-ter World War I. In 1928 Wood took over leadership of the company from Rosenwald; during the Great Depression, Wood managed to keep the firm growing. The company's Allstate automobile insurance business, estab-lished in 1931 after Wood's neighbor and fellow commuter suggested that Sears sell auto insurance, was a major success. In 1932 the company moved into its famous flagship store on State and Van Buren Streets in Chicago's Loop, where it would remain until 1986. Sears's annual sales neared $1 bil-lion by 1941. Meanwhile, Wood, a staunch political conservative, served as a leader of the isolationist America First movement, and he opposed ef-forts among Sears workers during the New Deal and World War II to join unions. In the seven years after the end of the war, the company opened nearly 100 new stores, including one in Mexico City, and expanded several others. By the time Wood retired in 1954, the company's annual sales had surpassed $3 billion, and Sears had become America's leading retailer. But by the beginning of the 1970s, although annual sales had risen to $10 bil-lion and although it was about to move its headquarters into the world's tallest building (the Sears, now Willis, Tower), the company's fortunes were declining. Discount retail chains such as Kmart were competing successfully against Sears, which by 1975 had over 850 stores and close to 400,000 employees (about 30,000 of them in the Chicago area). Between 1979 and 1986, the company spent about $100 million to defend itself against a lawsuit (in which Sears eventually prevailed) by the U.S. govern-ment for alleged discrimination against female and minority employees. By the early 1990s, the company's payrolls had shrunk by tens of thousands of workers. The company's annual sales stood at about $40 billion at the end of the 1990s, and Sears, headquartered in suburban Hoffman Estates, employed about 8,000 men and women in the Chicago area. The year 2001 was a milestone for Sears in Chicago, as it opened a large store on downtown State Street after having been gone from the historic location for 15 years. In 2002 the company purchased Lands' End, a mail-order company that had its beginnings in 1963 on North Elston Avenue. A year later Sears divested itself of its credit division, which had helped spur its growth 90 years earlier. The following year, it merged with Kmart to form the Sears Holding Company. With 2010 revenues of $43 billion and some 6,000 local employees, Sears was one of the Chicago area's largest firms.

**Sidley Austin LLP.** This law firm traced its roots to Williams & Thompson, a Chicago firm founded in 1866 by Norman Williams and John L. Thompson. The name Sidley—from William Pratt Sidley, who started working for the firm as a young lawyer in 1892—entered the firm's title in 1900, when it became Holt, Wheeler & Sidley. Edwin C. Austin joined the firm in 1914. By this time, the firm's list of clients included many of Chicago's largest businesses, including Pullman, Western Electric, and Illinois Steel. In 1916 the firm consisted of nine lawyers and their office staff. Four years later, the firm's offices moved from the Tacoma Building to the Roanoke Building, a newer skyscraper. Known as Sidley, McPherson, Austin & Burgess by 1941, it employed 32 lawyers. From 1950 to 1967, the firm was called Sidley, Austin, Burgess & Smith. In 1967, when it changed its name to Sidley & Austin, it consisted of 80 lawyers, half of whom were partners; two years later, the firm moved into new offices at One First National Plaza, a new skyscraper in Chicago's Loop. A 1972 merger with Liebman, Williams, Bennett, Baird & Minow, another large Chicago law firm, created a firm of 150 lawyers. Over the next 25 years, Sidley & Austin grew to rank consistently as one of Chicago's largest law firms and opened offices in other cities around the country. In 1999 it merged with competitor Brown & Wood to become Sidley Austin Brown & Wood LLP. Under its new name, the firm claimed 400 attorneys and 1,400 staff in its Chicago headquarters alone, with 14 additional offices nationwide. Since 2006 the firm has been known as Sidley Austin LLP and has over 500 attorneys in Chicago and over 1,600 in its other offices in the United States, China, Belgium, Germany, Switzerland, the United Kingdom, Australia, Singapore, and Japan.

**Signode.** In 1913 Ellsworth Flora and J. Fremont Murphy formed the Seal & Fastener Co. in Chicago. The company made steel strapping systems, which could be used to seal and reinforce large containers. In 1916 the company's name became Signode System. Seven years later, Signode Britain became its first foreign subsidiary; in 1936 Signode International Ltd. was formed to consolidate the company's international businesses. During World War II, with about 400 employees, the company made radar equipment and other military supplies; sales in 1945 approached $16 million. During the postwar era, Signode expanded nationwide and overseas. Starting in 1955, many of its operations were transferred to Glenview, northwest of Chicago. By the early 1960s, when annual sales reached $60 million, the company employed more than 1,000 people in the Chicago area. The company was renamed Signode Corp. in 1964 and opened a new plant in Bridgeview, southwest of Chicago. By this time, Signode had begun to sell nylon and plastic strapping, and annual sales had reached $100 million. In the mid-1980s, when the company became known as Signode Industries Inc., it employed nearly 2,000 people in the Chicago area, and annual sales reached about $750 million. Signode was purchased by another Chicago-area company, Illinois Tool Works, in 1986. In the new millennium, Signode was one of ITW's largest operating divisions, based in suburban Glenview.

**Skidmore, Owings & Merrill.** This architecture firm was founded in 1936 in Chicago as Skidmore & Owings by Louis Skidmore and his brother-in-law, Nathaniel Owings. Before creating this firm, Skidmore had served as the chief architect (Owings assisted him) for the 1933 Century of Progress Exposition in Chicago. The partners opened a New York office in 1937. After John Merrill joined the firm in 1939, the name changed to Skidmore, Owings & Merrill (SOM). By 1952 the firm was one of the few American architecture enterprises to employ more than 1,000 people around the country. During the 1960s and 1970s, it designed many large buildings in Chicago, including the Brunswick Building, the John Hancock Center, the Sears (now Willis) Tower, the main libraries for the University of Chicago and Northwestern University, and much of the University of Illinois at Chicago. Skidmore, Owings & Merrill employed about 700 people in Chicago in the late 1980s, making it the city's largest architecture firm at that time. At the end of the 1990s, Chicago-area projects accounted for about one-third of the firm's $90 million in annual billings across the country. Although a decline in new commercial construction in the early 2000s led to cutbacks in the firm's local workforce, it maintained offices in Chicago, New York, San Francisco, Washington, D.C., Los Angeles, London, Hong Kong, and São Paulo. In the first decade of the twenty-first century, the Chicago office of SOM helped to create the world's tallest building, the Burj Khalifa in Dubai, and the Trump International Hotel and Tower in Chicago.

**Standard Oil Co. (Indiana).** In 1889 John D. Rockefeller's Standard Oil Co. established an Indiana-based subsidiary. The next year, the company began to process oil at an enormous new refinery at Whiting, Indiana, southeast of Chicago. By the mid-1890s, the Whiting plant had become the largest refinery the United States, handling 36,000 barrels of oil per day and accounting for nearly 20 percent of the total U.S. refining capacity. During these years, the company's main product was kerosene, which was used in lamps. By 1910, when it was connected by pipeline to oil fields in Kansas and Oklahoma, as well as in Ohio and Indiana, the Whiting facility had about 2,400 workers. When the U.S. government forced Rockefeller to break up his oil giant in 1911, Standard Oil of Indiana—which had its main offices in downtown Chicago—emerged as an independent company; it soon began to purchase oil wells of its own. During the 1910s, the company pioneered a new thermal "cracking" process, in which crude oil was processed under pressure in order to produce higher yields of gasoline. By this time, the beginning of the automobile age, gasoline had become the leading product of oil refineries. Standard Oil of Indiana ranked as the third largest oil refiner in the United States by 1920, behind Standard Oil of New Jersey and Standard Oil of California. In 1925, when it already had more than 25,000 employees around the country, Standard Oil of Indiana merged with the American Oil Co. (Amoco). During the mid-1930s, the company employed about 7,000 people at its Whiting plant and Chicago offices. Standard Oil of Indiana ranked as the second largest American oil company at the beginning of the 1950s, when annual sales grossed $1.5 billion. In the early 1970s, when the company moved into new offices on East Randolph Drive near Chicago's lakefront, Standard Oil of Indiana still employed about 8,000 people in the area. Annual sales neared $30 billion in 1985, when the company changed its name to Amoco, which then ranked as the nation's sixth largest oil company. By that time, Amoco and other leading oil companies were huge global corporations that not only refined oil but also explored and drilled for it; Amoco also had a large chemicals division. At the end of the 1990s, when Amoco employed about 4,000 people in the Chicago area, it merged with British Petroleum (BP). While most of the company's jobs still remained in Chicago by the early 2000s, especially on its suburban Naperville and Cantera (Warrenville) campuses and its Whiting refinery, management of the company was directed from London.

**Stone Container Corp.** After emigrating from Russia to the United States around 1888, Joseph H. Stone made his way to Chicago, where he worked as a cigar maker. By the late 1910s, Stone was a wholesaler of paper products. In 1926 Stone and his sons Norman and Marvin formed J. H. Stone & Sons, a small enterprise that sold paper and twine. Their sales in 1927 amounted to about $70,000. During the late 1930s, the company built a large corrugated cardboard box factory at 42nd Place and Keeler Avenue in Chicago. Its name changed to Stone Container Corp. in 1945, by which time the company owned another plant in Philadelphia. By the early 1960s, annual sales reached $50 million, and Stone Container had over 1,000 employees in the Chicago area and hundreds more nationwide. Roger W. Stone, a son of Marvin, took charge of the company in the late 1970s,, leading it through a period of great expansion. The new chief made Stone bigger by buying other paper companies, including Consolidated-Bathurst of Canada, a newsprint maker acquired in 1989. Stone's annual sales rose from nearly $300 million in 1979 to about $6 billion in the mid-1990s, when it employed about 30,000 people around the world and ranked as the world's leading manufacturer of paper packaging. In 1998 Stone merged with the Jefferson Smurfit Corp., a smaller paper company based in St. Louis. The resulting entity was named Smurfit-Stone Container Corp., which at the end of the twentieth century grossed more than $7 billion in annual sales and employed about 1,200 people in the Chicago area, where it made its headquarters. Georgia-based Rock-Tenn Co. acquired Smurfit-Stone in 2011.

**Swift & Co.** During the 1850s, when he was still a teenager, Gustavus F. Swift started to work in the beef business in Massachusetts. In 1875 Swift began buying cattle in Chicago to send to his family's butcher operations back east. He quickly revolutionized the meat industry by using newly developed refrigerated railcars to ship fresh meat from Chicago to eastern markets. The company soon set up a national network of branch offices, which allowed it to control the distribution of its meat across the country. By 1886, when the company slaughtered more than 400,000 cattle a year, Swift employed about 1,600 people. Between 1887 and 1892, new packing plants were opened in Kansas City, Omaha, and St. Louis. By the time the founder died in 1903, his company grossed $200 million in annual sales and employed about 23,000 people across the country, including over 5,000 workers at its slaughtering plant in Chicago's Union Stock Yard. In 1908 Swift plants across the country slaughtered a total of about 8 million animals. By this time, Swift owned a fleet of nearly 5,000 refrigerated railcars. Annual sales reached $700 million by the late 1920s, when the total workforce of the company—which ranked as one of the largest industrial corporations in the United States—consisted of about 55,000 people. Swift stopped slaughtering in Chicago in 1953, but its corporate headquarters remained in the city. In 1973, by which time meat had become only one of its businesses, Swift became part of Esmark Inc., a holding company. During the 1980s, Esmark's meat division was spun off and moved to Texas. Swift, once one of Chicago's leading employers and largest companies, no longer has a presence in the city. From the early 1990s through the early 2000s, food conglomerate Conagra owned Swift's operations. Swift & Company's divisional headquarters were located in Greeley, Colorado.

**Telephone and Data Systems Inc.** This company, which grew by buying small independent telephone companies, was founded in 1969 by LeRoy T. Carlson, a Chicago native. In 1983, when Telephone and Data Systems (TDS) had its headquarters in Chicago, it created a subsidiary called U.S.

Cellular Corp., which grew into one of the ten largest wireless telecommunications companies in the country. After purchasing numerous smaller companies around the country, TDS claimed over 5 million customers in 35 states by the early 2000s. Led by one of LeRoy Carlson's sons at the LaSalle Street headquarters, the company grossed about $3 billion in revenues and employed over 8,000 people in the Chicago area at that time. By 2010 TDS had more than 7 million customers in 36 states and revenues of almost $5 billion. Chicago-based U.S. Cellular, still a majority-owned subsidiary of TDS, had revenues exceeding $4 billion, over 4 million customers, and almost 9,000 employees.

**Tootsie Roll Industries Inc.** The first Tootsie Roll candies were made in New York City during the early 1890s by Austrian immigrant Leo Hirschfeld. In 1922 Hirschfeld's company was renamed Sweets Co. of America. When brothers Bernard and William Rubin bought the company in 1935, it operated a large candy factory in New Jersey. In 1966 Tootsie Roll opened a large factory in the Ford City industrial park in southwest Chicago. Soon, all of the company's operations were centralized in Chicago, where it employed about 900 people by the mid-1970s. By that time, the company was led by Rubin's daughter Ellen Gordon and her husband, Melvin Gordon. In 1988 Tootsie Roll bought Charms Co., a maker of lollipops. By 1990, when annual sales were close to $200 million, Tootsie Roll was the nation's leading producer of lollipops. The company continued a pattern of solid growth through the 1990s, with annual sales of $400 million and about 1,700 employees in the Chicago area by the end of the decade, when sales began to flatten. In the early 2000s, the company was still headed by William Rubin's daughter and son-in-law. In 2010 Tootsie Roll's many brands of confections were marketed in over 75 countries, generating over $500 million in sales.

**Tribune Co.** The *Chicago Daily Tribune* newspaper was founded in 1847. In 1861, six years after Joseph Medill became associated with the paper, the name changed to the *Chicago Tribune*. After a few years in other pursuits, Medill regained control of the paper in 1874 and directed it until 1899. Medill's company had about 200 production workers in Chicago in 1880. During the 1910s, Medill's grandsons Robert R. McCormick and Joseph Medill Patterson took over the management of the company that owned the *Tribune*, which became more than just a publisher of a leading Chicago newspaper. In 1919 the Tribune Co. established a new paper in the country's largest city called the New York *News* (later the *Daily News*), led by Patterson, who had moved to New York. Back in Chicago, McCormick had made the *Tribune* the most widely read of the city's several daily newspapers, even as he built the Tribune Co. into a diversified media company. *Daily* circulation of the paper rose from about 230,000 in 1912 to 660,000 by 1925. The WGN radio station was launched in 1924, just before the company and its flagship newspaper moved into the new Tribune Tower on North Michigan Avenue in downtown Chicago, providing space for some 2,000 employees. The company's WGN television station was established in 1948, becoming Chicago's only "superstation" 30 years later, with broadcast outlets around the country. After McCormick died in 1955, the Tribune Co. continued to grow. During the 1960s, it purchased newspapers in Florida. It created a subsidiary called the Tribune Broadcasting Co. in 1981 and bought the Chicago Cubs baseball team from the Wrigley family. In 1983, as annual revenues approached $2 billion, the Tribune Co. began to sell stock to the public. The New York *Daily News* was sold off in 1991, and the Tribune Company's total workforce across the country dropped from nearly 19,000 in 1985 to about 10,000 in 1994. During the 1990s, the company launched an electronic version of the *Tribune* newspaper. At the end of the century, with over $3 billion in annual sales, the company expanded by purchasing the Times Mirror Co., publisher of the *Los Angeles Times* and other newspapers around the country. This acquisition turned the Tribune Co.—which owned 10 major papers—into the nation's third largest newspaper company in terms of total circulation. It also owned some 20 television stations nationwide. By 1999 the company employed nearly 6,000 people in the Chicago area. It continued to grow vigorously through the early 2000s, with annual revenues reaching over $5 billion. Sam Zell, chairman of Chicago-based Equity Group Investments LLC, bought the Tribune Co. in 2007 and turned it into a private company. A year later, the company filed for Chapter 11 bankruptcy protection, where it remained at the end of 2011. The company sold most of its interest in the Chicago Cubs and Wrigley Field in 2009. Still the owner of 20-plus television stations, a radio station, a cable station, 9 daily newspapers, 3 Spanish-language papers, and numerous other digital ventures, the Tribune Company's revenues in 2010 stood at $3.2 billion, and it employed some 3,200 people in the Chicago area and 13,000 nationwide.

**True Value Co.** In 1948 John Cotter, a veteran hardware salesman from St. Paul, Minnesota, created Cotter & Co., a wholesaler that supplied a co-operative of 25 hardware retailers in Illinois and other midwestern states. This company, which sold through catalogs, had about 200 employees and $20 million in annual sales by the beginning of the 1960s, when the retail network had expanded to about 500 stores. In 1963 Cotter spent $2.5 million to acquire the hardware operations and True Value trademark of the venerable Chicago hardware company Hibbard, Spencer, Bartlett & Co. This brought 400 new retailers into the Cotter cooperative and doubled the size of the business. Annual sales proceeded to grow from $100 million in 1966 to about $2 billion by the end of the 1980s, when the company employed about 1,000 people in the Chicago area. In 1997, after Cotter & Co. merged with Pittsburgh-based competitor ServiStar Coast to Coast Corp., the company became known as the TruServ Corp. Based in Chicago,

TruServ was a member-owned cooperative supplying over 10,000 independent hardware retailers worldwide; it had annual sales of over $4 billion and nearly 2,000 employees in the Chicago area. Renamed True Value Co. in 2005, the hardware cooperative in 2010 supplied 5,500 independent retailers in 54 countries, had revenues in excess of $1.8 billion, and employed some 800 persons in the Chicago area.

**Union Tank Car Co.** Founded in 1866 by one of Standard Oil Co.'s early competitors, J. J. Vandergrift, the Star Tank Line shipped oil from the fields of Pennsylvania to Chicago. The company was purchased by Standard Oil in 1873 and its headquarters moved to Ohio. Five years later, its name was changed to Union Tank Car Co. As part of John D. Rockefeller's innovative scheme to avoid state antitrust measures, Union Tank Car was incorporated in New Jersey in 1891 as a subsidiary of the newly incorporated Standard Oil Trust. By 1904 Union Tank Car owned a fleet of 10,000 railcars, far more than any other private car operator. It shipped products solely for its parent company until 1911, when the Standard Oil Trust was dissolved by the federal government. During the 1920s, when its fleet consisted of about 30,000 railcars, the company changed its name to UTCC and its headquarters were moved to Chicago. In 1931 it began shipping chemicals and producing tank cars. Over the next several decades, UTCC acquired other companies and became one of the world's largest tank carrier companies. By the early 1960s, when the company moved into the new Union Tank Car Building in Chicago's Loop, annual sales exceeded $100 million. A decade later, UTCC and its newly created holding company, Trans Union Corp., employed about 1,500 people in the Chicago area. Trans Union Corp. and its subsidiaries (UTCC included) were purchased by the Chicago-based Marmon Group investment company in 1981.

**United Airlines.** United Airlines and the modern American commercial airline industry were born out of small private companies that contracted in the 1920s with the U.S. postal service to deliver mail to the Pacific coast. One of these early airlines, the Boeing Air Transport Co., was founded by William Boeing in 1927; it flew between Chicago and San Francisco. By 1931 Boeing Air Transport—along with National Air Transport, another airline that flew out of Chicago—was part of the United Aircraft & Transport Corp., which included Boeing's airplane manufacturing operations. In 1934 a new federal law forced this company to split into separate, independent airline and aircraft manufacturing companies. The airline became United Air Lines Transport Corp., which was led by William Patterson. In 1939 the company built its headquarters next to Midway (then Chicago Municipal) Airport. During the middle of World War II, when it sold aircraft to the U.S. military, the company's name was shortened to United Air Lines. During the postwar era, United and the whole commercial airline industry grew rapidly. Annual revenues, which came primarily from passenger tickets, rose from about $16 million in 1940 to $130 million in 1951. By this time, the company employed about 600 female flight attendants. In 1959 United started to fly its first jets, which were DC-8 models. At the beginning of the 1960s, when the company's home moved from Chicago Midway to Chicago O'Hare, United owned a fleet of more than 200 airplanes and employed over 28,000 people worldwide. Soon United was grossing $500 million in annual sales and ranked as the world's largest passenger airline, ahead of competitors such as American and Eastern. In 1969 United Air Lines became part of a holding company named UAL Inc., which had its headquarters in Elk Grove Village, a suburb just west of O'Hare Airport. By the early 1970s, UAL employed about 10,000 Chicago-area residents, making it one of the region's leading employers. Despite financial difficulties and strikes by its workers, UAL continued to expand. By the end of the 1970s, annual revenues approached $4 billion, and the company employed over 70,000 people around the world. When the U.S. government deregulated the airline industry in 1978, United was the number one passenger carrier. By 1985, when United pilots engaged in a one-month strike, the company owned a fleet of over 300 planes. For a brief period during the late 1980s, United's name was changed to the Allegis Corp. In 1994 the company's employees became its new owners, as they received a majority of stock in exchange for wage concessions. By the end of the 1990s, when the company was once again the world's largest passenger airline, annual revenues had grown to about $18 billion. At this point, UAL employed about 100,000 people around the world, including about 21,000 Chicago-area residents. United's fortunes turned dramatically in the twenty-first century. Corporate policies, combined with the September 11, 2001, attacks that involved two United flights, weakened the company, which filed for bankruptcy protection in 2002. Nonetheless, United Airlines, at the end of that year, continued to employ some 18,000 persons in Chicago and 72,000 worldwide and had revenues in excess of $14 billion. The bankruptcy led the company to reduce its fleet, cut back services and employees, renegotiate contracts with employees, cancel its pension plan, create a low-cost carrier named Ted, and to expand its more profitable international routes. Emerging from bankruptcy in 2006, United began searching for a merger partner. Various efforts faltered until 2010 when it one again began talks with Houston-based Continental Airlines. After various approvals, the UAL Corporation, United's parent company, acquired Continental Airlines and changed its name to United Continental Holdings Inc. in October 2010. The combined airline retains the United name and will continue to be headquartered in Chicago, although O'Hare will no longer be its largest hub.

**United States Gypsum Co.** This leading maker of common construction materials such as wallboard and Sheetrock was established in Chicago in 1901. Created from a merger of several smaller operations, U.S. Gypsum started with $7.5 million in capital. Its operations around the country—which included a plant in East Chicago, Indiana—mined gypsum (hydrous calcium sulfate) and turned it into building products. By the mid-1930s, the East Chicago plant employed about 300 people. The company's annual sales rose from about $8 million in 1919 to $175 million in 1950. By the beginning of the 1960s, United States Gypsum had about 13,000 employees around the country, including over 1,000 in the Chicago area. In 1985 the company changed its name to USG Corp. By the end of the century, USG grossed about $3.6 billion in annual sales and employed some 1,200 Chicago-area residents. Facing almost 200,000 asbestos-related lawsuits, the company filed for Chapter 11 bankruptcy protection in 2001, but its sales continued to climb. The company emerged from bankruptcy in 2006; its 2010 revenues approached $3 billion, and it employed more than 9,200 workers in North America, Europe, the Middle East, New Zealand, and Asia.

**United Stationers Supply Co.** In 1921 Morris Wolf, Harry Hecktman, and Israel Kriloff bought the Utility Supply Co. and started selling office products in Chicago. By the 1930s, they had retail stores as well as wholesale and retail catalog operations. The company's annual sales rose from about $120,000 during its first year to $2 million by 1948, when mail-order sales accounted for about 40 percent of the business. In 1960, when it was still based in Chicago, the company changed its name to United Stationers Supply Co. When Howard Wolf, a son of the founder, became the president of the company in 1967, annual sales hit $10 million. By the early 1980s, when it had exited the retail business, United Stationers ranked as the nation's leading wholesaler of office supplies. Annual sales reached about $180 million by 1986. In 1995 an investment company called Wingate Partners bought a large piece of United Stationers and merged it with Associated Stationers, creating United Stationers Inc. By the end of the 1990s, the company grossed about $3.4 billion in annual sales; about one-sixth of its 6,000 employees nationwide worked in the Chicago area. During the following decade, United Stationers acquired several firms to broaden its product lines and expanded its e-business options. Headquartered in suburban Deerfield, the company had revenues over $4.8 billion in 2010.

**Veluchamy Enterprises.** In 1974 Indian native Pethinaidu Veluchamy began selling magazine subscriptions door-to-door while taking graduate courses at the University of Illinois, Chicago. As the enterprise became increasingly profitable, Veluchamy left his program, hired sales associates, and rented an office space in suburban Downers Grove, where his company could solicit magazine subscriptions by mail. By the late 1970s, Veluchamy began to acquire other Chicago-area direct-mailing companies as well as commercial and industrial real estate. By the late 1980s, Veluchamy Enterprises, as it became known, had developed a vertically integrated direct-marketing operation that included nine individual companies specializing in printing, data entry, automated mailing services, embossing, gift cards, and the encoding of credit and ATM cards. At that time it employed nearly 1,000 people around Chicago and had sales of about $60 million. In 1995 the company purchased the single branch of Security Bank. By the early 2000s, Veluchamy Enterprises owned and leased over 2 million square feet of retail and industrial real estate space, including the building that housed the former Michael Jordan's Restaurant downtown. It owned two banks with eight branches by that time. Still headquartered in Downers Grove, it owned nearly a dozen direct-marketing businesses in the Chicago area, and one each in New Jersey and India. With 1,500 Chicago-area employees, 1,500 more worldwide, and over $200 million in annual revenues, this family-owned and family-operated company was one of Chicago's largest minority-owned firms. In 2010 the slightly leaner corporation newly renamed VMark Inc. owned eight companies that generated $200 million in revenues and still employed 1,100 in the Chicago area.

**Walgreen Co.** In 1901 Charles R. Walgreen, the son of Swedish immigrants, started a small pharmacy at Cottage Grove and Bowen Avenues on Chicago's South Side. A second Walgreen store opened in 1909; over the next few years, the chain grew rapidly, until there were nearly 400 Walgreen pharmacies nationwide by 1929. The chain's annual sales rose from about $1.5 million in 1920 to nearly $50 million by 1929. By the mid-1930s, the company employed about 1,300 men and 1,400 women at its large manufacturing laboratory and warehouse on the South Side. After the founder died in 1939, his son Charles R. Walgreen Jr. led the firm. The company's first self-service store (a retailing design that would become the rule throughout the industry) opened on the South Side in 1952. Annual sales for the entire chain passed $200 million during the 1950s and $1 billion in the 1970s, when Charles R. Walgreen III led the company. By that time, Walgreens employed about 10,000 people in the Chicago area, and it was the nation's leading drug retailer, with 650 stores nationwide (most of them in the Midwest). The corporate headquarters moved to Deerfield in 1975. The company grew quickly during the last years of the twentieth century. By the early 2000s, Walgreens could boast nearly $25 billion in annual sales from over 3,000 stores nationwide. It employed over 14,000 people in the greater Chicago area. That growth continued into the twenty-first century, buoyed by the purchase of other pharmacy chains, including its subsidiaries Duane Reade in New York and drugstore.com. Its $67 billion in 2010 revenues made it Chicago's largest publicly held company as ranked by revenues. It employed almost a quarter of a million people nationwide (over 5,000 in its Deerfield headquarters alone) and operated over 8,000 stores in all 50 states, the District of Columbia, Puerto Rico, and Guam.

**Ward (Montgomery) & Co.** The world's first great mail-order retail company was founded in Chicago in 1872 by Aaron Montgomery Ward. Ward, a New Jersey native, arrived in Chicago in 1866 and found a job with Field, Palmer & Leiter, the large dry-goods business that would become Marshall Field & Co. After selling Field's products in hard-to-reach rural areas for several years, Ward decided to create an easier means to market merchandise. In 1892 Ward and his brother-in-law George R. Thorne invested $2,400 in a new mail-order business. Boosted by orders from members of the Patrons of Husbandry (or "Grange"), the midwestern farmers' association for which it served as an official supply house, the business grew rapidly. In 1874 the catalog was 32 pages long; by 1876 a 152-page Ward catalog listed 3,000 items. The slogan adopted in 1875, "Satisfaction guaranteed or your money back," proved to be appealing to consumers, who used Ward catalogs to order all sorts of goods, including clothing, barbed wire, saddles, windmills, and even steam engines. By 1897 annual sales had reached $7 million, and the catalog was nearly 1,000 pages long. In 1900 there were about 1,400 workers at the company's Michigan Avenue headquarters; ten years later, when annual sales stood at nearly $19 million, Ward employed more than 7,000 Chicago-area residents at its huge new facility along the North Branch of the Chicago River. As branches were added around the country, annual sales grew to over $100 million by 1920. The company entered a new era in 1926, when it decided to follow the lead of Sears, Roebuck & Co., its main rival, by opening retail stores. By 1931 there were more than 530 Montgomery Ward stores across the country. Led by Sewell Avery, the company continued to grow during the Great Depression: between 1928 and 1941, annual sales grew from $200 million to $600 million. Ward employed over 70,000 people nationwide by the early 1940s. During World War II, when Avery refused to recognize an employees' union that was backed by the government's War Labor Board, the U.S. Army seized much of the company's property. Although annual sales passed $1 billion in 1956, Ward grew much more slowly during the second half of the twentieth century than it had previously. In 1968 Ward merged with the Container Corp. of America, another Chicago-based company. In 1974, with about 450 stores across the country and nearly $900 million in annual sales, Ward was purchased by the Mobil Oil Corp. After Mobil sold Ward in 1985, the retailer became a private company. But profits proved elusive. At the beginning of the twenty-first century, when it grossed $7 billion in annual sales and still employed close to 7,000 people in the Chicago area, Ward announced that it would shut down permanently. After nearly 130 years in business as a major Chicago company and leading American retailer, the company founded by Aaron Montgomery Ward was gone.

**Waste Management Inc.** Dean Waste Management had its origins in the Dutch-dominated Chicago garbage business. In 1965 the U.S. Congress passed new laws that set stricter requirements for waste disposal, opening the field for new, larger companies in the industry. One of these companies was Waste Management, an Oak Brook–based enterprise founded in 1968 by Dean Buntrock and Wayne Huizenga through a merger of several garbage companies in Illinois, Wisconsin, and Florida. The annual revenues of this enterprise rose from about $5 million in 1968 to $17 million in 1971, when the company began to sell stock to the public under the name Waste Management Inc. The company grew at an extraordinary rate. At the beginning of the 1980s, when annual revenues neared $800 million, Waste Management owned about 4,500 vehicles and had about 12,000 workers worldwide. Waste Management had become the leading garbage disposal company in the United States. One of the company's divisions, Chemical Waste Management—which had a large laboratory in Riverdale, outside of Chicago—was spun off as an independent entity in 1986. By 1993, when the company changed its name to WMX Technologies, it was a giant international corporation claiming about $10 billion in annual revenues and some 75,000 employees around the world. In 1998 USA Waste Services Inc. of Houston, Texas, purchased WMX for nearly $19 billion; the new owner returned the company's name to Waste Management Inc.,

**Western Electric Co.** Gray & Barton, a telegraph industry supply company founded in 1869 by Elisha Gray and Enos Barton, moved from Cleveland to Chicago immediately after it was established. In 1872 the company changed its name to the Western Electric Manufacturing Co., which was located at Kinzie and State Streets. Led by Barton and company president Anson Stager, Western Electric expanded during the 1870s from 20 people in 1870 to a workforce of 105 men and 25 women by 1880. In 1881, when annual sales had already grown to nearly $1 million, the firm was purchased by the American Bell Telephone Co. (the company that would become AT&T); it was renamed the Western Electric Co. and became Bell's manufacturing arm. When Barton succeeded Stager as president in 1886, Western Electric was prospering at its new plant at Clinton and Van Buren Streets. By the turn of the century, this facility employed about 5,300 workers. In 1904, when annual sales neared $32 million, the company relocated to suburban Cicero, where it had built a large new manufacturing complex known as the Hawthorne Works. By 1917 this facility employed 25,000 people, many of them Cicero residents of Czech or Polish descent, making it one of the largest manufacturing plants in the world. In 1915 Western Electric was associated with one of the worst accidents in Chicago history, when the *Eastland*, a vessel filled with employees and their family members attending the company's annual outing, capsized at its dock in the Chicago River, killing more than 800 people. By the 1920s, when annual sales reached $300 million and the company opened a new plant in New Jersey, Western Electric supplied roughly 90 percent of all the telephone equipment used in the United States. At the same time, its Hawthorne Works became famous as a leader in the "scientific management" of employees and the production process. During the 1910s, researchers at the Hawthorne Works pioneered new technologies such as the high-vacuum tube, the condenser microphone, and radio systems for airplanes. During the Great Depression, the company laid off thousands of workers, but business recovered during World War II, when Western Electric became a leading producer of radar equipment. During the war years, when it was subject to federal rules for government contractors, the company began to employ African Americans for the first time. During the 1950s and 1960s, when its Hawthorne plant was one of several around the country, Western Electric continued to grow, as annual sales rose from about $1 billion to $5 billion. After 1970, when there were still 25,000 employees at the Hawthorne Works and another 190,000 workers world-wide, Western Electric slipped. As part of the Federal Communications Commission's ordered breakup of AT&T, Western Electric was subsumed under a new entity, AT&T Technologies, in 1984. The Hawthorne Works plant was closed for good, and Western Electric effectively ceased operations under its old name. In the mid-1990s, AT&T Technologies and its divisional branches joined Bell Labs to become New Jersey–based Lucent Technologies. By early 2001 Lucent employed about 11,000 people in Illinois, most of them in suburban Naperville and Lisle, but company-wide layoffs had cut that number in half within only two years. The French firm Alcatel SA purchased Lucent in 2006, creating Alcatel-Lucent. The firm continues to operate a training center in Naperville and an R&D and briefing center in Lisle.

**Wilson Sporting Goods Co.** This Chicago-based manufacturer of athletic gear began in 1913 as Ashland Manufacturing, a subsidiary of the Wilson & Co. meat company. At one point, the enterprise became known as the Thomas E. Wilson Co., taking the name of an early chief executive. In 1931 the name was changed to Wilson Sporting Goods Co. During the mid-1930s, the company's plant on Powell Avenue in Chicago employed about 800 people. By the middle of the century, Wilson had become the leading sporting goods manufacturer in the United States. The company's headquarters moved from Chicago to the suburb of River Grove in 1957. After LTV purchased Wilson & Co. in 1967, Wilson Sporting Goods was spun off as a separate company and grossed about $100 million in annual sales. In 1970 Wilson Sporting Goods was acquired by PepsiCo, the New York–based beverage giant. In 1985 the company reemerged as an independent entity, Wilson Sporting Goods Inc., which had its headquarters in River Grove and employed about 400 Chicago-area residents among its 4,200 workers nationwide. At the end of the 1980s, when Wilson Sporting Goods was purchased by the Amer Group of Finland, annual sales had exceeded $400 million. The executive offices were moved to Chicago's Northwest Side from River Grove in the early 1990s,. In 2010 Wilson employed some 1,600 individuals doing business in over 100 countries.

*John H. Long*

**Wirtz Corp.** This large family business was created in 1922 by Arthur M. Wirtz, who made money in real estate and liquor distribution in Chicago. After struggling through Prohibition and the Great Depression, Wirtz bought the large Judge & Dolph liquor wholesaler from the Walgreen Co. in 1945. The Wirtz Corp., headquartered in Chicago with branches around the city, continued acquiring liquor companies and real estate through the ensuing decades, serving as a holding company. When the founder died in 1983, his son William Wirtz, in charge of Judge & Dolph since 1950, took the reins of Wirtz Corp. By the end of the century, the Wirtz Corp. also owned Edison Liquor Co., distributed about half the liquor sold in Illinois, and ranked among the ten largest liquor distributors in the United States. Wirtz had annual revenues of $700 million and employed about 1,600 people in the Chicago area. The real estate arm of the corporation owned property in Illinois, Wisconsin, Mississippi, Texas, Nevada, and Florida at the beginning of the next century. Wirtz Corp. also owned the Chicago Blackhawks hockey team and co-owned the United Center arena—where the Blackhawks and the Chicago Bulls basketball team played—with Bulls majority owner Jerry Reinsdorf.

**Wrigley (William, Jr.) Co.** After working as a soap salesman for his father in Philadelphia, 29-year-old William Wrigley Jr. moved to Chicago in 1891. He continued to sell soap but soon offered other products, including baking soda. Wrigley's best-selling item proved to be chewing gum, which he started buying in 1892 from the Zeno Manufacturing Co. of Chicago. Among the early brands of gum made for Wrigley by Zeno were Lotta, Vassar, Juicy Fruit, and Spearmint. By 1897 Wrigley's annual gum sales passed $1 million, and Wrigley and Zeno together employed about 500 people. In 1910 Wrigley and Zeno formally combined their businesses, creating the William Wrigley Jr. Co. National advertising helped the company's annual sales rise to nearly $4.5 million in 1910, when Spearmint was the industry's leading brand. A new brand, Doublemint, was introduced in 1914. As the company's operations expanded nationally and overseas, annual sales grew to $27 million by 1919. Some of Wrigley's profits went toward the construction of the Wrigley Building, the Michigan Avenue tower that was Chicago's tallest structure when it was completed in 1921. Meanwhile, William Wrigley Jr. had become the primary owner of the Chicago Cubs baseball team, which now played in a stadium called Wrigley Field. In 1932, after the founder died, his son Philip K. Wrigley took charge of the company, which would continue to be headed by family members through the end of the twentieth century. During World War II, government-ordered rationing forced Wrigley to stop much of its normal production; the company temporarily and unsuccessfully introduced Orbit. Business recovered after the war, as annual sales grew from about $38 million in 1946 to over $100 million by 1961; the company employed over 1,000 people in the Chicago area during this period. Sales topped $500 million by the end of the 1970s, when new brands such as Freedent, Big Red, and Hubba Bubba helped Wrigley to maintain a hold over about one-third of the domestic market for gum. In 2008 William Wrigley's great-grandson oversaw the firm's acquisition by family-owned and Virginia-based Mars Inc. As a wholly owned subsidiary of Mars, Wrigley's global operations are still overseen from Chicago, although beginning in 2012 its headquarters will be moved from Michigan Avenue to Goose Island near its new Global Innovation Center. With 60 percent of its business occurring outside the United States, Wrigley employs over 16,000 employees worldwide (1,000 in Chicago) and has sales in excess of $5 billion.

**Yellow Cab Co. (of Chicago).** Chicago automobile salesman John Hertz entered the taxicab business with Walden W. Shaw in 1907 by transforming used trade-in cars into taxicabs. Hertz began painting the taxis yellow to attract the attention of would-be riders. Hertz, an Austrian native who grew up in Chicago, incorporated the Yellow Cab Co. in 1915 with a fleet of 40 taxis. By 1925, when publicly owned Yellow Cab was the largest taxi company in the world, the fleet had grown to 2,700 vehicles, most built by the Yellow Cab Manufacturing Co. During that time, the company, still controlled by Hertz, helped launch several important innovations: automatic windshield wipers, smooth-riding Firestone balloon tires, and telephone dispatching of taxis. In 1929 Hertz sold his share of Yellow Cab in order to focus on the rental car business he had purchased from fellow Chicagoan Walter L. Jacobs in 1923. The new majority owners of Yellow Cab, a partnership led by Russian-born Morris Markin, also owned Checker Taxi; its parent company, Checker Cab Manufacturing Co. of Kalamazoo, Michigan; and numerous smaller taxi companies in New York City, Minneapolis, and Pittsburgh. By 1935 the Markin partnership had turned Yellow Cab back into a privately held company and would maintain control of the company for the next seven decades. At the beginning of the 1960s, when it had about 3,000 employees and $16 million in annual revenues, Chicago Yellow Cab was formally merged into the Checker Motors Corp. During the middle and late 1990s, Yellow Cab changed hands several times and effectively ended its legal relationship with Checker. Yellow Cab eventually split into multiple companies across the nation bearing the Yellow Cab name. In Chicago, the Yellow Cab Management Co. operated a fleet of 2,000 taxis—the most in Chicago—leasing the cabs to drivers belonging to the Yellow Cab Association for about $150 a week. At the end of the century, Yellow Cab Management Co. founded the Wolley Cab Association ("yellow" spelled backward), a bright orange fleet of 120 taxis in Chicago. In 2006 the new owners of Yellow Cab purchased the assets of Checker Cab, then in bankruptcy and converted the Wolley cabs to Checkers. By 2011 Yellow had a fleet of some 1,700 vehicles.

**Zenith Electronics.** Karl Hassel and Ralph H. G. Mathews founded Chicago Radio Laboratory in 1919 as a small manufacturer of radio equipment.

The brand name Z-Nith came from the call letters of their small Chicago radio station, 9ZN. In 1923 Hassel, Mathews, and investor Eugene F. McDonald Jr. formed the Zenith Radio Corp., which soon moved into a large factory on the 3600 block of South Iron Street. The company pioneered the manufacture of portable radios in 1924, and in 1926 it introduced the first home radio receivers to operate on AC power instead of batteries. Annual sales grew from about $5 million in 1928 to $11 million in 1930. About 450 people worked at Zenith's Iron Street plant by the mid-1930s. During World War II, the company expanded as it filled military orders for bomb fuses and other devices. In the late 1940s, Zenith began to manufacture televisions, and it was the number one maker of black-and-white TV sets during the 1950s and 1960s. Annual sales reached $100 million in 1950 and approached $500 million by the mid-1960s, when Zenith had more than 15,000 employees, most of whom worked at factories around the Chicago area. Zenith's headquarters remained in Chicago at this time. The company still employed about 12,000 Chicago-area residents in the early 1970s, but international competition was beginning to take its toll. By 1984, when it was renamed Zenith Electronics, the company had laid off thousands of employees and moved some operations overseas. Thanks in part to a move into computer manufacturing, Zenith still employed about 5,000 Chicago-area workers by 1990. Losses mounted, however, and after a Chapter 11 reorganization, Zenith emerged from bankruptcy in 1999 as a wholly owned subsidiary of LG Electronics Inc., a South Korean company that gained a controlling stake in the corporation in 1995.

# IV.  Working in Chicago

**Work.** In the late nineteenth century, booming Chicago struck visitors as the "purest kind of commercial city," a place devoted to work and money-making. More than its notoriety for crime, corruption, and political machines, work has defined Chicago in popular and literary imagery, shaped the city's character, and served as the fulcrum of its history. As the city grew, work in Chicago underwent dramatic transformations, both in the type of industries that dominated and in the organization of work itself. Especially in the late nineteenth century, Chicago was both shaped by and helped to foment a nationwide revolution in work that first undermined and then remade the democratic promise of America. People flocked to Chicago to find work and fought there over what work should be. The changes wrought by large-scale corporate manufacturing and trade provoked battles over the character and control of work that spilled over into broader political fights over democracy, citizenship, and the rights of workers.

At first the work of Chicago was trade and—nearly equally important—speculation in real estate and in the city's future as the great metropolis of the frontier. Chicago's commercial and, eventually, industrial power depended on its linkages to the hinterland and other cities, first by lakes, rivers, and canals, then roads and railroads, which consolidated Chicago's central position until the ascendance of airpower and interstate highways after World War II. Although trade and transportation remained key, in the mid-nineteenth century small factories first began processing the products of the prairie—packing pork, sawing lumber, or milling flour—and then started making grain harvesters, furniture, and clothing for farmers and frontier towns. From 1870 to 1930, Chicago grew rapidly from bustling trading center to quintessential industrial complex, Carl Sandburg's "Hog Butcher for the World," "City of the Big Shoulders."

As the nation's transportation hub, Chicago also became the Midwest's primary labor market for rural and small-town job seekers and immigrant

Traffic on Dearborn and Randolph. The congestion and signage visible at the corner of Dearborn and Randolph in 1909 offers a picture of the jobs available in the Loop and the practical pressures to locate some businesses and industries away from the city center. Photo: Frank W. Hallenbeck. Courtesy of the Chicago History Museum (ICHi-04192).

workers—at first from Germany, Ireland, and Scandinavia, then from southern and eastern Europe. Beginning in World War I, they were joined by large numbers of African Americans from the South and, after 1965, by Latinos and Asians.

From its early days, Chicago was a place where everything happened fast. The town grew with amazing speed, generating jobs in construction and the manufacture of construction materials, but there was a high priority on doing things quickly and grandly in every other endeavor as well. This emphasis on speed and scale also encouraged businessmen to find faster, simpler ways to get things done, resulting in the standardization of products from grades of grain to sizes of lumber. Chicago's success lay partly in the ability of its businesses to make nature abstract in ways that transformed products of farms and forest more readily into commodities for the market. Chicago's grain merchants turned discrete bags of grain from specific fields into a standard type passing through the city's new grain elevators, financed in part by contracts for future delivery that formed the basis for a new financial services business.

Typical of most early nineteenth-century American industry, Chicago's earliest manufacturing took place in artisan workshops and manufactories where skilled craftsmen, aided by laborers or apprentices, dominated production. Manufacturers in Chicago, with rail access to abundant southern Illinois coal, turned to steam power for larger factories after the Civil War. As they did, they initiated changes in the nature of factory work and the relationship between those who owned the factories and those who worked there.

Chicago's competitive environment fostered a search for production methods that were faster and less expensive. Anxious to cut costs, businesses sought ways to trim the cost of labor. One important step was elaborating the division of labor. Dividing a job, such as building a house or butchering a pig, that had previously been executed by a master craftsman made it possible for employers to hire unskilled workers at lower wages. Equally important, it shifted control to the employer, who adopted a variety of strategies to respond to labor market supply, technological opportunities, and worker resistance.

In Chicago, major industries such as construction, meatpacking, garment making, and machinery manufacture followed distinctive courses. Although large contractors rather than master carpenters dominated Chicago building construction as early as the 1840s, carpenters were still skilled tradesmen who supplied their own extensive tool chests. In 1833 balloon-frame construction opened up the potential for increased reliance on factory mass production of building parts like sashes and doors. Even at the work site, contractors turned to piecework, fragmenting the work into specialties that required little training and offering lower pay tied to output. In meatpacking, the "disassembly line" arrived in Chicago soon after its introduction in Cincinnati. The industry relied on the line to fragment labor-intensive production and to organize meatpacking on a much larger scale than had previously been possible. The scale of operations, combined with the pressures of cost cutting and environmental complaints, fostered the growth of ancillary industries that used what otherwise would have been waste—"everything but the squeal." In the men's clothing industry, boosted by Civil War uniform contracts, small contractors would bid for work from "jobbers," who cut the cloth and then turned it over to workers at home or in small shops for different stages of sewing; competition among these workers based on price made for classic sweatshop conditions. There could be up to 150 separate operations divided among many workers in sewing a man's coat. By the late nineteenth century, major men's clothing retailers consolidated many sweatshops into larger factories to gain more control over quality, although contractor sweatshops persisted. At the McCormick reaper factory in 1886, company president Cyrus McCormick Jr. installed new pneumatic molding machinery to displace the skilled iron molders and their union, thereby securing management control. The machines turned out poor-quality castings, however, and nearly tripled labor costs in the short term.

As the new factory system challenged the craftsman's control, the foreman (and, to a lesser extent, labor brokers and employment agents) assumed new importance. The foreman—with his arbitrary and discriminatory power over hiring and firing, especially of pro-union workers or blacklisted "troublemakers"—was the key figure in the "drive system" that pushed workers to work faster, continuously, and more dangerously. His power provoked worker rebellions small and large.

Before the new factory system, hours of work were usually long, but work was sporadic and often paced by workers themselves. Until the 1930s, it was not unusual for Chicago factory or other manual workers to put in 10 hours or more a day, 6 days a week, with 12-hour days common in many industries, including steel. Yet the opposite condition was equally problematic: work continued to be irregular and unreliable. Many industries in the nineteenth and early twentieth century were seasonal, with meatpacking jobs more available in the winter and construction jobs in the spring through fall. Even within the seasons, work was erratic. For example, a few packinghouse workers were given steady jobs and, in return, were expected to show fervent loyalty to management. Most workers, however, did not know how much work they would have. They would show up outside the gates of the stockyards and wait to be called, then perhaps end up working very long hours early in the week but few or no hours at the end. Uncertain business cycles, panics, and depressions precipitated widespread cuts in wages for many and threw others out of work, forcing them to rely on limited private charity. During boom periods, workers in factories experienced extremely high turnover, as many expressed their frustrations and hopes by quitting. Immigrant workers complained that work in Chicago was harder than back home, and historians debate how much better off financially, if at all, immigrants were here, especially with employers' persistent efforts to drive down wages. Even when productivity soared, workers struggled to gain their share. At the McCormick Harvesting Machine Co. and its successor, International Harvester, for example, wages and benefits grew on average 0.1 percent a year during the non-union period but 3.85 percent a year when workers were organized into unions.

Historians often describe the change in work in late nineteenth-century Chicago as a homogenization of labor toward a low common denominator comparable to the homogenization of nature and standardization of products by Chicago's industries. As mechanization increased in factories, semi-skilled machine-operator positions grew in numbers, threatening the skilled workers, sometimes providing better jobs for unskilled workers, and complicating relationships between workers. But the intensified commodification of labor did not eliminate all distinctions. Employers maintained elaborately differentiated wage scales and increasingly designated certain jobs or departments within a factory as primarily the province of particular ethnic groups or genders. At a time when roughly two-thirds of Chicago factory workers were immigrants, employers pursued a variety of strategies to mix and separate different ethnic groups to the employers' advantage. While some divisions reflected skills and labor-market supply and demand, they were primarily part of a management strategy to control workers, discourage their organization into unions, exploit entrenched social discrimination, and create individualistic motivations to work harder. Just as Chicago gained fame as a center of unionism and worker radicalism in the mid- and late nineteenth century, the city's business leaders were equally notorious for their adamant opposition to unionization or other worker organization.

Workers did not submit meekly to the changes imposed on their work. They protested wage cuts and demanded the eight-hour day; they also challenged, from different perspectives, the legitimacy of the new industrial capitalist order. With the agitation about chattel slavery in the South and the Civil War vividly in their minds, nineteenth-century workers denounced the "wage slavery" to which they were subjected. Native-born American workers and union leaders commonly adopted a "labor republican" outlook, arguing that employers were robbing workers of the fruits of their labors while the emerging wage labor system denied their manhood and their rights as citizens. They called for a cooperative commonwealth of producers that would include farmers and some small businessmen. Immigrants, especially skilled German workers, brought with them socialist ideas about state ownership as a solution to the growing power of corporate industrialists. The influential Chicago anarchists, who supported insurrectionary action over politics, did not share the labor republican ideology but envisioned a future society that more resembled the cooperative commonwealth advocated by rural populists.

Unions fought for short-term gains, especially to restore wage cuts or to reduce hours of work. They also fought to maintain control of the shop floor, often through informal restrictions on output and the labor market, through closed union shops or union label campaigns. The movement for an eight-hour day, in which Chicago workers played a leading role, was not just an effort to reduce hours of hard-driven toil. Leaders saw it as a critical step to restore lost citizenship and to transform the wage labor system. Chicago unions were politically active, strongly influencing local political parties and usually securing neighborhood police neutrality in conflicts from the 1860s through the early 1880s. After the post-Haymarket collapse of the Great Upheaval of 1886, when the police and government more clearly acted against workers and for employer interests, unions tried forming labor parties but failed to displace the Democrats.

During the 1890s, unions increasingly turned away from attacks on the wage system to advocate a living wage that would guarantee workers an "American" standard of living, improved conditions at work, and regulation of the labor market. They found allies among some upper-class reformers, such as members of the Chicago Civic Federation, who joined with unions in support of legislation to protect women workers and exclude children from industry. As unions and reformers found common ground on regulation, employers enacted their own strategy to regulate markets by combining smaller firms into large corporations and oligopolies—from U.S. Steel and International Harvester to the group of dominant meatpackers. This strategy protected business from ruthless competition, but it further reduced workers' power. Powerful literary works like Upton Sinclair's *The Jungle* demonstrated that loss of power to readers around the world by identifying the "beef trust" as the chief oppressor of Jurgis Rudkus and his fellow workers.

In the early decades of the twentieth century, while many skilled trade unions moved toward a practical-minded "business unionism," efforts to build broad-based industrial unions in industries such as meatpacking, steel, railroads, and farm implement manufacture were dramatic but short-lived. Labor republicanism died out, but socialist ideas had wide appeal among workers, and into the 1920s the leaders of the Chicago labor movement advocated a labor party and industrial democracy as a response to corporate power. During the 1930s, Chicago workers finally succeeded in forming broad-based industrial unions in steel, meatpacking, farm implements, and other sectors. They also became linked to both the New Deal ideas of economic regulation and government provision of social welfare and the local Democratic machine, setting a pattern of reform and accommodation with a system their predecessors had reviled that persisted with modest changes throughout the century.

By 1880 Chicago was, after New York, the second most important manufacturing center in America. Factories in Chicago were, on average, larger than elsewhere. By 1900, 3 of the nation's 14 giant factories employing over 6,000 workers were in Chicago. In most cases, the big factories also employed the most advanced mechanization of work.

But Chicago was more than a center of manufacturing and trade in the natural products of the Midwest. From efforts to sell goods that both reflected and spread a new era of industrial capitalism into farms and small towns, Chicago became the center of new techniques in mass marketing, advertising, and consumer credit, epitomized by the giant catalog merchandisers, Montgomery Ward and Sears, Roebuck. Their mail-order catalogs, warehouses, and centralized sales staffs displaced not only many traveling salesmen but also small-town retail shops. The scale of these industrial and commercial enterprises, along with the broad coordinated networks formed by the railroads, contributed to further changes in management and the growth of a white-collar bureaucracy to administer large, complex enterprises.

Initially, men dominated the office workforce, but after the 1880s, the invention of the typewriter and the proliferation of business colleges opened certain jobs to women. At the same time, managerial strategies of dividing tasks and reducing required skills were extended from factories to offices. In nearly every case, women were paid substantially less than men who had previously done the same work. Gradually, lower-level office work was redefined as women's work, while men continued to dominate the upper ranks. Office jobs greatly expanded women's place in the labor market, which had previously been limited to extensions of what were seen as women's natural domestic and maternal roles. In 1870, two-thirds of female workers in Chicago were domestic servants. Over the next 30 years, the number of women working in clothing manufacture rose dramatically. The growth of Chicago women in clerical and sales work—especially in large department stores like Marshall Field's—was faster than in the nation as a whole. Even as women entered factories, their work was distinct from and less well paid than that of male workers. In 1900 domestic work was still the principal female occupation reported in the census, and many women still toiled at home tending to their families, taking in paid but unrecorded work, and managing the boarders common to working-class households.

The less than 2 percent of Chicago's 1890 population who were African American also worked primarily in domestic and personal service jobs. One of the most prestigious of such jobs was working as a railcar porter for the Chicago-based Pullman Company. Although African Americans were regularly denied regular jobs in factories, they were frequently hired to break strikes, as employers manipulated racial hostilities to stymie worker demands. When strikes ended, blacks often lost their jobs, which worsened smoldering racism.

Despite these conflicts—and many unions' prohibitions against African American members—blacks and whites sometimes did cooperate to improve working conditions. For example, black men made up roughly half of the restaurant and hotel waiters in late nineteenth-century Chicago. Like their white counterparts, black waiters were upset by job insecurity, pay inequities, and factory-like discipline. Excluded from white unions, however, blacks either identified with employers or formed their own unions. In 1890, an interracial Culinary Alliance went on strike with some success, only to watch employers fan racial tensions and bring in women strikebreakers—although until then women were not common in the trade. During World War I, when European immigration declined precipitously and employers turned to the rural South for workers, African Americans made important breakthroughs into industry. Between 1915 and 1920, blacks tripled their ranks in Chicago factories, especially meatpacking, when factory work surpassed service as the primary employment of black men. The formation of the Brotherhood of Sleeping Car Porters in 1925 was pivotal for the entire black community, but the organization of the multiracial industrial unions during the 1930s had an even broader impact on black workers' lives.

Although many Chicagoans continued to work in small stores and workshops or in the informal economy, by 1920 more than 70 percent of manufacturing wage earners worked for corporations employing 100 or more workers, a third for firms employing more than 1,000. The big corporations with their large factories, warehouses, and offices dominated the local economy and had the largest impact on changes in work. Most big companies continued to control workers with proven tools: strike-breakers, private detectives and spies, divisive tactics, deskilling technology, and the legal apparatus of the state. During the early decades of the twentieth century, partly in hopes of reducing both worker turnover and discontent, employers also moved toward more bureaucratic administration, scientific management, and efforts to motivate workers with more than the threats of the old drive system. Centralized management, used increasingly by most big companies, brought tighter financial accounting and, in the spirit of Frederick Winslow Taylor's "scientific management," a closer evaluation of individual workers.

George Pullman's model town and factory south of Chicago in 1880 had been one of the most prominent early examples of paternalistic control in the guise of providing for workers' welfare, but modified versions of the strategy grew increasingly common as corporations consolidated economic power and sought new ways to fight unionization. In 1901 McCormick/Harvester adopted "welfarism," including profit-sharing, pensions, and sickness and accident benefits, as a way to fight unions, win public approval, limit legal liabilities, and fend off antitrust action and other government regulation. In 1919, partly in reaction to a postwar strike wave, Harvester introduced its Works Council, a prominent example of the company-controlled unions that several major Chicago employers adopted in the 1920s, when Harvester, U.S. Steel, Armour, Swift, and Western Electric espoused what often was called "welfare capitalism" or "the American plan."

Companies sought innovative ways to increase productivity, reduce turnover, and resist unions. Western Electric, one of many firms that made Chicago a national leader in electronics manufacturing in the decades after 1920, initiated research on how adjustment of various physical factors, such as lighting, influenced work at its giant Hawthorne Works in Cicero. Instead, researchers found that the social organization of the work group and the attention given workers by researchers were both more important than physical variables. This study laid the foundations for a new school of centralized personnel management that gradually supplanted the foreman in organizing and controlling work.

Welfare capitalism and employee unions faltered in the Great Depression, but they provided additional legitimation for workers' belief that companies should treat them more fairly. Although many believed that the Depression demonstrated the failure of capitalism, a larger number were interested simply in a fairer, more moral capitalism regulated by a federal government that provided more economic security and better working conditions. The new industrial unions of the Congress of Industrial Organizations, as well as some American Federation of Labor craft unions, provided a voice for workers in the mass-production industries. They readily joined the labor movement during the Depression and World War II, despite continued resistance from employers that at times turned bloody, as in the Memorial Day 1937 police attack on Chicago's striking Republic steelworkers.

Demand for war material during World War II combined with labor shortages caused by troop mobilization opened industrial jobs for new workers, especially women, who were expected to return home after the war. Anxious to avoid strikes, the federal government pushed companies to recognize unions. In the postwar years, strong domestic demand kept unemployment low, and newly established unions raised wages and expanded benefits, including pensions and health insurance, which were tied to jobs rather than universally provided. Union contracts and government social safety nets combined to reduce the hardship for workers during recessions, and unionization provided new protection from arbitrary managerial decisions, especially through the use of seniority to determine jobs and grievance procedures to resolve disputes. Union contracts often set the standard for pay, benefits, and even personnel systems that non-union companies felt forced to approximate. Mechanization and fragmentation of work continued on its established trajectory, further undermining many manual skills, but employment was steadier and more lucrative for most workers than in the past.

In 1947 manufacturing employment in the city of Chicago peaked at 667,407 workers. It began to drop sharply in the 1950s, before stabilizing in the 1960s at roughly half a million. Manufacturing employment plummeted in the 1970s, falling to 147,000 by 2000. Chicago, whose boosters had long boasted that someone who couldn't find work there couldn't find work anywhere, began to consistently register unemployment rates higher than the national average.

Industries closed or dispersed to new locations. The largest companies found it easiest to relocate, leaving small suppliers stranded without their traditional customers. Many manufacturers relocated to the suburbs, seeking cheaper land and taking advantage of the new interstate highway system. By 1965 more than half of manufacturing jobs in the metropolitan area were located in the suburbs, jobs that made the Chicago metropolitan area home to the nation's largest concentration of manufacturing jobs in 1970. Suburban Chicago manufacturing employment continued to expand until the early 1980s. Other businesses, however, relocated factories to the Sunbelt. Meatpacking moved west, leading to the closing of the famed packing plants and stockyards in the mid-1960s. From the 1960s onward—when foreign competition began to cut into sales and employment in industries like steel, apparel, and consumer electronics—manufacturers increasingly located operations in foreign countries. In many cases, employers fled to escape unionization and to pay lower wages. The loss of central-city manufacturing jobs hurt African Americans hardest, as sociologist William Julius Wilson showed in his studies of the social devastation of concentrated poverty in Chicago's neighborhoods.

In the latter part of the twentieth century, Chicago's remaining factories were smaller, and major companies increasingly subcontracted production work to smaller firms. In the 1990s suburban-based Sara Lee exemplified the trend in announcing that it no longer intended to manufacture the products it sold. Manufacturing productivity increased as businesses invested in technology, including computers, and refined the organization of work, with measures including adoption from the Japanese of just-in-time production. Although manufacturing at the end of the twentieth century remained more important in Chicago (18 percent of all jobs) than for the national economy as a whole (15 percent), Chicago was no longer the manufacturing powerhouse it had been a century earlier. The limited career ladders of the nineteenth-century factory and office have been almost entirely displaced by requirements for formal education as a prerequisite for more-skilled and better-paid jobs. Debates about the future of work in Chicago increasingly focused on the adequacy of its educational system, even though most service and retail economy jobs demand little skill. Services—including health care, business services, finance, and retail work—had become the mainstays of employment in Chicago, each roughly providing as many or more jobs than manufacturing. While Chicago remains comparatively highly unionized, the labor movement is not the dynamic force it once was, even if it does raise questions about deindustrialization, globalization, inequality, and living wages.

Although efforts to preserve and nurture manufacturing in the central city continue, Chicago business and political leaders at the close of the twentieth century were more concerned with Chicago as part of a regional economy and its prospects as a "global city," a center of corporate administration, professional services, finance, government, communications, universities, and culture. But there are questions about whether Chicago could become part of a rarefied elite with London, New York, and Tokyo and about what that would mean for most Chicago workers. The economic transformations of globalization since the early 1970s have brought increasing economic inequality and less stable employment to both Chicago and the country as a whole. Although work is still more predictable than it was for most Chicagoans a century ago, there is increasing dependence on contingent (contract, part-time, or temporary) work at all skill levels and less job security even for white-collar employees. Once identified with companies like Swift and Armour that slaughtered cattle by the millions, Chicago—or, more precisely, suburban Oakbrook—is now more identified with McDonald's, whose global workforce flips burgers by the billions. While Chicago is the headquarters of many global corporate leaders, their employment—like that of technology giant Motorola—is spread throughout the world, not concentrated in the corporate backyard as was true of their predecessors. In a similar fashion, even many of the biggest Chicago banks and businesses (like Amoco) are owned and controlled by companies outside the city and even the United States. Not only have workers never regained the control over their work that union leaders in late nineteenth-century Chicago thought was essential for a citizen of a democratic republic; increasingly, local political leaders and business executives do not appear to control the city economy as they once did. As far as the future of work in Chicago is concerned, the "City of the Big Shoulders" has become the "Metropolis of the Big Question Mark."                                                    *David Moberg*

**Work Culture.** When 18-year-old Carrie Meeber, the title character of Theodore Dreiser's novel *Sister Carrie* (1900), steps off the afternoon train from Wisconsin onto the streets of Chicago, she enters a world of seemingly endless work possibilities. An industrial behemoth, Chicago bristled with crowded factories, bustling stockyards, brimming grain elevators, a rapidly growing labor force, and, most of all, complex cultures of work.

What Carrie saw was a remarkable diversity of opportunities shaped by the unique geography of the city. The centrality of Chicago to shipping and transportation routes by water and land made possible and profitable businesses of all kinds—and a correspondingly wide variety of workplaces. Carrie's brother-in-law Sven cleans refrigerator cars at the stockyards; her friend Drouet is a "drummer"—a traveling salesman; and his acquaintance Hurstwood is a well-to-do restaurant manager. Carrie finds her first job punching eyeholes into shoes at a factory on Van Buren Street. Their choices within this cornucopia of employment possibilities were determined by a combination of gender, age, education, ethnicity, race, and marital status.

Work cultures—that mix of practices and ideologies arising from the interactions of people with their work environments—have been shaped in Chicago above all by diversity: diversity of employment opportunities, population, and housing. The ways in which people find jobs, the rhythms of employment and unemployment, the size of the workplace, the process of getting to and from work, how the workday is organized, power relationships and hierarchies, how workers learn and manage their tasks, how they socialize and organize family life, how informal worker behavior interacts with sanctioned authority and rules—all these things constitute work culture. There are many different work cultures, reflecting the differences between skilled and unskilled labor, professional, white-collar, and service work, and workers' identities by race, gender, age, and ethnicity.

Policemen taking the sergeant's exam, ca. 1904. Courtesy of the Chicago History Museum (DN-0000739).

Work cultures have also changed as the nature of work has transformed over the past 150 years.

During the city's infancy, a fur-trading culture developed through interactions between Potawatomi and white traders. Intermarriage and custom led many whites to adopt Indian ways while never losing sight of the controlling hand of the American Fur Company. At the same time, white influence and trade goods altered traditional patterns of work and life for Native Americans. A mixture of frontier autonomy, native culture, entrepreneurial values, and financial dependence thus coexisted uneasily in one of the earliest work cultures of the city.

Throughout the nineteenth century, work for a huge pool of floating and unorganized labor was shaped by transience. The reliance on the products of nature for profit—agriculture, livestock, ice, and lumber—required men to move according to the rhythms of the seasons. They planted in the spring, harvested crops or timber in the fall, cut ice in the winter, and shepherded cattle and pigs through increasingly narrow roads into the city for processing and sale. Uncontrollable forces like drought or fire could instantly create or destroy opportunities for employment.

Transient laborers tended to be white, unmarried men. Answerable to a gang boss, men would work for a season, collect their pay, and move on to the next opportunity. This was not usually a life for families. Transient laborers often lived in cheap boardinghouses, able to pick up and follow work wherever it appeared.

One of the transient job opportunities in mid-nineteenth-century Chicago was lumber production. Lake Michigan lumbermen hired Chicago laborers on seasonal contracts, specifying work from sunrise to sunset daily. Workers were to bring their own axes and pay their passage to the timber fields across the lake, where they would haul logs, push them through blades, and stack lumber. In return, they received room, board, and from $100 to $200 yearly; on occasion their wives and children would be hired to do the "inside" work of cooking and cleaning. During hard times—such as the 1857 panic—these workers would be precipitously fired or offered store credit in place of currency for wages.

The nature of work in shops was very different. Through the early decades of the nineteenth century, workshops were small, with craftsmen hiring a few skilled handicraft workers at a time. Apprenticeship and later employment were personalized and individualized, as cabinetmakers, upholsterers, machinists, and others created items from design to finished product.

The coming of the canals by the 1840s and then the expansion of the first railroads by the 1850s increased the market range for the city from a few hundred miles to the length and breadth of the country, while providing the means to transport people and goods to and from far distances. Chicago became the nexus of a huge organization of products: lumber from Michigan, Wisconsin, and Minnesota; ores from Illinois, Minnesota, and Colorado; pigs, cattle, and grains from the Mississippi Valley. After the calamitous fire of 1871, the local economy experienced an unprecedented building boom, which led to work for timbermen, carpenters, laborers, and painters, and a concomitant need for local stores and services.

The growing demand for labor coincided with the influx of immigrants. Reflecting national patterns, the first waves of foreign immigrants to Chicago in the 1850s and 1860s included Irish, German, and Scandinavian newcomers. From the 1870s through the beginning of the twentieth century, people from eastern and southern Europe—Bohemians, Lithuanians, Italians, Russians, Greeks, Hungarians, Austrians, Poles, and eastern European Jews—flooded into Chicago looking for opportunity and work. Often unskilled and with limited English, these workers found work in the giant factories, particularly in the stockyards, ironworks, and steel industries. Chinese came in lesser numbers and looked especially to laundries as opportunities for self-employment. By the 1890s, three out of four Chicagoans were either immigrants or the children of immigrants.

But the city's newcomers were not only from distant lands. Tens of thousands of people from American small towns and farms sought the excitement and possibilities of life in the big city, creating a pool of migrants. Theodore Dreiser's fictional Sister Carrie came from "Columbia City"—a small town in Wisconsin, a state sending a multitude of migrants to Chicago. Young people from farms and rural towns in Minnesota, the Dakotas, Iowa, Michigan, and Indiana also turned to Chicago as an attractive alternative to what they perceived to be a dreary and limited future in the countryside.

The first significant numbers of African Americans came from the South during the 1890s. A majority of these black migrants, barred from higher-paying factory jobs, found work in domestic service or day labor. As industrial labor opened up to black workers during the 1910s, the Great Migration from the South would bring thousands more blacks and establish the city as a leading center of African American life.

Factory operatives needed little training, but they did have to be able to endure long hours in rough conditions. The majority of these workers were white male immigrants, except in the garment trades, which welcomed women. Factory workers found an increasingly impersonal life as "hands" or "operatives" laboring monotonously on a minuscule part of the production of an item for 10 to 14 hours, 6 days a week. The individualized and personal work culture of artisans faded as industry grew. By the end of the century, factories had become huge places of business. In 1880 over 75,000 Chicago workers labored in industries, including meatpacking, clothing production, iron and steel, beer and liquor processing, furniture manufacture, printing, and the manufacturing of foundry, machine, and agricultural implements. By 1920, 70 percent of workers in manufacturing trades were employed by companies of 100 workers or more, and one-third of these worked in establishments with over 1,000 employees. The personal relationship between upper management and workers became increasingly distant as the size of companies grew.

The plant foreman set the daily pace. His authority was absolute. He could raise or decrease the speed of work, determine pay, and assign hours and tasks of labor. He represented factory management to the operatives under his command and had the power to hire and fire at will. For his workers, the workday offered very little autonomy or sense of empowerment.

Finding work could be a complicated business. In Upton Sinclair's 1906 novel *The Jungle*, Jurgis Rudkus, a Lithuanian immigrant to Chicago, gets his first job by joining the morning crowd outside a Packingtown factory; a "boss" picks him out for the task of sweeping out cattle entrails on the killing floor of the plant. Similarly, Jurgis's cousin-in-law Marija Berczynskas wanders in and out of smaller factories in the district until she is hired by a "forelady" to paint cans of smoked beef. People could also find work through "intelligence" or personnel agencies, saloons and hiring halls, labor unions, newspaper advertisements, and employers' organizations. Kin and ethnic networks provided a time-honored resource for finding a job. Italian and Greek immigrants could also find work through the *padrone* system of labor agents steering them to unskilled work—for a price.

The cost of this unregulated industrial growth included the pollution of home and workplace. Workers labored long hours in unsafe conditions, sometimes standing all day in noisy, crowded, filthy, overheated, and unventilated rooms, always with the threat of dire poverty should injury or illness or unemployment stop a paycheck. There was no safety net.

Industrial workers, especially if they were white, tended to live near their jobs, in the shadow of the mills, stockyards, or factories. Within these neighborhoods, institutions like saloons brought men together with offers of fellowship, food and drink, and such essential services as check cashing and mailing addresses. Women, barred by custom from the world of the saloon, often instead found friendship, education, and social services through the neighborhood settlement houses, such as Hull House or Chicago Commons, which proliferated around the turn of the century. Other community institutions such as churches, barbershops, ethnic newspapers, mutual benefit societies, corner stores, and fraternal organizations preserved ethnic cultures and racial identities at the same time that the forces of "Americanization" were at work.

By the late nineteenth century, many Chicagoans looked to unions and labor federations to win influence over their working conditions. Strikes and lockouts could be violent, as indicated by labor disorders among stevedores, lumberyard workers, railroad workers, and stockyard laborers during the 1870s and 1880s. The growing success of labor legislation within the context of union activism—particularly minimum wages, maximum hours of work, unemployment compensation, and safety standards—changed the hierarchy of industrial relations as government regulatory agencies became influential participants. Factory inspectors, pioneered by Florence Kelley, attempted to enforce new labor laws meant to protect the health and well-being of workers from indifferent company policy. At the same time, some workers resisted the new protective labor legislation. Chicago women who worked as elevated railroad ticket agents, for example, protested in 1911 when their hours were cut from 12 to 10 a day because of a new law limiting the hours of women's employment.

Racial segregation kept the relatively few black factory workers in more distant parts of the city, forcing them to find daily transportation to and from their work and blocking channels of social interaction that might have reduced racial barriers. Until 1916 black factory workers were few and far between, though some did find employment on the killing floors of the stockyards or in the steel mills. More commonly, black men worked as unskilled day laborers, restaurant waiters, Pullman porters, bootblacks, and hotel redcaps, while black women filled the laundry trades and other forms of domestic service. Like industrial workers, unskilled laborers and service workers faced uncertain job security, as slack times led to staff reductions with no notice. Moreover, black employees of hotels, restaurants, and the railroads found themselves employed in places that would deny them and their families and neighbors service as customers.

White and educated native-born men more easily found employment possibilities in business and the professions. By the 1950s, studies of such new postwar suburbs as Chicago's Park Forest suggested that the culture of white-collar work for men had transformed. The workplaces of large corporations in business, government, and industry were staffed by bureaucratic "organization men" who evidenced a "group-mindedness" characterized by values of security and safety rather than initiative and risk. They identified their well-being with that of the company, and so long hours at work, and the belief that the company would reward loyalty with lifetime employment, fostered an environment of conformity that marginalized individual initiative and creativity.

The corporate environment at midcentury included few women or blacks. For women, there had always been a much smaller choice of jobs. With some notable exceptions, only the poorest of married women worked for wages before the middle of the twentieth century, while single women in most ethnic groups worked at least briefly. Poor women found jobs in garment, millinery, and shoe factories, or as domestic servants or laundry workers. Some turned to prostitution. Hilda Polacheck, a Polish Jew whose family had immigrated to Chicago in 1892, left school at the age of 14 to work in a knitting factory on State Street. Six days a week for over 10 hours a day she operated a machine—1 of 400 in a huge room—until she was fired for attending a union meeting. Hilda next worked at a shirtwaist factory, sewing shirt cuffs for 10 hours a day. Her description of this job as "deadly monotony" typified the difference between the earlier culture of artisans who could take pride in their work and newer conditions for industrial laborers.

Native-born white women also found opportunities in emerging occupations, such as the professional fields of education and librarianship and the white-collar areas of clerical and department store work. Wages were consistently lower for women than for men, and unionization far less frequent.

Jobs defined as women's work went through tremendous changes in the twentieth century. Clerical work, for example, once the domain of men, became feminized by the end of the nineteenth century after the invention of the typewriter and through the twentieth century grew to become the single largest job category for women of all races. Montgomery Ward—a mail-order firm whose workers had no direct public contact—employed the most black clerical workers in the country by 1920, when over 1,000 African American women worked for the Chicago company. As the size of office staffs enlarged, new management techniques originally developed for factories began to affect the lives of office workers. Domestic service, which at one time included a population of workers who lived in the homes or businesses of their employers, became more of a day job, increasingly perceived as temporary. Restaurant waitressing also grew as a category of low-paid, often transient unskilled work for women.

As the great urban department stores like Marshall Field's appeared during the second half of the nineteenth century, department store sales work also became a woman's profession. Managers trained "shopgirls" to become "professional" saleswomen skilled in everything from etiquette to merchandise. At Marshall Field's a personnel department was described as "a conscientious mother" working to influence the workers in the niceties of behavior and saleswomanship. Managing the business was a large-scale enterprise; by 1904 the workforce at Marshall Field's could reach 10,000 in a store that served up to a quarter of a million customers a day.

The work culture of this particular occupational group developed to express three identities of the saleswoman: worker, woman, and consumer. These identities, reflected through a set of unwritten rules followed on the job, illustrated the complexities of women's lives where private and public identities intersected. The interactions among managers, saleswomen, and customers—which favored skills of social interactions and initiatives—allowed these retail workers a relatively autonomous working environment.

Many of these workers were called "women adrift"—the term for unmarried women living outside of traditional family life before the 1930s. They created a kind of "working girls" subculture in the city, challenging Victorian prescriptions for behavior, influencing popular culture, and ultimately changing social mores. This heterogeneous group of women—young and old, black and white, native-born and immigrant—lived in boardinghouses, both supervised and unsupervised, and later in apartments and furnished rooms. They patronized restaurants, dance halls, and theaters. This population of workers was sharply delineated by race; boarding homes were often segregated, as were working girls' clubs. For example, in Chicago the Eleanor Clubs served white women, while the Phyllis Wheatley Home had a black clientele.

For most married women, the ideal was a one-wage-earner family economy. For middle-class women—both black and white—voluntary participation in civic culture through organizations like church, women's clubs, and school organizations like the Parent-Teacher Association constituted a kind of unpaid work that contributed to the community environment. Additionally, the housekeeping and child care they provided constituted unpaid labor for their families, although many through the 1920s relied on domestic servants as they organized household work.

More often, however, a man's salary was insufficient to support his family. Women often supplemented family income by such "off the books" homework as midwifery, keeping boarders and lodgers, doing laundry, selling goods door-to-door, or by manufacturing garments or other goods at home. Hilda Polacheck, for example, describes how women and children labored around kitchen tables in crowded West Side tenements to make cloth flowers for women's hats during the late 1890s.

Children have long been part of the work history of the city. As part of the family economy, children labored on farms and in rural areas. In the city, in the era before schooling became a longer part of life, children often left school at the age of 14 or much earlier and hawked newspapers, labored in sweatshops, traveled as messengers, or peddled goods on the streets. Their earnings were sometimes critical for family sustenance.

With the advent of the twentieth century, industrial work culture began to change. Scientific management came to many big corporations, such as the Pullman Palace Car Company, where from 1913 to 1919 efficiency experts brought modern techniques of manufacturing to the shop floor. As the century progressed, new standards of technology and factory organization greatly reduced the need for physical labor in the plants. Women and black men began to work in factories previously barred to them, although the type of work available was often still segregated by race and gender.

The population of the workforce changed along with the city. As new suburbs developed after the streetcar lines were built in the late nineteenth century, many city workers lived farther away from downtown; by 1913 some 123,000 suburban passengers arrived and departed the city daily, riding on 746 trains. The construction of such highways as the Kennedy and the Eisenhower expressways further accelerated suburban growth and a commuter culture. Work itself migrated to the new suburbs, as some large corporations left Chicago's downtown and as a high-technology corridor developed in suburban Cook and DuPage Counties. Computer technologies and wireless communications developed in the 1980s and 1990s allowed some workers new freedom of place, as they were able to work from home or on the road as well as in an office. Piecework, once the province of the factory or home worker, became high-tech.

Further decline of industrial manufactures occurred in the later twentieth century, as professional, technical, and service industry occupations increased. The growth of multinational corporations meant that many more professional and white-collar workers now found that job security and work definitions could be determined by distant executives from abroad instead of by a local foreman or manager; health care workers saw the rise of HMOs (health maintenance organizations) in the last two decades of the century change the nature of even professional workers' autonomy and decision-making power.

Additionally, the population of workers transformed. New immigrants arrived from Puerto Rico, Cuba, Mexico, Central America, Asia, and Africa. Child labor by the 1940s was no longer as accepted as it was earlier because of new legal requirements for longer schooling as well as changing cultural conceptions of childhood. Even more significantly, during the second half of the twentieth century, the labor-force participation rates for women in every age group under 65 increased, especially as married women began to work at higher rates. As more married women and mothers of young children entered the workforce, debates about policies on child care, extended school hours, and such conditions of work as flex-time were raised across a variety of occupations.

Since Chicago's earliest years as a fur-trading outpost on the midwestern prairie, the city's work culture has reflected the tremendous diversity of its people and its economy. Strongly shaped by geography and characterized by a remarkably varied population, Chicago's story has been no less than the larger saga of American economic and social development—continually changing and reflecting complex interactions between people and their workplaces. If the industrial city witnessed by Carrie Meeber at the end of the nineteenth century has vanished, still new forms of work and work culture have developed that just as surely shape the lives of Chicagoans and reflect the continuing evolution of the city itself.

*Lynn Y. Weiner*

**Leisure.** Chicago's leisure pastimes have been a product of several factors. Early Chicago's entertainment reflected its rough-edged frontier character, but as the village grew into a walking city, leisure options reflected its growing urbanity. After the Great Fire of 1871, Chicago became an industrialized radial city with a huge, heavily foreign-origin population. These factors had a major impact on working hours; discretionary income; the formation of subcultures differentiated by class, gender, race, and ethnicity; and changing spatial relationships, all of which helped shape the leisure patterns of metropolitan Chicago.

### LEISURE IN PRE-INDUSTRIAL CHICAGO

Recreation in pre-urban Chicago reflected frontier life. The Fort Dearborn community was made up of soldiers, French Canadians, and Native Americans who enjoyed rural sports, gambling, and drinking. They hunted wolves and wild fowl and honed their skills with marksmanship contests. At the time the town was founded in 1833, denizens sleighed, skated, danced, went to horse races, and attended monthly concerts of popular music. Mark Beaubien's Sauganash Hotel was the most important recreation center in the early 1830s, with dancing, drinking, card playing, roulette, and storytelling.

Chicagoans in the newly established walking city worked six days a week, leaving just Sunday and holidays for rest, most notably New Year's Day, May Day, the Fourth of July, Thanksgiving, and Christmas. The city charter empowered the municipality to license, regulate, or prohibit entertainment to encourage wholesome recreation, promote safety and morality, and raise revenue. The government originally banned billiards, shuffleboard, baiting sports, card playing, and prostitution to discourage gambling and to restrain the flourishing male bachelor subculture that frequented saloons, poolrooms, and brothels, although the revised 1851 charter licensed bowling alleys and billiard parlors, while other so-called "vile" amusements went on illegally. Prostitution flourished. By 1856, 1,000 women worked in 110 brothels. Lotteries were legal, gambling games were commonplace, and betting at the racetracks was popular. A temperance crusade against Irish and German drinkers resulted in stiffer licensing and Sunday closing laws that culminated in the Lager Beer Riot.

American middle-class reformers in the 1840s initiated the rational recreation movement that sought to substitute moral amusements for the evil pleasures of the male bachelor subculture in order to uplift people, reduce crime, and improve public health. In 1858 evangelist Dwight L. Moody set up a YMCA branch in Chicago to develop muscular Christians. New sports were introduced, particularly baseball, a simple team sport that would supposedly build morality, character, and health. One year after the Civil War, there were 32 teams sponsored by fraternal organizations, occupational groups, the companies, and neighborhood clubs. Businessmen like Marshall Field, who had earlier opposed baseball as deleterious to hard work, began to see it as a means to promote teamwork, discipline, sobriety, and self-sacrifice, and sponsored company nines. By 1870 civic boosters raised $15,000 for a professional baseball team, the White Stockings (Cubs), to enhance the city's image nationally.

Touring professional singers first appeared in Chicago in 1839, the Christy Minstrel shows were popular in the mid-1850s, and the first opera season occurred in 1853. In 1837 Chicago's first theatrical performances, starring the renowned Joseph Jefferson, were widely opposed as demoralizing and out of fear that the Sauganash Hotel where they were held might burn down. A weak economy further discouraged theater troupes. In 1847 the $11,000 brick Rice Theater was constructed, with patrons segregated by price and race, but it was surpassed by the $85,000 McVickers (1857) and by Crosby's Opera House (1865), with its 3,000-seat auditorium; all three were located in the heart of the city. Popular plays included the works of Shakespeare and Richard Sheridan and productions based on local topics and anti-southern themes.

Other occasional entertainment was provided by touring monologuists and illusionists, exhibitors of panoramas of events like the burning of Moscow, and circuses like Barnum's "Grand Colossal Museum and Menagerie," which charged adults 30 cents admission. There were also dime museums, whose exhibitions of freaks, wax reproductions of infamous crimes, and objects of historical curiosity were popular with the lower classes.

Ethnic groups had a significant impact on entertainment. German, Irish, and Scandinavian immigrants brought their own amusements, which promoted a sense of peoplehood, especially in terms of language and culture. Germans brought to America an intense love of classical music. In 1850 Julius Dyhrenfurth conducted Chicago's first symphonic concert, and in 1852 the Männergesangverein, the city's first male chorus, was founded. An important German theater was established at midcentury that staged German classics reminding audiences of the Old World. New plays were written that taught them how to cope with the New World. The Svea Society (1857) sponsored a Scandinavian theater where performances were often followed by dances. Tickets cost 50 cents.

The Germans and the Irish brought athletic traditions. The Irish emphasized boxing, which was part of their own male bachelor subculture and enabled them to fit in with the prevailing bachelor subculture. However, the Germans made a more distinctive contribution with the mainly working-class turnverein, which emphasized calisthenics and gymnastics and supported workingmen's interests. *Turnhalles* were community centers, often the largest building in the neighborhood, with a large gym and auditorium. By the 1890s, there were 5,000 turners in 34 units, the most of any American city. They provided a model for the establishment of similar organizations by Bohemians, Poles, and Ukrainians.

## LEISURE IN THE INDUSTRIAL RADIAL CITY, 1870–1920

Chicago's leisure patterns in the industrial radial era were influenced by industrial capitalism and its social structure, a heterogeneous population divided into ethnic communities, gender, changing spatial relationships, and a liberal enforcement of Sunday blue laws. The upper class had the greatest wealth and control of time. They used leisure activities for fun and social prestige by participating in and financing expensive high-status pastimes. Parties, clubs, and sports dominated their social calendar. Charity balls introduced debutantes and honored individuals. Parties were ostentatious multicourse meals at elegant hotels or luxurious mansions. Institutions of high culture like the Art Institute, founded in 1879, were established to promote civilization, boost Chicago's reputation, and enhance personal recognition.

Chicago's elites gathered in the Chicago Club (1869), where men socialized and did business, and the Fortnightly (1873), where women considered social issues and pursued educational topics. Sports clubs like the Chicago Yacht Club, the Chicago Athletic Club, and the Chicago Women's Athletic Club were less prestigious but enabled its new rich members to gain status and participate in expensive sports. Fascination with English country life and the new sport of golf, which was enormously popular in Chicago, resulted in the establishment of suburban country clubs, beginning with the Chicago Golf Club (1893). These organizations were particularly attractive to elite women who enjoyed golf, tennis, and parties at the clubs. The elite was very involved in equestrian sports, and a few owned thoroughbreds and belonged to the prestigious jockey club that operated the elegant Washington Park Race Track, founded in 1884.

The middle class, which made up 31 percent of the workforce in 1900, generally believed in hard work, domesticity, sobriety, and piety, and wanted to employ free time for self-improvement and self-renewal.

Middle-class men worked a five-and-a-half-day week and had sufficient income to pursue leisure activities. The new middle class of professionals and bureaucrats turned to their pastimes to demonstrate their creativity, self-worth, and manliness at a time when WASP birthrates were declining and culture seemed to be feminized by influential mothers and school-teachers. Men formed organizations that sponsored hobbies like the Chicago Philatelic Society (1886), the Chicago Camera Club (1904), and the Chicago Coin Club (1905). They became active sportsmen, joining groups like the Chicago Bicycle Club (1879), and became ardent ball fans. They had the time and money to attend White Stocking games played in the midafternoon. The team did not have Sunday games until 1893, originally because of league rules and then because owner Albert G. Spalding incorrectly assumed that middle-class fans opposed public amusements on the Sabbath.

Middle-class women also had substantial leisure time, as they seldom worked outside the home and many had servants to perform household chores. They read fiction, belonged to clubs, and shopped in downtown stores. Specialty shops and department stores like Marshall Field's made shopping an enjoyable experience with tearooms, fine restaurants, and free delivery. Increasingly, younger women also participated in sports, encouraged by physicians and female physical educators who recommended exercise to improve health and beauty. Such "feminine" sports as golf, tennis, horseback riding, cycling, and ice skating proliferated. Even certain active sports like basketball became women's sports, modified by special rules designed to conform to current notions of women's physical abilities.

Low wages and long working hours limited turn-of-the-century working-class leisure opportunities. Less-skilled workers regularly worked 60 hours per week, while more-skilled workers typically worked 54 hours. Yet the limited remaining free time was important, providing opportunities for self-expression, status, and even politics, with the eight-hour day movement.

Reflecting the immigrant character of Chicago (80 percent of Chicago's population in 1890 was of foreign origin), blue-collar recreation was ethnic, neighborhood, and family-based and tied to religious customs. Roman Catholic immigrants observed a Continental Sunday Sabbath, with afternoons free for moderate pleasures that contested local blue laws, while Jews observed the Sabbath on Saturdays and considered Sunday a working day. Traditional holidays were still observed, like the Italian festivals that honored patron saints in a carnivalesque atmosphere, providing continuity with the Old World. Houses of worship also provided space for weddings, sports, and clubs, most notably the Catholic Youth Organization, founded in 1930.

Gender was important in socializing and family gatherings that focused on the dinner table. Women prepared traditional foods, and afterward men and women socialized separately. The primary daily entertainment for working-class women was visiting with friends and neighbors at home, on the stoop, or in the street. Second-generation daughters were very closely supervised, at least until they were full-time wage earners, when they gained a little more freedom. Their brothers, by comparison, had far more liberty to hang out in the street or participate in neighborhood recreation. They played sports at ethnic social and athletic clubs, pool halls, bowling alleys, boxing gymnasiums, or settlement houses, where reformers sought to use athletics to socialize inner-city youth into the values of the host society.

Adult men socialized away from crowded homes at fraternal clubs or saloons, often the only recreation site in their neighborhoods. By 1915 there was one saloon for every 335 residents in Chicago. German taverns were family institutions, well-lit beer gardens that provided wholesome entertainment. Most others, however, were "poor man's clubs," highly particularistic institutions where men drank, ate free lunches, played games, and gambled. Irish saloons, for instance, were modest, dimly lit "stand-up" taverns whose customers were encouraged to drink excessively.

Gambling and prostitution were rampant in Chicago. Illegal betting occurred at neighborhood saloons, resorts in the South Side vice district, and downtown gambling halls and poolrooms that served as off-track betting parlors. Men of all classes visited houses of prostitution, the most famous of which was the Everleigh House, where an evening could cost $50. The Vice Commission identified 5,000 prostitutes working in 1,020 resorts in 1910. When Mayor Carter Harrison II closed the vice district shortly thereafter, prostitution moved into residential neighborhoods.

In the 1870s, celebrated traveling companies boasting stars like Henry Irving, Ellen Terry, Lily Langtry, and Sarah Bernhardt played the McVicker's, the Academy of Music, and the Grand Opera House, where Chicagoans paid 25 to 50 cents to see them. Vaudeville made its first Chicago appearance in the 1880s. Immigrants, who often brought with them a theatrical tradition, supported ethnic theaters in spite of weak scripts, inexperienced actors, and a limited audience base. The theater promoted their culture and ethnic pride, gained them respect from the host society, and helped newcomers become acclimatized to America. German theater dominated with *Volkstheaters* and classical scripts. The English press reviewed an 1889 performance of Schiller glowingly, and a 1903 performance of Goethe's *Faust* drew 3,600 spectators to the Auditorium Theatre.

Musical entertainment flourished between 1871 and 1920. Theodore Thomas first brought his chamber music orchestra to Chicago in 1869 and established the Chicago Symphony Orchestra in 1891. Certain dates were set aside for workingmen's concerts with reduced admissions. Popular vocal music emphasized light opera, and group singing was common at parties. There was growing interest in opera, and in 1885 over 100,000 enthusiasts attended the Chicago Opera Festival. The 4,300-seat Auditorium

Theatre, completed by 1890, had its first opera season in 1891 and continued to have opera every year through 1932, when the Civic Opera Company
went out of business. Choral music was very popular with ethnic groups,
especially Germans, Scandinavians, and Poles. The three major German
singing societies in 1900 consisted of over 200 singing clubs, but interest
sharply fell off during World War I, when Chicagoans identified German
culture as unpatriotic.

Dancing boomed in the early 1900s among all social and ethnic groups.
In 1911 an average of 86,000 people nightly attended one of the 275 dance
halls in Chicago, more than went to any other recreation. Especially popular with the most fashionable middle-class couples were cabarets, a type
of nightclub influenced by the old beer gardens, public dance halls, and
revues. Cabarets combined hot music, new dances, risqué shows, drinking, and smoking.

Ethnic leaders worried that the second-generation would become de-
bauched or meet the wrong people at public dances, so they organized
dances at ethnic clubs and neighborhood halls. Their young men and
women preferred modern commercial ballrooms with big bands but
maintained a sense of ethnicity. They preferred accessible halls where
their group dominated or controlled part of the floor. Rather than bringing formal dates, dancers often came in groups or met at the dance. The
girls usually danced with neighborhood boys or other fellows from the
same ethnic group. Many single immigrant men frequented taxi dance
halls, where they paid 10 cents per tune to dance with women employed
by the owner. By the late 1920s, Chicago had 36 taxi dance halls, which,
along with cabarets, were often accused of demoralizing young people.

Silent movies were a hugely popular entertainment based on a new
technology. Chicago's first theaters in the early 1900s were five-cent nickelodeons, simple storefronts in working-class neighborhoods. By 1908
there were more than 340 in the city, and admission had reached 10 cents.
Moralists' concerns about conduct in the dark theaters and about subject
matter resulted in the establishment of a film censorship code by 1909.
The cinema boomed in the mid-1910s with the popularity of feature-
length movies exhibited in elegant downtown and suburban theaters and
accompanied by stage shows and large orchestras.

African American newcomers welcomed the leisure options available
in Chicago, which they in turn shaped in important ways. However, African Americans encountered prejudice at theaters, dance halls, YMCAs,
public parks, beaches, and other entertainment venues. They had to rely
heavily on their own institutions in the Black Belt to sponsor recreations
and on entrepreneurs who established theaters, nightclubs, and baseball
teams. The first notable African American nightspot was the 900-seat
Pekin Theater at 2700 South State Street, established by policy kingpin
Robert T. Motts to diversify his operations. It became a showcase for black
musical talent. A stock company was established to perform dramatics,

operettas, and comic operas. Admission was 15 or 25 cents. The leading nightspots in the early 1910s were located on "the Stroll," State Street from 26th to 39th Streets. By 1920 as many as 1,000 couples went to the Royal Gardens Café (459 East 31st Street) every Friday to dine, dance, and listen to jazz and blues music.

Black ballplayers were barred from playing in organized baseball. While African Americans did attend games played by the Cubs and White Sox, most attended Sunday games played by local black semiprofessional teams like the Leland Giants, who were a source of community pride. In 1911 that club was supplanted by Rube Foster's American Giants, which became a charter member of the Negro National League in 1920. The team played at Schorling Park (39th and Wentworth), adjacent to the ghetto, where adult tickets cost 25 cents.

Other popular commercial entertainments of the time included museums, circuses, county fairs, and amusement parks. Fairs often publicized agricultural and scientific achievements, most notably the Interstate Industrial Exposition, held downtown from 1873 until 1892. The World's Columbian Exposition in 1893 attracted an estimated paid attendance of 21.5 million, who preferred the Midway's attractions to displays of technology or art. Buffalo Bill Cody's Wild West Show that summer played before 6 million spectators on a 14-acre site just across from the main entrance to the fair.

Major amusement parks included White City, established in 1905 at 63rd and South Park Way and emphasizing low-class pleasures like carnivals, bowling alleys, and a roller rink and roller coaster. By 1914 it provided year-round entertainment, including two dance floors that accommodated 5,000 people. It was partially destroyed by a fire in 1927 and went into receivership six years later. Riverview (1904–67) was the North Side equivalent, with thrill rides, freak shows, dance halls, and a beer garden.

A much-needed park system was funded by the legislature in 1869. The new large parks were Jackson and Washington, south of the city; Douglas, Central (Garfield), and Humboldt on the West Side; and Lincoln Park, the largest, at the city's northern border. These suburban parks, at first accessible only to middle-class residents of nearby communities and train riders, originally emphasized receptive recreation. But parkgoers wanted active recreation, and in the 1880s baseball diamonds and tennis courts were constructed. Lakefront beaches were opened for public use after 1895. Park space was also set aside for the Garfield Park Conservatory and the Lincoln Park Zoo.

Unfortunately, the system lagged behind population growth. In 1899 one-third of the population lived more than a mile from any park. The suburban parks in the 1890s had become more accessible to better-paid workers once carfare on the expanding streetcar system dropped from 15 to 5 cents, yet this was still too expensive for the poor. Reformers organized a small-park movement in the 1890s to alleviate the inner city's need for play and breathing spaces, leading to the municipality funding neighborhood parks in 1904. The *Plan of Chicago* of 1909 stimulated future recreation by recommending the extension of Grant Park and the building of beaches, Municipal (Navy) Pier (1914), forest preserves (1914), and lakefront museums.

## LEISURE IN THE INTERWAR ERA, 1920–45

In the 1920s the average Chicagoan enjoyed a higher standard of living than ever before. By 1920 the blue-collar workweek had shortened by about 10 hours compared to 1914, plus wages had appreciated significantly, averaging about $1,000 a year for unskilled workers and $2,000 for skilled. During the Great Depression, incomes plummeted and workers experienced of unwanted free time. The national standard of a 40-hour workweek was established in 1938 by the Fair Labor Standards Act.

In the 1920s, leisure was heavily influenced by the greater freedom of young women, some of whom smoked, drank liquor, wore short dresses, danced the Charleston, and dated men with automobiles, which provided privacy for dating couples as well as greater access to suburban recreational opportunities. During this decade, ethnic peer groups mediated mass culture through sponsored dances, clubs, and sports. But by the 1930s, white industrial workers were generally Americanized and the ethnic factor was less prominent, although clubs, parades, and holidays were (and remain) significant.

There was a growing reliance on commercial entertainment by the 1920s. Blue-collar workers spent on average $22.56 a year on movies, more than the middle class and more than one-half of their amusement budget. Neighborhood theaters competed with downtown movie palaces with cheaper admission, films that reflected community tastes, and larger playhouses primed for a middle-class audience. In 1921 the city's largest cinema was the 3,000-seat Tivoli Theater (Cottage Grove and 63rd), which had a marble lobby and charged $1 admission. Sound was introduced in 1927, and within three years all the big theaters had it. Sound altered the ambience at neighborhood theaters, where audiences that in the silent era had been pretty loud quieted down to hear the actors. There was a movie seat for every nine Chicagoans during the Depression, when movies took in about one-third of all entertainment expenditures. Neighborhood prices for adults ranged from 15 to 25 cents, half the price of downtown theaters. Sound films hurt the once-flourishing legitimate stage, which barely survived the early Depression, mainly with Broadway shows.

Radio became ubiquitous during the 1920s. Eighty percent of programming presented musical shows and comedy sketches. Nonprofit ethnic, religious, and labor stations supplemented commercial stations. The Radio Act of 1927 promoted station consolidation but did not kill ethnic programming, which in the mid-1930s accounted for 5 percent of local broadcasts. Families bought Victrolas, often on credit, so they could play their favorite music at home. Sales of ethnic music swelled as Italians bought records of Caruso singing operas, Mexicans purchased recordings of Mexican music, and African Americans bought "race" records made by jazz and blues artists.

Nightlife flourished in the 1920s despite Prohibition and the demise of the workingmen's saloon. Illegal drinking became an exciting middle-class pastime at speakeasies. When Mayor William Dever closed many clubs in the mid-1920s, roadhouses in Cicero, Stickney, and Burnham that offered liquor, sex, and gambling replaced them. Exotic "black and tan" night-clubs in the South Side ghetto, like the Plantation Cafe, offered integrated audiences excellent music and the thrills of being naughty and dangerous by drinking illegal liquor, dancing to hot jazz, and rubbing shoulders with celebrities or gangsters. The center of the ghetto's nightlife shifted from the Stroll to 47th Street, where the first large commercial dance hall for African Americans, the Savoy, was opened in 1927, followed two years later by the 3,500-seat Regal Theater. These were a part of the "chitlin' circuit" of black theaters in the United States. Forty-Seventh Street was home to the big bands in the 1930s and 1940s and rhythm-and-blues music in the mid-1950s.

Chicagoans relied heavily on public resources for entertainment, particularly sites envisioned by the 1909 *Plan of Chicago*. The Field Museum moved in 1921 to Grant Park, and next door the $6.5 million Soldier Field was opened in 1924 and completed five years later along with the John G. Shedd Aquarium and, a year after that, the Adler Planetarium. Soldier Field was the site of the 1927 Dempsey-Tunney rematch, seen by 104,000 spectators, and the 1937 Austin-Leo high school football championship, attended by over 110,000. In 1933 the Museum of Science and Industry opened with popular presentations of scientific and industrial subjects. Museum attendance dropped off sharply during the Depression; Field Museum crowds dropped by one-third between 1933 and 1936, with 90 percent coming on free days. An exception was the Century of Progress Exhibition of 1933 and 1934, which drew 40 million people. In 1934 the Brookfield Zoo opened, and 22 different park districts were merged into the 5,416-acre Chicago Park District, comprising 84 parks and 78 fieldhouses, along with golf courses and swimming pools.

The sports boom of the 1920s fell off during the Depression. The Cubs were a popular attraction, winning four pennants from 1927 to 1938; the Bears began playing at Wrigley Field in 1921; and the Blackhawks began playing in 1926 at the Coliseum, moving to the Chicago Stadium three years later. Boxing and horse racing were legalized in 1926, and several tracks soon opened, including Arlington Park in 1927. Participatory sport also expanded. There were 55 metropolitan golf courses, including elite clubs whose initiation fees cost from $3,000 to $5,000. Bowling alleys and billiards halls boomed among the working class until the Depression, when one-third of the former and one-half of the latter closed.

## LEISURE IN METROPOLITAN CHICAGO SINCE 1945

The leisure activities of postwar Chicago were influenced by the same variables as in earlier periods, particularly a rising standard of living, along with technological innovations, fashions and fads, age, race, gender, and homesite. Two-day weekends were the norm along with increased vacation time. By the 1980s, Chicagoans were spending about 6 percent of their income on leisure, double the 1901 proportion. Class became less important, although differences in taste remained significant. The upper middle classes who lived in fashionable neighborhoods like Lincoln Park and Hyde Park and the wealthier suburbs were the main clients at theaters, concerts, golf courses, and college football games. Lower-class Chicagoans devoted relatively more attention to such sports as baseball, boxing, and horse racing, and to TV, whose rise hurt movies, radio, and reading. Race played a big factor, with differences in musical tastes and nightlife. Racial discrimination hindered opportunities, reflected by uneven park development in different neighborhoods. The feminist movement that emerged in the 1960s encouraged women to work, secure higher-paying jobs, become sexually liberated, and participate in sports, a sphere from which they had been largely absent since the early 1900s.

Chicago enjoyed a rich nightlife, which flourished in the 1950s on Rush Street at nightclubs like Mister Kelly's and at South Side blues halls, which declined with the coming of rock 'n' roll. In the 1970s, most of the remaining old clubs died in the wake of disco, urban decay, and the expense of booking name entertainers. Blues revived in the 1990s with new clubs on the African American South Side and especially with trendy North Side locales like Kingston Mines and Blue Chicago. Jazz had a big following with places like the Green Mill in Uptown and the London House (360 North Michigan Avenue), a showcase for Ramsey Lewis, Oscar Peterson, and Stan Getz. Chicagoans had a choice of many comedy clubs, most notably the Second City. Eating out became an important recreation in the 1960s, with ethnic restaurants for the budget conscious as well as fine dining. Since 1980, Chicagoans have combined their love of music and cuisine in the annual Taste of Chicago lakefront festival.

High culture prospered in this era. In 1953 the Lyric Opera was organized, restoring a tradition of outstanding opera and, with the Chicago Symphony, making the city an internationally renowned center of classical music. Dance companies and especially theater proliferated. By 1998 Chicago was home to about 50 theater companies, from community and experimental theaters and suburban dinner playhouses to Loop theaters that charged Broadway prices for Broadway-style productions.

Interest in participatory and spectator sports has grown substantially.

Especially since the 1970s, Chicagoans have taken advantage of public beaches, bicycle paths, volleyball courts, and soccer fields to improve fitness and to socialize. From the 1950s through the 1970s, the Blackhawks regularly sold out the Chicago Stadium, and attendance at racetracks, Bears games, and major league baseball rose, the latter abetted by extensive TV coverage and the ambience of Wrigley Field. Interest in basketball was mainly at the collegiate level until the Bulls became popular in the 1970s and achieved fanatic support once they became title contenders in the late 1980s. The cost of attending sport events, however, rose dramatically in the 1990s, making them unaffordable for many Chicagoans.

CONCLUSION

Chicago's leisure patterns have been historically influenced by the city's growth and maturation. Leisure opportunities were a product of economic development, which, on the one hand, shaped the social structure, income levels, and available free time and surplus income, and, on the other, a product of urbanization, which reshaped urban space and was accompanied by a booming population. Leisure patterns were further affected by entrepreneurs who commercialized recreation, by politicians who promoted public parks and festivals, and by immigrants and southern African Americans, who brought with them their own cultural traditions and values. At the same time, leisure activities became an increasingly larger segment of Chicago's economy, driven not only for Chicagoans but also by the domestic and international tourists who came to the city. As a result, sites of leisure became places of work for an increasing number of the region's residents.                                    *Steven A. Riess*

**Schooling for Work.** The relationship between schools and the preparation of the next generation of workers became a major issue in American education at the beginning of the twentieth century as the nation was transformed by new kinds of industry. In Chicago, a deep and bitter conflict over the relationship of schooling to the workplace revealed the conflicting class interests that were threatening to rend the city's social fabric. At the same time, the conflict demonstrated the issues that deeply divided two groups of reformers, both of whom thought of themselves as "progressives." One group, followers of Jane Addams and her associates at Hull House, saw themselves as humanitarians who wanted to use schooling as a tool for helping immigrants and the poor adapt to the new harsh industrial system while softening its rigors. Another group of progressives, largely composed of businessmen and concerned with social efficiency, wanted to modernize the schools to prepare workers for the new factories that were beginning to dominate the city's economy. Addams and her followers sought to maintain older, community values within a new system of production, while the social-efficiency progressives strove to prepare workers to fit into the rapidly developing, impersonal system of mass production without any effort to alter it. Both sets of reformers agreed that some form of vocational education was needed to increase the "holding power" of the schools—to make them more attractive to children who were likely to drop out because they lacked either academic interests or abilities.

The need for schools to adjust to the new industrial age was not at issue. Few people thought that the schools should merely replicate the traditional curriculum. As John Dewey pointed out in a series of lectures at the University of Chicago at the end of the nineteenth century, the rapid changes that industrialization brought with it required a radically different education. The new industrial society had disrupted the natural transition from childhood into the world of work. Children no longer learned about work through informally observing their parents, and, in Dewey's

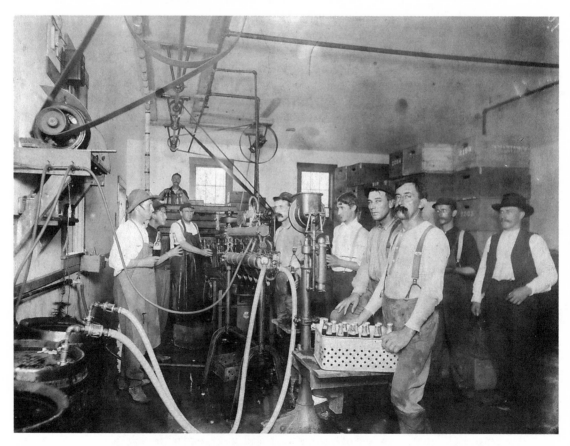

Dr. John E. Siebel's brewing academy, ca. 1902–4. In 1868 Siebel opened his Chemical Laboratory devoted to brewing research. He began offering brewing instruction in the 1880s at what is still known as the Siebel Institute of Technology. When this photograph was taken, the company was offering regular courses on brewing in both English and German. Courtesy of the Chicago History Museum (ICHi-17537).

words, the school had become the legatee institution and needed to take on an expanded role, providing an education that went well beyond the traditional three R's. For Dewey, this would not include preparing children for any specific occupation but rather for the ability to respond to new needs and new tasks. The study of occupations would be a central part of the curriculum in Dewey's laboratory school—important not as vocational training but as a way of helping children to understand the new industrial world around them.

At the same time, members of Chicago's powerful business community also recognized that schools could play a crucial role in preparing the next generation of workers. They argued that schools should offer a vocational curriculum to future factory and office workers while, at the same time, inculcating the habits necessary for work. The schools also needed to undertake the essential task of Americanizing the large number of immigrants who were increasingly providing the city's labor needs. For schools to socialize the children of immigrants and the poor, they needed to develop a curriculum that would keep them in school longer. A "practical" course of study that offered a path to employment was the answer.

At first, Chicago's businessmen agreed with educational reformers like Dewey and welcomed the idea of manual training in schools. Giving children a basic knowledge of how to use tools was important. But by the early years of the twentieth century, as the demand for more highly trained labor became ever more imperative, they began to argue that schools should go beyond manual training and teach actual trades. Impressed by the growing commercial competition from European nations and especially Germany, the Chicago Commercial Club (Chicago's most prestigious business club) commissioned former superintendent of schools Edwin Cooley to visit Europe to study their systems of vocational education. In the wake of his report of 1911, businessmen increasingly supported a differentiated system of vocational education, with high schools preparing the "noncommissioned officers" of an industrial army and vocational schools furnishing the well-trained soldiers that modern industry required. The new vocational education, as differentiated from manual training, would "consist of the actual trade processes" and produce "articles of commercial value" under "conditions of the occupation outside the school." Such vocational programs would be gender-specific, preparing children for careers in a highly differentiated job market.

In 1912 the Chicago Public Schools adopted the new philosophy and introduced a differentiated curriculum, encouraging sixth graders to choose between an academic and an industrial track. The latter would lead to a two-year high school vocational program. The Board of Education also established different kinds of high schools—technical schools with both two-year and four-year programs that prepared students for skilled laboring positions or technical colleges. In these schools, even the "academic" subjects took on a workplace orientation. Instead of history, for example, they offered "industrial history." Overtly vocational education also infiltrated general high schools, and by 1913, 16 of the city's 21 high schools had become composite high schools offering vocational courses in addition to academic work. The board also offered "continuation" courses in which children already in the workforce could improve their work skills and enhance their ability to find more highly skilled jobs. At the same time, again at the behest of businessmen, the board instituted a program of commercial courses—such as bookkeeping, typing, and business English—in high schools. The commercial program eventually included more specialized courses in selling and advertising. By 1914, one-third of Chicago's high school students were enrolled in day and evening commercial courses.

Although the radical shift in the program of the schools did not arouse immediate opposition, it led to a great debate and a political crisis in 1913. Supported by members of Chicago's business elites, former superintendent Edwin Cooley recommended that Illinois establish a state system of vocational education. Cooley's proposal would have established full-time vocational schools and, for youngsters already in the workforce, continuation schools, in a school system that would be fully separated from the regular public schools. The new program would be governed by independent boards, made up of men with practical experience in industry and commerce, and funded by a special tax. Promoters of the Cooley plan had an additional agenda: a major goal of the new venture would be to shape the ideology of the working class as a way of fighting radicalism, promoting the morality of hard work, and instilling such industrial virtues as punctuality.

The Cooley bill, introduced several times between 1913 and 1917, was strenuously opposed by Superintendent Ella Flagg Young (a disciple of Dewey), the Chicago Teachers Federation, and the Chicago Federation of Labor. First and foremost, opponents protested that the Cooley plan was undemocratic; it would lead to permanent class divisions by stifling social mobility. Opponents shared the opinion of the Illinois State Federation of Labor, which charged that the specialization it would encourage would prevent children from "acquiring the skills and training necessary to the continued development, or even proper maintenance of various trades and callings." Moreover, labor leaders saw the plan as an ill-disguised attempt to turn the public schools into institutions that would supply industry with a well-trained and docile (non-union) workforce. It would weaken trade unions by taking away their role in admitting new workers to apprenticeship programs. Unionists saw the new vocational schools as little more than potential "scab factories." Professional educators bristled at Cooley's assumption that vocational education, to be efficient, had to be "kept out of the hands of the old fashioned school master."

The critics were correct in pointing out that the new vocational education plan constituted a radical reorientation of public education. Horace Mann and the common school reformers of the pre–Civil War period had seen education as the great equalizing institution, bringing rich and poor, immigrants and native-born, together in the same classroom, where they would be offered equal opportunities for advancement. Dewey, too, saw the classroom as the basic unit for building a democratic community. For him, manual training was a gateway to understanding the modern industrial world, not preparation for a specific trade. Contrary to the educational reformers' vision, advocates of the new vocationalism would divide children at an early age; those who were thought destined for factory or clerical work would go to different schools from those who would be offered academic courses. The children of the poor and immigrants would be relegated to the dead-end vocational track.

Businessmen countered the argument that the new program was undemocratic by contending that offering children the chance to learn a trade fostered economic mobility and reduced potential class conflict. Indeed, preparing children for a specific trade was now a requirement for citizenship education. They also argued that in a separate school system men with practical experience (as opposed to educational credentials) could be hired to teach.

Although the business-minded reformers lost the battle over the Cooley bill, they were able to attain many of their objectives with the federal Smith-Hughes Act (1917). This provided funds for vocational education and, like the ill-fated Cooley bill, allowed states to establish separate vocational education boards. Under the auspices of Smith-Hughes, businessmen attained their primary goal—a program of training students for specific skills, directed by people of practical experience.

The divisions revealed by the Cooley bill resurfaced in 1923, when a new, efficiency-minded superintendent, William McAndrew, proposed a system that introduced the first junior high schools. When teacher representatives asked him if the junior high schools would offer terminal programs for children not headed for high school, McAndrew was evasive, and it became clear that these new schools could easily become vehicles for tracking children of the laboring classes into vocational programs while the children of the higher classes were being prepared for high school (this, in effect, was what they believed had happened in the schools of Rochester, New York). McAndrew, who believed that teachers should follow orders rather than give advice, went ahead with his plans and tried to avoid further consultations with them. Instead, it became clear that he was eager to consult the businessmen who had supported the Cooley plan. The board adopted the new program, despite the opposition of many of those who had united to oppose the Cooley plan. Although the worst fears of the opponents were not realized by the junior high schools, the controversy was significant because it revealed once more the way in which the issue of schooling for work could uncover the tensions between business and labor in Chicago.

The Great Depression had a devastating impact on all aspects of Chicago's public schools, including its vocational programs. No major city in the United States was in worse financial condition when the crisis began. The impact of the national crisis was exacerbated by the high degree of corruption and racketeering that had infected the administration of Chicago's schools as well as persistent revenue battles between Chicago politicians and representatives of downstate Illinois. In 1933, faced with a disastrous financial crisis, the Board of Education increased teachers' workloads, slashed their pay, and cut many programs, including most vocational courses. In 1936, however, while the schools were still suffering under the draconian cuts imposed by a highly politicized school board, a new attempt to promote vocational education revived the bitter battles that had been fought over the Cooley bill. William H. Johnson, who became superintendent after the death of the popular William J. Bogan, was a man who was distinguished largely for his personal ambition and his subservience to an economy-minded board. Faced with the continuing financial crisis, he saw that a new emphasis on vocationalism could be a money-saving proposition. First he cut back the number of "major" academic subjects that high school students could take. He then boldly proposed allowing only 20 percent of Chicago public school students to enter academic programs and sending the others into vocational courses. Since the salaries of vocational teachers were heavily subsidized by the state and federal governments under the Smith-Hughes Act, replacing teachers of academic subjects with vocational teachers would relieve some of the financial pressure on the Board of Education.

Johnson's proposal was even more restrictive than the Cooley plan. It not only threatened the democratic ideal of equal access to academic opportunities; it also directly attacked teacher tenure. Like his predecessors Cooley and McAndrew, Johnson was a moralist who sought to use vocational programs as a way of shaping the working classes. After a great storm of popular protest, which included charges that the plan to use the educational system to sort students into occupational niches was a "fascist" device, Johnson claimed that his original proposal had been "misunderstood" and he withdrew the plan. The proposal indicated once more, however, that there were still those who saw public education as a way of sorting children into appropriate vocational categories, and, despite the failure of the Cooley and Johnson plans, this was, in fact, how vocational education often functioned in Chicago.

The increased use of vocational education as a sorting device was facilitated by the fact that during the Depression, the Chicago labor movement, which had been a leading force in opposing the creation of a dual-track educational system, had abandoned its concern for such broad educational issues. Organized labor was in large measure co-opted by Chicago's powerful Democratic political machine. The Chicago Federation of Labor now concentrated on getting its share of political rewards by emphasizing such bread-and-butter issues as the salaries of school custodians and maintaining labor representation on the school board. It no longer sup-ported the teachers' demand for increased school funds or their campaign for a more democratic system of education.

The use of vocational education to sort children became central to a program for "pre-vocational" education in the upper elementary grades with the establishment of vocational centers for children who were 14 or older and still enrolled in the sixth grade. Beginning in 1913, these chil-dren were offered special vocational classes—one set for boys and a dif-ferent set of courses deemed appropriate for girls. While the intent of the program was expressed in the language of John Dewey as appealing to the interests and needs of the child, in their actual operation, pre–high school vocational schools became disproportionately the schools for children seen as lacking the intellectual abilities for the regular academic program. In addition, children who were troublesome for the schools—chronic truants and children who misbehaved—were increasingly shunted into these programs. As a result, of course, the reputation of the vocational programs suffered. Good students were discouraged by their parents from attending these schools, and they became virtually reform schools. By 1941 (a typical year), the average IQ of children attending the Chicago Public Schools' vocational centers was 79.

After World War II, it became clear that Chicago's vocational program (as in so many other cities) was highly segregated by race. The best pro-grams with the best connections to the job market were in white neigh-borhoods. As late as the 1960s, Washburne Trade School, which accepted only students who had been granted apprenticeships by the notoriously racist unions of the building trades, had an enrollment that was 99 per-cent white. When, in the 1980s, pressured by a federal consent decree, Washburne finally opened its doors to minorities, a number of the skilled unions drastically cut their programs or withdrew completely from Wash-burne. African American youth were served by Dunbar Vocational Center (which was not promoted to high school level until 1952) and other voca-tional schools that had inferior equipment and instruction. Dunbar's cur-riculum followed the highly segregated Chicago labor market by offering only programs leading to the less desirable, lower-paid trades.

Deindustrialization dealt an even more serious blow to meaningful schooling for work in Chicago's African American neighborhoods. As the steel mills and meatpacking industry left the South Side, new industries did not replace them, and by the 1970s it was clear that there were few jobs for which even the most successful vocational programs could provide an entry. As unemployment in the vast ghettoes of Chicago climbed, school-ing for work became ever less relevant to the young people growing up in a community that was increasingly isolated from the rest of the metro-politan area.

Reformers who valued social efficiency eventually won the battles over vocational education in the Chicago Public Schools that had begun early

in the twentieth century. While the best of the vocational programs succeeded in preparing workers for the industrial and commercial needs of
the city, for many children, especially the poor, vocational education provided a relatively inexpensive way to meet the requirements of compulsory attendance laws.

After World War II, as the world became more and more reliant on
technology, much of the focus on schooling for work shifted to community and junior colleges and their vocational centers, administered by the
City Colleges of Chicago. Malcolm X College—founded in 1911 as Crane Junior College and located on the West Side near Cook County and St. Luke's
Presbyterian Hospitals—offered a large number of vocational programs
in the health sciences, in addition to courses in computer science and
the child care professions. Truman College, located in the Uptown neighborhood, advertised itself as the most "richly diverse" of any community college in Illinois. Building on an institution begun in 1956, Truman
has served Native Americans and immigrants from Latin America, Asia,
and Poland. It offered, among other vocational programs, nursing, pre-
engineering, chemical-industry technology, and child development. The
City Colleges also established a number of job skills centers. The one established by Olive-Harvey College, located in the African American community in the Southeast Side's Pullman neighborhood, trained workers
for entry-level jobs such as counter person, bank teller, nurse's assistant,
and security guard.

The public school system was by no means the only source for vocational education in Chicago. From the earliest days, Americans have gone
to school to prepare for specific careers by attending private, entrepreneurial schools, and in the dynamic economy of early twentieth-century
Chicago, these schools proliferated. By 1898 a Chicago directory listed
schools as varied as the Chicago School of Assaying, the Chicago Nau-
tical School, and at least four shorthand schools. Schools listed in later
directories include several millinery schools, the Chicago School of Bookkeeping, as well as the Wahl-Henius Institute of Fermentology and the
Zymotechnic Institute and Brewing School. While these schools differed
in quality, their persistence indicates a continuing demand by Chicagoans for schooling directed toward preparation for specific careers.

Perhaps the best known of Chicago's entrepreneurial schools was
founded in 1931 by Herman A. DeVry, a pioneer in developing motion-
picture projectors. With a loan from a friend, DeVry purchased a defunct
school with 25 students and 3 employees. Its purpose was to train students
for technical work in electronics, motion pictures, radio, and, eventually,
television. The DeVry Institute has trained thousands of people and now
awards college degrees as well as certificates. Purchased by Bell and Howell in 1967 and by the Keller-Taylor Corporation in 1987, the school (renamed DeVry University in 2002) rapidly expanded beyond its Chicago
base and established campuses in several other states as well as Canada.

Schooling for work in Chicago also involved a great number of post-graduate institutions. Foremost among these were programs in teacher education, initially offered as part of the public school program. The metropolitan area also offered graduate training in law, medicine and nursing, and business. Except for teacher and nursing education, these programs were quite different from most schooling for work in that they attracted mostly middle-class participants. And unlike pre-collegiate vocational education, they provided genuine opportunities for social mobility.

The story of schooling for work in Chicago is, of course, one aspect of a national problem. Vocational education has never been simply a way of preparing youngsters for work; it has also been called upon to serve children who are unmotivated or lack academic abilities in a system that requires them to be in school. The great pressures to deal with the second problem have meant that the first motive often has gotten lost. Another limit on schooling for work within the public school system has been finding the flexibility to deal with a rapidly changing job market. The Smith-Hughes Act compounded this by its emphasis on agricultural work and other trades that rapidly became irrelevant to the needs of employers. Absent the requirement of serving as a means of keeping unmotivated and frequently troublesome children in school, however, the Chicago City Colleges and the private, entrepreneurial schools were able to concentrate on preparing people for new jobs—and this they have done with notable success.                                                        *Arthur Zilversmit*

**Building Trades and Workers.** The modern construction industry and organizations of journeymen and contractors originated in the commercial, industrial, and urban transformations of the early nineteenth century. As large-scale merchant builders took over from the master artisans in the various special crafts required to erect a building, they relegated many to the position of labor subcontractors. These changes were well under way by midcentury, when Chicago experienced its greatest growth. With the advent of factory-made materials, many workers, especially those in the carpentry trade—the largest of the construction crafts—became little more than installers of prefabricated products, often paid by the piece. Under the "piecework" system, speculators bypassed masters and their broadly trained journeymen, allowing easily trained, lower-paid "greenhorns" who were often recent immigrants to threaten the integrity of the crafts.

By the 1870s, unions of skilled building tradesmen had taken root in almost all city crafts. Though they were at first little more than makeshift bodies relying on the enthusiasm of the moment, these early unions embodied a basic labor demand: that all journeymen receive a standard minimum wage. Payment of a standard wage would remove contractors' incentive to employ lower-paid pieceworkers and cement class solidarity among journeymen.

No building trades unions won stable contracts until the great eight-hour day movement surrounding the Haymarket Tragedy of 1886. By that time, many unions employed paid walking delegates (now called business agents), required initiation fees and dues, and offered burial, sick, and other benefits.

In 1887, after the bricklayers and carpenters had won the eight-hour day, the contractors formed strong employers' associations and mounted an open shop counterattack to destroy the power of the walking delegates to enforce union standards at the widely scattered building sites. After a short but bitter battle, Judge Murray F. Tuley arbitrated a precedent-setting trade agreement in which the bricklayers and mason contractors agreed to regularized collective bargaining for the first time. By 1890 the bricklayers and other trades had joined together in the first viable Building Trades Council. Under its leadership, journeymen from all organized trades could strike a building under construction in unison—the "sympathy strike"—leaving the contractor without a workforce. They were often aided by a hands-off approach from Chicago police.

In 1890–91, during construction of the World's Columbian Exposition, carpenters, painters, plumbers, steam fitters, ironworkers, and others in the building trades used their favorable bargaining position and newfound strike methods to win agreements similar to those of the bricklayers.

During the 1890s, the contractors' associations fell into disarray. Under the two-fisted leadership of Martin "Skinny" Madden, the unions parlayed their ability to mount sympathy strikes into union control over the industry. The depression from 1893 to 1897, however, forced the unions to accept agreements to work only for association contractors, thus artificially strengthening their employers. Soon the agreements were expanded into three-cornered arrangements in which unions and the associations of contractors and material manufacturers gained monopolies within their respective markets.

In 1900–1901, the contractors locked out the unions, claiming that these exclusive agreements raised material prices to exorbitant levels and that sympathy strikes created intolerable unpredictability in the market for contractors. Under intense pressure from Chicago business, Democratic mayor Carter Harrison II used the police to protect strikebreakers, and the Great Lockout of 1900–1901 ended in union defeat. Though most labor gains from the late nineteenth century remained, the exclusive agreements were abolished and the unions accepted "the eight cardinal principles" in which they acknowledged the supremacy of the contractors in the industry.

The first 11 years of the twentieth century were years of peace in the construction industry and accomplishments such as the establishment of jointly run apprenticeship programs. But gradually the rise of new construction methods led to union rivalry over control of the new work. By 1913 fully 75 percent of all work stoppages resulted from jurisdictional disputes between unions. In 1915 general contractors led by the Builders' Association were able to initiate a lockout and force the unions to accept a "uniform form of agreement" as the basis of all labor agreements and a Joint Conference Board, which still functions to resolve disputes.

The last great episode of industrial conflict in the Chicago construction industry occurred in the early 1920s. The city's largest employers and builders combined to impose the open shop on contractors and unions alike. Using many unions' unwillingness to abide by Judge Kenesaw Mountain Landis's 1921 arbitration award, outside employers established a Citizens Committee that labeled as "outlaw" any unions that rejected the award and that bound contractors not to bargain with them.

No struggle in the history of the construction industry in the city was fought with more bitterness and violence. The carpenters and painters split from the Building Trades Council and led successful opposition to the Landis award. A major reason for their victory was the massive 1920s building boom in which speculative builders operating in the outlying

Construction workers, Chicago Daily News building, at Madison, Washington, Canal, and the Chicago River, 1928. © Chicago History Museum. Photo: *Chicago Daily News*. Courtesy of the Chicago History Museum (DN-0085101).

residential areas employed the journeymen outlawed by the Citizens Committee. A troubling by-product of the conflict was the use by many building trades unions of professional thugs to intimidate non-union workers and contractors through bombings and beatings. By the late 1920s, Al Capone and his gangsters had turned the tables on union members by taking control of many of the smaller building trades unions.

By the end of the decade, most contractors returned to union recognition. An extended era of cooperation and non-adversarial bargaining relations began, which was reinforced by two developments. The first was the pro-collective-bargaining legislation of the New Deal in the 1930s and 1940s. Second, after World War II, a 30-year building boom, whose yearly average of residential units built approached that of the 1920s, permitted contractors to pass union wages onto the public. In the early 1980s, the construction industry was hit with a major recession, followed by substantial expansion from the late 1980s to the end of the century.

Most worrisome to labor has been the decline, beginning in the 1970s, of general contractors employing all the basic trades (carpenters, painters, ironworkers, laborers, cement masons, bricklayers) to build a building. General contractors have been replaced by project managers whose entire business is brokering bids to subcontractors. As a result, there is more specialization in the basic trades, more cutthroat bidding, a resurgence of piecework, and more white-collar middlemen in the industry. Though union contractors still control a majority of residential, industrial, and commercial work in the metropolitan area, the short duration of most contracts makes it difficult for business agents to police collective-bargaining agreements and has allowed small immigrant-owned non-union firms a niche in the basic trades.

Since the 1970s, the building trades have opened their doors, reluctantly at first, to African American, Latino, and even a trickle of women workers. By the 1980s, apprenticeship programs had been integrated and many unions had outreach programs. The carpenters district council claimed at the end of the century that approximately 20 to 25 percent of its membership was black or Latino. Union leadership, however, remained largely white and male.                                                *Richard Schneirov*

**Clerical Workers.** Chicago's explosive growth and economic development during the late nineteenth century multiplied the demand for office workers. Clerks of many sorts, bookkeepers, typists, stenographers, and receptionists found positions in expanding bureaucracies in the service and business sectors. Many of these new workers were women. The male clerk—the young, aspiring company man who was a common feature of small nineteenth-century offices—was gradually replaced by the young female, who was expected, or allowed, to remain at her job only until she got married.

This transition derived from a combination of Chicago's characteristics. As a terminus for immigrants and migrants, Chicago attracted young women looking for work. For women who had the right qualifications—which at that time meant literate, young, and white—positions in office work did seem appealing given the limited opportunities available. The newly invented typewriter was paired with stenography to create the stenographer-typist just as a large number of Chicago's private business colleges began teaching these skills. Chicago was home to the nation's first skyscrapers, urban workspaces that women believed were modern, safe, and clean. Despite the concerns of female reformers like Jane Addams, who warned of the dangers faced by solitary working girls, many philanthropic and benevolent organizations like the YWCA, the Eleanor Association, and the Woman's City Club created service institutions, residential clubs, and rest areas in the Loop to accommodate the needs of this new feature of the downtown business district: the working girl. By the 1920s, courses in all the skills necessary for the office became regular and popular in a variety of curricula offered by the Chicago Board of Education in the city's public school system.

In this era of transition, Chicago's female clerical workers experienced a wide range of working conditions. Public stenographers had their own offices in large office blocks or hotels and contracted for work from the various office suites. A stenographer-typist might work for a single boss much like a private secretary today, or she might work in a large office with many other stenographer-typists in a more factory-like setting. A clerk or bookkeeper could also find herself in a wide range of possible jobs depending on size and type of firm or the type of office machinery she could operate. Even though women could expect only very limited job mobility, young white women flocked to these positions, especially stenography-typing, since it offered the best wages, hours, and working conditions for women without professional training.

Chicago witnessed some of the earliest efforts to organize clerical workers. Organizing Chicago's stenographer-typists was on the agenda of Chicago's branch of the Women's Trade Union League from the start. In 1905 the Stenographers' and Typewriters' Union No. 11691 appeared in a directory of unions affiliated with the Chicago Federation of Labor. Until 1912, when the union ceased to exist, it provided a wide range of services to its several hundred members.

By 1920 the majority of Chicago's clerical workers were U.S.-born white females of foreign or mixed parentage and under the age of 24. Companies employing these clerical workers were challenged to create separate occupational hierarchies and in some cases even separate workspaces for men and women. Some Chicago companies, particularly railroads, attempted to bar women from employment because employers did not want to have to promote women within their ranks. The new larger office staff prompted many companies to adapt scientific management techniques originally designed for factories. Nevertheless, for immigrant daughters, clerical work might have been seen as a way to escape the danger and degradation of the factory and the slum or ghetto. They saw clerical work, as well as other white-collar occupations such as clerking in department stores and teaching, as a way to "Americanize" themselves.

Since 1920 the clerical labor force has become more demographically diverse, even though individual firms or industries, until quite recently, have discriminated on the basis of age, marital status, race, and ethnicity. Because of the civil rights movements and legislation of the 1950s and 1960s, minority women made some inroads into a wider variety of office positions. As a result, women of all backgrounds have used clerical jobs for self-support and to provide vital income for their families. Recently, computer technology has accelerated the trend toward factory-like office work. Early efforts at unionizing clerical workers in the 1930s were revived in the 1960s and 1970s, as the concentration of large numbers of women in typing pools or word-processing centers along with the recent women's movement created favorable conditions for this activity.

The importance of clerical workers in Chicagoland's twenty-first-century economy was underscored in the 2010 census. By that year, over 16 percent of all workers in the Chicago-Naperville-Joliet area worked in office and administrative support jobs.                    *Lisa Michelle Fine*

**Domestic Work and Workers.** The explosive economic growth of the latter half of the nineteenth century transformed Chicago into the nation's leading interior metropolis. Men and women of the burgeoning urban middle class sought to display their prosperity through the hiring of domestic servants to perform daily cooking, cleaning, and child care chores. By 1870 one in five Chicago households employed domestic workers, who accounted for 60 percent of the city's wage-earning women. Over the next half century, domestic service represented the leading occupation of women in Chicago and the nation.

Domestic servants usually lived with the employing family, performing a multitude of household tasks (such as laundry, ironing, cooking, cleaning, and serving) in exchange for a modest wage plus room and board. Domestic workers were usually young, single women from working-class families whose terms of service lasted until marriage. While comparable or superior in pay to other jobs open to poor, uneducated females, domestic work attracted few native-born women because of the long hours, low status, lack of freedom, and close supervision. Consequently, domestic servants often came from the ranks of the most desperate members of the community, either those too poor to pay for housing or those excluded from other vocations. In late nineteenth-century Chicago, domestic work was increasingly performed by Irish, German, Scandinavian, and Polish women.

By the turn of the twentieth century, domestic work had changed little in either substance or status. When a Chicago newswoman went undercover as a live-in servant in 1901, she reported toiling 15 hours daily and performing every household chore except laundry, which was sent out. She made $2.75 per week plus room and board. While her wage was a $1.50 less than the average, similar conditions compelled some domestic workers to form the Working Women's Association of America (WWAA) in the same year. Aided by reformers such as Jane Addams, the group pushed employers to raise wages, lower hours, allow home visitors, and agree to an established grievance procedure. But the personalized, decentralized nature of domestic work made organizing difficult, and the WWAA disbanded after enrolling only 300 of the city's 35,000 domestic servants. Later efforts at unionizing domestic workers also proved unsuccessful.

In the wake of World War I, changes in the national economy and labor market precipitated a transformation in the structure of domestic work and those who performed it. New opportunities for white women in the expanding clerical and sales sectors, restrictions on European immigration, and the great migration of African Americans to urban cities in the North significantly altered the labor market for domestic work. Already in 1900, African American women, only 4 percent of the wage-earning female population in the city, represented 30 percent of domestic workers, and their numbers grew over the next 40 years.

Racially excluded from most occupations, black women soon dominated the domestic service sector in Chicago. Despite limited options, black domestic workers still experienced an improvement in wages compared to similar positions in the South, where it took three weeks to earn the same amount as in one week in Chicago in the 1910s. In contrast to earlier domestic servants, black women were often married with children and hence preferred day work to a live-in situation. By 1920 more domestic workers were living at home than boarding with their employer. By reducing the hours that domestic workers were available for personal service, day work fostered the introduction of electric labor-saving appliances into middle-class homes, further transforming the nature of household work.

While a step up economically from the South, Chicago nonetheless presented newly arrived African American domestic workers with difficult conditions. As late as the 1930s, domestic servants complained of employers offering day work to the lowest bidder at the notorious "slave pens" at the corner of Halsted and 12th Streets. While single white women often utilized domestic work as a temporary stop on a track of upward mobility, most African American women were forced to make careers as domestic day workers or laundresses.

In the post–World War II period, domestic work receded from prominence as a privilege in middle-class families and an occupational option for working-class women. Commercial facilities outside the home increasingly performed much of the household labor, as in the case of child care centers, nursing homes, and fast-food restaurants. Even the enduring practice of day work was contracted out to cleaning agencies, who might send a worker once or twice a week to a specific home. Still, while the structure of domestic work had changed, the low pay and status associated with it remained the same. In her 1999 investigations, journalist Barbara Ehrenreich found that corporate cleaning companies paid between $5 to $6 per hour on average. And in Chicago, as elsewhere in the United States, cleaning, cooking, and child care for pay continued to be performed by poor, immigrant, and nonwhite women.        *Daniel A. Graff*

**Health Care Workers.** Efforts to organize health care workers in the United States, including the 100,000 workers employed in Chicago's 70 hospitals in the 1990s, have been hampered by long-standing divisions between doctors, nurses, and other hospital staff, as well as a series of U.S. Supreme Court rulings dividing hospitals into eight different bargaining units. Union organizers have also cited the increasing corporatization of American hospitals as an obstacle to organizing efforts.

Hospital organizing efforts surged nationwide in the 1970s, but results varied from region to region. For example, in the late 1990s, two-thirds of New York City's hospital workers were members of unions or professional organizations, while only 20 percent of their colleagues in Chicago were organized. Half of these were members of Local 73 of the Service Employees International Union (SEIU), accounting for 40 percent of the local's 25,000 members. Other workers—including occupational therapists, technical employees, office clerks, and skilled and semi-skilled maintenance workers—have been organized by the American Federation of State, County and Municipal Employees (AFSCME), the International Brotherhood of Electrical Workers, and the International Brotherhood of Teamsters. The most original feature of local health worker unionization in Chicago was a joint effort by Local 73 of the SEIU and Teamster Local 743, which resulted in the founding of the Hospital Employees Labor Program (HELP) in 1966. In its first five years, HELP concentrated on organizing low-paid service and maintenance workers, most of whom were African American. Later non-service and clerical workers were recruited.

Many nurses in the United States have traditionally preferred professional organizations over traditional union structures. Local nurses have been organized by the Illinois Nurses Association (INA), the local affiliate of the American Nurses Association (founded in 1901), and unions affiliated with the AFL-CIO like the SEIU and AFSCME; as well as teachers' unions such as the National Educational Association, the American Federation of Teachers, and the Chicago Teachers Federation. By the spring of 1999, 7,000 of Illinois's approximately 130,000 nurses—70 percent of whom worked in the Chicago metropolitan area—were members of the INA.

Most doctors and their national organization, the American Medical Association, have traditionally opposed unionization. By 1999 only 30,000 of the nation's 680,000 doctors had joined unions. In the 1970s, friction between doctors and insurance companies stimulated interest in collective bargaining. In 1973, 15 Chicago-area doctors founded the Illinois Physicians Association (IPA), chartered by the AFL-CIO. However, organizers cited difficulties in mobilizing doctors to attend meetings, and the IPA dissolved by 1979. Interest in collective bargaining by doctors, anxious to negotiate with health maintenance organizations over reimbursement amounts for medical procedures and drug coverage policies, rose once again in the 1990s. The Illinois State Medical Society voted to form a union in April 1999. By the first decade of the twenty-first century, organizing efforts among physicians grew, and in 2009 the AMA voted to support a national organization for doctors.

More recently, SEIU has been particularly active in organizing Chicago-area doctors, nurses, and other health care workers. In 2008 three of its health care–related unions voted to merge to create SEIU Healthcare Illinois Indiana, an organization of 85,000 members in the two states who worked in the home care, child care, and health care industries.

*Keith Andrew Mann*

**Housekeeping.** From all over the world, Chicago's many in-migrants have brought with them an immense variety in ways of keeping house. For every new household, there has been someone, usually a woman, who has negotiated the choices between old and new ways of eating, of housecleaning, and of purchasing household necessities. Having learned one set of skills—and housewifery was a highly skilled undertaking until well into the twentieth century—she had to learn another set that might be very different in Chicago. Thus, the pace of a family's assimilation to life in the city has owed in substantial part to mundane daily decisions by a housewife. To whose standards of cleanliness would she adhere? Where would she find the ingredients for her family's holiday dinner? Hundreds of thousands of Chicago women have pondered such issues over the generations and in this way have played a major role in shaping the character both of their families' lives and of the city's neighborhoods.

Some of those neighborhoods have constituted a particularly difficult challenge for a housewife—none more so than the famed Back of the Yards. Said two sociologists in 1911 of the area adjacent to the stockyards: "No other neighborhood in this, or perhaps in any other city, is dominated by a single industry of so offensive a character." The people who lived near the yards confronted filthy conditions: stench, decaying carcasses, pollution of many sorts. A plethora of packinghouses discharged their wastes into Bubbly Creek, a fork from the South Branch of the Chicago River that traversed Back of the Yards.

Upton Sinclair described the problems vividly in *The Jungle*, published in 1906. His fictional Lithuanian immigrants, arriving in Back of the Yards, see housing worse than any they had heretofore encountered. Their landlady's home is "unthinkably filthy," with a "fetid odor" permeating the area. The thick swarms of flies, the terrible overcrowding—there is even a flock of chickens in the house—are all described in nauseating detail. The sociological report of 1911 stated that researchers had found one residence in the neighborhood in which a single toilet [EDW: chances are good that the report called it a water closet. Is it necessary to change? If not, I would leave it as is.] was provided for 47 persons.

With so many thousands coming to Chicago in the late nineteenth century, frequently to confront appalling housing conditions, it is not surprising that in 1889 this city gave birth to the American settlement house movement with Jane Addams's founding of Hull House. Addams, her Chicago colleagues, and those they inspired in other parts of the country, usually middle-class women, took up residence in homes in impoverished immigrant neighborhoods and tried to teach those in the vicinity about standards of cleanliness, among other things. Scholars still debate the extent to which the settlement house workers were busybodies—as opposed to being genuinely helpful—but what is incontrovertible is that thousands of working-class Chicago housewives were struggling and needed relief. Even if they were fortunate enough to live some place other than Back of the Yards, they might well be doing piecework at home, thus creating another set of challenges for maintaining a clean and pleasant domestic environment. In her memoir *Twenty Years at Hull-House*, Jane Addams left no doubt that she found the homes in the Hull House neighborhood as disturbing as Sinclair had found those in Back of the Yards: they were located on streets that were "inexpressibly dirty," suffered from "unenforced sanitary legislation," and were adjacent to "stables foul beyond description."

Dirt, diseases such as tuberculosis that correlate with unclean conditions, and demoralization—all these afflicted many homes at the same time that Chicago played host to the World's Columbian Exposition of 1893—the White City. The great fair, with alabaster buildings sited to create a pristine and orderly environment, stood in ironic contrast to the disorder and grime that plagued so many households in nearby areas. Most Americans cities contained stark contrasts between tenements and opulent households, but with the fair, Chicago flaunted its capacity to create an island of ideal beauty in a sea of squalor.

Such unhappy contrasts are part of the story of keeping house in Chicago, but they are not the whole story. Chicago came into being just as the first of many significant changes was taking place in household technology: the transition from open-hearth cookery to the stove. A dazzling array of further changes in the nineteenth century—the sewing machine and improved refrigeration, for example—were in place by the time of the world's fair and were featured in the fair's catalog. Moreover, displays at the White City's Electricity Building suggested possibilities for the future such as electric stoves, electrified pans, washing machines, and ironing machines.

In the nineteenth century, working-class housewives struggled to maintain homes under highly adverse conditions while their middle-class sisters fretted about the "servant problem"—which became more intense as working-class white women began to enjoy employment options better paid and less stigmatized than domestic service. Middle-class women could look to technology for relief from their burdens. Working-class housewives would have to wait longer for relief from this quarter, because it was not until the 1920s that such consumer goods as household electrical appliances began to be widely disseminated throughout the society (owing both to lower prices and to the increasing use of installment buying).

Scholars who have studied domestic work have found that the women who waited upon other women and their families bore the heaviest housekeeping burden of all. At first Chicago servants were drawn primarily from the ranks of immigrants, and then as increasing numbers of African Americans began to move north, black women began to be the largest component of the domestic service workforce. Servants' days were long, they were poorly paid, and they could not count on being treated with dignity. Conflicts must have been common between middle-class housewives with their standards for how things should be done, and servants fresh off the boat or the farm with no notion of the niceties that might be expected in their new employment.

The trends of the twentieth century and the first decades of the twenty-first century can be summarized briefly. Ever fewer households employed servants, and those that did used them fewer days per week than in the past. Shrinking numbers of servants plus smaller families meant that average household size continued the decline it had begun in the early nineteenth century. Since more women than ever were gainfully employed outside the home, they looked to technology and new products—and probably to their partners—to help with the demands of housekeeping. Hence homes became both more mechanized and more commodified. All forms of household work became deskilled as busy people increasingly used convenience foods or fast food for meals, while newer fabrics and clothing styles simplified laundry and virtually eliminated ironing. Some things remained constant: home was the place where children are reared, and a home was still something people dreamed of owning, their most valuable possession if they were already owners, and the place where newcomers mediated between the old and new ways.        *Glenna Matthews*

**Ironworkers and Steelworkers.** As early as 1847, Chicago had six iron foundries. Steelmaking in Chicago began in 1865. As steel production grew nationwide during the late nineteenth century, steel production in Chicago grew too. For decades, immigrants came to Chicago because of the high wages available in the mills. Steel companies specifically recruited many of them.

The first wave of immigrants to the mills—mostly Scots, Irish, and Germans—came in the 1870s and 1880s. The second wave was Slavic immigrants, mostly Poles and Serbs, who first arrived in the 1890s and continued to arrive until the beginning of World War I. The third wave, African Americans from the South and Mexicans, began during World War I. The Europeans tended to settle in largely homogeneous ethnic neighborhoods near the mills along the Calumet River on the South Side, although the dominant group in particular neighborhoods has changed over time. These areas have prospered and declined along with the firms that ran the mills. African American employment in the Chicago steel industry increased sharply after World War II, but hostility from white residents forced these workers to settle on the western and northern fringes of this area.

Around the turn of the century, the largest mills in Chicago were the South Works, built by the North Chicago Rolling Mill Company in 1880, and the Wisconsin Steel Works, built by International Harvester in 1902. When U.S. Steel formed in 1901, it took control of the South Works. Unable to expand its steelmaking operations in Chicago proper, U.S. Steel began work on building the city of Gary, Indiana, in 1906 so that it could continue to take advantage of the Chicago region's proximity to railroad and barge routes. Other mills that took advantage of these same geographic conditions operated in Gary, Joliet, even Milwaukee.

Chicago steelworkers played an important role in the industry's two most important strikes of the early twentieth century. The National Committee for Organizing Iron and Steel Workers, chaired by Chicago Federation of Labor president John Fitzpatrick, began an organizing drive in Chicago during World War I. This push culminated in an unsuccessful nationwide steel strike in 1919. The industry's use of African Americans as strikebreakers during this dispute, particularly in Chicago and Gary, enflamed racial tensions among steelworkers for decades afterward. In the late 1930s, the Steel Workers Organizing Committee of the Congress of Industrial Organizations (CIO) began the first industry-wide union organization since 1892. As part of this effort, employees at Republic Steel in Chicago participated in the unsuccessful Little Steel Strike of 1937. Police attempts to keep demonstrators at bay resulted in the Memorial Day Massacre.

Employees at the South Works were the first beneficiaries of U.S. Steel's attempt to improve safety in its mills, with a plan adopted throughout the corporation in 1906 as part of its welfare capitalism efforts. Workers at Wisconsin Steel were among the first in the industry to belong to an employee representation plan (or ERP), which critics derisively referred to as a company union. Management used the ERP as a way to give workers limited collective-bargaining rights without recognizing an outside union. Given the opportunity to join the CIO in the late 1930s and early 1940s, Wisconsin Steel employees repeatedly voted instead to maintain

Open-hearth blast furnace, U.S. Steel Company's South Works, ca. 1952. Courtesy of the Chicago History Museum (ICHi-37058).

the ERP. Even though the National Labor Relations Board forced Wisconsin Steel to sever its ties to the ERP, it lived on for decades, having evolved into an independent organization.

As late as the 1970s, there were 130,000 members of the United Steelworkers of America (AFL-CIO) in the Chicago-Gary area. In recent decades, ironworkers and steelworkers in Chicago have suffered a fate common to iron- and steelworkers across the nation. Wisconsin Steel went out of business in 1980. U.S. Steel closed the South Works in 1992. Plant shutdowns like these have devastated the economy of the entire South Side. They hurt not only steelworkers and their families but steel industry suppliers and other area businesses that depended upon the wages of steelworkers for their livelihood. Most of the iron and steel plants operating in Chicago at the turn of the century were small producers of specialty steel, not the basic steel producers of old that helped build the railroads, buildings, and automobiles of a bygone era. By the end of the first decade in the twenty-first century, large-scale steel production in the Chicago area was located exclusively in the northwest Indiana suburbs.

*Jonathan Rees*

**Railroad Workers.** Chicagoans began working on the railroad in 1848, when building began on the Galena & Chicago Union Railroad. By the 1870s, railroads employed some 2,700 workers, about 9 percent of Chicago's labor force. Over 15,000 Chicagoans worked for railroads in 1900 and almost 30,000 in 1930.

Railroad workers ranged from unskilled freight handlers to locomotive engineers to those who built and repaired the rolling stock. In the early days of Chicago railroading, most engineers and conductors were native-born men. European immigrants built and repaired track, with the Irish predominating early, followed by Italians and, by the 1910s, Romanians and Mexicans. African Americans worked as Pullman porters and in other often segregated unskilled jobs; starting in the twentieth century, women were hired for some clerical and telegraphy jobs, as car cleaners, and as on-train maids. Employment offices on Madison, Canal, and Halsted Streets recruited track laborers for jobs throughout the region.

Railroad workers put in long hours; a 1907 law restricted train crews to 16 hours work out of every 24. Well into the twentieth century, work was unsteady and unsafe. One railroad worker in every 357 nationally died on the job in 1889. Though some track workers preferred their outdoor work to regimented factories, turnover was high. Railroads responded to this and to labor unrest by adopting bureaucratic forms of labor discipline and record-keeping and employee welfare programs well before other economic sectors.

Railroad workers dominated many Chicago and suburban communities. Pullman is the best-known example; others include Aurora, Blue Island, Fuller Park, and Brighton Park. Chicago's Burnside region, home to car building and repair shops and rail yards of several roads, was an industrial complex of 5,000 workers by 1910. Home-ownership was common there. On the other hand, Cook and DuPage County track workers, most of them Mexicans, lived in at least 26 company labor camps in 1928. Conditions in these camps, often consisting of boxcars, ranged from wretched to barely adequate. Despite this, residents frequently developed a strong community life, raised gardens, and held religious services.

As early as 1856, Chicago's railroad master mechanics established unions to represent their interests. In 1863 engineers went on strike for the first time against the Galena railroad. By the 1880s, operating workers, in Chicago as elsewhere, had achieved a high degree of union organization and maintained relatively good pay and some job security. Chicagoans played a major role in the 1888 strike of the Brotherhood of Locomotive Engineers against the Burlington lines.

Chicago, home to several rail unions, was also at the center of other important rail strikes. Chicago rail workers and residents in the communities in which they lived participated in the Great Railroad Strike of 1877, while in 1886 thousands of unorganized railroad freight handlers went on strike for an eight-hour day, as did track workers and switchmen. In the Pullman Strike of 1894, neighborhood residents in city and suburbs aided members of the American Railway Union (ARU) in their unsuccessful boycott of Pullman cars. Many joined in violence against railcars, strikebreakers, and police in such diverse places as Blue Island, Hammond, and Back of the Yards. ARU president Eugene Debs was jailed in Woodstock. Chicago rail workers of all skill levels participated in the expansion of unionism during and after World War I, when the railroads were under federal control, a buildup that included the all-black Railwaymen's International Industrial Benevolent Association. In 1922 Chicago unionists were at the center of a national strike of some 400,000 repair shop workers, and in 1925 the Brotherhood of Sleeping Car Porters launched what would be a successful effort to organize the Pullman Company's African American workforce of porters and maids.

During the 1930s, railroad workers took advantage of new federal legislation to join unions, many of which admitted African Americans for the first time. Newly unionized railroad workers enjoyed better pay, and railroad work grew increasingly safe. The U.S. Railroad Retirement Board provided railroad workers with retirement benefits even before Social Security. Most unskilled employees and repair shop workers had unionized by 1941. Federal law mandated a 40-hour work week for non-operating workers in 1949.

Railroad employment peaked in the 1920s, declined during the Great Depression, rose during World War II, and then dropped precipitously as railroads succumbed to competition from cars, buses, trucks, and airplanes. Meanwhile, railroad companies adopted diesel locomotives, track-laying machinery, and other innovations that cut their labor forces, often after bitter disputes with rail unions. Corporate reorganization and deregulation contributed to this job loss. Between 1920 and 1995, national rail employment dropped by 89 percent, although the proportion of white-collar and skilled jobs grew. Union membership remained high and pay scales were good, but the shock of downsizing damaged morale at some railroads. Civil rights gains occurred slowly, just as overall rail employment was dropping. Pullman porters, for example, finally won their civil rights suit against the Pullman Company after the company had stopped operations. Chicago's railroad workers' neighborhood communities broke up, as central-city depots, yards, and shops were closed or reorganized and workers dispersed to homes distant from workplaces. By 2010 the census identified only 1,550 individuals working in the yards, on trains, or in railroad-related positions.                          *Christopher Thale*

**Retail Workers.** Chicago's explosive development in the wake of the Civil War propelled the city to preeminence as the leading manufacturing, transportation, and retail metropolis in the nation's interior, rivaled only by New York for much of the twentieth century. Retail giants Mar-

A Palace of Art and Industry, 1873. This engraving reflects the gendered landscape of the nineteenth-century retail environment. The clerks are all men; the shoppers, almost all women. From *Land Owner*, March 1873. Courtesy of the Newberry Library.

shall Field & Co., Sears, Roebuck & Co., and Montgomery Ward all called Chicago home. These and other Chicago firms played leading roles in the creation of American consumer society; they also became leading employers of thousands of men and women in the city. By 1904, for example, Marshall Field's State Street store employed nearly 10,000 individuals.

Throughout Chicago's history, the variety of retail establishments demanded a diverse workforce, from individuals working alongside owners in specialty and neighborhood shops to the thousands toiling for large department stores with complex occupational hierarchies. Early retail clerks were primarily men who operated a small store from open to close and often slept on the counter to accommodate customers throughout the night. Beginning with the Civil War, retailers began employing women, a trend that continued with the emergence of large department and discount stores. From the early twentieth century, women have occupied a majority of retail positions, though men have continued to dominate supervisory jobs. Until the 1960s, when the federal government began enforcing equal opportunity laws, most employers practiced overt racial discrimination, refusing to hire persons of color for positions requiring contact with the public.

Retail workers faced poor working conditions and pay, especially before the passage of the Fair Labor Standards Act in 1938. Sales clerks served unusually long hours, toiling from 6 a.m. to 9 p.m. daily, plus a half-day on Sundays. Responsible for opening and closing the store, keeping shelves stocked, sweeping the sales floor, and devoting personal attention to each customer, retail workers toiled under sweatshop-like conditions. In an 1899 study, Annie MacLean of the University of Chicago went undercover to experience the life of a retail worker in a Chicago department store. MacLean reported that saleswomen were forced to stand the entire day, eat their lunches in cramped rooms, and survive on below-subsistence wages, prompting many to turn to prostitution. MacLean concluded that only unionization would solve the problems of overwork and low pay.

Male retail workers in Chicago had attempted to organize as early as 1841, when downtown retail store and brokerage clerks banded together to form an Early Closing Association, forcing employers to adopt an 8 p.m. closing time. By the early 1890s, the Retail Clerks International Protective Association (RCIPA) boasted a local in Chicago, though organizers made more headway in grocery stores than in dry-goods establishments and department stores. Although the union officially demanded equal pay for women, the RCIPA failed to promote the organization of saleswomen, who made up a large chunk of the department store workforce by the 1920s.

Despite the low pay, poor work conditions, and indifference of organized labor, working-class white women flocked to retail occupations by the turn of the twentieth century. Sales jobs offered white-collar respectability and pay commensurate with clerical positions, while granting a degree of autonomy not available outside of nursing and teaching. If the first half of the twentieth century represented the heyday of the American department store, it also witnessed the rise of the saleswoman as a legitimate profession in the eyes of the industry. Though still underpaid in comparison to men, saleswomen achieved a status according to which their skills in selling products and cultivating customer loyalty were recognized as central to their firms' success.

The increasing size of department stores and their workforces led to greater attempts at unionization in the 1930s, led by the newly formed United Retail, Wholesale, and Department Store Employees of America. Though unsuccessful at penetrating the huge emporiums on State Street, the union did organize the workers of mail-order king Montgomery Ward in 1940, precipitating the most notorious labor conflict of World War II. When Ward's chairman Sewell Avery refused to renew the union's contract in 1944, President Roosevelt's National War Labor Board authorized the U.S. Army to seize the company to guarantee the flow of consumer goods. The union then won a recertification election in a landslide. In the long run, however, retail unions have been unable to overcome employer resistance to organize sales clerks on a significant scale in Chicago.

In the post–World War II era, the changing nature of the retail industry reshaped the character of retail work. While in 1940 large, urban department stores featured active salespeople, by the end of the century major chains preferred smaller, suburban stores relying on television advertising and self-service displays. Although retail workers now benefited from federal minimum-wage and maximum-hour legislation, employers increasingly turned to a part-time, seasonal workforce to lower labor costs. While State Street and Michigan Avenue's "Magnificent Mile" still beckoned urban shoppers and tourists to Chicago, the city's retail workforce toiled primarily for companies whose headquarters were located elsewhere.

*Daniel A. Graff*

**Unemployment.** Great turbulence, marked by periods of economic dislocation and grassroots movements for social insurance programs, has characterized Chicago's unemployment history. In 1819 Illinois enacted poor laws that provided for overseers of the poor. However, recurrent panics brought unemployment and poverty so severe as to require municipal attention. In the depression of 1857, 20,000 Chicago workers and their dependents faced starvation, and relief was inadequate. On Christmas Day in the depression year of 1873, police dispersed crowds of unemployed begging for food at the Relief and Aid Society.

Four years later, during the Great Railroad Strike, unemployed workers joined strikers to battle police and U.S. troops. The American Federation of Labor Convention in Chicago in 1893 resolved that the government had a duty to provide jobs when economic conditions, like then, made them difficult to find. In the spring of 1894, Jacob Coxey, an Ohio businessman and reformer, organized the jobless into "Coxey's Army" and led a march on Washington, D.C. Declaring Coxey a "demagogue," the *Chicago*

*Tribune* (April 24, 1894) editorialized that "action must be taken at once to suppress" his movement. That call was followed by two decades of intermittent violence and confrontation between Chicago police and the unemployed. During these same years, however, police stations provided shelter to hundreds of thousands of homeless people, many of them unemployed workers.

In 1899 Illinois became the fifth state to establish a State Employment Service. Compulsory unemployment insurance became an objective of reformers. A committee at the University of Chicago sponsored by the American Association for Labor Legislation called for a state or national unemployment insurance program in 1912.

Labor's agitation for the abolition of unemployment was the strongest in Illinois, where the Illinois Federation of Labor and the powerful Chicago Federation of Labor, under the progressive leadership of John Fitzpatrick, formed the core for a local, state, and national labor party movement. In the spring of 1919, Chicago leaders ran state and local tickets on a reform manifesto called "Labor's Fourteen Points," which demanded full pay for the jobless and comprehensive social insurance.

Unions also attempted to set up their own system of unemployment insurance between 1919 and 1928, as the Amalgamated Clothing Workers of America and the International Ladies' Garment Workers' Union adopted progressive unemployment insurance plans. The depression of 1920–22 terminated these "Chicago Plan" developments, but the unions managed to pay reduced unemployment insurance through the mid-1930s.

The stock market crash of 1929 brought new turmoil and organization. Almost half a million in Illinois were unemployed by the end of 1930. By mid-1932, the Communist-led Chicago Workers Committee on Unemployment had organized 25,000 jobless in 60 locals to fight for jobs and adequate relief. They marched on relief stations in the city and in industrial suburbs like Melrose Park. Early in 1933, the unemployed planned a statewide hunger march to Springfield. More than 1,000 relief demonstrators from Chicago and Rockford formed a cavalcade of automobiles and trucks ultimately repulsed by state police.

Despite this burgeoning right-to-work movement, there was no nationwide organization of the unemployed until April 1936, when the Workers Alliance of America was formed, merging with the Unemployed Council, the Unemployed League, and some independent organizations. The alliance's protest activities served to support increased appropriations for the New Deal's work programs, such as the Works Progress Administration (WPA), created by executive order of the president on May 6, 1935.

The Wagner-Peyser Act (1933) established the federal-state system of public employment services and the Veterans' Employment Service. The Social Security Act of 1935 mandated unemployment insurance in the United States. Illinois was the last state to adopt the unemployment insurance law in 1937.

Nationally unemployment dropped to an all-time recorded low of less

Unemployed men's club distributing cabbage to members and their families, October 1932. Courtesy of the Chicago History Museum (ICHi-20837).

than 2 percent during World War II. Postwar national economic stabilization policies prevented massive unemployment, but joblessness remained a major problem, especially as the burden of unemployment shifted. Relatively fewer workers were out of work, but those who were unemployed were for longer spells, and young people and minorities were increasingly affected. Their plight was cited as a major factor behind rioting during the 1960s; federally funded jobs programs mitigated the problem but failed to solve it. Limited education, inadequate transportation, and persistent hiring discrimination have brought substantial long-term unemployment to many minority communities, causing high poverty rates, housing abandonment, and other problems. Economic downturns in the 1970s and 1980s exacerbated these problems, which, coupled with technological innovation and foreign competition, devastated some long-established Chicago industries and the industries dependent on them. The unemployment rate in Gary in 1990, for instance, was 17 percent. In September 2002, 261,600 workers were unemployed in metropolitan Chicago, or 6.3 percent of the civilian workforce.

In the first decade of the twenty-first century, unemployment reflected the broader economy, with a substantial rise visible beginning in 2008.

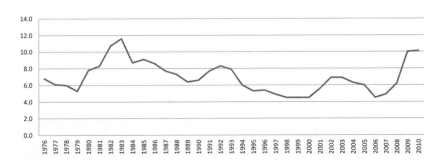

**Average Annual Unemployment, 1976-2010**
**Chicago-Naperville-Joliet Metropolitan Division**
Source: Yearly Averages, Illinois Department of Employment Security; Counties: Cook, DeKalb, DuPage, Grundy, Kane, Kendall, McHenry, Will

Recession, corporate reorganizations, the collapse of the housing market, as well as a longer-term rise in worker productivity contributed to one in ten workers being jobless by 2009. Official jobless rates hovered around 10 percent through 2011.                            *Alan Harris Stein*

**Unionization**. Chicago's historic reputation as a labor town is somewhat misleading. Workers have built some of the strongest organizations in the country, but unions have often struggled against well-organized, militant employers, and racial and ethnic diversity has shaped the movement's character as much as the dynamics of social class. How do we explain the broader patterns of labor organization in terms of the city's distinctive characteristics? What factors contributed to the rise, changing character, and decline of the movement, and what are its prospects at the dawning of a new century?

With the shifting composition of its working-class population and the diversity of its metropolitan economy, Chicago has presented both enormous challenges and special advantages for labor organizers. Heavy immigration from the mid-nineteenth century through the early 1920s, and then again in the postwar era and especially after the Immigration Act of 1965, required labor to carry its message in diverse languages to people from vastly different cultures. Likewise, the Great Migration of black southerners, immigration from Mexico and other Latin American nations, Puerto Rican migration, and the influx of East and South Asian immigrants in the late twentieth century have forced organizers to confront race issues for most of the movement's history. Yet racial and ethnic minorities have often played key roles in building and transforming the movement.

The city's largest employers in the late nineteenth and first half of the twentieth century were building construction and maintenance companies, railroads, and a range of manufacturing concerns characterized by increasing concentration in a few large firms—slaughtering and meat-packing, metalworking, garment manufacturing, iron and steel production, lumber and woodworking, electrical manufacturing, and a variety of food-processing factories. Chicago also built a large printing and publishing industry; and as a corporate, legal, and medical center, the city claimed an increasingly large population of white-collar and technical workers beginning in the late nineteenth century. Such variety led to the conventional wisdom that "anyone can make a living in Chicago," but it also required that any successful labor movement embrace a diverse range of workers. Immigrants and workers of color often have been more difficult to organize, not because of any intrinsic qualities, but because they have tended to be among the least skilled and the poorest paid—and as such particularly vulnerable in periods of economic crisis and employers' offensives.

One of the Chicago movement's distinctions, then, was that well into the mid-twentieth century it generated considerable power amid this social, cultural, and occupational complexity. Another was the movement's division between conservative and often corrupt elements, concentrated disproportionately in the Building Trades Council, and progressive, often radical elements. In the late nineteenth century, the radicals were represented above all by the German-speaking Marxists; in the early twentieth century, by the mainstream labor progressives around Chicago Federation of Labor (CFL) president John Fitzpatrick; and in the Great Depression and war years, by the activists involved in the creation of the new Congress of Industrial Organizations (CIO) unions. Such progressives provided the movement with an aggressive, innovative leadership that helps to explain organized labor's relative success in Chicago. They were particularly important in expanding the movement to those otherwise left behind—women, the unskilled, and racial minorities.

As elsewhere, skilled workers led the move to permanent organization. In the 1850s and 1860s, printers, shipwrights and caulkers, iron molders, machinists and blacksmiths, and others established craft unions that were often linked to some of the earliest national organizations. By the late 1860s, Chicago workers supported more than 20 unions aimed at higher wages and shorter working hours; a lively newspaper, the *Workingman's Advocate*; numerous producers' cooperatives; and a network of Eight Hour Leagues, which organized in municipal, state, and congressional elections, winning both city and state eight-hour laws. As with later legislative successes, however, the laws worked only where unions were strong enough to enforce them, a rare scenario during the 1873–77 depression.

Until the 1880s, the city's unskilled—Irish, Bohemian, and Polish lumber shovers, brickyard workers, coal heavers, and construction and track laborers—found their voice only sporadically, often in violent strikes and riots, as in the 1877 Great Railroad Strike. The "Great Upheaval" of the mid-1880s brought a dramatic expansion of unionism among virtually all occupations, including craftsmen. The big breakthrough, however, came in the organization of the Irish and other unskilled workers in the ranks of the Knights of Labor, by far the largest and most important late nineteenth-century labor reform movement. As craftsmen poured into the Knights' trade assemblies and laborers into its mixed assemblies, the movement grew from 2,300 in 1882 to more than 40,000 by 1886. Led by Elizabeth Rodgers, the Knights also organized thousands of women. Working together, the radical Central Labor Union's German and Bohemian socialists and anarcho-syndicalists, the immigrant and native-born craftsmen in the mainstream Trades and Labor Assembly, and the Knights created perhaps the strongest and most radical movement in the United States. They sponsored labor newspapers in various languages, a vibrant cooperative movement, and a United Labor Party, which seemed poised to win control of the city government. More than 40,000 workers joined a general strike for the eight-hour day in May 1886, and throughout the world Chicago became a great symbol of labor solidarity.

A number of factors explain the destruction of this movement. First, a series of crushing defeats, particularly among the unskilled in the stockyards and elsewhere, reversed the movement's expansion. Second, internal conflicts, especially within the Knights of Labor, eviscerated the movement's vitality. Finally, the radical socialist and anarchist wing, especially strong in Chicago and a key to the organization of unskilled immigrants, was decimated in the political repression following the events at Haymarket Square in 1886. By 1887 many of the radicals were in prison, blacklisted, or dead, while the Knights had shrunk to 17,000 members.

A new movement emerged in the 1890s. While the Knights lost 75 percent of their membership between 1886 and 1887 and the revolutionary organizations were badly disrupted, many of the craft unions survived. The new American Railway Union emerged to organize both skilled and unskilled workers in the early 1890s. Greater federation through the formation of the Building Trades Council (1890) and the Chicago Federation of Labor (CFL; 1896) brought more planning and coordination and an era of effective sympathy strikes. Thus, the movement emerged from the historic defeat of the Pullman Boycott in 1894 and the depression of the 1890s with renewed strength. At the turn of the century, organization spread once again to the less skilled—in the stockyards and steel plants; in machine shops; in candy, garment, and box factories; among scrubwomen, waitresses, and teachers. By the end of 1903, more than half of the city's workers—245,000 people—were affiliated with the CFL, including 35,000 women in 26 different occupations. Strikes mushroomed amid new calls for a shorter workday. Federation leaders claimed that theirs was the "best organized city in the world."

Yet much of this movement, particularly among the unskilled, had been destroyed by 1905. In the building and metal trades, among transport owners and garment manufacturers, and elsewhere, well-organized employers declared their establishments open shops and waged war on the city's unions. Spectacular lockouts in the midst of heavy unemployment in 1904 weakened organization among the skilled and extinguished it among immigrant laborers in meatpacking and other factories around the city. Except for the clothing and garment industry, where strikes in 1909 and 1910 led to the expansion of the International Ladies' Garment Workers Union (ILGWU) and the foundation of the Amalgamated Clothing Workers of America (ACWA) in 1910, new organization was minimal until World War I.

The CFL attracted national attention again from 1917 to 1919, spawning successful national organizing drives in both steel and meatpacking and launching the Cook County Labor Party, the linchpin for the national labor party movement of the postwar years. Again, a combination of mainline progressives around CFL president John Fitzpatrick and secretary Edward Nockels and with syndicalists and other radicals associated with William Z. Foster provided much of the leadership for these movements, and they made special efforts to integrate immigrant and African American laborers. However, a number of factors shattered the movement: political repression in the form of the Red Scare (1919–22), unemployment, the Race Riot of 1919, and a powerful employers' open-shop drive employing court injunctions, lockouts, and blacklists. While organization persisted under fire throughout the 1920s in the building trades, among other craftsmen, and on the railroads, most of the breakthroughs among the unskilled in basic industries were eradicated by 1922, and political innovation stagnated for most of the next decade.

One important community of workers was largely absent from this movement even at its height. While it reached out to unskilled immigrant women as well as men, Chicago's labor movement largely excluded or segregated African Americans. There were important exceptions, as in the garment and meatpacking industries, but on the eve of World War I, more than a third of the CFL's constituent unions excluded blacks entirely or segregated them into Jim Crow locals. Many other unions practiced more subtle forms of discrimination. The cynicism among black

Workers throughout Chicago and its suburbs took part in the nationwide movement for an eight-hour day with strikes, meetings, and parades in early to mid-1886. Reflecting the city's economic and social geography, labor activity was concentrated in industrial areas along the Chicago River and in nearby working-class neighborhoods. Tens of thousands went on strike, and many strikers marched from workplace to workplace, displaying solidarity and summoning fellow workers to join them. On two separate days, thousands of railroad freight handlers marched for miles from one terminal to another. But worker processions were more often neighborhood affairs, centered on local employment concentrations and sometimes displaying ethnic clustering. To avoid strikes, many employers agreed to worker demands. Though most labor activity was peaceful, violent confrontations with the police also occurred. A clash on May 3 between workers and police near the McCormick Reapers Works (*left*) led to the call for a protest meeting at the Randolph Street Haymarket. The Haymarket (*upper center*) was the starting point for two parades and the scene of a May 4 protest meeting that ended in violence. In the aftermath, the eight-hour movement came to a resounding halt for the time being.

# Labor Unrest in Chicago, April 25–May 4, 1886

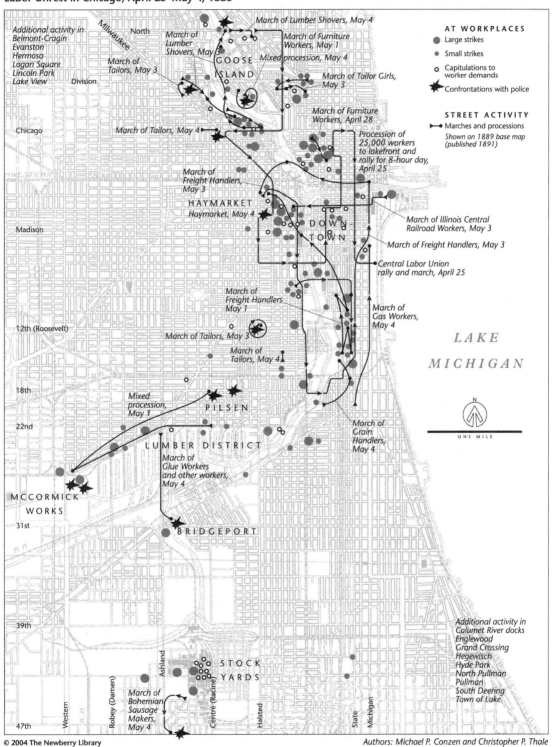

Additional activity in
Belmont-Cragin
Evanston
Hermosa
Logan Square
Lincoln Park
Lake View

March of Lumber Shovers, May 4

March of Lumber Shovers, May 3

March of Furniture Workers, May 1

March of Tailors, May 3

Mixed procession, May 4

GOOSE ISLAND

March of Tailor Girls, May 3

March of Tailors, May 4

March of Furniture Workers, April 28

Procession of 25,000 workers to lakefront and rally for 8-hour day, April 25

March of Freight Handlers, May 3

HAYMARKET
Haymarket, May 4

DOWN-TOWN

March of Illinois Central Railroad Workers, May 3

March of Freight Handlers, May 3

Central Labor Union rally and march, April 25

March of Freight Handlers May 1

March of Gas Workers, May 4

March of Tailors, May 3

March of Tailors, May 4

Mixed procession, May 1

PILSEN

LUMBER DISTRICT

March of Grain Handlers, May 4

March of Glue Workers and other workers, May 4

MCCORMICK WORKS

BRIDGEPORT

STOCK YARDS

March of Bohemian Sausage Makers, May 4

LAKE MICHIGAN

## AT WORKPLACES

- ● Large strikes
- ● Small strikes
- ○ Capitulations to worker demands
- ★ Confrontations with police

## STREET ACTIVITY

- ►● Marches and processions

*Shown on 1889 base map (published 1891)*

N

ONE MILE

Additional activity in
Calumet River docks
Englewood
Grand Crossing
Hegewisch
Hyde Park
North Pullman
Pullman
South Deering
Town of Lake

North

Milwaukee

Division

Chicago

Madison

12th (Roosevelt)

18th

22nd

31st

39th

47th

Western

Robey (Damen)

Ashland

Centre (Racine)

Halsted

State

Michigan

Authors: Michael P. Conzen and Christopher P. Thale

workers that grew from such experiences created a serious problem once the massive migration of the war years and the 1920s created a large black labor force in meatpacking, steel, and elsewhere. The ultimate destruction of promising organizations in basic industry during the 1919–22 era can be explained largely in terms of postwar unemployment and another aggressive open-shop campaign, but the unions' unsuccessful efforts to integrate the black migrants helps to account for the relative weakness of Chicago unions during the 1920s and the early Depression years. Industrial organization emerged in meatpacking, steel, agricultural machinery manufacturing, and elsewhere only in the late 1930s and during World War II, when the new CIO unions stressed civil rights in strenuous organizing campaigns among African Americans, Mexicans, and other minority workers. In turn, these workers provided some of the strongest bases of support for the new industrial unions. Yet some building trade unions continued to discriminate long after the civil rights legislation of the mid-1960s and were forced to integrate only through federal government pressure and protests from the Coalition of Black Trade Unionists and other local groups.

The story of Chicago's building trade unions represents many of the strengths and weaknesses of Chicago labor. Strong craft organizations flourished in a decentralized industry where technological limits and a series of building booms created a persistent demand for skilled manual labor. By the end of the nineteenth century, more than a score of unions had federated into a powerful Building Trades Council (BTC), which co-ordinated a complex range of work rules and crippling sympathetic strikes on sites throughout the city. Federated contractors copied the model, launching lockouts in 1900 and 1921, but union control persisted. In some trades, union power came along with graft and collusion. Most building trades became closely allied with the emerging Democratic political machine and several with organized crime. Throughout most of the twentieth century, conservative leaders from the building trades excluded women and minorities from their lucrative apprenticeship programs and dueled with progressive elements in the CFL.

The initiative for the new CIO unions of the late 1930s and the World War II era lay in some of the older and more progressive AFL unions, notably the ILGWU and ACWA, which had completely organized the clothing industry by the mid-1930s, and among radical rank-and-file organizations—notably affiliates of the Communist Trade Union Unity League, in steel, farm implement, furniture, and electrical manufacturing and in meatpacking and other food-processing plants. By 1939 the Packinghouse Workers Organizing Committee (PWOC, later the United Packinghouse Workers of America–CIO [UPWA]) had organized the giant Armour plant and built a membership of 7,550, or about 40 percent of the Chicago industry's workers. As in packing, the Steel Workers' Organizing Committee (SWOC, later the United Steel Workers of America–CIO [USWA]) had one major breakthrough in the late 1930s: U.S. Steel and its subsidiaries in 1937. In May of that year, however, SWOC faced a major setback in its campaign to organize the independent "Little Steel" firms when police killed ten workers and wounded dozens of others in the Memorial Day Massacre at Republic Steel. This violence and a return of unemployment in the period from 1937 to 1939 slowed the organizing, and SWOC ended the 1930s with a membership of less than 21,000, about one-third of the region's steelworkers. Other CIO beachheads were established when the Farm Equipment Workers (FE) won representation rights at the giant International Harvester plant (6,300 workers) and the United Electrical Workers (UE) won contracts in a number of electrical manufacturing plants.

As late as the beginning of the Second World War, Chicago's labor movement was still dominated by the AFL unions, which had a 1939 membership of over 330,000 compared to the CIO's 60,000. The new industrial unions benefited, however, from a massive increase in defense production and federal policies that facilitated union formation and expansion during World War II. USWA District 31 grew from 18,000 in 1940 to 100,000 in 1945 and the UPWA, FE, and UE all experienced comparable expansion, as did the ILGWU and ACWA.

Following a massive strike wave in 1946–47 involving more than 2.5 million workdays lost, labor relations stabilized, but union fortunes remained uneven in the postwar period. Mayor Richard J. Daley's tenure (1955–76) is often thought of as a golden age for organized labor, and, in fact, with the economy booming and collective bargaining largely accepted by employers, most unions thrived. The politically well-connected building trades prospered most. In the midst of a sustained boom in building construction, construction journeymen enjoyed a 250 percent increase in real wages between 1945 and 1980. Signs of trouble emerged as early as the late 1950s, however, with the gradual decline of manufacturing employment, a trend that accelerated in the next two decades. Moreover, the high-wage, unionized manufacturing industries were declining just as large numbers of African Americans and Latinos were entering the city's labor force. Major strikes reemerged in the late 1960s and 1970s, and the labor movement was clearly in decline by the time of Daley's death in 1976.

In the same years, however, changes in state law and in Chicago's occupational structure and the racial and ethnic composition of its population led to a dramatic transformation. As older manufacturing-based unions like the UPWA, USWA, and the garment workers' unions declined as a result of technological change and low-wage competition abroad, government and service workers created a new movement. Public employees poured into the American Federation of State, County and Municipal Employees (AFSCME), and health care and service workers, into the Service Employees International Union (SEIU). These industries included large numbers of women, African Americans, and Latinos. By 1980 nearly half of all Chicago truck drivers were black or Latino, while minority representation in the Teamsters Warehouse and other locals tended to be much higher. In the same years, SEIU Local 73, with 18,000 health care workers, became the largest AFL-CIO local union in the state.

Women have been active in the city's labor movement at least since the formation of the Chicago Working Women's Union (CWWU) in the mid-1870s and were instrumental in efforts to organize the clothing trades and other industries with substantial female labor forces. The growing proportion of women in the labor force after World War II, together with the shift in the city's occupational work structure from industrial to service and clerical jobs, the rise of feminism over the past three decades, and the subsequent struggles for women's rights have all created a larger and more important role for women in the local movement during the second half of the twentieth century. Chicago activists have also played important roles in the national movement. A long legacy of women's activism—from the CWWU, through the Knights and the Women's Trade Union League, to CIO industrial unions and early efforts to organize clerical and service workers—made Chicago the natural birthplace of the national Coalition of Labor Union Women (CLUW) in 1974. CLUW has pursued not only better wages and working conditions but also broader social issues and the special needs of working women, including child care.

The challenges facing Chicago labor are those facing workers throughout the United States—and the same ones they have faced in the past. Will unions be able to integrate wage earners from vastly different backgrounds on the basis of class solidarity? Can they develop new forms of organization and protest better suited to the technological and occupational facts of the twenty-first century than the old craft or industrial unions and the traditional strike? Answers to these questions will emerge within the context of Chicago's historic reputation as a labor town, its progressive political heritage, and the striking diversity of its working-class population.                                                                      *James R. Barrett*

**Anti-Unionism.** From the late nineteenth century on, Chicago was one of the most heavily unionized American cities, but not for lack of ardent opposition by employers. Their strategies, reflecting both insistence on total managerial control typical of American large-scale business and reaction to the radicalism and militancy of Chicago's workers, often made the city as much a global center of anti-unionism as it was a "trade union capital of the world." Meatpacker Philip Armour in 1879 captured the managerial ethos: "As long as we are heads of our own houses, we shall employ what men we choose, and when we can't, why, we'll nail up our doors—that's all."

Anti-unionism took two basic forms: repression and paternalism. Repressive tactics included firing and blacklisting union sympathizers (Marshall Field & Co. fired workers for being in the company of a union member); recruiting strikebreakers; deploying spies, thugs, and private security forces (including the infamous Chicago-based Pinkertons); locking out workers to break their union; vilifying unionists as "anarchists" or "communists"; and exacerbating ethnic conflicts to divide workers. Frequently, owners took advantage of recessions to cut wages, then broke unions by relying on the desperate unemployed to cross picket lines (as the meatpackers did in 1904, destroying a newly created union movement). To present a united front against workers, employers formed associations, such as the railroads' General Managers Association in the 1890s, and to exert business influence over local government, they formed political groups, such as the Citizens' Association of Chicago in 1874.

Business owners frequently turned to the government to suppress unions and strikes through laws against political radicalism, conspiracy, restraint of trade, and even vagrancy; court injunctions against strikes, picketing, and other union activities; police protection of business property and strikebreakers; jailing of labor leaders; and violent—even deadly—attacks on union gatherings, including the police killing of ten men at a peaceful rally in southeast Chicago near the anti-union Republic Steel plant on Memorial Day 1937.

In the first decades after the Civil War, businessmen viewed Chicago's police as unreliable—or, in other words, occasionally neutral during strikes. In the 1870s and 1880s, they formed private armed militias and secured construction of armories and forts for state militia and federal troops, who were called in to suppress major strikes against the railroads in 1877 and against Pullman in 1894. They sought to "professionalize" the police to eliminate working-class sympathies, but the result was a police force whose willingness to support strikebreaking was seldom limited by a concern for civil liberties.

Despite profound business-class influence, local government was not consistently anti-labor: a few politicians, including Mayor Carter Harrison and Governor John Peter Altgeld, were largely sympathetic to the labor movement, and twentieth-century machine Democrats relied on union support despite their opposition to union contracts for most public workers. While businesses could count on many elite institutions, including churches and the press, to oppose unions, a few editors, religious leaders, and intellectuals—such as Henry Demarest Lloyd, Jane Addams, and Clarence Darrow—broke ranks to support unionization.

While most Chicago businesses openly fought unions, some tried to avoid unionization through paternalism, treating workers more humanely to instill loyalty. George Pullman conceptualized his model factory town south of Chicago to avoid labor unrest, but, like most paternalistic efforts, his idea fell victim to a gap between promise and reality, leading workers to strike in 1894. After World War I, when unionizing efforts in steel and meatpacking collapsed in the face of internal divisions and employer opposition (reinforced in the steel strike with deadly public and private force), businesses in Chicago joined in the national employer effort to roll back recent union gains with an open shop campaign. Many businesses embraced "welfare capitalism," which attempted to avoid the irritating aspects of paternalism and, rather than simply avoid unionism, adopted some union principles, but under management control. U.S. Steel, International Harvester, Swift, Armour, and Western Electric were among leading Chicago businesses that provided individualized pay, insurance and promotion incentives (including stock ownership), company-dominated employee representation plans, and family-oriented recreation. Companies, reversing earlier strategies, often broke up close-knit ethnic work groups as potentially subversive. Some, like Western Electric, initiated surveys and studies to identify sources of worker discontent.

While much of welfare capitalism collapsed with the Great Depression, some programs survived. Sears, Roebuck combined the "soft" and "hard" approaches to union avoidance, using worker surveys as well as the tough tactics of consultant Nathan W. Shefferman, who headed off Teamster organizing through payments to union president Dave Beck. Shefferman pioneered the modern anti-union consulting industry through his techniques of ferreting out union sympathizers and individually pressuring workers to oppose unionization. Shefferman mixed legal and illegal tactics to fight union organizing drives, and his disciples opened influential consulting businesses in Chicago.

Throughout Chicago history, a few businessmen, such as banker Lyman Gage in the late nineteenth century, have argued for a détente with the unions. The largely middle-class Civic Federation of Chicago, inspired in 1893 by reformer William Stead, promoted social cooperation, including alliances between reformers and labor. The National Civic Federation, founded in Chicago in 1900, became a leading advocate of a labor-capital bargain to recognize unions but assure unhindered production. At times, such as during World War I and II and from 1945 to the late 1960s, businesses generally were willing to accommodate unions, either because of government pressure or the power of organized labor. But from the 1960s on, many business operations, especially manufacturing branches of large national or multinational corporations, indirectly fought unions by relocating—either to the Sunbelt, where unions were weak, or to foreign countries, often ones with anti-labor regimes. Other large businesses, such as Motorola, tried to avoid unionization by matching union wages and devising human-relations strategies to defuse the buildup of grievances. By the late 1970s and early 1980s, businesses—often relying on specialist anti-union consultants—became more openly aggressive in fighting unionization and breaking unions, as witnessed during the 1985 printing unions' strike at the *Chicago Tribune*. At the close of the twentieth century, unions were losing influence over the city's workforce as emerging industries resisted unionization and new, non-union firms undercut union dominance in previously well-organized industries.     *David Moberg*

**Strikes.** Perhaps no city in the United States exceeded Chicago in the number, breadth, intensity, and national importance of labor upheavals in the period between the Civil War and 1919. Overall, there have been six important strike waves or labor upheavals in Chicago history that were notable for their social impact.

On May 2, 1867, Chicago's first Trades Assembly (formed in 1864) sponsored a general strike by thousands of workers to enforce the state's new eight-hour day law. Though the one-week strike was unsuccessful, it capped a four-year mobilization of local workers that encouraged political parties to incorporate labor demands into their platforms and appeals.

In July 1877, Chicago workers struck again as part of a nationwide railroad strike. Though lacking unions, thousands of working men, women, and teenagers thronged the streets, marching from factory to factory behind brass bands calling employees out to strike. At the height of the conflict, police and militia forcibly dispersed crowds of Irish, Bohemian, and German strikers while the U.S. Army waited in readiness. By the time the

Messenger boys strike, 1902. Young boy messengers were an important means of communication between downtown offices. Here a group of striking messenger boys walk down a sidewalk in 1902. Photo: *Chicago Daily News*. Courtesy of the Chicago History Museum (DN-0000022).

strike had been suppressed, 30 workers lay dead and 200 were wounded. The strike was significant, not just for the class bitterness it engendered, but for the unprecedented participation and solidarity of workers across skill, gender, and ethnic lines. Meanwhile, as the only group supporting the strikers, socialists emerged as the voice for local workers, and Chicago became the nation's strongest center of socialism.

In 1886 Chicago was the center for another labor upheaval. Approximately 88,000 workers in 307 separate strikes demanded the eight-hour day that year, most of them on May 1. Industry was paralyzed, and the city "assumed a sabbath like appearance." The Haymarket Affair of May 4 triggered widespread anti-labor repression. Moreover, the failure of the movement to spread much beyond Chicago made it easier for employers who competed in national markets to ignore labor demands.

As the tide of the Great Upheaval receded in the late 1880s, the character of strikes began to change. Until then, strikes often mobilized large numbers of immigrant men, women, and children within ethnic communities such as Irish Bridgeport and Bohemian Pilsen. Easily replaced unskilled workers, in particular, relied on crowd actions to intimidate strikebreakers. To avoid riots and capture the vaunted "labor vote," 1880s politicians such as Mayor Carter Harrison began to restrain police from intervening in strikes called by well-connected local unions. As the mass strike subsided, craft unions spread among skilled workers employed by small-scale employers in local and regional markets. A metropolitan unionism took hold particularly among the building trades, the building service workers, and the teamsters. For the most part, strikes were not spontaneous but were called, coordinated, and supported by the strike funds of permanent unions and aided by a hands-off attitude of the police. By the turn of the century, labor was a recognized interest in local politics and Chicago had became a "union town."

The most important early attempt of the new unionism to penetrate the domain of corporate-run industry came in 1894 when the American Railway Union (ARU), an industrial union founded by Eugene V. Debs, mounted a boycott of the nation's Pullman railway cars. With much of the nation's transportation at a standstill, a federal court granted the railroads an injunction declaring the strike illegal, and President Grover Cleveland dispatched 2,000 federal troops and over 5,000 U.S. marshals to Chicago, precipitating widespread violence. Despite a general strike by 25,000 Chicago unionists, the ARU was crushed.

In the aftermath of the Pullman Strike, employers increasingly resorted to injunctions to bring in the federal government on their side in strikes, especially sympathy strikes and boycotts. A particular object of the courts' ire was the Teamsters union, which in the early part of the century used its control over the distribution of local goods to support and spread local unionism via the sympathy strike. In the 1910s, the struggle for union recognition by workers in the emerging corporate-run, mass-production sector of the economy precipitated renewed upheavals. In 1919 workers in Chicago's packinghouses, steel mills, and ready-made clothing and agricultural equipment industries engaged in tumultuous strikes marked by race riots and government repression. The defeat of these strikes unleashed a powerful employer counterattack in the form of an open shop movement that kept strikes to a minimum during the 1920s.

In the late 1930s, workers in basic industry finally won union recognition. Congressional legislation stopped the courts from issuing labor injunctions during strikes and enforced the right of workers to be represented by the union of their choice. For the first time, large numbers of African American, eastern European immigrant, and female semi-skilled industrial workers were organized in permanent industrial unions under the wing of the Congress of Industrial Organizations. But victory was achieved amidst a series of bitter strikes, notably the Little Steel Strike of 1937 in which police shot to death ten strikers in the Memorial Day Massacre. Local industrial workers were also heavily involved in the great nationwide wave of strikes in 1946.

From the end of World War II through the early 1970s, strikes continued to be widespread; but with the acceptance of collective bargaining, they did not precipitate social upheavals nor did they generate the enormous class hostility that they had earlier. In the 1970s, the postwar liberal accord between capital and labor began to unravel. The strength of labor weakened as automation and the export of jobs overseas by corporations took its toll in heavily unionized Chicago. Industrial work increasingly gave way to service-sector work that was largely non-union. Then, following the example of President Ronald Reagan in the 1981 Air Traffic Controllers Strike, private employers, especially those facing global competition and deregulated markets, returned to the union-busting tactics of their forebears. For much of the rest of the twentieth century, with the exception of public-sector unions such as the Chicago Teachers Union, large strikes were scarce in Chicago. In the early years of the new century, strike activity rose as unionization activity increased in the service, health care, and other expanding areas of the economy.

*Richard Schneirov*

# Bibliography

Below are many of the most relevant and easily accessible books that individual authors selected for inclusion with their entries in the *Encyclopedia of Chicago*. Also included are several more recent publications that were particularly useful in updating entries for this volume, as were the digital versions of *Crain's Chicago Business*, the *Chicago Tribune*, the *Wall Street Journal*, and the *New York Times*.

Achilles, Rolf. *Made in Illinois: A Story of Illinois Manufacturing*. 1993.

Ackerman, William K. *Early Illinois Railroads*. 1884.

Addams, Jane. *Twenty Years at Hull-House*. 1910.

Advertising Age. *How It Was in Advertising: 1776–1976*. 1976.

Aldrich, Mark. *Safety First: Technology, Labor, and Business in the Building of American Work Safety, 1870–1939*. 1997.

Amalgamated Clothing Workers of America. Research Department. *The Clothing Workers of Chicago, 1910–1922*. 1922.

American Medical Association. *Caring for the Country: A History and Celebration of the First 150 Years of the American Medical Association*. 1997.

Anderson, Nels. *The Hobo: The Sociology of the Homeless Man*. 1923.

Andreas, A. T. *History of Chicago*. 3 vols. 1884. Reprint, 1975.

Avrich, Paul. *The Haymarket Tragedy*. 1984.

Bachin, Robin F. *Building the South Side: Urban Space and Civic Culture in Chicago, 1890–1919*. 2004.

Badger, Reid. *The Great American Fair: The World's Columbian Exposition and American Culture*. 1979.

Bae, Youngsoo. *Labor in Retreat*. 2001.

Baird, Russell, and A. T. Turnbull. *Industry and Business Journalism*. 1961.

Baker, Robert Osborne. *The International Alliance of Theatrical Stage Employees and Moving Picture Machine Operators of the United States and Canada*. 1933.

Bardolph, Richard. *Agricultural Literature and the Early Illinois Farmer*. 1948.

Barrett, James R. *Work and Community in the Jungle: Chicago's Packinghouse Workers, 1894–1922*. 1987.

Barrett, Paul. *The Automobile and Urban Transit: The Formation of Public Policy in Chicago, 1900–1930*. 1983.

Barth, James R. *The Great Savings and Loan Debacle*. 1991.

Bates, Beth Tompkins. *Pullman Porters and the Rise of Protest Politics in Black America, 1925–1945*. 2001.

Beadling, Tom. *A Need for Valor: The Roots of the Service Employees International Union, 1902–1992*. 1992.

Beckner, Earl R. *A History of Illinois Labor Legislation*. 1929.

Belcher, Wyatt Winton. *The Economic Rivalry between St. Louis and Chicago, 1850–1880*. 1947.

Bennett, Larry. *Fragments of Cities: The New American Downtowns and Neighborhoods*. 1990.

———. *The Third City: Chicago and American Urbanism*. 2010.

Bensman, David, and Roberta Lynch. *Rusted Dreams: Hard Times in a Steel Community*. 1987.

Benson, Susan Porter. *Counter Cultures: Saleswomen, Managers, and Customers in American Department Stores, 1890–1940*. 1986.

Berger, Molly W. *Hotel Dreams: Luxury, Technology, and Urban Ambition in America, 1829–1929*. 2011.

Berry, Brian. *Commercial Structure and Commercial Blight: Retail Patterns and Processes in the City of Chicago*. 1963.

Bodfish, H. Morton, ed. *History of Building and Loan in the United States*. 1931.

Bogue, Allan G. *From Prairie to Cornbelt: Farming on the Illinois and Iowa Prairies in the 19th Century*. 1963.

Bonner, Thomas N. *Medicine in Chicago, 1850–1950: A Chapter in the Social and Scientific Development of a City*. 1957.

Breese, Gerald W. *The Daytime Population of the Central Business District of Chicago, with Particular Reference to the Factor of Transportation*. 1949.

Brody, David. *The Butcher Workmen: A Study of Unionization*. 1964.

Brooks, John. *Telephone: The First Hundred Years*. 1976.

Brown, Emily Clark. *Book and Job Printing in Chicago*. 1931.

Budrys, Grace. *When Doctors Join Unions*. 1997.

Burnham, John C. *Bad Habits: Drinking, Smoking, Taking Drugs, Gambling, Sexual Misbehavior, and Swearing in American History*. 1993.

Cain, Louis P. *Sanitation Strategy for a Lakefront Metropolis: The Case of Chicago*. 1978.

Calder, Lendol. *Financing the American Dream: A Cultural History of Consumer Credit*. 1999.

Callahan, Raymond. *Education and the Cult of Efficiency: A Study of the Social Effects That Have Shaped the Administration of the Public Schools*. 1962.

Carsel, Wilfred. *A History of the Chicago Ladies' Garment Workers' Union*. 1940.

Caskey, John P. *Fringe Banking: Check-Cashing Outlets, Pawnshops, and the Poor*. 1994.

Cavan, Ruth Shonle. *Business Girls: A Study of Their Interests and Problems*. 1929.

Cayton, Horace, and George S. Mitchell. *Black Workers and the New Unions*. 1939.

Chandler, Alfred Dupont. *The Visible Hand: The Managerial Revolution in American Business*. 1977.

Chateauvert, Melinda. *Marching Together: Women of the Brotherhood of Sleeping Car Porters*. 1998.

Chicago Medical Society. *History of Medicine and Surgery and Physicians and Surgeons of Chicago*. 1922.

Chicago Recreation Commission. *The Chicago Recreation Survey*, 1937, 5 vols. 1937–40.

Clark, John. *The Grain Trade in the Old Northwest*. 1966.

Clemen, Rudolf. *The American Livestock and Meat Industry.* 1923.

Cobrin, Harry A. *The Men's Clothing Industry: Colonial through Modern Times.* 1970.

Cody, Thomas G. *Strategy of a Megamerger: An Insider's Account of the Baxter Travenol–American Hospital Supply Combination.* 1990.

Cohen, Lizabeth. *Making a New Deal: Industrial Workers in Chicago, 1919–1939.* 1990.

Colten, Craig E. *Industrial Wastes in the Calumet Region, 1869–1970: An Historical Geography.* 1985.

Condit, Carl W. *Chicago, 1910–29: Building, Planning, and Urban Technology.* 1973.

———. *Chicago, 1930–1970: Building, Planning, and Urban Technology.* 1974.

Connor, John M., and William A. Schiek. *Food Processing: An Industrial Powerhouse in Transition.* 2nd ed. 1997.

Conzen, Michael P., ed. *Chicago Mapmakers: Essays on the Rise of the City's Map Trade.* 1984.

Conzen, Michael, et al. *Studies on the Illinois and Michigan Canal Corridor.* 1987–94.

Cremin, Lawrence. *American Education: The Metropolitan Experience.* 1988.

———. *The Transformation of the School: Progressivism in American Education, 1876–1957.* 1962.

Cronon, William. *Nature's Metropolis: Chicago and the Great West.* 1991.

Cross, Gary. *Kids' Stuff: Toys and the Changing World of American Childhood.* 1997.

Cudahy, Brian J. *Destination Loop: The Story of Rapid Transit Railroading in and around Chicago.* 1982.

Currey, J. Seymour. *Manufacturing and Wholesale Industries of Chicago.* 3 vols. 1918.

Cutler, Irving. *Chicago: Metropolis of the Mid-Continent.* 3rd ed. 1982.

Darling, Sharon. *Chicago Furniture: Art, Craft, and Industry, 1833–1983.* 1984.

David, Henry. *The History of the Haymarket Affair.* 1936. Rev. ed., 1958.

Derber, Milton. *Labor in Illinois: The Affluent Years, 1945–80.* 1989.

Dewey, John. *School and Society.* 1900. Rev. ed., 1915. Reprint, 1956.

Diehl, Leonard J., and Floyd R. Eastwood. *Industrial Recreation: Its Development and Present Status.* 1940.

Drake, St. Clair, and Horace R. Cayton. *Black Metropolis: A Study of Negro Life in a Northern City.* 1945.

Dreiser, Theodore. *Sister Carrie.* 1900.

Drury, John. *Dining in Chicago: The Century of Progress Authorized Guide.* 1933.

Dudden, Faye E. *Serving Women: Household Service in Nineteenth-Century America.* 1983.

Duis, Perry R. *Challenging Chicago: Coping with Everyday Life, 1837–1920.* 1998.

Eastwood, Carolyn. *Chicago Jewish Street Peddlers: Toehold on the Bottom Rung.* 1991.

Ebner, Michael. *Creating Chicago's North Shore: A Suburban History.* 1988.

Edmunds, R. David. *The Potawatomis: Keepers of the Fire.* 1978.

Edmunds, R. David, and Joseph L. Peyser. *The Fox Wars: The Mesquakie Challenge to New France.* 1993.

Emmet, Boris, and John E. Jeuck. *Catalogues and Counters: A History of Sears, Roebuck and Company.* 1950.

Endres, Kathleen L., ed. *Trade, Industrial, and Professional Periodicals of the United States.* 1994.

Epstein, Dena J. *Music Publishing in Chicago Before 1871: The Firm of Root & Cady, 1858–1871.* 1969.

Epstein, Ralph C. *GATX: A History of the General American Transportation Corporation, 1898–1948.* 1948.

Ferris, William G. *The Grain Traders: The Story of the Chicago Board of Trade.* 1988.

Findling, John E. *Chicago's Great World's Fair*. 1994.

Fine, Lisa M. *The Souls of the Skyscraper: Female Clerical Workers in Chicago*. 1990.

Folsom, Franklin. *Impatient Armies of the Poor: The Story of Collective Action of the Unemployed, 1808–1942*. 1991.

Fox, Stephen. *The Mirror Makers: A History of American Advertising and Its Creators*. 1984.

Fraser, Steve. *Labor Will Rule: Sidney Hillman and the Rise of American Labor*. 1991.

Gazel, Neil R. *Beatrice: From Buildup through Breakup*. 1990.

Gems, Gerry. *Windy City Wars: Labor, Leisure, and Sport in the Making of Chicago*. 1997.

Giddens, Paul H. *Standard Oil Company (Indiana): Oil Pioneer of the Middle West*. 1955.

Gillespie, Richard. *Manufacturing Knowledge: A History of the Hawthorne Experiments*. 1991.

Godfried, Nathan. *WCFL: Chicago's Voice of Labor, 1926–78*. 1997.

Goldsborough, Robert. *The Crain Adventure: The Making and Building of a Family Publishing Co*. 1992.

Goode, J. Paul. *The Geographic Background of Chicago*. 1926.

Goodrum, Charles, and Helen Dalrymple. *Advertising in America: The First 200 Years*. 1990.

Grant, H. Roger. *The North Western: The Chicago and North Western Railway System*. 1996.

Green, Adam P. *Selling the Race: Cultural and Community in Black Chicago, 1940–1955*. 2006.

Grossman, James R. *Land of Hope: Chicago, Black Southerners, and the Great Migration*. 1989.

Hales, Peter Bacon. *Silver Cities: The Photography of American Urbanization, 1839–1915*. 1984.

Halpern, Rick. *Down on the Killing Floor: Black and White Workers in Chicago's Packinghouses, 1904–1954*. 1997.

Halpern, Rick, and Roger Horowitz. *Meatpackers: An Oral History of Black Packinghouse Workers and Their Struggle for Racial and Economic Equality*. 1996.

Harris, Neil, et al. *Grand Illusions: Chicago's World's Fair of 1893*. 1993.

Harris, William H. *Keeping the Faith: A. Philip Randolph, Milton P. Webster, and the Brotherhood of Sleeping Car Porters, 1925–1937*. 1977.

Haynes, Williams. *American Chemical Industry*. 6 vols. 1945–54.

Heinz, John P. *Chicago Lawyers: The Social Structure of the Bar*. 1982.

Hendrickson, Robert. *The Grand Emporiums: The Illustrated History of America's Great Department Stores*. 1979.

Herrick Mary J. *The Chicago Schools: A Social and Political History*. 1971.

Higdon, Hal. *The Business Healers*. 1969.

Hirsch, Arnold R. *Making the Second Ghetto: Race and Housing in Chicago, 1940–1960*. 1983.

Hirsch, Susan, and Robert Goler. *A City Comes of Age: Chicago in the 1890s*. 1990.

Hogan, David. *Class and Reform: School and Society in Chicago, 1880–1930*. 1985.

Holli, Melvin G., and Peter d'A. Jones, eds. *Ethnic Chicago: A Multicultural Portrait*. 4th ed. 1995.

Hoover, Edgar M., Jr. *Location Theory and the Shoe and Leather Industries*. 1937.

Hotchkiss, George W. *History of the Lumber and Forest Industry of the Northwest*. 1898.

Hoy, Suellen. *Chasing Dirt: The American Pursuit of Cleanliness*. 1995.

Hoyt, Homer. *One Hundred Years of Land Values in Chicago, 1830–1933*. 1933.

Hughes, Thomas P. *Networks of Power: Electrification in Western Society, 1880–1930.* 1983.

Industrial Chicago. *The Building Interests.* Vols. 1 and 2. 1891.

James, F. Cyril. *The Growth of Chicago Banks.* 2 vols. 1938.

Johnson, David R. *Policing the Urban Underworld: The Impact of Crime on the Development of the American Police, 1800–1887.* 1979.

Kantowicz, Edward R. *True Value: John Cotter, 70 Years of Hardware.* 1986.

Karamanski, Theodore J. *Schooner Passage: Sailing Ships and the Lake Michigan Frontier.* 2000.

Katzman, David M. *Seven Days a Week: Women and Domestic Service in Industrializing America.* 1978. Reprint, 1981.

Katznelson, Ira, and Margaret Weir. *Schooling for All: Class, Race, and the Decline of the Democratic Ideal.* 1985.

Keating, Ann Durkin. *Building Chicago: Suburban Developers and the Creation of a Divided Metropolis.* 1988.

Kinzie, Juliette. *Wau-Bun: The "Early Day" in the North-West.* 1932.

Kirkland, Joseph. *The Story of Chicago.* 1892.

Kirstein, George G. *Stores and Unions: A Study of the Growth of Unionism in Dry Goods and Department Stores.* 1950.

Klebaner, Benjamin J. *Commercial Banking in the United States: A History.* 1974.

Kogan, Herman. *Lending Is Our Business: The Story of Household Finance Corporation.* 1965.

———. *Proud of the Past, Committed to the Future.* 1985.

———. *The Long White Line: The Story of Abbott Laboratories.* 1963.

Kogan, Herman, and Rick Kogan. *Pharmacist to the Nation: A History of Walgreen Co., America's Leading Drug Store Chain.* 1989.

Kogan, Rick. *Brunswick: The Story of an American Company from 1845 to 1985.* 1985.

Koval, John P., et al., eds. *The New Chicago: A Social and Cultural Analysis.* 2006.

Kusmer, Kenneth L. *Down and Out, on the Road: The Homeless in American History.* 2002.

Lamb, John. *A Corridor in Time: I&M Canal, 1836–1986.* 1987

Lambert, Emily. *The Futures: The Rise of the Speculator and the Origins of the World's Biggest Markets.* 2011.

Law Bulletin Publishing Company. *Century of Law: 1900–2000.* 1999.

Leidenberger, Georg. *Chicago's Progressive Alliance: Labor and the Bid for Public Streetcars.* 2006.

LesStrang, Jacques. *Cargo Carriers of the Great Lakes.* 1985.

Levenstein, Harvey. *Revolution at the Table: The Transformation of the American Diet.* 1988.

Levine, Peter. *A. G. Spalding and the Rise of Baseball: The Promise of American Sport.* 1985.

Lewis, Robert. *Chicago Made: Factory Networks in the Industrial Metropolis.* 2008.

Licht, Walter. *Working for the Railroad: The Organization of Work in the Nineteenth Century.* 1983.

Lurie, Jonathon. *The Chicago Board of Trade, 1859–1905: The Dynamics of Self Regulation.* 1979.

Madigan, Charles, ed. *Global Chicago.* 2004.

Marsh, Barbara. *A Corporate Tragedy: The Agony of International Harvester Company.* 1985.

Matthews, Glenna. *"Just a Housewife": The Rise and Fall of Domesticity in America*. 1987.

Mayer, Harold M. *The Port of Chicago and the St. Lawrence Seaway*. 1957.

Mayer, Harold M., and Richard C. Wade. *Chicago: Growth of a Metropolis*. 1969.

Mayo, James M. *The American Grocery Store: The Business Evolution of an Architectural Space*. 1993.

McDermott, Charles H. *A History of the Shoe and Leather Industries of the United States*. 1918.

McGreevy, John T. *Parish Boundaries: The Catholic Encounter with Race in the Twentieth-Century Urban North*. 1996.

Meyerowitz, Joanne J. *Women Adrift: Independent Wage Earners in Chicago, 1880–1930*. 1988.

Miller, Donald L. *City of the Century: The Epic of Chicago and the Making of America*. 1996.

Miranti, Paul J., Jr. *Accountancy Comes of Age: The Development of an American Profession, 1886–1940*. 1990.

Monchow, Helen Corbin. *Seventy Years of Real Estate Subdividing in the Region of Chicago*. 1939.

Monroe, Day. *Chicago Families: A Study of Unpublished Census Data*. 1932.

Montgomery, Royal E. *Industrial Relations in the Chicago Building Trades*. 1927.

Murphy, Marjorie. *Blackboard Unions: The AFT and NEA, 1900–1980*. 1990.

Murray, George. *Madhouse on Madison Street*. 1965.

Nelson, Daniel. *Managers and Workers: Origins of the Twentieth-Century Factory System in the U.S., 1880–1920*. 1995.

——. *Unemployment Insurance: The American Experience, 1915–1935*. 1969.

Newell, Barbara Warne. *Chicago and the Labor Movement: Metropolitan Unionism in the 1930s*. 1961.

O'Shea, James, and Charles Madigan. *Dangerous Company: The Consulting Powerhouses and the Businesses They Save and Ruin*. 1997.

Ogilvie, William Edward. *Pioneer Agricultural Journalists*. 1927. Reprint, 1973.

Oursler, Will. *From Ox Carts to Jets: Roy Ingersoll and the Borg-Warner Story*. 1959.

Ozanne, Robert W. *A Century of Labor Management Relations at McCormick and International Harvester*. 1967.

Pacyga, Dominic A. *Chicago: A Biography*. 2009.

Pacyga, Dominic A., and Ellen Skerrett. *Chicago, City of Neighborhoods: Histories and Tours*. 1986.

Parker, William N. *Europe, America, and the Wider World: Essays on the Economic History of Western Capitalism*. 2 vols. Vol. 2. 1991.

Philpott, Thomas Lee. *The Slum and the Ghetto: Neighborhood Deterioration and Middle-Class Reform, Chicago, 1880–1930*. 1978.

Pierce, Bessie Louis. *A History of Chicago*. 3 vols. 1937–57.

Platt, Harold L. *The Electric City: Energy and the Growth of the Chicago Area, 1880–1930*. 1991.

Porter, Glenn, and Harold Livesay. *Merchants and Manufacturers: Studies in the Changing Structure of Nineteenth-Century Marketing*. 1971.

Previts, Gary J., and Barbara D. Merino. *A History of Accounting in America: An Historical Interpretation of the Cultural Significance of Accounting*. 1979.

Priest, Patricia Joyner. *Public Intimacies: Talk Show Participants and Tell-All TV*. 1996.

Puth, Robert C. *Supreme Life: The History of a Negro Life Insurance Company*. 1976.

Putnam, James. *The Illinois and Michigan Canal: A Study in Economic History*. 1918.

Quaife, Milo M. *Chicago and the Old Northwest, 1673–1835.* 1913.

———. *Chicago's Highways Old and New: From Indian Trail to Motor Road.* 1923.

Rabinovitz, Lauren. *For the Love of Pleasure: Women, Movies, and Culture in Turn-of-the-Century Chicago.* 1998.

Rader, Benjamin. *American Sports: From the Age of Folk Games to the Age of Spectators.* 1983.

Randall, Frank A. *A History of the Development of Building Construction in Chicago.* 1949.

Reckitt, Ernest. *Reminiscences of Early Days of the Accounting Profession in Illinois.* 1953.

Regan Printing House. *The Story of Chicago in Connection with the Printing Business.* 1912.

Regnery, Henry. *Creative Chicago: From the Chap-Book to the University.* 1993.

Rice, Mary Jane Judson. *Chicago: Port to the World.* 1969.

Riess, Steven. *City Games: The Evolution of American Urban Society and the Rise of Sports.* 1989.

———. *Touching Base: Professional Baseball and American Culture in the Progressive Era.* 1980.

Roell, Craig H. *The Piano in America, 1890–1940.* 1989.

Rust, Brian. *The American Record Label Book.* 1978.

Rydell, Robert W. *All the World's a Fair: Visions of Empire at America's International Expositions, 1876–1916.* 1984.

———. *World of Fairs: The Century of Progress Expositions.* 1993.

Schneirov, Richard. *Labor and Urban Politics: Class Conflict and the Origins of Modern Liberalism in Chicago, 1864–97.* 1998.

Schneirov, Richard, and Thomas J. Suhrbur. *Union Brotherhood, Union Town: The History of the Carpenters' Union of Chicago, 1863–1987.* 1988.

Scranton, Philip. *Endless Novelty: Specialty Production and American Industrialization, 1865–1925.* 1997.

Seligman, Amanda I. *Block by Block: Neighborhoods, Public Policy, and "White Flight" in Richard J. Daley's Chicago.* 2004.

Shattuc, Jane. *The Talking Cure: Women and Daytime Talk Shows.* 1996.

Siry, Joseph. *Carson Pirie Scott: Louis Sullivan and the Chicago Department Store.* 1988.

Skaggs, Jimmy K. *Prime Cut: Livestock Raising and Meatpacking in the United States, 1607–1983.* 1986.

Skilnik, Bob. *The History of Beer and Brewing in Chicago: 1833–1978.* 1999.

Sleeper-Smith, Susan. *Indian Women and French Men: Rethinking Cultural Encounter in the Western Great Lakes.* 2001.

Smalley, Orange A., and Frederick D. Sturdivant. *The Credit Merchants: A History of Spiegel, Inc.* 1973.

Smith, Alice E. *George Smith's Money: A Scottish Investor in America.* 1966.

Smith, Carl. *Urban Disorder and the Shape of Belief: The Great Chicago Fire, the Haymarket Bomb, and the Model Town of Pullman.* 1995.

Smith, Henry Ladd. *Airways: The History of Commercial Aviation in the United States.* 1942.

Solberg, Carl. *Conquest of the Skies: A History of Commercial Aviation in America.* 1979.

Southern, Eileen. *The Music of Black Americans: A History.* 1981.

Staley, Eugene. *History of the Illinois State Federation of Labor.* 1930.

Stamper, John W. *Chicago's North Michigan Avenue: Planning and Development 1900–1930.* 1991.

Stover, John F. *American Railroads.* 1961.

Suttles, Gerald D. *The Man-Made City: The Land-Use Confidence Game in Chicago*. 1990.

Tanner, Helen Hornbeck, ed. *Atlas of Great Lakes Indian History*. 1987.

Taylor, Charles H., ed. *History of the Board of Trade of the City of Chicago*. 3 vols. 1917.

Teaford, Jon C. *Cities of the Heartland: The Rise and Fall of the Industrial Midwest*. 1993.

Tebbel, John. *A History of Book Publishing in the United States*. 4 vols. 1972–82.

Terkel, Studs. *My American Century*. 1997.

———. *Working: People Talk about What They Do All Day and How They Feel about What They Do*. 1974.

Thornton, Harrison John. *The History of the Quaker Oats Company*. 1933.

Truax, Charles. *Mechanics of Surgery*. 1899.

Tyack, David. *The One Best System: A History of American Urban Education*. 1974.

Viskochil, Larry A. *Chicago at the Turn of the Century in Photographs*. 1984.

Wade, Louis Carroll. *Chicago's Pride: The Stockyards, Packingtown, and Environs in the Nineteenth Century*. 1987.

Weems, Robert E., Jr. *Black Business in the Black Metropolis: The Chicago Metropolitan Assurance Company, 1925–1985*. 1996.

Wendt, Lloyd. *Chicago Tribune: The Rise of a Great American Newspaper*. 1979.

Wendt, Lloyd and Herman Kogan. *Give the Lady What She Wants!: The Story of Marshall Field & Company*. 1952.

Westbrook, Robert B. *John Dewey and American Democracy*. 1991.

White, Richard. *The Middle Ground: Indians, Empires, and Republics in the Great Lakes Region, 1650–1815*. 1991.

Whyte, William H., Jr. *The Organization Man*. 1956.

Williamson, Harold F., and Arnold R. Daum. *The American Petroleum Industry: The Age of Illumination*. 1959.

Williamson, Harold F., et al. *The American Petroleum Industry: The Age of Energy, 1899–1959*. 1963.

Williamson, Jefferson. *The American Hotel*. 1930.

Wilson, William J. *When Work Disappears: The World of the New Urban Poor*. 1996.

Wirth, Louis. *The Ghetto*. 1928.

Witte, Ann D. "Beating the System?" In *Exploring the Underground Economy*, edited by Susan Pozo. 1996.

Worthy, James. *Shaping an American Institution: Robert E. Wood of Sears, Roebuck*. 1984.

Wrigley, Julia Wrigley. *Class Politics and Public Schools: Chicago, 1900–1950*. 1982.

Young, David M. *Chicago Transit: An Illustrated History*. 1998.

Zilversmit, Arthur. *Changing Schools: Progressive Education Theory and Practice*. 1993.

Zorbaugh, Harvey Warren. *The Gold Coast and the Slum: A Sociological Study of Chicago's Near North Side*. 1929.

# Index